D1472535

Experiences in Biochemical Perception

I. C. GUNSALUS

Experiences in Biochemical Perception

Edited by

L. NICHOLAS ORNSTON

Department of Biology
Yale University
New Haven, Connecticut

STEPHEN G. SLIGAR

Department of Molecular Biophysics and Biochemistry
Yale University
New Haven, Connecticut

1982

ACADEMIC PRESS

A Subsidiary of Harcourt Brace Jovanovich, Publishers

New York   London
Paris   San Diego   San Francisco   São Paulo   Sydney   Tokyo   Toronto

ACAP 1982

Library,
I.U.P.
Indiana, Pa

574.192 Ex 71p
c.1

COPYRIGHT © 1982, BY ACADEMIC PRESS, INC.
ALL RIGHTS RESERVED.
NO PART OF THIS PUBLICATION MAY BE REPRODUCED OR
TRANSMITTED IN ANY FORM OR BY ANY MEANS, ELECTRONIC
OR MECHANICAL, INCLUDING PHOTOCOPY, RECORDING, OR ANY
INFORMATION STORAGE AND RETRIEVAL SYSTEM, WITHOUT
PERMISSION IN WRITING FROM THE PUBLISHER.

ACADEMIC PRESS, INC.
111 Fifth Avenue, New York, New York 10003

United Kingdom Edition published by
ACADEMIC PRESS, INC. (LONDON) LTD.
24/28 Oval Road, London NW1 7DX

Library of Congress Cataloging in Publication Data
Main entry under title:

Experiences in biochemical perception.

In honor of I. C. Gunsalus.
Includes bibliographies and index.
1. Biological chemistry--Addresses, essays, lectures.
2. Microbiological chemistry--Addresses, essays,
lectures. 3. Gunsalus, I. C. (Irwin Clyde), Date
I. Ornston, L. Nicholas. II. Sligar, Stephen G.
III. Gunsalus, I. C. (Irwin Clyde), Date
[DNLM: 1. Biochemistry. 2. Metabolism. QU 4 E96]
QP509.E89   574.19'2   82-1614
ISBN 0-12-528420-9   AACR2

PRINTED IN THE UNITED STATES OF AMERICA

82 83 84 85   9 8 7 6 5 4 3 2 1

Contents

Contributors   xv
Preface   xix

I   METABOLISM

1   The Search for the Mechanism of Pyruvate Oxidation in 1951

SEVERO OCHOA

Enzymatic Synthesis of Citrate   4
Pyruvate Oxidation   4
References   7

2   A Decade of Pyruvate Systems

D. J. O'KANE

Text   9
References   13

**3   Early Studies on Respiration and the Coenzyme
     Form of Vitamin B$_6$**

W. W. UMBREIT

Text   15
References   20

**4   Branched-Chain Ketoacid Dehydrogenase
     of *Pseudomonas putida* PpG2**

JOHN R. SOKATCH

Introduction   24
Purification   26
Requirement of Branched-Chain Ketoacid Dehydrogenase
    for Lipoamide Dehydrogenase from *P. putida* Grown
    on Valine   29
Effect of L-Valine on Kinetics of Branched-Chain Ketoacid
Dehydrogenase   31
Discussion   32
References   34

**5   A Movable Feast with Gunny:
     An Early History of the Mandelate Pathway**

R. Y. STANIER

Text   35
References   42

6   Our Microbial World

S. DAGLEY

Text   45
References   55

7　Bacteria and the Challenge of Cyclic Molecules

P. W. TRUDGILL

I.	Introduction	59
II.	Effects of Camphor Vapor	60
III.	Metabolism of Cyclohexanol and Cyclopentanol	63
IV.	Metabolism of Alicyclic Acids	66
V.	Camphor Revisited	69
	References	72

8　Microbial Metabolism of Anthracycline Antibiotics

VINCENT P. MARSHALL

I.	Introduction	75
II.	Microbial Metabolism of Anthracycline Antibiotics	78
III.	Conclusion	81
IV.	Personal Note	82
	References	83

9　Fatty Acid and Electron Transport in Pseudomonads

RICHARD A. HARTLINE AND WILLIAM A. TOSCANO, JR.

The First Generation	86
The Second Generation	90
References	96

II　GENETICS

10　Order and Disorder in Genome Arrangement

BRUCE HOLLOWAY

Introduction	101
Mapping the Bacterial Genome	102

The Genetics of Bacteria Other than *E. coli* K12   102
The Genetics of *P. putida*   103
The Promiscuous Plasmid   104
Gene Arrangement and Regulatory Patterns   106
The Plasmid—Nature's Wild Card   107
References   108

11   Plasmids and Nutritional Diversity

A. M. CHAKRABARTY

Regulation of Plasmid-Coded Enzymes   112
Evolution of Degradative Plasmids   116
References   119

12   Communication among Coevolving Genes

L. NICHOLAS ORNSTON

Rearrangements among Structural and Regulatory Genes   124
Extensive Divergence of Homologous Genes as They
    Coevolve within a Cell Line   125
Similar Amino Acid Sequences in Enzymes with Different
    Catalytic Activities   125
References   126

13   Mixed Regulation in a Biosynthetic Pathway: Learning How to Listen

IRVING P. CRAWFORD

   I. Discovery   129
  II. Attempt to Characterize Tryptophan Synthase Regulation in
     P. putida by Genetic Analysis   133
 III. Cloning Certain *P. aeruginosa trp* Genes in *E. coli*   135
 IV. Unsolved Problems and Future Experiments   139
  V. Envoi   141
    References   142

III REGULATION

14 Regulation of L-Threonine Dehydrase by Ligand-Induced Oligomerization: An Odyssey Born of the Pyridoxal Phosphate Era

D. J. LEBLOND, R. C. MENSON, AND W. A. WOOD

Results	152
Summary	163
References	163

15 Organization and Expression of an *E. coli* Cluster of Genes Involved in the Translation Process

MARIANNE GRUNBERG-MANAGO

Organization and Expression of the Initiation Factor IF3 *E. coli* Gene Cluster	168
Translational Initiation Pathways	169
Isolation of a Thermosensitive Strain Containing a Thermolabile IF3	171
Order of the Genes in λp2 as Studied by Their Segregation Pattern in Deleted Phages	175
Physical Location of the Genes on λp2	178
Transcription of the Genes around *infC*	181
The Expression of the Genes around *infC* Is Differently Regulated	186
Conclusion	186
References	187

16 Posttranscriptional Control of Protein Synthesis during Substrate Adaptation

LEWIS A. JACOBSON AND LINDA JEN-JACOBSON

Text	191
References	203

17   From Bacterial Camphor Metabolism to Mammalian Protein Kinase Systems Regulated by Cyclic AMP, Cyclic GMP, and Calcium

J. F. KUO

I.	Introduction	205
II.	A Bacterial Dehydrogenase in Camphor Oxidation	206
III.	Mammalian Protein Kinase Systems	207
IV.	Concluding Remarks	216
	References	216

18   Phosphorus–Nitrogen Bonds in Proteins

ROBERTS A. SMITH

Text	219
References	231

19   Regulation of Glutamine Synthetase Degradation

C. N. OLIVER, R. L. LEVINE, AND E. R. STADTMAN

I.	Introduction	233
II.	Results	237
III.	Discussion	244
	References	248

IV   CYTOCHROME P450 AND ELECTRON TRANSPORT

20   From Stars to Organic Chemistry via Cytochrome P450

STEPHEN G. SLIGAR

Introduction	253
The Illinois Biochemistry/Biophysics Group, 1972–1977	254
References	264

21 Purification and Characterization of Adrenal P450 Cytochromes

MASAYUKI KATAGIRI AND KATSUKO SUHARA

I.	Introduction	267
II.	Purification of the Two P450 Proteins	269
III.	Catalytic Activity of Adrenal P450	271
IV.	Molecular Properties of the Two Cytochrome P450 Proteins	272
V.	Comparison of Substrate Specificity and Spectral Properties	274
VI.	Adrenal Steroid Hydroxylases as Second Model P450 Systems	275
	References	276

22 Application of Affinity and Photoaffinity Probes to Cytochromes $P450_{cam}$ and $P450_{11\beta}$: New Insights into the Mode of Substrate Binding and Orientation

KARL M. DUS, JOHN A. BUMPUS, AND RALPH I. MURRAY

I.	Introduction	279
II.	The Substrate-Binding Site of Cytochrome $P450_{cam}$	280
III.	The Substrate-Binding Site of Cytochrome $P450_{11\beta}$	287
IV.	Applicability of the Two-Site Hypothesis to P450 Heme Proteins	290
	References	291

23 NADH Peroxidase of *Streptococcus faecalis*

M. I. DOLIN

I.	Oxygen as Electron Acceptor for *Streptococcus faecalis*	293
II.	NADH Peroxidase from Fermentatively Grown *S. faecalis*, 10C1: Demonstration of an Enzyme-Substrate Complex	298
III.	NADH Peroxidase from Aerobically Grown *S. faecalis*	299
IV.	Conclusions	304
	References	305

24 Biochemical Investigations at Subzero Temperatures

PIERRE DOUZOU

I.	Introduction	310
II.	Temporal Resolution of Enzyme-Catalyzed Reactions	311
III.	Purification of Reaction Intermediates and Structural Studies	318
	References	324

25 Dynamic Proteins

PETER G. DEBRUNNER AND HANS FRAUENFELDER

Conformational Substates—Concepts and Existence	328
Conformational Transitions	331
The Spatial Structure of Conformational Substates	334
Structure and Function	337
Reaction Theory	339
A Dynamic Model for Ligand Binding	342
References	343

V MICROBIOLOGY

26 The Microbes' Contribution to Nutritional Science

HERMAN C. LICHSTEIN

Introduction	349
Studies on Biotin	351
The Microbes' Contribution to Nutritional Science	355
References	359

27   *Pseudomonas aeruginosa*—**A Highly Evolved Aerobe**

JACK J. R. CAMPBELL

Text   361
References   366

Index   369

Contributors

Numbers in parentheses indicate the pages on which the authors' contributions begin.

John A. Bumpus (279), Department of Biochemistry, St. Louis University Medical School, St. Louis, Missouri 63104

Jack J. R. Campbell (361), Department of Microbiology, University of British Columbia, Vancouver, British Columbia V6T 1W5, Canada

A. M. Chakrabarty (111), Department of Microbiology and Immunology, University of Illinois Medical Center, Chicago, Illinois 60612

Irving P. Crawford (129), Department of Microbiology, College of Medicine, University of Iowa, Iowa City, Iowa 52242

S. Dagley (45), Department of Biochemistry, University of Minnesota, St. Paul, Minnesota 55108

Peter G. Debrunner (327), Department of Physics, University of Illinois, Urbana, Illinois 61801

M. I. Dolin (293), Department of Microbiology and Immunology, University of Michigan, Ann Arbor, Michigan 48104

Pierre Douzou (309), Institut de Biologie Physico-Chimique, 75005 Paris, France

Karl M. Dus (279), Department of Biochemistry, St. Louis University Medical School, St. Louis, Missouri 63104

Hans Frauenfelder (327), Department of Physics, University of Illinois, Urbana, Illinois 61801

Marianne Grunberg-Manago (167), CNRS, Biochemistry Department, Institut de Biologie Physico-Chimique, 75005 Paris, France

Richard A. Hartline (85), Department of Chemistry, Indiana University of Pennsylvania, Indiana, Pennsylvania 15705

Bruce Holloway (101), Department of Genetics, Monash University, Clayton, Victoria 3168, Australia

Lewis A. Jacobson (191), Department of Biological Sciences, University of Pittsburgh, Pittsburgh, Pennsylvania 15260

Linda Jen-Jacobson (191), Department of Biological Sciences, University of Pittsburgh, Pittsburgh, Pennsylvania 15260

Masayuki Katagiri (267), Department of Chemistry, Kanazawa University, Kanazawa 920, Japan

J. F. Kuo (205), Department of Pharmacology, School of Medicine, Emory University, Atlanta, Georgia 30322

D. J. LeBlond (147), Department of Biochemistry, Michigan State University, East Lansing, Michigan 48824

R. L. Levine (233), Laboratory of Biochemistry, National Heart, Lung, and Blood Institute, National Institutes of Health, Bethesda, Maryland 20205

Herman C. Lichstein (349), Department of Microbiology, College of Medicine, University of Cincinnati, Cincinnati, Ohio 45267

Vincent P. Marshall (75), Research Laboratories, The Upjohn Company, Kalamazoo, Michigan 49001

R. C. Menson (147), Department of Biochemistry, Michigan State University, East Lansing, Michigan 48824

Ralph I. Murray (279), Department of Biochemistry, St. Louis University Medical School, St. Louis, Missouri 63104

Severo Ochoa (3), Roche Institute of Molecular Biology, Nutley, New Jersey 07110

D. J. O'Kane (9), Department of Biology, University of Pennsylvania, Philadelphia, Pennsylvania 19104

C. N. Oliver (233), Laboratory of Biochemistry, National Heart, Lung, and Blood Institute, National Institutes of Health, Bethesda, Maryland 20205

L. Nicholas Ornston (121), Department of Biology, Yale University, New Haven, Connecticut 06511

Stephen G. Sligar (253), Department of Molecular Biophysics and Biochemistry, Yale University, New Haven, Connecticut 06511

Roberts A. Smith (219), Department of Chemistry and The Molecular Biology Institute, University of California, Los Angeles, California 90024

John R. Sokatch (23), Department of Microbiology and Immunology, University of Oklahoma Health Sciences Center, Oklahoma City, Oklahoma 73190

E. R. Stadtman (233), Laboratory of Biochemistry, National Heart, Lung, and Blood Institute, National Institutes of Health, Bethesda, Maryland 20205

R. Y. Stanier (35), Unité Physiologie Microbienne, Institut Pasteur, 757724 Paris, France

Katsuko Suhara (267), Department of Chemistry, Kanazawa University, Kanazawa 920, Japan

William A. Toscano, Jr. (85), Department of Toxicology, Harvard University School of Public Health, Boston, Massachusetts 02115

P. W. Trudgill (59), Department of Biochemistry, University College of Wales, Aberystwyth SY23 3DD, Dyfed, Wales, United Kingdom

W. W. Umbreit (15), Department of Biology, Rutgers University, New Brunswick, New Jersey 08903

W. A. Wood (147), Department of Biochemistry, Michigan State University, East Lansing, Michigan 48824

Preface

This volume honors I. C. Gunsalus, a gifted and versatile biochemist. The breadth of his contributions is reflected in the papers included in this work in which authors trace scientific insights they have gained as a result of their interreactions with Gunny.

Evident throughout this volume is Gunny's insistence on mastery of the technique most applicable to the problem at hand. Our knowledge is poor when compared with the wealth of the unknown, and, in seeking understanding, we are well advised to take whatever is available. Thus, genetics, enzymology, microbiology, chemistry, and spectroscopy combine to form the following narratives.

Gunny typically examined seemingly simple processes and followed them through to novel conclusions that swiftly became textbook generalizations. This volume begins with a description of metabolic processes as Ochoa and O'Kane describe the study of pyruvate oxidation. Umbreit then illustrates how studies of microbial respiration led to the discovery of pyridoxal phosphate, and Sokatch reviews dehydrogenases that participate in the dissimilation of branched-chain aromatic acids. Stanier communicates the flavor of correspondence with Gunny in a review of early discoveries in the mandelate pathway.

Outgrowths of Gunny's interest in metabolism are then presented in reviews by Dagley, Trudgill, and Marshall. Hartline and Toscano present a unified description of fatty acid and electron transport in *Pseudomonas*. The nutritional diversity of these organisms raised questions about their genetic organization, and these topics are addressed by Holloway, Chakrabarty, and Ornston. As described by Crawford, the genetic investigation of tryptophan biosynthesis in *Pseudomonas* has revealed novel regulatory mechanisms.

Wood and his associates introduce a section on regulation with a description of control of L-threonine dehydrase. Grunberg-Manago describes genes associated with the translation of messenger RNA; Jacobson and Jen-Jacobson present evidence for posttranscriptional control of protein synthesis. A description of protein kinases by Kuo follows, and Smith gives an account of the phosphorus–nitrogen bond in phosphorylated proteins. Stadtman and his associates show that the inactivation of glutamine synthetase is in part mediated by cytochrome P450.

Studies of cytochrome P450 have correlated protein structure with electron transport. Sligar gives a description of life in the Gunsalus laboratory during the P450 years. Katagiri and Suhara describe adrenal cytochrome P450 molecules, while Dus reviews the binding of substrates to cytochrome P450. The function of another electron-transport protein, NADH peroxidase, is described by Dolin. Douzou describes the use of low temperature techniques to explore the mechanism of cytochrome P450. Debrunner and Frauenfelder relate the mechanism of electron transport to protein structure and document the interface between the Gunsalus laboratory and the physicists.

The volume concludes with two microbiological reviews: Lichstein describes elucidation of the function of the coenzyme biotin and generalizes about the use of bacteria in nutritional studies, while Campbell (Gunny's first graduate student) comments on discoveries that have been made with *Pseudomonas,* a favorite subject of Gunny's research.

Fresh perspective brings new knowledge, and the articles in this volume enrich one another. As would be expected in a volume honoring Gunny, the contributions bring insight into biochemistry past, passing, and to come.

L. Nicholas Ornston
Stephen G. Sligar

I

Metabolism

1

The Search
for the Mechanism
of Pyruvate Oxidation
in 1951

Severo Ochoa

I may have met Gunny earlier but our friendship dates from 1949. That summer I gave a graduate course in Biochemistry at Berkeley and was fortunate to have Gunny as my Microbiology counterpart. We often attended each other's lectures and spent much time together either by ourselves or in the company of our friends, Horace Barker, Michael Doudoroff, Zev Hassid, Roger Stanier, and Barker's bright graduate student, Earl Stadtman. I think it was Gunny who introduced me to Case van Niel; we went together several times to Pacific Grove to listen to van Niel's scholarly lectures and discussions with his students. Gunny's breadth of knowledge, intelligence, imagination, and his warm, engaging personality made it a real pleasure, as well as a great experience, to talk science with him. Moreover, our common interest in the enzymology of intermediary metabolism was an important factor in strengthening the ties of our beginning friendship.

The following year Gunny spent a few months in my laboratory at New York University during his tenure of a Guggenheim Fellowship. The collaboration between him, Seymour Korkes, Joe Stern, and myself brought some light into the mechanism of pyruvate oxidation in bacteria and animal tissues. At that time this was rather obscure. The use of bacterial extracts and bacterial enzymes was

3

EXPERIENCES IN BIOCHEMICAL PERCEPTION
Copyright © 1982 by Academic Press, Inc.
All rights of reproduction in any form reserved.
ISBN 0-12-528420-9

chosen at the outset and Gunny's know-how and experience in bacteriology were essential for this approach.

ENZYMATIC SYNTHESIS OF CITRATE

It was clear from the classical work of Krebs (1950) that in animal tissues pyruvate is oxidized via the citric acid cycle. Krebs had established that oxaloacetate was a precursor of citrate but the mechanism of citrate synthesis was unknown. It was believed that citrate was formed by condensation of oxaloacetate either with pyruvate to give rise to a 7-carbon precursor, or with a 2-carbon compound at the oxidation level of acetate. In 1951 we isolated crystalline condensing enzyme from pig heart (Ochoa *et al.*, 1951). We found that citrate was formed on incubation of pig heart extracts with acetyl phosphate and oxaloacetate in the presence of catalytic amounts of CoA. Since Stadtman (1950) had shown that transacetylase catalyzed the reaction

$$\text{Acetyl phosphate} + \text{CoA} \rightleftharpoons \text{acetyl-CoA} + \text{phosphate}$$

and since CoA was present only in catalytic amounts, it was clear that the synthesis of citrate occurred through a reaction between acetyl-CoA and oxaloacetate to yield citrate and CoA. This was confirmed by the finding (Stern *et al.*, 1952) that the condensing enzyme catalyzed the synthesis of citrate from oxaloacetate and the acetyl-CoA that Lynen had isolated from yeast (Lynen *et al.*, 1951).

PYRUVATE OXIDATION

In the oxidation of foodstuffs through the citric acid cycle, acetyl groups for citrate synthesis are generated by oxidation of pyruvate and fatty acids (Ochoa, 1951) and it thus became apparent from our work that pyruvate and fatty acid oxidation must lead to the formation of acetyl-CoA. Acetyl-CoA would also be formed by breakdown of β-keto fatty acids which were known to yield acetyl groups for citrate synthesis (Ochoa, 1951; Stern and Ochoa, 1951). We next turned our attention to the mechanism of pyruvate oxidation which, insofar as it occurred via the citric acid cycle, at least in animal tissues, should involve formation of acetyl-CoA.

We found (Korkes *et al.*, 1950, 1951), provided that inorganic phosphate was present, that extracts of *Escherichia coli* and *Streptococcus faecalis* catalyzed the conversion of two molecules of pyruvate to one of acetyl phosphate, one of CO_2, and one of lactate. With dialyzed extracts the reaction required the addition of NAD. Therefore, the reaction could be formulated as an NAD-linked dismutation (see below) between two molecules of pyruvate, catalyzed by pyruvate dehydrogenase [reaction (1)] and lactate dehydrogenase [reaction (2)].

$$\text{Pyruvate + phosphate + NAD}^+ \rightleftharpoons \text{acetyl phosphate + CO}_2 + \text{NADH + H}^+ \qquad (1)$$

$$\text{Pyruvate + NADH + H}^+ \rightleftharpoons \text{lactate + NAD}^+ \qquad (2)$$

$$\text{Net result: 2 Pyruvate + phosphate} \rightarrow \text{acetyl phosphate + CO}_2 + \text{lactate} \qquad (3)$$

Lactate dehydrogenase was present in both *E. coli* and *S. faecalis* extracts. A further requirement of this reaction was thiamin pyrophosphate. Such a requirement was not apparent when the bacterial extracts were dialyzed against neutral buffer solutions but it appeared after dialysis against pyrophosphate buffer, pH 8.6. This dialysis was followed by dialysis against neutral buffer to remove the pyrophosphate. In the absence of phosphate, the rate of dismutation reaction was sharply reduced and no acetyl phosphate was formed. However, if condensing enzyme and oxaloacetate were added, the dismutation proceeded at the same or higher rate as in the presence of phosphate and citrate was formed according to reaction (4). These results proved that oxidation of pyruvate

$$\text{2 Pyruvate + oxaloacetate} \rightarrow \text{citrate + CO}_2 + \text{lactate} \qquad (4)$$

yields directly acetyl groups for citrate synthesis, without the intermediary formation of acetyl phosphate, and also that phosphate was not an intermediate in the oxidation of pyruvate. The model we proposed is shown in Fig. 1.

In an effort to obtain further evidence for the above model we tried to purify the enzyme(s) involved in pyruvate oxidation. Extracts of lyophilized *E. coli* cells were treated with $MnCl_2$ to remove excess nucleic acid and fractionated with ammonium sulfate. This yielded two fractions, A and B, precipitating between 0 and 45% and 60 and 100% ammonium sulfate saturation, respectively. Brief heating destroyed the transacetylase present in the fractions. Both fractions were needed for pyruvate dismutation whether to acetyl phosphate, CO_2, and lactate, in the presence of transacetylase and orthophosphate, or to citrate, CO_2,

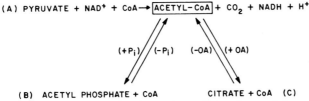

Fig. 1. Pyruvate oxidation and its coupling with acetyl phosphate and citrate synthesis. The overall reaction (A) is catalyzed by the pyruvate dehydrogenase complex. Reaction (B) is catalyzed by transacetylase, reaction (C) by the condensing enzyme. P_i, orthophosphate; OA, oxaloacetate (Korkes *et al.*, 1951).

and lactate, in the presence of condensing enzyme and oxaloacetate. The addition of NAD (not replaceable by NADP) was also required in both cases. There was also an absolute requirement for CoA. Taken all together these results strongly suggested that, in the presence of CoA, thiamin pyrophosphate, and NAD, pyruvate is oxidized to acetyl-CoA and CO_2 with concomitant reduction of NAD^+ to $NADH + H^+$ [Fig. 1, reaction (A)]. When CoA is present in catalytic amounts, as was the case in our experiments and is the case in the cell, this reaction cannot proceed to a significant extent unless the acetyl group is passed on to another acceptor, thus releasing CoA for further reaction. In our experiments this occurred in either of two ways. In the presence of transacetylase, acetyl-CoA was split by phosphate to form acetyl phosphate and CoA [Fig. 1, reaction (B)]. In the presence of condensing enzyme, acetyl-CoA was split by oxaloacetate to yield citrate and CoA [Fig. 1, reaction (C)]. Under the conditions of our experiments, the NADH formed by reaction (A) was oxidized by another molecule of pyruvate to form lactate and regenerate NAD. This reaction is catalyzed by lactate dehydrogenase which was present in the bacterial fractions. For this reason, and short of further purification of the system, it was not possible at the time to assay reaction (A) spectrophotometrically, i.e., by following the reduction of NAD^+ at 340 nm wavelength. Gunsalus had shown the requirement for a further cofactor (lipoic acid) in bacterial pyruvate oxidation, a factor that was later characterized as dithioctanoic acid (O'Kane and Gunsalus, 1948).

Further work in our laboratory (S. Korkes, A. del Campillo, and S. Ochoa, unpublished experiments, cited in Korkes et al., 1951) provided evidence that reaction (A) (Fig. 1) was catalyzed by enzyme preparations from pig heart. Ammonium sulfate fractionation of the heart extracts yielded a fraction, precipitating between 60 and 100% ammonium sulfate saturation which, like the E. coli fraction B, could be coupled with the E. coli fraction A to reconstruct the pyruvate oxidation system when supplemented either with transacetylase–orthophosphate or with condensing enzyme–oxaloacetate. The heart fraction precipitating between 0 and 45% saturation with ammonium sulfate could not be resolved into two distinct components. It was apparently contaminated with sufficient enzyme(s) of fraction B to give maximal reaction rates without addition of the latter. In other respects, however, the heart system appeared very similar to that of E. coli in its requirements for CoA, NAD, and an acetyl acceptor system as seen in Fig. 1.

As shown quite early by Lipmann (1946) some bacteria oxidize pyruvate to acetyl phosphate and CO_2 due to the presence of transacetylase. However, animal tissues that lack transacetylase but contain condensing enzyme, can oxidize pyruvate only via formation of citrate in the presence of oxaloacetate. This explained why pyruvate did not disappear aerobically in dialyzed heart homogenates unless a dicarboxylic acid (which could be oxidized to oxaloacetate), or oxaloacetate itself was added (Ochoa, 1944). On the other hand, E. coli, containing both transacetylase and condensing enzyme, was capable of converting pyruvate to either acetyl phosphate or citrate and could also convert acetyl phosphate to citrate (cf. Fig. 1).

The 1950 work outlined in this essay in honor of I. C. Gunsalus was carried out in part with his active and stimulating collaboration. It represented a modest but significant contribution to the unraveling of the complex mechanism of biological pyruvate oxidation. This work established the nature of the basic overall reaction of pyruvate oxidation and its requirement for three cofactors: thiamin pyrophosphate, NAD, and CoA. Lipoic acid and FAD were still to be added to the list. Gunny's participation in this endeavor made it more exciting and enjoyable than it would have been without him.

REFERENCES

Korkes, S., Stern, J. R., Gunsalus, I. C., and Ochoa, S. (1950). Enzymic synthesis of citrate from pyruvate and oxaloacetate. *Nature (London)* **166**, 439–441.

Korkes, S., del Campillo, A., Gunsalus, I. C., and Ochoa, S. (1951). Enzymatic synthesis of citric acid. IV. Pyruvate as acetyl donor. *J. Biol. Chem.* **193**, 721–735.

Krebs, H. A. (1950). The tricarboxylic acid cycle. *Harvey Lect.* **44**, 165–199.

Lipmann, F. (1946). Acetyl phosphate. *Adv. Enzymol.* **6**, 231–267.

Lynen, F., Reichert, E., and Rueff, L. (1951). Zum biologischen Abbau der Essigsäure. VI. "Aktivierte Essigsäure," ihre Isolierung aus Hefe und ihre Chemische Natur. *Justus Liebigs Ann. Chem.* **574**, 1.

Ochoa, S. (1944). A ketoglutaric dehydrogenase of animal tissues. *J. Biol. Chem.* **155**, 87–100.

Ochoa, S. (1951). Biological mechanisms of carboxylation and decarboxylation. *Physiol. Rev.* **31**, 56–106.

Ochoa, S., Stern, J. R., and Schneider, M. C. (1951). Enzymatic synthesis of citric acid. II. Crystalline condensing enzyme. *J. Biol. Chem.* **193**, 691–702.

O'Kane, D. J., and Gunsalus, I. C. (1948). Pyruvic acid metabolism. A factor required for oxidation by *Streptococcus faecalis*. *J. Bacteriol.* **56**, 499.

Stadtman, E. R. (1950). Coenzyme A-dependent transacetylation transphosphorylation. *Fed. Proc., Fed. Am. Soc. Exp. Biol.* **9**, 233.

Stern, J. R., and Ochoa, S. (1951). Enzymatic synthesis of citric acid. I. Synthesis with soluble enzymes. *J. Biol. Chem.* **191**, 161–172.

Stern, J. R., Ochoa, S., and Lynen, F. (1952). Enzymatic synthesis of citric acid. V. Reaction of acetyl coenzyme A. *J. Biol. Chem.* **198**, 313–321.

2

A Decade
of Pyruvate Systems

D. J. O'Kane

To return to Cornell in February, 1946 after some 50 months in the army was an exciting experience that I had been seriously planning since V-J Day. Returning to old haunts is always pleasant. I had been an undergraduate at Cornell and had been an NYA boy in the department (National Youth Administration—the New Deal version of the work-study student) and had worked for Gunny and for Dr. Sherman, the chairman. Gunny had been my major advisor; through his skillful direction and effective advocacy with the college officials I had been able to take a curriculum richer in hard sciences than was normal. The army had assigned me to a project in the Veterinary School at Cornell for most of 1943 so I could keep up relationships over lunches and evenings. We even did some experiments evenings, and demonstrated what is now known as sucrose phosphorylase, during an attempt to prepare a polysaccharide-synthesizing system from *Leuconostoc*. Our elation was short-lived; the paper of Doudoroff and his colleagues (1943) describing this enzyme soon appeared.

Wayne Umbreit, with whom I had worked for a masters' degree at Wisconsin, joined the Cornell group in 1944. A great deal of progress had been made on the pyridoxal phosphate problem, and some aspects were still being studied. A marvelous interaction between Gunny and Wayne characterized the laboratory

9

EXPERIENCES IN BIOCHEMICAL PERCEPTION
Copyright © 1982 by Academic Press, Inc.
All rights of reproduction in any form reserved.
ISBN 0-12-52840-9

and combined with the eagerness of the veterans joining the laboratory to produce an exciting atmosphere.

Sherman's long-standing interest in the streptococci pervaded the laboratory. As undergraduates, we heard of and rejoiced in the remarkable agreement between Sherman's physiological classification and Lancefield's serological one (Sherman, 1937). For a long time Sherman's students had each isolated a collection of streptococci and studied the collection. As his reputation in streptococci grew, others sent in cultures that puzzled them. A great deal of knowledge and a large number of cultures accumulated. As sometime custodian of the culture collection, I am particularly aware of the numbers!

Another influence was Otto Rahn, who taught bacterial physiology, and had long advocated the usefulness of simple organisms, such as bacteria, to elucidate fundamental processes that were much more difficult to recognize in the welter of reactions in complex organisms (Rahn, 1932).

The ideas of Kluyver (1931) and Fildes (1940), that all organisms shared the same fundamental reactions, were becoming more generally accepted. Fildes' "essential metabolite" that is either synthesized or must be provided was an idea finding increasing experimental support. My master's thesis had shown that the autotrophic *Thiobacillus thiooxidans* contained several B vitamins and phosphorylated intermediate characteristics of heterotrophic metabolism, so it was no longer necessary to consider the chemosynthetic autotrophs as metabolically unique (O'Kane, 1942). Thus, there was a general feeling of unity of metabolic reactions and the usefulness of bacteria as organisms for study was developing—very different from today's ubiquity of microorganisms as experimental material.

Against this background of the laboratory and the scientific world, Gunny and his students studied metabolic problems, particularly in the streptococci, but not confined to them. The growth conditions required to produce metabolically active cells were worked out by A. J. Wood (Wood and Gunsalus, 1942), organic acid metabolism by J. J. R. Campbell (Campbell *et al.*, 1943), and the distribution of pyruvate oxidation ability by Miller (1942). This was a surprising finding to us and we had expressed our skepticism about lactic acid bacteria oxidizing pyruvate to Lipmann at a conference in 1941 (Lipmann, 1939), an occasion he recalled to us after we presented our first paper on pyruvate oxidation by *Streptococcus faecalis* in 1947 (O'Kane and Gunsalus, 1947).

Synthetic media were either not worked out or too expensive, so we began with the partially synthetic medium used by Bellamy and Gunsalus (1944). When acid-hydrolyzed casein was substituted for acid-hydrolyzed gelatin, neither growth nor pyruvate oxidation were very good in this medium devised for apotyrosine decarboxylase production by a different strain of *S. faecalis*. Miller (1942) had used a tryptone-yeast extract medium to produce cells capable of oxidizing pyruvate, so we tried adding yeast extract to the medium; this improved both growth and pyruvate oxidation. Further manipulations of the medium, chiefly the addition of trypsin-hydrolyzed casein and higher levels of purines and pyrimidines to media without yeast extract, produced good crops of cells unable to oxidize pyruvate, but these cells would oxidize pyruvate if yeast extract was added to the Warburg cups, and the response was proportional to the amount of yeast extract over a reasonable range.

Here we have evidence for a factor required for pyruvate oxidation and an assay—what should we do next? In the discussion that ensued, Wayne held out for recording this interesting finding and going on to something else. Gunny and I, even though we thought we were aware of the difficulties of fractionation, held out for going ahead with it. Wayne then bowed out of that particular collaboration, settling the question that had bothered me for some time: "Who would be my thesis advisor?" The choice between these two would have been difficult indeed, since I was indebted to each for significant parts of my education.

Before plunging into the fractionation we established that the factor, pyruvate oxidation factor (POF), was removed from the oxidation medium by the cells and was required for the anaerobic dismutation, as well as the aerobic direct oxidation of pyruvate. Glucose oxidation did not require the factor, and none of the known growth factors or vitamins nor any described stimulatory preparations contained the factor. Both brewer's and bakers' yeast contained the factor, as did various liver preparations (O'Kane and Gunsalus, 1948).

Although we considered ourselves well equipped, and we probably were, the conditions would be almost unimaginable by today's standards. It must be remembered that the country was emerging from almost two decades dominated first by the great depression and then by war. Universities had limited spending for a long time, research grants were almost unknown, and many things we take for granted now were then unavailable. We made our own ATP and phosphorylated intermediates and many other compounds. There was a DU spectrophotometer in the Federal Nutrition Laboratory that was available to us for limited periods. At that time spectrophotometers were run by storage batteries, preferably by a freshly charged one, so the battery-charging routine set further constraints on the use of the instrument. We did a great deal of improvising; one of Gunny's favorite dicta, which combines challenge and confidence in proportions fine-tuned to the occasion, still rings in my ears: "A good bright boy could figure that out."

We did at least two full Warburg runs a day, calculating the data between readings and extrapolating ahead of the experiment to plan what to do next. Washing up, experimentation, media making, fractionation, etc., were done in between and at night. The living cell assay worked best with 12-hour cells, so inoculations were made at 8 PM and midnight. Only later, at other institutions, did we face this inconvenience—Gunny with a dried cell assay (Gunsalus et al., 1953) and I with a portable incubator. Saturdays we only worked part of the day;

what else we did depended chiefly on the season, and frequently included swimming, sailing, and a picnic at Gunny's place on the west side of Lake Cayuga. Sunday was almost a whole day of leisure: up late, leisurely breakfast with the papers, drift to the lab in the early afternoon, do some preparations for Monday, but mostly listen to Dr. Sherman, who always came around the labs on Sunday afternoon prepared to talk science, history, philosophy, or what have you.

Gunny shared his ideas and philosophy with us on a less regular, but equally steady, basis. He also shared his reading with us in discussions at lunch or other breaks. I particularly remember three, but am unable to date them accurately. One was on the history of Grant's campaigns—Grant's aggressiveness and his preference for battle rather than remaining in camp and taking a similiar number of casualties from disease particularly impressed Gunny. Another was a work of John Dewey on problem solving. For some time, we tried to fit all problems, large or small, into Dewey's system. I have before me the reprint Gunny gave me of Carl Becker's lecture at the 75th anniversary celebration of the Charter of Cornell University titled "The Cornell Tradition: Freedom and Responsibility" (Becker, 1940). These themes arose again and again and were applied repeatedly to all sorts of situations.

Many projects were going on at the same time—some with pyridoxal phosphate, others exploring new areas. Among those in the Gunsalus–Umbreit group were Herman Lichstein, W. A. Wood, Carol Foust, Doreen Jeffs (later O'Kane), and in other nearby laboratories Eugene Delwiche, Margaret Dyer, and Harry Seeley. We all worked hard, played hard, and helped and supported each other. Through it all Wayne and Gunny, but particularly Gunny, prodded, advised, warned, encouraged, and generally made the whole experience exciting and interesting.

The fractionation went slowly; we found the factor to be extremely acid stable and extractable under acidic conditions with organic solvents. In yeast extract only about half the activity could be extracted, but after hydrolysis 100% could be extracted. By various means a product 1500 times purer than yeast extract was obtained (Gunsalus *et al.*, 1952). Then I started writing my thesis which went through the usual revisions. One Sunday morning, Gunny phoned about seven, and asked Doreen, "Does Dan have his thesis home? The building's on fire." Fortunately I did, but the laboratory and all it contained was lost. This physically ended what had already been decided on another level—Wayne was going to Merck & Co., Gunny to Indiana, and I to the University of Pennsylvania.

Gunny continued the purification at Indiana. At Penn, as the second member of the microbiology unit that was organizationally within the Botany Department (although was physically apart from it), I had to cope with teaching responsibilities as well as setting up a metabolism laboratory in a building that had been closed for much of the war. I can still remember how elated I was the first time I reproduced the pyruvate oxidation factor assay there! I then studied the glucose oxidation by *S. faecalis* cells unable to oxidize pyruvate; the pyruvate produced by the oxidation of 3-glyceraldehyde phosphate was converted to acetoin and carbon dioxide (O'Kane, 1950).

A number of my students studied microbial pyruvate systems over the next several years. The intent, of course, was to understand the reactions, but a more immediate question was, Is lipoate (POF) involved? Harris Moyed studied the *Proteus* oxidative system. Cell-free extracts convert pyruvate to acetate and carbon dioxide, reducing oxygen or artificial electron acceptors such as ferricyanide or 2,6-dichlorophenol indophenol. Moyed was able to separate the preparation into two protein fractions required for activity. One was a cytochrome-containing particulate that could be replaced by the synthetic acceptors. Fraction II oxidized pyruvate to acetate and carbon dioxide in the presence of Fraction I or one of the synthetic acceptors. Only carboxylase and divalent cations needed to be added for activity, and other cofactors such as CoA, pyridine nucleotides, flavins, or lipoate were not required (Moyed and O'Kane, 1952a,b, 1956).

Another pyruvate system, that of *Clostridium,* was studied by Ralph Wolfe. The native system carried out the following reaction:

$$\text{Pyruvate} + \text{phosphate} \rightarrow \text{acetyl phosphate} + CO_2 + H_2$$

The extreme lability of the hydrogen-producing system made it necessary to bypass hydrogen production by the reduction of neotetrazolium. Appropriate treatments produced inactive extracts that could be activated by the addition of cocarboxylase, CoA, and Fe^{2+}. Lipoate was about 1/25 of the level found in *S. faecalis* capable of similar rates of pyruvate oxidation. Arsenite, a potent inhibitor of lipoate systems, only inhibits the *Clostridium* system 6% at levels that inhibit the *S. faecalis* system 100% (Wolfe and O'Kane, 1955). Somewhat later, Norris Wood studied the formate-producing system of *S. faecalis* by following formate exchange. This system is very labile, especially in cell-free extracts, but also seems not to require lipoate. Wood has continued work on this reaction in his laboratory in Rhode Island (Wood and O'Kane, 1964).

This is a brief summary of a little over a decade of studying pyruvate systems all directly stimulated by the original pyruvate studies done with Gunny.

REFERENCES

Becker, C. (John Stambaugh Professor of History) (1940). The Cornell Tradition: Freedom and Responsibility. Address delivered on the 27th of April 1940 the 75th anniversary of the charter of Cornell University, Ithaca, N.Y. Printed for the University.

Bellamy, W. D., and Gunsalus, I. C. (1944). Tyrosine decarboxylation by streptococci: Growth requirements for active cell production. *J. Bacteriol.* **48,** 191–199.

Campbell, J. J. R., Bellamy, W. D., and Gunsalus, I. C. (1943). Organic acids as substrates for streptococci. *J. Bacteriol.* **46**, 573.

Doudoroff, M., Kaplan, N., and Hassid, W. Z. (1943). Phosphorolysis and synthesis of sucrose with a bacterial preparation. *J. Biol. Chem.* **148**, 67–75.

Fildes, P. (1940). A rational approach to chemotherapy. *Lancet* **1**, 955–957.

Gunsalus, I. C., Struglia, L., and O'Kane, D. J. (1952). Pyruvic acid metabolism. IV. Occurrence, properties, and partial purification of pyruvate oxidation factor. *J. Biol. Chem.* **194**, 859–869.

Gunsalus, I. C., Dolin, M. I., and Struglia, L. (1952). Pyruvic acid metabolism. III. A manometric assay for pyruvate oxidation factor (lipoic acid). *J. Biol. Chem.* **194**, 849–857.

Kluyver, A. J. (1931). "The Chemical Activities of Microorganisms." Univ. of London Press, London.

Lipmann, F. (1939). An analysis of the pyruvic and oxidation system. *Cold Spring Harbor Symp. Quant. Biol.* **7**, 248–259.

Miller, A. K. (1942). Pyruvic acid metabolism by *Streptococcus faecalis* (IOCI). Thesis, Cornell Univ., Ithaca, New York.

Moyed, H. S., and O'Kane, D. J. (1952a). Fractionation of pyruvate oxidase of *Proteus vulgaris. J. Biol. Chem.* **195**, 375–381.

Moyed, H. S., and O'Kane, D. J. (1952b). The enzymes of the pyruvate oxidase system of *Proteus vulgaris. Arch. Biochem. Biophys.* **39**, 457–458.

Moyed, H. S., and O'Kane, D. J. (1956). Enzymes and coenzymes of the pyruvate oxidase of *Proteus. J. Biol. Chem.* **218**, 831–840.

O'Kane, D. J. (1942). The presence of growth factors in the cells of the autotrophic sulphur bacteria. *J. Bacteriol.* **43**, 7.

O'Kane, D. J. (1950). Influence of the pyruvate oxidation factor on the oxidative metabolism of glucose by *Streptococcus faecalis. J. Bacteriol.* **69**, 449–458.

O'Kane, D. J., and Gunsalus, I. C. (1947). Acessory factor requirement for pyruvate oxidation. *J. Bacteriol.* **54**, 20.

O'Kane, D. J., and Gunsalus, I. C. (1948). Pyruvic acid metabolism. A factor required for oxidation by *Streptococcus faecalis. J. Bacteriol.* **56**, 499–506.

Rahn, O. (1932). "Physiology of Bacteria." McGraw-Hill (Blakiston), New York.

Sherman, J. M. (1937). The streptococci. *Bacteriol. Rev.* **1**, 3–97.

Wolfe, R. S., and O'Kane, D. J. (1955). Cofactors of the carbon dioxide exchange reaction of *Clostridium butyricum. J. Biol. Chem.* **215**, 637–643.

Wood, A. J., and Gunsalus, I. C. (1942). The production of active resting cells of streptococci. *J. Bacteriol.* **44**, 333.

Wood, N. P., and O'Kane, D. J. (1964). Formate–pyruvate exchange reaction in *Streptococcus faecalis. J. Bacteriol.* **87**, 97–103.

3

Early Studies
on Respiration
and the Coenzyme Form
of Vitamin B₆

W. W. Umbreit

It has been my experience that when I read the history of some discovery or project with which I have been associated, I hardly recognize either the characters or obtain any reliable view of their contributions to the discovery. The problem seems to be that the historian either is only partly familiar with the development considered or lives in such a more advanced environment with such considerably increased knowledge of the problem being approached, that the actual knowledge available at the time the work was done, the intellectual and physical climate, the concepts and methods available, and the constraints under which the discovery was made, are generally not considered. It is clearly true that our paradigms change, as indeed they should, and what is acceptable proof for one generation is not suitable for the next. Who, today, for example, would regard the melting point of two derivatives to be adequate characterization of an unknown compound? To capture the mood, the materials, and the approach of time long past, requires the abilities of a novelist rather than those of a scientist.

It was just about 40 years ago that Gunsalus ("Gunny") spent a summer working with me at the University of Wisconsin. We had a nice little laboratory—clearly primitive by today's standards but one could get some things done in it anyhow. We had an Evelyn photoelectric colorimeter, but no Beckman. We had a Warburg, a Sharples steam-driven flow-through centrifuge

15

EXPERIENCES IN BIOCHEMICAL PERCEPTION
Copyright © 1982 by Academic Press, Inc.
All rights of reproduction in any form reserved.
ISBN 0-12-528420-9

(whose whine would reverberate through the building), no refrigerated centrifuge or fermentors. Column chromatography was just coming into use (we had heard of it, but had had little experience with it), but paper chromatography was far in the future as an everyday laboratory operation. We did not have isotopes of any kind available (nor did most other laboratories). The concept of phosphate bond energy had just been proposed (Lipmann, 1941; Kalckar, 1941) and there was a certain amount of argument over its validity. The Neuberg concept that methylglyoxal was the major intermediate in the pathway from glucose to lactic acid had just been eliminated experimentally on what today looks like rather flimsy grounds.

Gunny wanted to work on a streptococcus that oxidized glycerol. As I recall he had active cell suspensions ("washed, nongrowing cells") which oxidized glycerol but not glycerol phosphates and he hoped to make cell-free enzyme preparations which could do this. Our methods for liberating enzymes from bacterial cells were not particularly sophisticated. One made acetone preparations by dispersing the cells in ice-cold acetone and collecting the precipitate, or vacuum-dried preparations, by lyophilizing from the frozen state. One then ground whole cells or such dried preparations with ground glass or finely divided alumina (losing a great deal of the enzymatic activity adsorbed to the glass) and there were various mills available (which we did not possess) for grinding cells. I remember Gunny describing the process of grinding with ground glass in a chilled mortar and pestle as continuing until three men were tired.

The reason for interest in the respiration of this organism was that the oxidation of glycerol proceeded at a very rapid rate in an organism that did not possess a cytochrome system. At this time, known systems for the uptake of oxygen which did not employ the cytochrome system were very sluggish and could not nearly approach the rate found in this streptococcus. We only managed a little progress in knowledge of this system over the summer, as I recall, but since we worked on it subsequently at Cornell, I do not remember how much was done by Gunny at Wisconsin and how much was done subsequently at Cornell (Gunsalus and Umbreit, 1945). The net result of the study was, however, that the pathway was glycerol → glycerol phosphate → glyceraldehyde 3-phosphate → lactic acid, the system glycerol phosphate $+O_2$ → glyceraldehyde 3-phosphate $+H_2O_2$ being catalyzed by an enzyme, clearly not a cytochrome type, but capable of reacting with oxygen at a very rapid rate. It was only many years later that the enzyme could be proved to be a flavoprotein in which the flavin was very tightly bound to the enzyme (Koditschek and Umbreit, 1969). The important point was that there existed among the bacteria respiratory systems capable of rapid oxygen uptake which did not involve the cytochrome pathway.

There were two graduate students in the laboratory at the time, D. J. O'Kane and G. A. LePage, both working on the autotrophic bacterium *Thiobacillus thiooxidans*. This organism was capable of growth on an inorganic salts medium using sulfur as its source of energy and CO_2 as its carbon source, producing very considerable quantities of sulfuric acid to which it was clearly resistant. One approach to the question of how life under the conditions mentioned was possible, was to make a comparison of the properties of this organism with more conventional heterotrophs. The question then arose, "Does this unusual organism possess the intermediates of the Meyerhoff scheme?" We had, therefore, devised an analytical system depending on precipitation of the barium salts for the separation and estimation of the major phosphate esters of the Meyerhoff scheme (it was not really called the Meyerhoff-Embden system then).

The situation was such that many people felt that whereas the Meyerhoff scheme might apply to muscle and to yeast, it probably did not apply to bacteria. This was partly due to an innate hunch that bacteria might well be different (which was later to be expressed in the prokaryote-eukaryote separation) and partly due to the experimental observations which showed very little phosphate exchange (insofar as it could be measured) in bacteria. Gunny felt that his streptococcus (or a close relative) would be the ideal organism, and he and I persuaded O'Kane (we were in a position to do so) that he ought to apply the methods for determining organic phosphate esters, which LePage and he had developed for autotrophic bacteria, to these heterotrophic forms. O'Kane grew up 10-20 liter batches of cells, harvested them through the Sharples and made heavy washed cell suspensions to which glucose was added, the acid neutralized periodically, and samples taken at intervals and analyzed for the various phosphate esters according to the method described by LePage (LePage and Umbreit, 1943). This study was not without some difficulties. I vividly remember a day when Gunny and I retired to the Pine Room (a small coffee shop in the basement of an adjacent dormitory), partly to escape the incessant high-pitched whine of the steam-driven centrifuge, and over danish and coffee planned how the cells that O'Kane was harvesting could best be used in the "critical definitive experiment." After an hour or so we were joined by O'Kane, drenched in sweat and slightly befuddled (we thought) from too close contact with the centrifuge. We blandly told him what was the best thing to do with his cells. We were surprised to find that he had another, not too effective, thing he suggested we could do with his cells. Eventually, he somewhat calmed, we somewhat chastened, did get our experiments underway. This work was eventually published without Gunny's name on it (O'Kane and Umbreit, 1942) and this has been a source of regret to me all my life for clearly Gunny had contributed at least as much as I to this work, and he never got any credit for it. (I should add neither did O'Kane nor I.) In the long run it made, I hope, no real difference but it is something that still bothers me.

The summer ended, and although Gunny returned to Cornell, we continued correspondence. In the summer of 1944, Dr. Sherman, head of the department at Cornell, was able to provide some modest funds and I was able to go to Cornell to work in Gunny's lab for the summer. I wanted to work on the study of a theory

I had about the lag phase of bacterial culture. I felt that when an organism was transferred to media under conditions where lag occurred, it was necessary for the cells to build up a level of ATP within themselves before they could begin cell division and that, therefore, the ATP/ADP ratio per cell should markedly increase during the lag phase. The methods for measuring ATP and ADP were rather crude (we did not yet have a Beckman spectrophotometer) and were based on the ratio of Δ^7-phosphate (inorganic phosphate released by heating in 0.1 N HCl at 100°C for 7 minutes) in the barium-insoluble compared to the barium-soluble, alcohol-insoluble fraction. To do this one would inoculate 10 liters of media (with perhaps a 10% inoculum from the stationary phase). After 30 minutes, the cells from 8 liters were centrifuged; after one hour, the cells from 1.5 liters were centrifuged; after 2 hours from 200 ml, and after 3 hours from 100 ml. Using this type of rather laborious method, I was able to show in about four experiments that there was a marked rise in the ATP/ADP ratio during lag phase. Indeed, there seemed to be perhaps 10 times as much ATP in the lag phase as in mid-log. I was happy with this, but Gunny was skeptical. He thought that possibly the bacteria were concentrating nucleosides or nucleotides from the complex media employed. At considerable expense and difficulty, he prepared a large quantity of synthetic media, using some of his very limited supply of SLR factor (a folic acid) to do so—and his hunch proved correct. There was no rise in ATP in the lag phase and what I had been seeing was probably a mere concentration of nucleosides from the complex medium.

This result shot rather a "large hole" in what I had planned for the summer, and since it was somewhat late for me to start a new project, I volunteered to help Bellamy and Gunsalus in a project they were working on. During the early stage of the war (which was still going on), certain cheeses made in New York State (and elsewhere) proved to contain hallucinatory amines, especially tyramine. It was shown that this was due to the presence in the cheese of fecal rather than dairy streptococci. The fecal streptococci had a tyrosine decarboxylase which was responsible for the formation of tyramine. Bellamy and Gunsalus had been working out the nutritional requirements of such tyrosine decarboxylase-containing streptococci and had found a medium that would permit good growth, but no tyrosine decarboxylase activity was formed unless a vitamin-like factor was provided. After an incredibly complex set of experiments, the factor required for tyrosine decarboxylase activity was traced to pseudopyridoxine, and shortly before that final summer it had been identified as pyridoxal (Gunsalus and Bellamy, 1944b; Bellamy and Gunsalus, 1944, 1945).

Gunny obtained a small quantity of pyridoxal from Snell (1944) from a small supply made available by Merck & Co., whose laboratories had just recently synthesized pyridoxine (vitamin B_6) and related substances (Harris et al., 1944a,b). Gunsalus and Bellamy (1944a) had already identified the nutritional factor required for tyrosine decarboxylation, earlier called pseudopyridoxine, as pyridoxal. Further, they showed that resting cells, taken from a medium deficient in vitamin B_6, whose ability to decarboxylate tyrosine was low, could be stimulated to perform this function by the addition of pyridoxal to the resting cells (Gunsalus and Bellamy, 1944a; Bellamy and Gunsalus, 1945), i.e., growth (or protein synthesis) was not necessary. It appeared that the enzyme tyrosine decarboxylase was produced during growth but was inactive because it lacked a coenzyme somehow derived from pyridoxal.

A few milligrams of a dried preparation from cells grown on complex medium would rapidly decarboxylate tyrosine. However, when a similar preparation was attempted from cells grown in the absence of any form of vitamin B_6, no tyrosine decarboxylation activity could be found. Addition of pyridoxal (or other available B_6 derivatives) did not have any great effect. However, the addition of heat-killed cells grown on yeast extract, as well as yeast extract itself, markedly enhanced the production of CO_2 from tyrosine. Presumably this coenzyme present in cells grown on complex media had something to do with vitamin B_6. So, in the time remaining, I set about trying to activate pyridoxal in some way to form the coenzyme. About August 20, 1944, I found that with a dried preparation actually prepared by Bellamy (consisting of vacuum-dried cells grown in the absence of vitamin B_6), the addition of ATP and pyridoxal to the preparation markedly increased decarboxylation of tyrosine. The actual values were (Q_{CO_2})—no additions, 4.0; + 13 μg pyridoxal, 4.5; + 3 μg pyridoxal + 1 mg ATP, 20.5. There is nothing like being in the right place at the right time with the right experiment (however unlikely). One may note that the publication of the note (Gunsalus *et al.,* 1944) appeared in October, the original ATP activation having been observed near the end of August.

At that time only the structures of "coenzyme I" ("cozymase") (NAD), "coenzyme II" (NADP), and the flavin nucleotides were known. It would be a reasonable assumption that the vitamin B_6 coenzyme would also be a nucleotide. As I remember, we thought of ATP as an energy source and as an agent of phosphorylation (glucose to glucose 6-phosphate, for example) rather than as a source of the adenylate moiety. Gunny, therefore, proposed that we should try to synthesize the "coenzyme" by putting a phosphate on the 5-hydroxyl (rather than the 3-hydroxyl) of pyridoxal. I do not recall why we picked the 5 (which later evidence proved to be correct) or really that our methods would have made any real distinction between the two hydroxyls.

At that time, Gunny had about 5 mg of pyridoxal (actually 4.68 mg) which he made up to 25 ml. Ten milliliters were set aside as our standard pyridoxal, and the remaining 15 ml were used for coenzyme synthesis. We used 10 ml (1.86 mg) for synthesis via thionyl chloride because I had been very much impressed by the value of this reagent in chlorinating hydroxyls, especially since excess reagents could be removed by evaporation *in vacuo*. I, therefore, attempted to replace 5-hydroxyl with a chlorine and to replace the chlorine with phosphate using silver hydrogen phosphate as described by Lipmann and Tuttle (1944). The method is essentially that later described by Baddily and Gale (1945). Gunny took the remaining 5 ml, added 0.1 ml 90% phosphoric acid, evaporated off the water, and put under vacuum over Drierite for 16–18 hours. Both preparations were active, although they were not as good as pyridoxal plus ATP. On this basis, with certain other experiments, we concluded that pyridoxal 5-phosphate was the coenzyme of tyrosine decarboxylase. At about this time, Gale and Epps (1944) provided evidence that a natural coenzyme existed (termed "codecarboxylase") (Baddiley and Gale, 1945; Umbreit *et al.*, 1945) and this was soon shown to be pyridoxal phosphate.

All of these discoveries, i.e., that ATP was involved in the synthesis of the coenzyme form of vitamin B_6 and the synthesis of the active phosphorylated form, occurred within a single week. It is hard to describe the excitement and stimulus that these experiments provided. Of course, a great deal more work had to be done, i.e., the proof that the natural coenzyme described by Gale and Epps was indeed pyridoxal phosphate, and the extension of knowledge of the activity of pyridoxal phosphate in other decarboxylases, to transaminase, and its relation to animal deficiencies in vitamin B_6, etc. Clearly, this astonishing week put the entire subject on the right track.

One may speculate as to what forces, what chances, what skills, and what insights converged at this point—but possibly we shall never know. Surely, I have inevitably provided a picture no more closely related to the actual facts than is usual—it would take a skilled novelist to recreate the mood and the ambiance which existed at the time. But even this inadequate picture shows Gunny as a careful and imaginative observer, a persistent and critical experimenter, and a young man with a grasp of the important and relevant. It does not show his ready wit and his sometimes penetrating insights, but enough comes through, I hope, to give some picture of "the artist as a young man." At least I hope that he will recognize it as a tribute and that it will recall to him an exciting time from a period now long gone—which was both simpler and more complex than we imagined at the time.

REFERENCES

Baddily, J., and Gale, E. F. (1945). Codecarboxylase function of 'pyridoxal phosphate.' *Nature (London)* **155**, 727–728.

Bellamy, W. D., and Gunsalus, I. C. (1944). Tyrosine decarboxylation by streptococci: Growth requirements for active cell production. *J. Bacteriol.* **48**, 191–199.

Bellamy, W. D., and Gunsalus, I. C. (1945). Tyrosine decarboxylase. II. Pyridoxine-deficient medium for apoenzyme production. *J. Bacteriol.* **50**, 95–103.

Gale, E. F., and Epps, H. M. R. (1944). Bacterial amino acid decarboxylases. III. Distribution and preparation of codecarboxylase. *Biochem. J.* **38**, 250–256.

Gunsalus, I. C., and Bellamy, W. D. (1944a). A function of pyridoxal. *J. Biol. Chem.* **155,** 357–358.

Gunsalus, I. C., and Bellamy, W. D. (1944b). The function of pyridoxine and pyridoxine derivatives in the decarboxylation of tyrosine. *J. Biol. Chem.* **155,** 557–563.

Gunsalus, I. C., and Umbreit, W. W. (1945). The oxidation of glycerol by *Streptococcus faecalis. J. Bacteriol.* **49,** 347–357.

Gunsalus, I. C., Bellamy, W. D., and Umbreit, W. W. (1944). A phosphorylated derivative of pyridoxal as the coenzyme of tyrosine decarboxylase. *J. Biol. Chem.* **155,** 685–686.

Harris, S. A., Heyl, D., and Folkers, K. (1944a). Vitamin B$_6$ group. II. The structure and synthesis of pyridoxamine and pyridoxal. *J. Am. Chem. Soc.* **66,** 2088–2092.

Harris, S. A., Heyl, D., and Folkers, K. (1944b). The structure and synthesis of pyridoxamine and pyridoxal. *J. Biol. Chem.* **154,** 315–316.

Kalckar, H. M. (1941). The nature of energetic coupling in biological systems. *Chem. Rev.* **28,** 71–178.

Koditschek, L. K., and Umbreit, W. W. (1969). α-Glycerophosphate oxidase in *Streptococcus faecium* F24. *J. Bacteriol.* **98,** 1063–1068.

LePage, G. A., and Umbreit, W. W. (1943). Phosphorylated carbohydrate esters in autotrophic bacteria. *J. Biol. Chem.* **147,** 263–271.

Lipmann, F. (1941). Metabolic generation and utilization of phosphate bond energy. *Adv. Enzymol.* **1,** 99–162.

Lipmann, F., and Tuttle, L. C. (1944). Acetyl phosphate: Chemistry, determination and synthesis. *J. Biol. Chem.* **153,** 571–582.

O'Kane, D. J., and Umbreit, W. W. (1942). Transformation of phosphorus during glucose fermentation by living cells of *Streptococcus faecalis. J. Biol. Chem.* **142,** 25–30.

Snell, E. E. (1944). Vitamin activities of "pyridoxal" and "pyridoxamine." *J. Biol. Chem.* **154,** 313–314.

Umbreit, W. W., Bellamy, W. D., and Gunsalus, I. C. (1945). The function of pyridoxine derivatives: A comparison of natural and synthetic codecarboxylase. *Arch. Biochem.* **7,** 185–199.

4

Branched-Chain Ketoacid Dehydrogenase of *Pseudomonas putida* PpG2

John R. Sokatch

I had the good fortune to be a graduate student in Gunny's laboratory during the time that the work on the pyruvate dehydrogenase was at its greatest intensity. The excitement then was something like the atmosphere on a football team during a winning streak. My own research was on the gluconate fermentation by *Streptococcus faecalis* so that I was not directly involved, but we all shared in the anticipation of the almost daily new information on the structure and function of lipoic acid. Maybe we all remember our graduate student days with more nostalgia than accuracy, but there is no question that these were important times. One of the other things that contributed to the enjoyment was an unusually compatible group of graduate students and postdoctoral fellows. The fact that W. A. Wood's laboratory was a stone's throw away and that Luria and Speigelman were right around the corner, made it an unusual learning opportunity.

It became clear quickly that Gunny was a person of unusual scientific breadth. We have all had the opportunity to meet and know first-class scientific minds, but I never cease to be amazed at the information at his fingertips. He is able to discuss organic chemistry and genetics on fluent terms with the practitioners of those arts. The current research in his laboratory, which is some of the best of an incredibly productive career, is an example. I have made the habit of using Gunny as a resource for pieces of information that are difficult to obtain any-

23

EXPERIENCES IN BIOCHEMICAL PERCEPTION
Copyright © 1982 by Academic Press, Inc.
All rights of reproduction in any form reserved.
ISBN 0-12-528420-9

where else. I thought at first that it might be just coincidence that our laboratory is working on a ketoacid dehydrogenase and using *Pseudomonas putida* PpG2, but on reflection, it is apparent that Gunny is one of the giants who has contributed to the scientific foundation on which we build our work.

INTRODUCTION

The metabolism of branched-chain amino acids in bacteria is outlined in Fig. 1 (Massey *et al.*, 1976). The reactions in mammals are virtually identical. Pseudomonads can grow with either D- or L-branched-chain amino acids as the sole carbon source. The first three or four enzymes of the pathway are common to the metabolism of valine, leucine, and isoleucine. L-Branched-chain amino acids are deaminated by transamination with 2-ketoglutarate as the amino acceptor (reaction 1, Fig. 1). D-Branched-chain amino acids are deaminated by a membrane-bound D-amino acid oxidase which is linked to a *b*-type cytochrome (reaction 2, Fig. 1). Reaction 3, Fig. 1, is catalyzed by branched-chain ketoacid dehydrogenase, the subject of this chapter. Branched-chain ketoacid dehydrogenase is produced during growth on any of the three branched-chain amino acids, but the specific inducers are the branched-chain ketoacids, 2-ketoisovalerate, 2-ketoisocaproate, and 2-keto-3-methyvalerate (Marshall and Sokatch, 1972). Reaction 4 is assumed to be the result of a acyl-CoA dehydrogenase, but this enzyme has never been studied, as far as we are aware.

The unsaturated fatty acyl-CoA esters of valine and isoleucine metabolism are hydrated by enoyl-CoA hydratase (Roberts *et al.*, 1978) and the hydroxy fatty acyl-CoA esters then undergo reactions that are specific for their individual pathways (Fig. 1). The unsaturated fatty acid which is an intermediate in leucine metabolism, 3-methylcrotonyl-CoA, is carboxylated, then metabolized to acetoacetyl-CoA and acetyl-CoA.

Branched-chain ketoacid dehydrogenase is an obligatory enzyme in the metabolism of all three branched-chain amino acids by *P. putida*. Mutants that lack this enzyme are unable to grow on any of the three branched-chain amino acids as carbon and energy sources (Martin *et al.*, 1973). These mutants also lose the ability to oxidize all three branched-chain ketoacids but oxidation of pyruvate and 2-ketoglutarate are unaffected (Martin *et al.*, 1973). Before this study began, there were no highly purified preparations of branched-chain ketoacid dehydrogenase and therefore very little was known about the nature of the enzyme. There were, however, several interesting questions that could be asked:

1. Is this ketoacid dehydrogenase a multienzyme complex on the order of pyruvate and 2-ketoglutarate hydrogenases of *Escherichia coli* and mammals (Reed and Cox, 1970)? If so, the corresponding subunits would be a branched-

Library,
I.U.P.
Indiana, Pa.

574.192 Ex 7/p
c.1

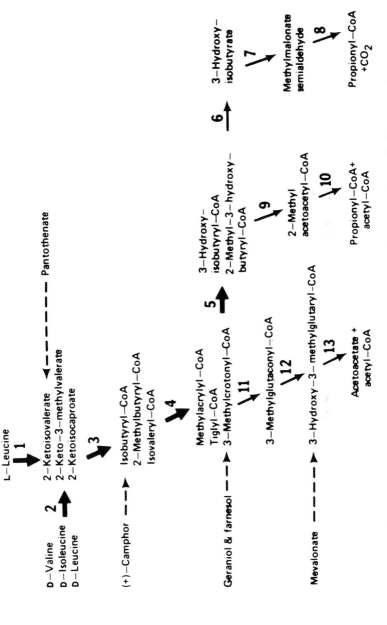

Fig. 1. Pathways for the catabolism of branched-chain amino acids in pseudomonads. (Massey et al., 1976.)

chain ketoacid dehydrogenase decarboxylase (E1), branched-chain acyltrans-
acylase (E2), and lipoamide dehydrogenase (E3).

2. Pyruvate and 2-ketoglutarate dehydrogenases of *E. coli* share the same
lipoamide dehydrogenase (Guest, 1978). Assuming that branched-chain ketoacid
dehydrogenase is a multienzyme complex, is its lipoamide dehydrogenase subunit the same one which serves pyruvate and 2-ketoglutarate dehydrogenases?

3. Is branched-chain ketoacid dehydrogenase a regulated enzyme? Considering its position as the first enzyme common to the metabolism of both D- and
L-branched chain amino acids, it appears to be a likely candidate for regulation.
The mammalian pyruvate dehydrogenase is tightly regulated by phosphorylation
and dephosphorylation (Barrera *et al.*, 1972).

4. Can anything be learned about the human genetic disease, maple syrup
urine disease, by a study of the purified bacterial enzyme? The lesion in this
disease is in branched-chain ketoacid dehydrogenase (Dancis *et al.*, 1963). It is
too soon to even speculate about this question, but the recent progress in purifying the bovine enzyme (Pettit *et al.*, 1978) and the bacterial enzyme (Roberts and
Sokatch, 1978; Sokatch *et al.*, 1981) makes us hopeful.

PURIFICATION

Our early attempts to purify branched-chain ketoacid dehydrogenase from *P.
putida* were frustrated because of large losses of enzyme activity. These losses
were due to the disassociation of lipoamide dehydrogenase and thiamin
pyrophosphate from the enzyme and due to the then unrecognized stimulation of
enzyme activity by L-valine.

The requirement for a heat-stable factor became apparent during assay of the
pellet which was formed after centrifugation at 176,000 g. When the soluble
fraction from this step was heated at 100°C for 5 minutes, and then added to the
pellet, there was consistent stimulation of enzyme activity (Fig. 2). The soluble
factor passed through a membrane filter with an exclusion limit of 1000, indicating that its molecular weight was relatively low. Several potential effectors were
tried and ruled out including AMP, ADP, ATP, FAD, and dihydrolipoamide.
However, all three branched-chain amino acids stimulated enzyme activity,
L-valine being the most effective (Roberts and Sokatch, 1978). Assuming that
stimulation of branched-chain ketoacid dehydrogenase by the heat-treated fraction was due entirely to valine, we estimated that the concentration of valine in
the filtrate would have been approximately 0.5×10^{-3} M. The concentration
of amino acids in the filtrate were determined with the amino acid analyzer and
were: glycine, 0.21×10^{-3} M; alanine, 0.23×10^{-3} M; valine, 0.51×10^{-3} M;
isoleucine, trace; and leucine, 0.02×10^{-3} M. In separate experiments it was
found that neither glycine nor alanine stimulated enzyme activity. Therefore, all

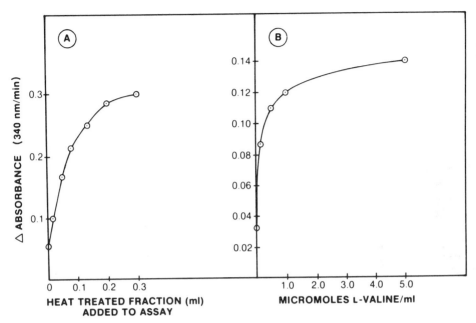

Fig. 2. Stimulation of the standard assay by the heat-treated fraction (A). The amount of enzyme was 0.34 mg protein at a specific activity of 0.135 μmoles NADH/min/mg protein. (B), the stimulation of the standard assay by L-valine. There was 0.12 mg protein in these assays at a specific activity of 0.188 μmoles NADH/min/mg protein (Roberts and Sokatch, 1978.)

the stimulation of the filtrate could be explained by the presence of valine. We also found that crude extracts were deficient in lipoamide dehydrogenase and this component was added to all assays, either as the heat-treated preparation made from the first Sepharose CL-4B pool (Table I) or as the highly purified lipoamide dehydrogenase (Sokatch *et al.*, 1981). All of these components must be added to the assay in order to detect increases in specific activity. It is possible that one of the other subunits, E1 or E2, also disassociates during purification and this possibility is now being studied. Once these requirements were identified, it was possible to purify the complex by conventional methods (Table I).

The purified enzyme separated into three major bands during SDS–gel electrophoresis. The molecular weights of these subunits were 51,000, 47,000 and 39,000, and there were five to six minor bands. When the enzyme was stored in the cold (but not frozen) over a period of weeks, a subunit with the molecular weight of 35,000 appeared. The purified enzyme was active with all three branched-chain ketoacids; the ratio of activities being 2-ketoisovalerate; 2-ketoisocaproate: 2-keto-3-methylvalarate = 1.48; 1.14:10, which is similar to that obtained by Pettit *et al.* (1978) with the enzyme purified from bovine kidney

John R. Sokatch

TABLE I

Purification of Branched-Chain Ketoacid Dehydrogenase from *P. putida*[a]

Fraction	Total protein (mg)	Total units	Specific activity (units/mg)
90k g Supernatant	432	172	0.399
176k g Pellet	164	139	0.848
Pool from Sepharose CL-4B column	82	131	1.6
Pool from DEAE-Sepharose CL-6B column	14	41	3.0
Pool from second Sepharose CL-4B column	2.3	19	8.3

[a] The 90k g supernatant fraction contained 29 units of pyruvate dehydrogenase and 18 units of 2-ketoglutarate dehydrogenase. The final preparation contained 1.5 units of pyruvate dehydrogenase and 0.84 units of 2-ketoglutarate dehydrogenase.

mitochondria. Because of the enzyme data presented here and the genetic data obtained earlier (Martin *et al.*, 1973), we believe that a single enzyme is responsible for the oxidation of all three branched-chain ketoacids. The final enzyme preparation usually contained some pyruvate and 2-ketoglutarate dehydrogenases. For example, one enzyme preparation contained 19 units of branched-chain ketoacid dehydrogenase, 1.5 units of pyruvate dehydrogenase, and 0.84 units of 2-ketoglutarate dehydrogenase. It is possible that some of the pyruvate dehydrogenase activity is inherent to branched-chain ketoacid dehydrogenase, but we believe that the 2-ketoglutarate dehydrogenase activity is due to contamination since we have obtained enzyme preparations without 2-ketoglutarate dehydrogenase activity.

The purified enzyme had absolute requirements for NAD and CoA and almost

TABLE II

Activator and Cofactor Requirements of Branched-Chain Ketoacid Dehydrogenase

Assay conditions	Specific activity (μmoles/min/mg protein)
Complete assay	6.50
L-Valine	2.70
Thiamin pyrophosphate	0.32
Magnesium chloride	0.51
CoA	0.00
Lipoamide dehydrogenase	1.67
Substitute D-valine for L-valine	2.51
Substitute L-leucine for L-valine	3.79
Substitute L-isoleucine for L-valine	4.82

absolute requirements for thiamin pyrophosphate and magnesium. Addition of lipoamide dehydrogenase, purified to the extent that there was only one protein detectable, stimulated enzyme activity nearly fourfold (Table II). L-Valine stimulated activity 2.4-fold; D-valine did not stimulate the enzyme; L-leucine and L-isoleucine were much less effective as stimulators of branched-chain ketoacid dehydrogenase. The activity of L-valine as a regulator of branched-chain ketoacid dehydrogenase is discussed later. The enzyme catalyzed the formation of 1 mole each of isobutyryl-CoA, NADH, and carbon dioxide from 2-ketoisovalerate (Sokatch *et al.*, 1981). Considering the subunit composition of the enzyme and the stoichiometry of the reaction catalyzed, it was clear that this was indeed a multienzyme complex similar to pyruvate and 2-ketoglutarate dehydrogenases.

REQUIREMENT OF BRANCHED-CHAIN KETOACID DEHYDROGENASE FOR LIPOAMIDE DEHYDROGENASE FROM *P. putida* GROWN ON VALINE

One unusual feature of pyruvate and 2-ketoglutarate dehydrogenases of *E. coli* is that they share the same lipoamide dehydrogenase subunit. This interesting topic is covered in the review by Guest (1978), whose laboratory was responsible for much of the research on this subject. Pettit and Reed (1967) purified lipoamide dehydrogenase from both ketoacid dehydrogenases of *E. coli* and found that they were chemically and physically indistinguishable. Later, Guest and Creaghan (1973) and Alwine *et al.* (1973) isolated lipoamide dehydrogenase mutants of *E. coli* which were also deficient in pyruvate and 2-ketoglutarate dehydrogenases. Both ketoacid dehydrogenases could be activated by purified lipoamide dehydrogenase. The locus for lipoamide dehydrogenase was contiguous to the locus for the transacetylase subunit of pyruvate dehydrogenase, *aceF*, but some 14 minutes from the loci for E1 and E2 of 2-ketoglutarate dehydrogenase (*succA* and *succB*; Guest, 1974). This background naturally leads to the question, "Does branched-chain ketoacid dehydrogenase share a common subunit with pyruvate and 2-ketoglutarate dehydrogenases?"

We attacked the problem from two directions. First, I attempted to isolate lipoamide dehydrogenase mutants of *P. putida* while on sabbatical leave in the laboratory of Professor H. L. Kornberg at Cambridge University and under the exacting eye of Maurice Jones-Mortimer. Using the procedure of Guest and Creaghan, we isolated some 20 mutants. None of the mutants had an absolute requirement for acetate + succinate as did the *E. coli lpd* mutants, but rather their lag time was shortened, usually by succinate only. None of these mutants were able to grow on the branched-chain amino acids as the sole carbon source. We were able to demonstrate 2-ketoglutarate dehydrogenase deficiencies in four

John R. Sokatch

TABLE III

Requirement for Lipoamide Dehydrogenase from *P. putida* Grown on Valine

	Nanomoles of NAD reduced/min	
Additions to assay	−Valine	+Valine
None	4.6	4.9
Lipoamide dehydrogenase from *P. putida* grown on valine	7.2	13.2
Lipoamide dehydrogenase from *P. putida* grown on glucose	3.5	3.8

[a] The components of the assay were as described in Sokatch *et al.* (1981) with 4.75 μg branched-chain ketoacid dehydrogenase with a specific activity of 4.8 μmoles NADH formed/min/mg protein. The enzyme had been passed over a Sephadex G-25 column to remove L-valine added during the purification. Lipoamide dehydrogenase prepared from *P. putida* grown on L-valine had a specific activity of 16 μmoles NADH oxidized/min/mg protein. Lipoamide dehydrogenase prepared from *P. putida* grown on glucose had a specific activity of 4.0 μmoles NADH/min/mg protein and yielded only one band in SDS–gel electrophoresis. The details of this purification and the properties of the two lipoamide dehydrogenases will be described in a subsequent publication.

mutants, but none had a deficiency to pyruvate dehydrogenase alone. Four mutants, JS30, JS61, JS94, and JS97, had apparent defficiencies in both pyruvate and 2-ketoglutarate dehydrogenases; JS30 and JS61 appear to be regulatory mutants, JS94 and JS97, lacked both pyruvate and 2-ketoglutarate dehydrogenases and had low levels of lipoamide dehydrogenase. An enzyme preparation from *P. putida* grown on valine enriched in lipoamide dehydrogenase but lacking ketoacid dehydrogenases was prepared by heat-treating the pool from the first Sepharose CL-4B column (Table I). *Pseudomonas putida* grown on glucose does not form branched-chain ketoacid dehydrogenase and the corresponding heat-treated Sepharose CL-4B pool contains lipoamide dehydrogenase only from pyruvate and 2-ketoglutarate dehydrogenases. Both heat-treated enzyme preparations stimulated pyruvate dehydrogenase, but the preparation from glucose-grown bacteria was much more effective. In no case were we able to resurrect 2-ketoglutarate dehydrogenase and we believe that JS94 and JS97 are either deletion or polar mutants unable to form 2-ketoglutarate dehydrogenase.

The second approach was to purify lipoamide dehydrogenase from pyruvate and 2-ketoglutarate dehydrogenases and compare it with the enzyme from branched-chain ketoacid dehydrogenase which we had already prepared (Sokatch *et al.*, 1981). The purification procedure was basically the same as that used to prepare lipoamide dehydrogenase from cells grown on valine. The behavior of lipoamide dehydrogenase from glucose cells during purification was similar to the enzyme from valine cells except that the former was retained more tightly by the Affi-Gel Blue column. The two enzymes differed slightly in molecular weight; the enzyme from glucose cells had a molecular weight of 57,000, whereas the enzyme from valine cells had a molecular weight of 52,000. The specific activity of the enzyme from glucose cells was 4 μmoles NADH oxidized/min/mg protein compared to 33 for the enzyme from valine cells. The significant finding, however, was that only the enzyme from valine cells stimulated branched-chain ketoacid dehydrogenase—the enzyme from glucose cells had no effect at all (Table III). It appears, therefore, that the lesion in JS97 is in the *lpd* locus.

EFFECT OF L-VALINE ON KINETICS OF BRANCHED-CHAIN KETOACID DEHYDROGENASE

The purpose of the previous work was to isolate and characterize the enzyme; however, a study of the kinetics provided some revealing data about the action of L-valine. The Michaelis constants (K_m) and maximum velocity (V_{max}) for 2-ketoisovalerate, are shown in Table IV. Both the Michaelis constant for ketoisovalerate and maximum velocity changed when valine was added to the assay. However, the Michaelis constants for NAD and CoA were not changed when valine was present although the maximum velocity increased in both cases by about the same percentage. The Michaelis constants for 2-ketoisocaproate and 2-keto-3-methylvalerate also decreased when valine was present in the assay. These latter studies were made with other preparations of branched-chain ketoacid dehydrogenase. The addition of valine to the assay did not effect the Hill coefficients for any of these substrates which was approximately 1.0 for 2-ketoisovalerate, NAD, and CoA.

TABLE IV

Michaelis Constants (K_m) and Maximum Velocity (V_{max}) for Substrates of Branched-Chain Ketoacid Dehydrogenase

Substrate	−Valine		+Valine	
	K_m	V_{max}	K_m	V_{max}
2-Ketoisovalerate	0.46	1.27	0.059	2.13
NAD	0.12	1.17	0.13	2.19
CoA	0.033	1.49	0.26	2.38

DISCUSSION

There is no longer any question that the branched-chain ketoacid dehydrogenases of *P. putida* (Sokatch *et al.*, 1981) and bovine kidney (Pettit *et al.*, 1978), are multienzyme complexes. The reaction can be represented as shown in Fig. 3. The branched-chain ketoacid dehydrogenase of *P. putida* has three subunits, one of which has been identified as lipoamide dehydrogenase. Presumably the other two are the decarboxylase–dehydrogenase (E1) and the transcylase (E2), which would mean that there is no regulatory subunit. It is interesting that the highly purified bovine kidney branched-chain ketoacid dehydrogenase has four subunits, E1 being composed of two nonidentical subunits, molecular weights 46,000 and 35,000. The molecular weight of E2 is 52,000. The bovine kidney branched-chain ketoacid dehydrogenase is unaffected by the addition of L-valine to the assay. The other properties of the two enzymes were similar, both catalyzed the oxidation of all three branched-chain ketoacids, and the Michaelis constants for the keto acids were approximately 50 mM for both enzymes.

Probably, the singular most interesting feature of branched-chain ketoacid dehydrogenase from *P. putida* is its stimulation by valine. Although we have thus far been concerned mostly with the structure of the enzyme, one significant fact has emerged concerning its regulation. The Michaelis constants for branched-chain keto acids were substantially reduced by the presence of valine, but these for NAD and coenzyme A were unaffected. We have not obtained any evidence for a regulatory subunit, but we consider this to be an open question until we have characterized all the subunits. Although the double reciprocal plots were occasionally curved, the deviations from a straight line were at low enzyme rates which were difficult to measure accurately. Therefore, the present evidence points to a mode of action for L-valine which tightens the binding of branched-chain ketoacids to E1.

Regulation of branched-chain ketoacid dehydrogenase by L-valine could be a beneficial regulatory feature of the enzyme. When *P. putida* grows in a medium that lacks valine, this amino acid is synthesized *de novo* with 2-ketoisovalerate as the immediate precurser. If the concentration of 2-ketoisovalerate become high enough to induce the branched-chain ketoacid dehydrogenase, the ketoacid will be protected until the concentration of L-valine becomes high enough to stimulate enzyme activity. The fact that branched-chain ketoacid dehydrogenase is induced by branched-chain keto acids rather than amino acids, may also be significant. This mechanism of induction would pervent induction of branched-chain ketoacid dehydrogenase by amino acids of the cell's pool.

The second interesting feature of the enzyme is the apparent requirement for its own lipoamide dehydrogenase. It is curious that lipoamide dehydrogenase from glucose cells has absolutely no activity with branched-chain ketoacid dehydrogenase. Some additional work is needed to establish this conclusion, but it

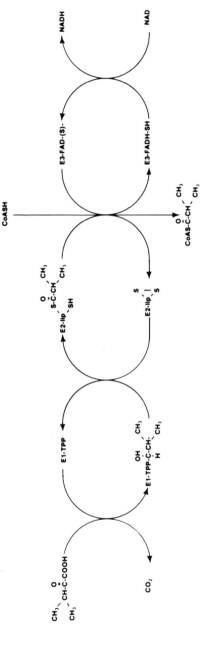

Fig. 3. The oxidation of 2-ketoisovalerate by branched-chain ketoacid dehydrogenase of *P. putida*. E1 is the decarboxylase–dehydrogenase, E2 is the transacylase, and E3 is lipoamide dehydrogenase. The branched-chain ketoacid attaches to thiamin pyrophosphate of E1, decarboxylates, and then transfers to a lipoic acid sulfhydryl of E2. The isobutyryl group then transfers to CoA and the sulfhydryl groups of lipoic acid are oxidized to the disulfide by lipoamide dehydrogenase.

seems the most likely possibility at this time. It is possible, for example, that the lipoamide dehydrogenase from glucose-grown *P. putida* lacks a minor component of the branched-chain ketoacid dehydrogenase which is present in the enzyme prepared from cells grown on valine. It is also possible that there is only one locus for lipoamide dehydrogenase and that is modified for use by branched-chain ketoacid dehydrogenase. There is no reason to believe that branched-chain ketoacid dehydrogenase of bovine kidney requires its own lipoamide dehydrogenase (Pettit *et al.,* 1978). If mutant JS97 is a polar mutant, this would suggest that the *lpd* locus is adjacent to the *succA* and *succB* loci which would be very different from *E. coli.*

REFERENCES

Alwine, J. C., Russell, F. M., and Murray, K. N. (1973). *J. Bacteriol.* **115,** 1.

Barrera, C. R., Namihira, G., Hamilton, L., Munk, P., Eley, M. H., Linn, T. C., and Reed, L. J. (1972). *Arch. Biochem. Biophys.* **148,** 343.

Dancis, J., Hutzler, J., and Levitz, M. (1963). *Pediatrics* **32,** 234.

Guest, J. R. (1974). *J. Gen. Microbiol.* **80,** 523.

Guest, J. R. (1978). *Adv. Neurol.* **21,** 219.

Guest, J. R., and Creaghan, I. T. (1973). *J. Gen. Microbiol.* **75,** 197.

Marshall, V. P., and Sokatch, J. R. (1972). *J. Bacteriol.* **110,** 1073.

Martin, R. R., Marshall, V. P., Sokatch, J. R., and Unger, L. L. (1973). *J. Bacteriol.* **115,** 198.

Massey, L. K., Sokatch, J. R., and Conrad, R. S. (1976). *Bacteriol. Rev.* **40,** 42.

Pettit, F. H., and Reed, L. J. (1967). *Proc. Natl. Acad. Sci. U.S.A.* **58,** 1126.

Pettit, F. H., Yeaman, S. J., and Reed, L. J. (1978). *Proc. Natl. Acad. Sci. U.S.A.* **75,** 4881.

Reed, L. J., and Cox, D. J. (1970). In "The Enzymes" (P. D. Boyer, ed.), 3rd ed., Vol. 1, pp. 213-240. Academic Press, New York.

Roberts, C. M., and Sokatch, J. R. (1978). *Biochem. Biophys. Res. Commun.* **82,** 828.

Roberts, C. M., Conrad, R. S., and Sokatch, J. R. (1978). *Arch. Microbiol.* **117,** 99.

Sokatch, J. R., McCully, V. M., and Roberts, C. M. (1981). *J. Bacteriol.* **148,** 647.

5

A Movable Feast
with Gunny:
An Early History of
the Mandelate Pathway

R. Y. Stanier

One of the multiple casualties of the late twentieth century is the death of scientific correspondence: the sort of intimate, spontaneous unguarded scientific writings that form one of the pleasures of a more leisurely age. My scientific correspondence properly speaking with Gunny, stretched from ca. 1948 to 1954. Trained as a microbiologist in the very permissive school of Kees van Niel (1939–1942) I had lazily concentrated on completing my training as a microbiologist, to the total detriment of my biochemical education, which was manifestly defective.

When Gunny first crossed my path, during the summer of 1948 and in the course of a relatively long stay in Berkeley (which was a rare event for Gunny), I was hard at work exploring the oxidation of aromatic compounds by fluorescent pseudomonads. I had uncovered the phenomenon of ''simultaneous adaptation'' and was investigating this process as a technique for the study of metabolic pathways (Stanier, 1947). The argument may be summarized as follows (Stanier, 1950):

> The complete oxidation of even a relatively simple organic molecule must necessarily involve the formation of many intermediate substances, each successive step being under specific enzymatic control. In order to grasp the idea of simultaneous adaptation it is only necessary to combine this concept with another one: namely, that in the case of adaptive

35

EXPERIENCES IN BIOCHEMICAL PERCEPTION
Copyright © 1982 by Academic Press, Inc.
All rights of reproduction in any form reserved.
ISBN 0-12-528420-9

oxidations, not only the initial enzyme E_A acting on the primary substrate A but also the enzymes E_B, E_C, E_D, etc., acting upon the series of intermediates B, C, D, etc., produced successively from A, may well be adaptive. In such an event, the provision to the cells of an adaptively-attacked primary substrate A will act as a trigger mechanism not merely for the synthesis of the single enzyme E_A, but for the synthesis of a whole series of enzymes acting in succession on the intermediates formed from A. In other words, by providing a new adaptively attacked substrate we redirect large segments of the enzymatic constitution of the cell into new patterns. . . .

Despite its ingenuity (and speaking with hindsight) I should characterize the technique of simultaneous adaptation as a sort of "biochemistry without tears"—a last chance to elude the rigors of biochemical analysis by the use of the near-classical technique of manometry with intact, "resting cells."

I should recall that in 1947, there was no very satisfactory general procedure to obtain enzymatically active, cell-free preparations from bacteria. McIlwain (1948) soon remedied this deficiency. It was an absurdly simple and effective technique that cost nothing, save a certain amount of muscle power. One mixed a suspension of wet, packed bacterial cells with dry alumina and started grinding. After 3–4 minutes, a certain tackiness denoted an active, cell-free preparation.*

McIlwain's procedure was the breakthrough. There was no question about it: despite my ignorance of biochemical procedures, I simply had to acquire the rudiments of biochemistry. I shall always remember with profound gratitude Gunny's determinant role. He dealt with me with gentleness and simplicity, and he helped immensely by extending a hand that enabled me to acquire the elements of a biochemical education.

Gunny, listening with that sensitive third ear of his, summed up the situation correctly: here is an excellently trained microbiologist, but almost totally ignorant of biochemistry. Why not help him out?

In 1948–1949, Gunny had encountered a problem of great difficulty and importance: the enzymatically complex oxidative decarboxylation of pyruvate, terminating in acetyl-CoA. It is in all the textbooks now, as a model system for the terminal oxidation of α-keto acids via the citric acid cycle (1950). Indeed, no fewer than three coenzymes coupled with three apoproteins participate in this reaction. Gunny even succeeded in synthesizing a new coenzyme, lipoic acid.

To drop all this, in favor of the belated postdoctoral training in biochemistry of a microbiologist, argues great generosity of spirit. But Gunny has always been generous: he had a deep, if disinterested respect for scientific ability.

It was somewhat later (1951–1952) that I succeeded in working in Gunny's

---

*I note with astonishment that the technique of McIlwain (1948), despite its simplicity, effectiveness, and economy, was not introduced in our laboratory until 3 years later (Hayaishi and Stanier, 1951). In order to obtain enzymatically active, cell-free preparations from tryptophan-adapted cells, Hayaishi and Stanier (1951) systematically tried a variety of procedures: acetone drying; slow vacuum drying over P_2O_5; and autolysis of heavy cell suspensions. Of all these procedures, McIlwain's technique proved far superior. Perhaps it was *too* simple, cheap, and effective!

and Carol Gunsalus' laboratory at the University of Illinois on the pathway of mandelate oxidation, while I was a recipient of a Guggenheim Fellowship. We worked at least 14 hours a day, 7 days a week. I had absolutely no other commitments, save to turn myself into a biochemist. Poor Carol had definite commitments as Gunny's wife and could not keep up with me. Indeed, I remember with compunction an incident of stomach cramps near the end of my fellowship tenure. This was not unrelated to Carol's apparent failure to demonstrate two benzaldehyde dehydrogenases, one NAD-linked and one NADP-linked.

During my short stay in Illinois, out of mandelate-adapted cells (*Pseudomonas putida* A.3.12) we succeeded in fishing no fewer than five enzymatically active fractions, all with activities strictly inducible and very highly specific for the conversion of mandelate to benzoate from a cell-free extract (Fig. 1). Essentially, it was a

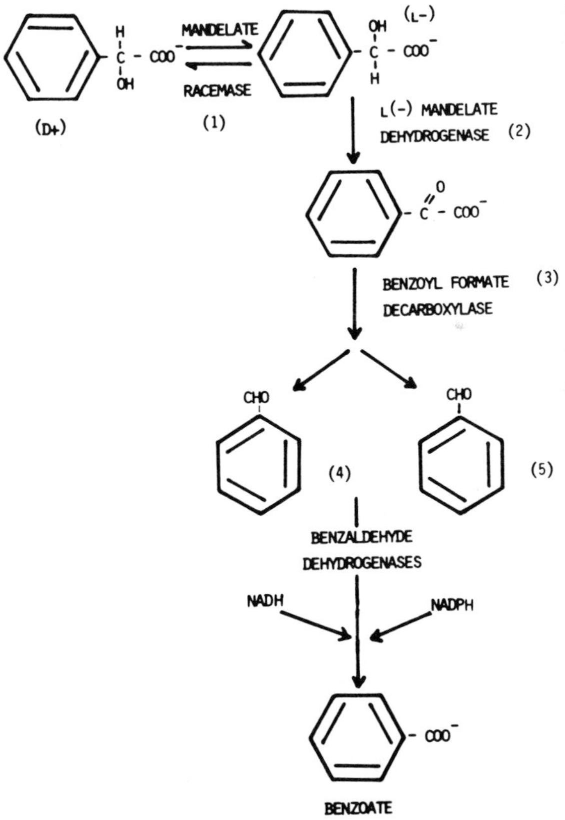

Fig. 1. A schematic diagram of the mandelate oxidative pathway. All five enzymes that constitute the pathway are inducible and very highly specific.

vindication at the enzymatic level of the technique of simultaneous adaptation (C. F. Gunsalus *et al.*, 1953; I. C. Gunsalus *et al.*, 1953; Stanier *et al.*, 1953).

The background thus briefly sketched, I shall let Gunny speak for himself. Here are a few passages from some of Gunny's correspondence prior to my stay in his laboratory.

Indiana University

October 25, 1948

Dear Roger:

May I take this opportunity to thank you for your kindness and hospitality during my stay in Berkeley. I certainly enjoyed the visit both from the standpoint of talking general matters with you and from the scientific viewpoint. It certainly is heartening to see a first rate scientific group which is going somewhere. As a matter of fact, as you well know, my whole stay on the West Coast contributed not only to my education but to general spirits as well. I hope you will not consider my tardiness in writing any indication of my true appreciation. Upon returning here I find the usual multitude of miscellany to be cleaned up. The boys are doing decent research in the lab but needed a considerable amount of time and attention, as a matter of fact they still do and I am having trouble reducing the myriad of petty details so that the proper amount of attention can be given to important items.

. . .

Again, Roger, thanks for all your hospitality. It was a real pleasure to have a more extended chance to talk with you and I hope to see you again. With best regards,

Gunny

Indiana University

April 18, 1949

Dear Roger:

Thanks for your abstracts. I will try to get them together and out by the end of the week, but first am going to the Federation Meetings and hope to have a chance to talk to Spiegelman, Wood, and Lederberg there.

As to time, Nungester figures that about two hours is right for the round table, but I think we can plan on two and a half or a little longer if we work things right. This being the case, I think we could expect four approximately 30-minute talks and still have the necessary time for discussions, etc. Lipmann has sent in a very nice general outline leading to some very specific items with respect to the utilization of energy rich phosphorus compounds in synthetic reactions, with the general tone being the utilization of microorganisms for the solution of enzyme problems in biochemistry, or the solution of biochemistry problems in microbiology, whichever you please. Josh has pretty well outlined the chemical aspects of the genetic studies with coli in relation to lactose fermentation. I think this will fit in well with Mike's, and that with your introduction, which, in addition to stressing the points of your method of approach, will introduce most of the types of concepts which the others will handle.

With regard to what I will need for teaching this summer, I had been intending to ask you when you come through here what these people will have as a background, both microbiochemically and chemically, and about how many there are likely to be, in order to know what would be most appropriate. I had rather been toying with the idea of spending a little time on the general aspects of getting bugs in good shape for doing biological experiments, which in high-toned language might be said to be a narrow minded chemical view of certain aspects of physiology, and then to spend most of the time on the application of general biochemical knowledge to various groups of microorganisms and to various types of reactions, as for example the energy processes, the reactions of pyruvate, what is known about reactions in amino acid synthesis, etc. Are these people on a primitive enough level so that Gale's book would be helpful to them? Are most of the reviews (bacteriological, chemical, and the advances in enzymology, protein chemistry, etc.) available so that some of the better reviews in these could more or less be used as chapters for the study of specific topics?

If there is no hurry about this I would like to talk to you at meeting time, since I am willing to cut the cloth to cover the corpse. Otherwise, if you will give me a little orientation as to what these people want, I will do the best I can in outlining what will be needed.

Indiana University

August 10, 1949

Dear Roger:

. . .

1. Benzaldehyde is oxidized rapidly with an oxygen uptake of one-half mole per mole substrate if one adds NAD to your second dried prep. This being the case, it looks as though several of the preparations may not be deficient in enzymes but only in carriers. The Benzaldehyde–benzoic system is also placed in the cell-free extracts and can be connected to NAD as indicated by spectrophotometer readings at 340. The oxidation of mandelate in the presence of an excess of NAD goes nearly to 1 oxygen, but in spite of the fact, we have made up several batches of substrate and it appears to fall a little short in some experiments. Whether this involves a slowness in the decarboxylation, i.e. the second step, or some other cause is not clear.

2. We got out some benzoyl formic using the large dialyzed prep but haven't the melting points or derivatives, etc., on this yet. It also appears to be decarboxylated but I would like to crystallize it again before being too confident.

We have rather precise data on the various steps now but probably will not have time to finish up all experiments with cell-free enzymes which might be desirable. Carol will do a couple of more experiments while I pack up books, etc., and will probably drop another note and some more curves to you on Saturday or so and then will take off for the East.

Indiana University

August 30, 1949

Dear Rog:

Thanks for your letter which I found this morning on returning to the lab. We were also worried about the apparent difference in the saturation of the mandelate and the benzaldehyde systems with NAD. The only hypothesis I could muster at the moment is that the dissociation of the coenzyme from the benzaldehyde system is much higher than from the mandelate. It is possible that neither is saturated but that more mandelate enzyme is present than benzaldehyde enzyme (this would also be of interest in terms of the effect of small amounts of substrate in enzyme formation). These, of course, would be subject to test. Now with the picture fairly well blocked out, it seems to me that it would be worth while to take both the benzaldehyde and mandelate enzymes out cell free, separate them by fractionation, determine their activity spectrophotometrically, and incidentally the dissociation constant for NAD. This would remove any doubt as to the direct action of NAD as the prosthetic group of the enzymes, and not leave the work based on too many postulates.

If you want to grow the cells and send them, I think we could readily get the enzymes out with a sonic oscillator, and if they are as stable as they seem to be, could probably even lyophilize them in case you wish to have some.

Since you are writing up the other work, I will put the pieces together so that I will be able to see what other facts may be needed, and also to give you a basis for criticism. Work will pile up deeper than I anticipate, but if at all possible I would like to see this finished before February.

. . .

Indiana University

September 30, 1949

Dear Roger:

. . .

A short time ago I had the good fortune to come by two small samples of mandelate, i.e., the resolved D- and L-isomers. I would like to check them in the polarimeter to be sure and then will ship them to you so that you can grow cells, etc. I would guess that the adaptation to D and L forms will be distinct. I am enclosing a rough sketch of my understanding of the present status of the oxidation of tyrosine by animal tissue. This is unpublished data which was explained to me in response to a suggestion of your ideas of the mechanism of the breaking of the benzine ring, i.e., the compounds as outlined, not the intimate mechanism as you visualized it. I was wondering if this might not be of value in terms of route of the phenylacetic oxidation. I haven't been thinking enough to have any sensible comments on your other pieces of information, but will try to do so.

. . . I wish now that I had time to talk to you about a couple of problems, but will let them slide, hoping you will come East. As a matter of fact, I need to talk to somebody quite often about bugology and biochemistry, and miss you and the California crew for this purpose.

University of Illinois

September 13, 1950

Dear Roger:

Thanks for your letter of August 30. It gave me the best kind of greeting on arriving in Urbana last night. Your and Josh's experiments on the effect of UV on adaptation is very exciting. As you said, it will be a practical tool, but I hope you also have some good ideas—no doubt you do—as to how this may be accomplished. . . .

. . . Incidentally, during the last two weeks I was able to separate the pyruvate dehydrogenase system into three portions of which one was transacetylase and the other two are in ammonium sulphate fractions, but as yet no dependable tests for their action have been devised, i.e., all three fractions are necessary for pyruvate dehydrogenase; the dependencies on co-enzyme A etc., were demonstrated with these preparations. I wish I had another couple of weeks—I really could have done something with the purification of one of the fractions which I was able to separate completely devoid of the others in good yield and at a fairly high level of purity. I feel that this problem is cracked now and will really require further fractionation and cleaning up of the enzymes and co-enzymes in order to know what does go on. To make life really interesting, I ran the *Leuconostoc* fermentation at Brookhaven with labelled glucose and also found that a new enzyme system is involved here. I am not sure whether we have discussed this, but the heterolactics, especially the cocci (Betacocci of Orla-Jensen) will ferment glucose and yield one molecule each of lactate, ethanol and CO_2. We have been unable to divorce this from the 1:1:1 ratio, thus I suspected a lack of mixing of the trioses. DeMoss has fractionated dried cell preparations and has been able to demontrate aldolases, triosephosphate dehydrogenase, lactic dehydrogenase and ethanol dehydrogenase, but has been unable to show any isomerase action. Fermentation of position one labelled glucose by resting cell-suspensions yielded labelled carbon entirely in the CO_2. Fermentation of 3:4 labelled glucose with similar preparation yielded the label better than 99%, and the carboxyl position of lactate (presumably the 4 carbon) in the CH_2OH of ethanol. Thus it looks like we are going to have some fun working out the enzyme systems which form the ethanol and CO_2 in this organism.

The mandelate is not forgotten. By high-speed centrifugation in Ochoa's laboratory (the preparation I made up for Joe to run the condensation experiments), the DPN Hn2 oxidation can be almost completely removed, thus satisfying the last criterion for which we were searching. This is an interesting system which some day should be studied in detail especially with respect to reversibility and phopshate requirement.

University of Illinois

November 27, 1950

Dear Roger:

. . .

We will answer your other letter shortly. I am glad to hear that Hayaishi is there and that you are making progress on the tryptophan system. We expect to get into our laboratory this weekend where we will have more room to work and also a more convenient order of things. In addition I won't have to answer questions as to where pipes should be put, why we have to have distilled water, etc. and as a result can spend more time on the type of thing which I am built to do. We are inching forward on the pyruvate problem and hope to accelerate the pace of this beginning this week especially since now we have accumulated most of the necessary enzymes to supplement our studies.

University of Illinois

January 23, 1953

Dear Roger:

The manuscript on mandelate, in which I would call a semi-finished form, has finally been typed and is on its way. As I indicated before, I think everything is in fairly good form with the exception of the benzaldehyde data. I have enclosed the best tables I can make from yours and Carol's collected efforts. If you want the notebooks to pick from further, I will be glad to send them. It is quite likely that we should insert a paragraph describing the benzaldehyde system more clearly.

It is quite clear that parts of this work are not finished, but from the standpoint of blocking out the enzymes in a sequence, including at least five, describing one new one and amplifying considerably the particle situation, it seems to me that this is a meritorious contribution. I shall get together the racemase data including the labeled experiments, written in JBC style, and ship them off to you as the Spring progresses.

There are a number of interesting problems which would bear discussion, but I hope that we can visit about these when you stop, either in April or May. The first week in April is the Federation Meetings in Chicago, so that if it would suit your plans, we would prefer that you stop in early May and spend a week with us. This fits for Luria as well as us. There have been many changes in the past year which will bear both further thinking and discussion.

University of Illinois

February 27, 1953

Dear Roger:

Luria was in the other day worrying about schedules before the Federation meetings. In addition I now have your letters of February 22 and 25. In view of your uncertainty about stopping on the return trip, I think we should make every effort to get together on the Mandelate papers, get them finished and off to press. The best re-arrangement I can make on my schedule is to be back in Urbana not later than April 1. I think we shall go to Chicago late on the 6th or early on the 7th, but cannot decide definitely until we see the Federation program. If you can make it, we will be tickled to have you any or all of the time from the 2nd to the 6th. The discussion of the papers can wait until your manuscript returns. I have always liked to put the first of the series in the J. Bact.: (a) to get the chemists more aware of bacteriological work and workers, and (b) if nothing else, to educate the peasants and to give the graduate students something to think about which, at least in my interests, can be more definitive than much which appears in the J. Bact. However, I will reserve judgement. I don't believe we should plan too much on Carol finishing experiments to complete the manuscripts since this draws out the time element and I don't believe at the moment will lead to better definition. This too we can discuss when you get here.

The letters concerning Gunny's participation with the mandelate pathway end here. Later on, Gunny and I collaborated on our five-volume treatise, "The Bacteria" (1960-1964). Gunny not only helped me immeasurably through his knowledge and experience, but even more through his moral support and esteem.

REFERENCES

Gunsalus, C. F., Stanier, R. Y., and Gunsalus, I. C. (1953). The enzymatic conversion of mandelic acid to benzoic acid. III. Fractionation and properties of the soluble enzymes. *J. Bacteriol.* **66,** 548–553.

Gunsalus, I. C., Gunsalus, C. F., and Stanier, R. Y. (1953). The enzymatic conversion of mandelic acid to benzoic acid. I. Cross fractionation of the system into soluble and particulate components. *J. Bacteriol.* **66,** 538–542.

Hayaishi, O., and Stanier, R. Y. (1951). The bacterial oxidation of tryptophan. III. Enzymatic activities of cell-free extracts from bacteria employing the aromatic pathway. *J. Bacteriol.* **62,** 691–709.

Korkes, S., Stern, J. R., Gunsalus, I. C., and Ochoa, S. (1950). Enzymatic synthesis of citrate from pyruvate and oxalacetate. *Nature (London)* **166,** 439.

McIlwain, H. (1948). Preparation of cell-free bacterial extracts with powdered alumina. *J. Gen. Microbiol.* **2,** 288–291.

Stanier, R. Y. (1947). Simultaneous adaptation: A new technique for the study of metabolic pathways. *J. Bacteriol.* **54,** 339–348.

Stanier, R. Y. (1950). Problems of bacterial oxidative metabolism. *Bacteriol. Rev.* **14,** 179–191.

Stanier, R. Y., Gunsalus, I. C., and Gunsalus, C. F. (1953). The enzymatic conversion of mandelic acid to benzoic acid. II. Properties of the particulate fractions. *J. Bacteriol.* **66,** 543–547.

6

Our Microbial World

S. Dagley

In 1963–1964 it was my good fortune to spend a year as Visiting Professor in Urbana. Gunny and I had previously shared a mutual interest in bacterial citrate lyase (Gillespie and Gunsalus, 1953; Dagley and Dawes, 1953). What was more important was that our friendship had been fostered during a period when a succession of my graduate students, Peter Chapman, John Sykes, and Peter Trudgill, crossed the Atlantic to become postdocs in the Division of Biochemistry, as it was then designated, of the Chemistry Department of the University of Illinois. At a later date, they were to be joined by David Gibson and John Wood who took up similar appointments in Burrill Hall, across the way from the Roger Adams building.

Although I retained an interest in aromatic metabolism, my attention in 1963 was chiefly focused upon two recently discovered metabolites with common features of structure: α-ketoglutarate semialdehyde and tartronate semialdehyde. Friends in England had shown that the latter compound is a metabolite of bacteria utilizing glycolate (Kornberg and Gotto, 1961; Gotto and Kornberg, 1961) and oxalate (Quayle *et al.*, 1961), and our group had explored its role in the metabolism of *Pseudomonas* growing with glycine as a sole carbon source (Dagley *et al.*, 1961). On arrival in Urbana I was pleasantly surprised to find that Ralph Wolfe, of the Department of Microbiology, was also engaged in assigning

EXPERIENCES IN BIOCHEMICAL PERCEPTION
Copyright © 1982 by Academic Press, Inc.
All rights of reproduction in any form reserved.
ISBN 0-12-528420-9

a place to tartronate semialdehyde in the metabolism of glyoxylate by *Streptococcus allantoicus* (Valentine *et al.*, 1964). As for α-ketoglutarate semialdehyde, this compound had been synthesized by Peter Trudgill, and identified as a metabolite arising when various hexaric acids and pentoses are degraded (Dagley and Trudgill, 1965). We were soon to become aware of work underway in the United States, proving that α-ketoglutarate semialdehyde was a bacterial metabolite of L-arabinose (Stoolmiller and Abeles, 1966) and of hydroxyproline (Singh and Adams, 1965). Despite the fascination and importance of these new biochemicals, however, my attention quickly reverted to aromatic catabolism. There were two reasons for this, one scientific and the other geographical, as I shall explain.

In those days, a topographical feature of the city of Urbana was the Boneyard Creek, and between its muddy banks there meandered a stream of legendary pollution. Such was its fame that I once read an article in (of all journals) the *Transactions of the Leeds Literary and Philosophical Society*, where mention was made of the last date when a live fish had been discovered in its water. The writer believed that the finder was the victim of a hoax. But whatever the status of higher forms of life, there was no doubt that the Boneyard supported a rich and catabolically versatile microbial flora, and that I had the advantage of unimpeded access. We lived in a house built upon a concrete raft that spanned the creek with the rich microbial habitat below; the house has since been demolished, and the stream enclosed for most of its length. Under those favorable circumstances, I soon isolated *Pseudomonas* U, an organism that eventually proved useful to investigators in laboratories ranging from Melbourne, Australia to Bangor, Wales. For our own group, the benefits were immediate. David Gibson had already isolated and characterized 4-hydroxy-2-ketovaleric acid, a meta-fission catabolite of catechol. Extracts of a Leeds pseudomonad had previously been useful for his purpose, since aldolase activity was feeble and the compound in question accumulated; but there the matter rested until he received, by airmail, a culture of the far livelier organism from the Boneyard. Gibson was able to study, immediately, an active aldolase for his compound and so complete a description of the metabolic route to pyruvate. Other studies followed, and our review of the new pathways of bacterial catabolism was published during that year (Dagley *et al.*, 1964).

The scientific impetus for the revival of my interest in aromatics was provided by the atmosphere of Gunny's laboratories. There, the intense concentration upon microbial catabolism of camphor baffled most visitors, and Gunny himself was content simply to observe that it would be fun to find out how bacteria managed to engulf such a little "grease-ball." For me it became a matter of increasing significance that *even* compounds such as camphor were rapidly drawn into the carbon cycle by microbial enzymes that could activate dioxygen without risk. Later, as a member of the Gunsalus Committee, set up to advise the

Secretary of Agriculture about the problems of maintaining and improving the quality of our environment, I was urged to think about the limitations of these enzymes when confronted with man-made chemicals (Dagley, 1972). In any event, only a person completely ignorant of the way that our understanding of metabolism has developed over three decades would dream of dismissing any of Gunny's hunches on the grounds that the program appeared to be somewhat esoteric. Thus, part of a mixed function methylene hydroxylase system employed by *Pseudomonas putida* to attack the little grease-ball turned out to be a cytochrome P450, a discovery which, at the time, riveted the attention of many mammalian biochemists and all pharmacologists. With few words and one attractive photograph, the crystallization of this elusive protein was reported (Yu and Gunsalus, 1970) and it was shown to consist of a single polypeptide chain of molecular weight 45,000, attached through acid-labile linkages to one molecule of ferriprotoporphyrin IX (Dus *et al.*, 1970). As the cytochrome was purified and characterized, the tools of modern physics were being recruited to reveal the detailed events of its operation.

However, other mighty oaks had previously grown from Gunny's little acorns. One of these was a study of the growth requirements of *Streptococcus faecalis* (Bellamy and Gunsalus, 1943), a title which, with a change of name, served many an average Ph.D. thesis in the 1940's. But in this case, full advantage was taken of conditions that yielded cells which contained the protein tyrosine decarboxylase, but were inactive because they lacked its coenzyme. For full activity to be expressed, it was necessary to provide them with ATP as well as pyridoxal (Gunsalus *et al.*, 1944). In a few short, decisive papers, not only were Gunsalus and Umbreit and their colleagues able to establish that pyridoxal phosphate was the coenzyme form of the vitamin: they also proved that a very distinguished organic chemist was backing the wrong chemical structure (Umbreit and Gunsalus, 1949; Karrer and Viscontini, 1947). Another important advance in general biochemistry began with the observations of Snell *et al.* (1937) that acetate stimulates growth of certain lactic acid bacteria. Ten years later, O'Kane and Gunsalus (1947, 1948) discovered a factor required for the oxidation of pyruvic acid by *S. faecalis*. Shortly afterward, Snell and Broquist (1949) proved that this same factor was very active in promoting growth of *Lactobacillus casei* in the absence of acetate. These separate lines of investigation finally coalesced when the group at Urbana joined forces with Lester J. Reed and his colleagues at Austin, Texas, and were able to crystallize and characterize α-lipoic acid from liver concentrates supplied by Eli Lilly and Company (Reed *et al.*, 1951).

As these examples prove, experiments with bacteria have enabled an investigator of exceptional insight to go straight to the heart of problems in mammalian biochemistry. In this chapter I shall try to show how the evolution of life itself has depended upon chemical activities of bacteria. Having this bold objective, I have made use (by modifying the title) of an inspiring book (Stanier *et al.*,

1963) so aptly described as "marvellous" by Fritz Lipmann (1976). Our own world, I believe, is a microbial world, so much have microbes contributed toward its existence. I also hope to show that, in the process of shaping it, the bacteria themselves have acquired a chemical decisiveness, a directness of approach, of great help to investigators. We tend to develop an instinctive feeling that if a proposed bacterial reaction sequence is not economical, simple to the point of elegance, then it is probably wrong. Bacterial investigations have been economical in another sense. Immediately preceding one of the decisive publications of Umbreit and Gunsalus using pyridoxal-deficient bacteria, we find a report of work with biotin-deficient turkeys: fruitful, but more expensive and less convenient.

Let us first consider how microbes played an essential part in setting the stage for the evolution of higher forms of life. For this process to operate effectively, a carbon cycle is essential. Organisms are born and bred; successful species are selected; all the time, organisms die and decay; and their biochemicals, being no longer of use, are recycled. Long before twentieth century man began to worry about the limitations of earth's resources, and was tempted into "cloud-cuckoo land," dreaming of escape to another home in outer space, nature had made the most of these constraints, and man himself emerged.

A carbon cycle operates within an energy gradient. At the bottom of this gradient is carbon dioxide, the stablest carbon compound in an atmosphere containing 20% of oxygen. At the top are biochemicals, conserving solar energy that was trapped by green plants. All of the earth's organic chemicals are thermodynamically unstable insofar as they can furnish energy when oxidized. All of them have been synthesized by a living organism: by a plant or an organic chemist. This was pointed out long ago by George Wald (1954) when writing of Wöhler's synthesis of urea. Oxygen was not only thermodynamically appropriate for its role in setting up an energy gradient; it was also kinetically appropriate. It is a relatively sluggish molecule under physiological conditions: it exists in a triplet state, with unpaired electron spins; and consequently, concerted reactions with the singlet carbon atoms of biochemicals are forbidden. To react, dioxygen must be transformed to an active state by a source of energy, such as sunlight, or by the action of a suitable enzyme. Without such a convenient barrier against spontaneous reactivity it is obvious that, in an atmosphere containing dioxygen, biochemicals would never have persisted long enough for evolution to have taken place. In fact, with all the promise it held for future developments, the advent of oxygen brought its attendant hazards. Some of the enzymes of present-day aerobic organisms, notably some flavoproteins, give rise to a reactive and toxic form of oxygen (the superoxide anion) when their normal function is, of course, far removed from involvement in this accidental occurrence. Protection is afforded by the enzyme superoxide dismutase (Fridovich, 1974) which removes the radical before it can do any damage by itself, or can give rise to even more dangerous forms (Kellog and Fridovich, 1975). Strict anaerobes lack this enzyme (McCord *et al.*, 1971); they never became equipped to venture forth and take advantage of the energy gradient that oxygen had provided; in consequence they have lurked in the mud throughout all ages, remaining strict conservatives because they could never tolerate radicals. Nevertheless, hazardous though it may be, the activation of dioxygen to give forms of the element capable of attacking carbon directly was necessary in order to establish a carbon cycle, as the following considerations demonstrate.

While it ensured the accumulation of atmospheric oxygen, photosynthesis also gave rise to other products that might have posed problems for the establishment of a carbon cycle. These products included the lignin, a biopolymer needed in evolutionary development insofar as it served as structural material for higher plants, enabling them to stand erect and make use of solar radiation. Lignin, and many other plant products such as the "little grease-ball," camphor, are biochemically unreactive compounds. Unlike carbohydrates, fats, proteins, and nucleic acids they are not degraded by primitive catabolic enzymes such as aldolases and hydrolases. For their rapid degradation, direct attack by dioxygen is called for, incorporating oxygen into carbon skeletons. Admittedly, some benzenoid compounds can be degraded by consortia of anaerobic organisms, but lignins are not included in this category: in anaerobic sewage fermentations they are both a nuisance and a challenge, representing, as they do, a potential source of methane (and energy) that the microorganisms have failed to release. The safely controlled enzymic activation of dioxygen on a global scale became the responsibility of microbes. By fixing oxygen, catabolic routes are initiated. Inert aliphatic hydrocarbons give fatty acids; aromatic hydrocarbons are converted into dihydric phenols and their benzene rings are opened by further oxygenase attack; atoms of oxygen are inserted into aliphatic ring structures such as those of camphor and cyclohexanone, etc. (Dagley, 1978). Once the appropriate number of oxygen atoms has been inserted, the product is usually open to attack by hydratases, aldolases, hydrolases, and other types of enzymes that living forms have always used for catabolism. The development of photosynthesis, therefore, raised these problems, but it also provided the chemical reagent, dioxygen, required for their solution. Microorganisms, with their vast array of oxygenases, put the reagent to work.

It may also be observed that bacteria not only set the stage for life processes by their role in the carbon cycle, but were also, apparently, instrumental in providing some of the essential equipment for eukaryotic evolution. I refer to the stimulating views of Dickerson *et al.* (1976) who used X-ray analysis to determine the shapes that are found to be taken up by the folding of the polypeptide chains of cytochrome c's from various species. Cytochrome c from tuna fish, c_{550} from *Paracoccus denitrificans*, c_{558} from *Euglena,* and c_2 from purple non-sulfur bacteria formed such a close-knit family that one could not identify the origin of a given sample for certain, if the choice were based solely on shape and amino acid sequence. These strong indications of common ancestry formed the basis of a suggestion as to how the Krebs cycle, and terminal respiratory chains, came to assume their present functions in aerobic organisms. Purple sulfur bacteria were probably among the first forms of life to use a cytochrome chain. They lived an anaerobic existence with hydrogen sulfide as a source of reducing power, the generation of ATP being coupled to electron flow from quinones to bacterial chlorophyll. A balance was maintained between the two requirements, those for reducing power and energy, by returning a portion of the electron flow from excited chlorophyll back to quinones. Significant modifications of this system occurred in the ancestors of the purple non-sulfur bacteria as the first atmospheric oxygen began to make its appearance. The cyclic aspects of the photosynthetic cytochrome chain were retained, but NADH now replaced hydrogen sulfide as a source of reducing power, electrons being passed through the chain back to chlorophyll. By providing, in addition, a route from what is now designated cytochrome c_2 to a cytochrome a/a_3 oxidase system, a complete cytochrome chain became available for electron flow from NADH to atmospheric oxygen. In other words, it is suggested that the earliest respiratory chain made use of a segment of an existing photosynthetic chain, a pool of quinones, shared by both, being susceptible to reduction by NADH and succinate, as well as by excited chlorophyll. Such a situation exists today in *R. spheroides* and similar organisms (Marrs and Gest, 1973a,b; Dutton and Wilson, 1974; Jones and Plewis, 1974). Mutations that led to loss of the photosynthetic part of the dual functioning system would not be detrimental as the concentration of oxygen increased; respiration would take over to satisfy the energy requirements of the cell. Thus we can see how the cytochrome c_{550} of the respiratory chain of *Paracoccus* might have come to resemble cytochrome c_2 of the purple non-sulfur bacteria so closely as to make it difficult to tell them apart. We need not follow the argument beyond the point of taking note that, of all prokaryotes, *Paracoccus denitrificans* most closely resembles the mitochondria of eukaryotic organisms (John and Whatley, 1975).

Purple non-sulfur bacteria operate a complete Krebs cycle and can grow aerobically in the dark at the expense of various organic compounds; these can also be photoassimilated. Therefore, it is a consequence of this view of evolution, presented by Dickerson *et al.* (1976), that sections of the Krebs cycle existed before the purple non-sulfur bacteria came into being. These sections were put together by ancestors of the organisms so that, functioning as a complete cycle, NADH could be generated by the oxidation of organic substrates as they became available. Most reactions of the Krebs cycle are catalyzed by green and purple sulfur bacteria of the present time, but they do not function in a cyclic manner: they operate for the synthesis of glutamate and the fixing of carbon dioxide.

The cycling of carbon in the biosphere occurs continually on a massive scale, but until recently has not received attention commensurate with its importance. When the microbial world is confronted with man-made chemicals that cannot be brought into the carbon cycle, those compounds will persist in the environment and may become hazardous to man. Biodegradability and recalcitrance have attracted great attention in the last decade, but they cannot be profitably discussed without some reference to the scope and limitations of microbial catabolism; and a simple appreciation, if no more, of factors that determine that the nature of the environment should be part of man's intellectual equipment in a technological society.

Since microbes have been engaged in the task of degrading lignins and their constituent monomers for time immemorial, it is not surprising that well-worn channels of aromatic catabolism have become established. The principal pathways used are summarized in Fig. 1. A great many naturally occurring benzenoid compounds are degraded to give, ultimately, one of the dihydric phenols shown; the product will not always possess the two hydroxyl groups required, and in such a case, the ring-fission substrate will be generated from it by the action of hydroxylases, each exhibiting stringent substrate specificity. The most striking feature of Fig. 1 is the separation of catabolic routes. Not only are the ring-fission dioxygenases, (a)-(g), specific for their substrates insofar as they have little or no action upon the other dihydric phenols, but, in addition, the enzymes that convert ring-fission products into Krebs cycle metabolites or their precursors are equally stringent. Thus, despite the similarity in structure of protocatechuate and homoprotocatechuate, and of their catabolites, the enzymes of one sequence do not catalyze the homologous reactions of the other. Likewise, homogentisate is degraded by a suite of enzymes that does not serve for gentisate, although types of reactions used are the same. Derepression mechanisms are also separate. Thus, when a strain of *Acinetobacter* was grown with 4-hydroxyphenylacetic acid, the substrate was hydroxylated at C-3 and then catabolized by the homoprotocatechuate route. When grown with 3-hydroxyphenylacetic acid, hydroxylation occurred at C-6 and the homogentisate pathway was taken, the reactions being catalyzed by a totally different set of enzymes.

The exclusion from one particular pathway of most of the compounds involved in the others does not imply absolute substrate specificity. Thus, alkyl group substituents are tolerated in the catechol meta-fission route, and in gentisate degradation. Pathways for several alkyl- or aryl-substituted catechols have, in fact, been thoroughly investigated since they are involved in the degradation of compounds of environmental or industrial significance. The same *types* of meta-fission reactions are involved as those used for unsubstituted catechol, and products can be predicted using the diagrams of Fig. 2, the basis of which was established during my visit to Urbana in 1963–1964. However, a word of caution is needed at this point. As I have stated, catalysis of similar reactions does not imply identity of enzymes. Indeed, the fact that these substituted catechols may

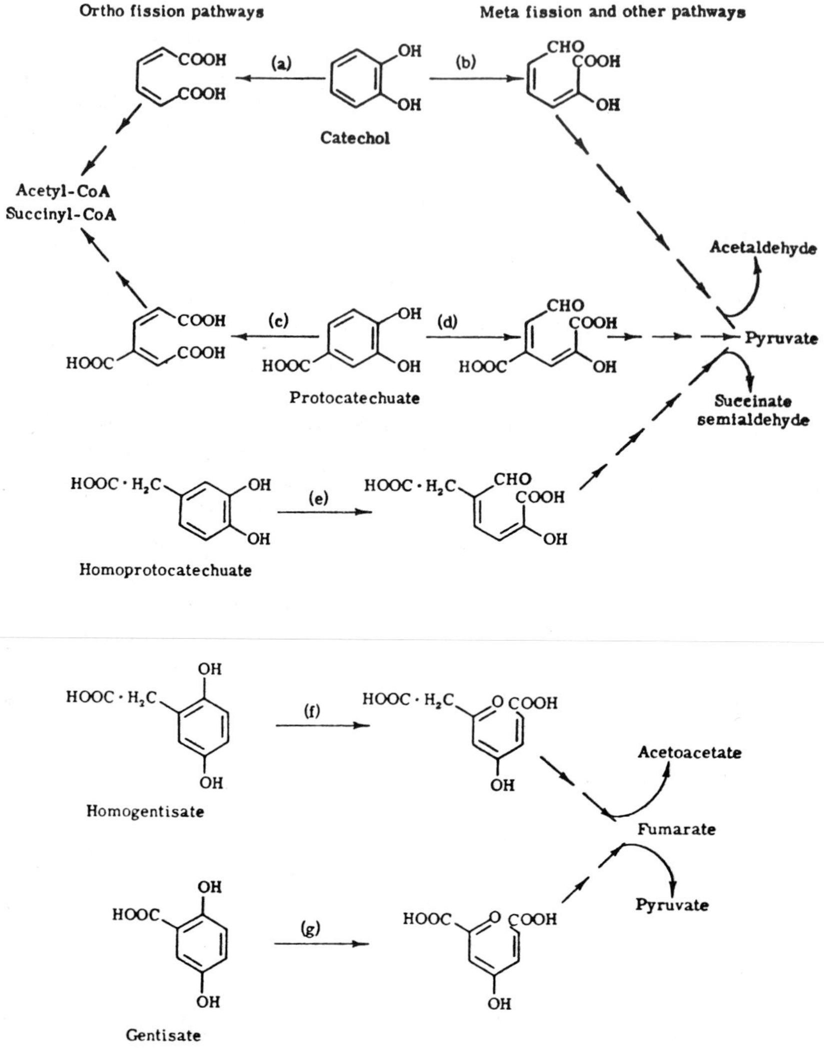

Fig. 1. Bacterial catabolism of benzenoid compounds. Separate suites of enzymes are used to degrade each dihydric phenol (Dagley, 1978, by permission).

be formed from man-made compounds renders it likely that at least some of the enzymes are plasmid-borne. The substrates involved are, at most, of peripheral significance in nature; those of Fig. 1 are central, and their catabolic enzymes are chromosomal. A beautiful demonstration of this point is furnished by the work of Williams and Murray (1974) who showed that the enzymes for degrading toluic acids, in *P. putida (arvilla)*, were carried on the TOL plasmid and catalyzed meta-fission reactions. Pseudomonads have also been isolated (Williams and Worsey, 1976), which metabolize toluene, methyl-substituted toluenes (xylenes), and their catabolites; and these enzymes are plasmid-borne. The methyl group of toluene was oxidized to carboxyl, giving benzoic acid, and xylenes gave methyl-substituted benzoic acids. Now benzoic acid is an important natural metabolite; toluic acids are not. The most convenient way to "cure" *P. putida (arvilla)* of the plasmid was to grow cultures in benzoic acid medium, when chromosomal (and, incidentally, ortho-fission) enzymes took over and degraded the substrate faster than did the plasmid-borne enzymes. In this connection, I recall that back in 1963 Gunny told me of his conviction that the microbial world owed its catabolic versatility to the fact that populations could "talk to each other," passing around their information on little bits of DNA.

Earlier, I gave examples to show how convenient it had been to use bacteria in general metabolic studies. For providing the outline of a catabolic pathway, no technique has been more rapid and convenient than Simultaneous Adaption (Se-

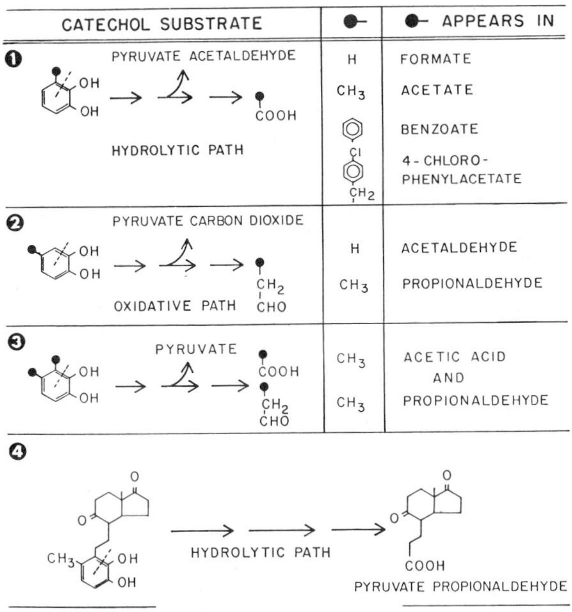

Fig. 2. Products of degradation of substituted catechols using meta-fission reactions. Ring cleavage by a dioxygenase is shown by the broken lines. In the oxidative pathway, the aldehyde group formed by ring cleavage is oxidized to carboxyl, and this carbon atom is released as carbon dioxide. In the hydrolytic pathway, the corresponding carbon appears in a carboxylic acid. Other reactions of the two routes are of similar types. Sequence (4) is a special example of (3) taken from steroid catabolism (Gibson *et al.*, 1966).

quential Induction); this is especially true for aromatic catabolism, for it was in this area that the method was first applied (Stanier, 1947). The foregoing discussion shows why this should be. Due to the separation of pathways and the specificity of their mechanisms of derepression, the investigator can be reasonably sure that if the gentisate pathway is taken, he will find that suspensions of benzoate-grown bacterial cells will oxidize gentisate, but will scarcely attack catechol or protocatechuate which lie on feasible alternative pathways. However, recent investigations in my laboratory using a yeast, *Trichosporon cutaneum*, have shown that we have never fully appreciated this obliging feature of bacterial behavior. When grown with benzoate, this yeast was fully adapted to oxidize catechol and protocatechuate as well as gentisate; and for good measure it also readily oxidized 2-, 3-, and 4-hydroxybenzoates. Cells did not oxidize phenylacetic acid unless they grew with this substrate, but when they did, homogentisic and homoprotocatechuic acids were immediately oxidized, as well

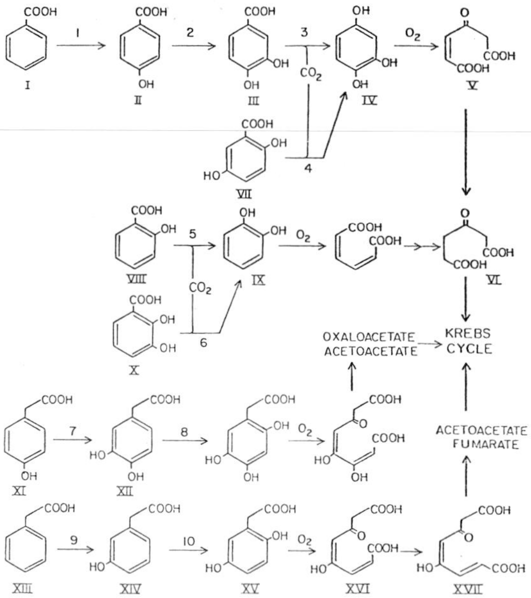

Fig. 3. Catabolism of benzoate (I), gentisate (VII), salicylate (VIII), 2,3-dihydroxybenzoate (X), phenylacetate (XIII), and 4-hydroxyphenyl acetate (XI) in *T. cutaneum*. All reactions shown by arrows were catalyzed by cell extracts, except 1 and 9 which were shown for intact cells using ^{14}C substrates. Reactions 2 and 7 were catalyzed by hydroxylases requiring NADPH specifically, whereas hydroxylases for reactions 3, 4, 5, 8, and 10 required NADH, replaced less effectively by NADPH. Reaction 6 is a specific nonoxidative decarboxylation requiring no dissociable cofactor; reactions 4 and 5 were catalyzed by the same hydroxylase (Anderson and Dagley, 1979, reproduced by permission of the American Society for Microbiology).

as each one of the monohydroxyphenylacetic acids. These broad inductive patterns left one more appreciative of the specificity of bacterial derepression. While it is true that no metabolic route can be established solely by Simultaneous Adaptation, the technique is useful in preliminary investigations of bacterial systems. In this case it was entirely without value, and outlines of possible pathways in *T. cutaneum* had to be sketched by determinations of stoichiometry for final product formation, and NADH and oxygen utilization using cell extracts. These observations were strengthened by tracing C-14 as it passed from initial substrates into catabolites during experiments with intact cells. Some pathways of aromatic catabolism proposed for *T. cutaneum* are shown in Fig. 3 (Anderson and Dagley, 1979). The organism metabolizes a wide range of such compounds, despite the fact that, in sharp contrast to bacteria, it elaborates no ring-fission dioxygenases for protocatechuate, homoprotocatechuate, or gentisate, although the cells do, in fact, oxidize these phenolics. This is achieved, for these compounds and others, by introducing a third hydroxyl group into the nucleus when the two already in place are not positioned to the yeast's liking. These and other activities of *T. cutaneum* suggest marked biochemical eccentricity, taking bacteria as the norm. Since this is the first eukaryote to be investigated displaying catabolic versatility worthy of a pseudomonad, I suspect that future research will modify this judgment. After all, the idea that we now know all that there is to know about metabolism never did make much headway in Urbana, Illinois.

ACKNOWLEDGMENT

I wish to acknowledge the support my research has received, for many years, from the National Institutes of Environmental Health Service, and of Arthritis, Metabolism and Digestive Diseases. I thank Mrs. Bonnie Allen for help in preparing this manuscript.

REFERENCES

Anderson, J. J., and Dagley, S. (1979). Catabolism of aromatic acids in *Trichosporon cutaneum*. *J. Bacteriol*. **138,** 425–430.

Bellamy, W. D., and Gunsalus, I. C. (1943). Growth requirements of *Streptococcus fecalis* for tyrosine decarboxylation. *J. Bacteriol*. **46,** 573.

Dagley, S. (1972). Summary. *In* "Degradation of Synthetic Organic Molecules in the Biosphere," pp. 336–347. Natl. Acad. Sci., Washington, D.C.

Dagley, S. (1978). Pathways for the utilization of organic growth substrates. *In* "The Bacteria" (L. N. Ornston and J. R. Sokatch, eds.), Vol. 6, pp. 305–388. Academic Press, New York.

Dagley, S., and Dawes, E. A. (1953). Citric acid metabolism of *Aerobacter aerogenes*. *J. Bacteriol*. **66,** 259–265.

56 S. Dagley

Dagley, S., and Trudgill, P. W. (1965). The metabolism of galactarate, D-glucarate and various pentoses by species of *Pseudomonas*. *Biochem. J.* **95**, 48–58.

Dagley, S., Trudgill, P. W., and Callely, A. G. (1961). Synthesis of cell constituents from glycine by a *Pseudomonas*. *Biochem. J.* **81**, 623–631.

Dagley, S., Chapman, P. J., Gibson, D. T., and Wood, J. M. (1964). Degradation of the benzene nucleus by bacteria. *Nature (London)* **202**, 775–778.

Dickerson, R. E., Timkovich, R., and Almassy, R. J. (1976). The cytochrome fold and the evolution of bacterial energy metabolism. *J. Mol. Biol.* **100**, 473–491.

Dus, K., Katagiri, M., Yu, C.-A., Erbes, D. L., and Gunsalus, I. C. (1970). Chemical characterization of cytochrome P-450$_{cam}$. *Biochem. Biophys. Res. Commun.* **40**, 1423–1430.

Dutton, P. L., and Wilson, D. F. (1974). Redox potentiometry in mitochondrial and photosynthetic bioenergetics. *Biochim. Biophys. Acta* **346**, 165–212.

Fridovich, I. (1974). Superoxide and evolution. *Horiz. Biochem. Biophys.* **1**, 1–37.

Gibson, D. T., Wang, K. C., Sih, C. J., and Whitlock, H. (1966). Mechanisms of steroid oxidation by microorganisms. IX. On the mechanism of ring A cleavage in the degradation of 9,10-seco steroids by microorganisms. *J. Biol. Chem.* **241**, 551–559.

Gillespie, D. C., and Gunsalus, I. C. (1953). An adaptive citric acid desmolase in *Streptococcus faecalis*. *Bacteriol. Proc.* p. 80.

Gotto, A. M., and Kornberg, H. L. (1961). The metabolism of c_2 compounds in microorganisms. 7. Preparation and properties of crystalline tartronic semialdehyde reductase. *Biochem. J.* **81**, 273–284.

Gunsalus, I. C., Bellamy, W. D., and Umbreit, W. W. (1944). A phosphorylated derivative of pyridoxal as the coenzyme of tyrosine decarboxylase. *J. Biol. Chem.* **155**, 685–686.

John, P., and Whatley, F. R. (1975). *Paracoccus denitrificans* and the evolutionary origin of mitochondria. *Nature (London)* **254**, 495–498.

Jones, O. T. G., and Plewis, K. M. (1974). Reconstitution of light-dependent electron transport in membranes from a bacteriochlorophyll-less mutant of *Rhodopseudomonas spheroides*. *Biochim. Biophys. Acta* **357**, 204–214.

Karrer, P., and Viscontini, M. (1947). Synthetische krystallisierte codecarboxylase. *Helv. Chim. Acta* **30**, 52–58.

Kellog, E. W., and Fridovich, I. (1975). Superoxide, hydrogen peroxide and singlet oxygen in lipid peroxidation by a xanthine oxidase system. *J. Biol. Chem.* **250**, 8812–8817.

Kornberg, H. L., and Gotto, A. M. (1961). The metabolism of c_2 compounds in microorganisms. 6. Synthesis of cell constituents from glycollate by a *Pseudomonas* sp. *Biochem. J.* **78**, 69–82.

Lipmann, F. (1976). Reflections on the evolutionary transition from prokaryotes to eukaryotes. *In* "Reflections on Biochemistry in Honour of Severo Ochoa" (A. Kornberg, B. L. Horecker, L. Cornudella, and J. Oró, eds.), pp. 33–38. Pergamon, Oxford.

McCord, J. M., Keele, B. B., and Fridovich, I. (1971). An enzyme-based theory of obligate anaerobiosis: The physiological function of superoxide dismutase. *Proc. Natl. Acad. Sci. U.S.A.* **68**, 1024–1027.

Marrs, B., and Gest, H. (1973a). Genetic mutations affecting the respiratory electron-transport system of the photosynthetic bacterium *Phodopseudomonas capsulata*. *J. Bacteriol.* **114**, 1045–1051.

Marrs, B., and Gest, H. (1973b). Regulation of bacteriochlorophyll synthesis by oxygen in respiratory mutants of *Rhodopseudomonas capsulata*. *J. Bacteriol.* **114**, 1052–1057.

O'Kane, D. J., and Gunsalus, I. C. (1947). Accessory factor requirement for pyruvate oxidation. *J. Bacteriol.* **54**, 20–21.

O'Kane, D. J., and Gunsalus, I. C. (1948). Pyruvic acid metabolism. A factor required for oxidation by *Streptococcus faecalis*. *J. Bacteriol.* **56**, 499–506.

Quayle, J. R., Keech, D. B., and Taylor, G. A. (1961). Carbon assimilation by *Pseudomonas oxalaticus* (OX1). 4. Metabolism of oxalate in cell-free extracts of the organism grown on oxalate. *Biochem. J.* **78**, 225–236.

Reed, L. J., DeBusk, B. G., Gunsalus, I. C., and Hornberger, C. S., Jr. (1951). Crystalline α-lipoic acid: A catalytic agent associated with pyruvate dehydrogenase. *Science* **114**, 93–94.

Singh, R. M. M., and Adams, E. (1965). Isolation and identification of 2,5-dioxovalerate, an intermediate in the bacterial oxidation of hydroxyproline. *J. Biol. Chem.* **240**, 4352–4356.

Snell, E. E., and Broquist, H. P. (1949). On the probable identity of several unidentified growth factors. *Arch. Biochem.* **23**, 326–328.

Snell, E. E., Tatum, E. L., and Peterson, W. H. (1937). Growth factors for bacteria. III. Some nutritive requirements for *Lactobacillus delbrückii*. *J. Bacteriol.* **33**, 207–225.

Stanier, R. Y. (1947). Simultaneous adaptation: A new technique for the study of metabolic pathways. *J. Bacteriol.* **54**, 339–348.

Stanier, R. Y., Doudoroff, M., and Adelberg, E. A. (1963). "The Microbial World." Prentice-Hall, Englewood Cliffs, New Jersey.

Stoolmiller, A. C., and Abeles, R. H. (1966). The formation of α-ketoglutarate semialdehyde from L-2-keto-3-deoxyarabonic acid and isolation of L-2-keto-3-deoxyarabonate dehydratase from *Pseudomonas saccharophila*. *J. Biol. Chem.* **241**, 5764–5771.

Umbreit, W. W., and Gunsalus, I. C. (1949). Codecarboxylase not pyridoxal 3-phosphate. *J. Biol. Chem.* **179**, 279–281.

Valentine, R. C., Drucker, H., and Wolfe, R. S. (1964). Glyoxylate fermentation by *Streptococcus allantoicus*. *J. Bacteriol.* **87**, 241–246.

Wald, G. (1954). The origin of life. *Sci. Am.* **191**, 45–53.

Williams, P. A., and Murray, K. (1974). Metabolism of benzoate and methylbenzoates by *Pseudomonas putida (arvilla)* mt-2: Evidence for the existence of a TOL plasmid. *J. Bacteriol.* **120**, 416–423.

Williams, P. A., and Worsey, M. J. (1976). Ubiquity of plasmids in coding for toluene and xylene metabolism in soil bacteria: Evidence for the existence of new TOL plasmids. *J. Bacteriol.* **125**, 818–828.

Yu, C.-A., and Gunsalus, I. C. (1970). Crystalline cytochrome P-450$_{cam}$. *Biochem. Biophys. Res. Commun.* **40**, 1431–1436.

7

Bacteria
and the Challenge
of Cyclic Molecules

P. W. Trudgill

I. INTRODUCTION

In September 1963 I left the University of Leeds in northern England to board
a Boeing 707 for Chicago on the trans-Atlantic phase of a journey that was
ultimately destined to end at Urbana, Illinois, and the Department of Biochemistry at the State University. A foretaste of the change of the biochemical environment that I was about to encounter was heralded by the change of climatic
conditions as the cool and, at best, unreliable climate of my home city gave way
to the steady hamburger-grilling sunshine of Illinois—and the mountains which
had been so familiar to me were replaced by a Polder-flat landscape.

The first few days after arrival in Urbana were inevitably taken up with the
necessity of finding suitable accommodations for my family and the initial process of acclimatization. In all of this we were generously helped by Professor S.
Dagley who had been my research director when I was a postgraduate student at
Leeds and who had preceded me to Urbana. Once these preliminary problems
had been overcome, my thoughts willingly returned to science and were
catalyzed by my first meeting with Gunny. Although it was a lunch date in the
Urbana Lincoln Hotel (in danger of being demolished at the time of my last visit
to Urbana), it was characterized by a continual flow of scientific ideas, observa-

EXPERIENCES IN BIOCHEMICAL PERCEPTION
Copyright © 1982 by Academic Press, Inc.
All rights of reproduction in any form reserved.
ISBN 0-12-528420-9

tions, and suggestions, frequently punctuated by relevant anecdotes, which would prove to be a continual stimulus to laboratory activity.

At that time a major effort in the laboratory was devoted to understanding the mechanism by which bacteria degrade (+)−camphor and related compounds. Such a research interest might have appeared on casual encounter to be esoteric and abstruse but, characteristically, Gunny realized that this natural product could provide the answers to fundamental questions concerning the biodegradation of alicyclic structures in nature, that some of the enzyme systems were very likely to be of considerable interest, and that the problem was amenable to available techniques. Although the microbial degradation of aromatic structures was understood in considerable detail, both in terms of reaction sequences and enzymology (Dagley et al., 1964), knowledge of the degradation of even simple alicyclic structures was sparse, with the exception of the developing understanding of (+)−camphor oxidation.

II. EFFECTS OF CAMPHOR VAPOR

I started work in Gunny's laboratory by completing a study of the microbial degradation of galactaric and glucaric acids (1,6-dicarboxylic acids derived from galactose and glucose). This had been initiated at the University of Leeds and was part of an extended study of bacterial degradation of hydroxydicarboxylic acids undertaken in conjunction with Professor Dagley (Dagley and Trudgill, 1965). However, continual exposure to camphor vapor soon exerted its magical effect and I was drawn into this very active research area, helped and guided by Peter Chapman, who was then putting the finishing touches to the elucidated pathway for (+)−camphor degradation by Mycobacterium rhodochrous T1 (Chapman et al., 1966). This pathway (Fig. 1, pathway A) is of particular interest since hydroxylation of the camphor ring at C6, followed by dehydrogenation, yields a β-diketone which is amenable to hydrolytic cleavage of a carbon-carbon bond as with 3-formylpyruvate (Watson et al., 1974). Cleavage of the second ring of (+)−camphor by M. rhodochrous T1 and, in all probability, cleavage of both rings by Pseudomonas putida (Fig. 1, pathway B) (Conrad et al., 1965a), is mediated by insertion of ring oxygen adjacent to a keto group with the consequent formation of lactones that may be inherently unstable or undergo hydrolytic cleavage.

In 1963 work was well advanced and these reaction sequences involved in the degradation of alicyclic structures were the subject of a major research effort. David Cushman, a postgraduate student, was engaged in unraveling the secrets of one of the enzymes from P. putida C1B involved in setting up the ring for the cleavage reaction, the (+)−camphor 5-exohydroxylase; although he had established the multicomponent nature of the system, the true identity of all the

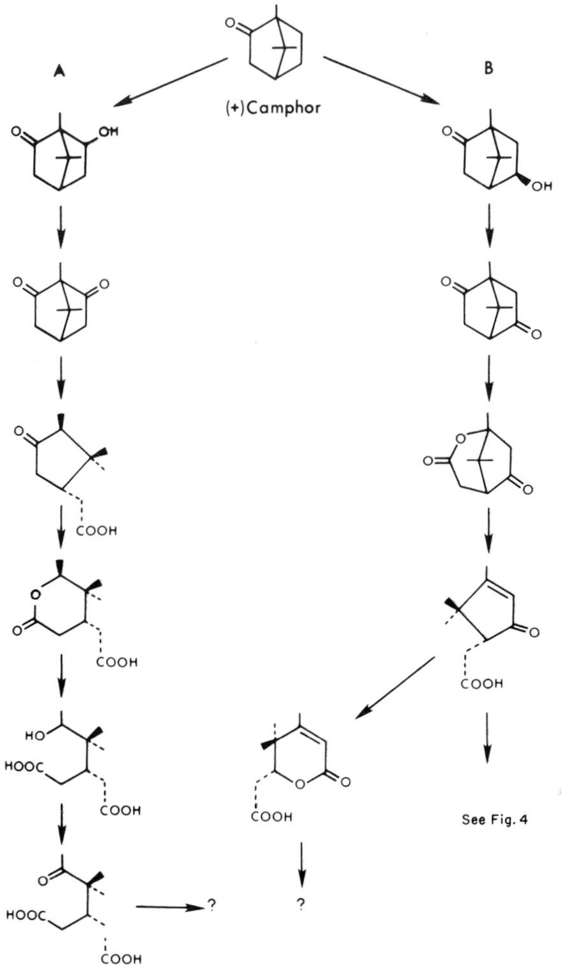

Fig. 1. Pathways of (+)−camphor degradation by *M. rhodochrous* T1 (pathway A) (Chapman *et al.*, 1966) and *P. putida* C1B (pathway B) (Bradshaw *et al.*, 1959). Although acyclic metabolites have been identified in camphor degradation by *M. rhodochrous* T1, the fate of the lactone 1-oxa-2-oxo-4,5,5-trimethyl-6-carboxymethyl-Δ³-cyclohexene formed by *P. putida* C1B is still somewhat uncertain.

individual pieces was still cryptic (Cushman *et al.*, 1967). Subsequent studies that have revealed the detailed nature of this hydroxylating system, including the involvement of the soluble cytochrome P_{450} component (Gunsalus *et al.*, 1974) have fully justified Gunny's initial perceptive and whole-hearted commitment to the project. Studies of the enzymology of the first ring cleavage step catalyzed by extracts of *P. putida* C1B had been initiated by Ed Conrad working in close association with Gunny. A hydrolytic cleavage of 5-hydroxycamphor or 2,5-diketocamphane is not feasible on mechanistic grounds, and it had become clear that ring cleavage was catalyzed by a reaction best described as a biological manifestation of the Baeyer-Villiger reaction (Conrad *et al.*, 1961).

Conrad's departure from the group left a body of substantial work (Conrad *et al.*, 1965a,b), which inevitably raised many tantalizing questions. The ring oxygen-inserting enzyme (1,2-monooxygenase) was a multiprotein complex, sensitive to non-heme iron-chelating agents and with quite a broad ketone substrate specificity but an absolute specificity for NADH as an electron donor and a tendency to loose flavin upon purification. Attempts to purify the complex had been thwarted by its readiness to dissociate irreversibly so that characterization of the system had proved elusive. This, then, was the situation when I transferred my allegiance from linear molecules to alicyclic structures.

The Camphor, 1,2-Monooxygenase

Although it had been established that the camphor 1,2-monooxygenase complex was fragile, one protein component, an NADH dehydrogenase, was readily assayable by virtue of its ability to transfer electrons to free FMN—this was chosen as a potentially resolvable system. Growth of vast quantities of *P. putida* in a 100-liter fermenter coupled with the enthusiastic assistance of René DuBus, encouragement and advice from Gunny, and an endless stream of distinguished and interested scientists who visited the department eventually resulted in the establishment of a suitable purification procedure that yielded pure protein. A regular supply of this pure material enabled the enzyme to be characterized as an NADH dehydrogenase of low molecular weight (36,000) with an ability to reversibly bind a catalytically active molecule of FMN with a particularly high dissociation constant ($4.5 \times 10^{-7} M$). In addition, FAD is even more weakly bound at an additional noncatalytic site with the result that purification always leads to the preparation of the apoprotein (Trudgill *et al.*, 1966a). It was reasonably concluded that this small flavoprotein was an intermediate electron carrier between NADH and the oxygenating component of the enzyme—of considerably greater interest. Conrad had earlier shown (Conrad *et al.*, 1965b) that components of the dissociated oxygenating complex could, in very impure states, be reassociated rather inefficiently so that oxygenation could be assayed. Unfortunately, because of the poor level of recoupling obtained, such systems were not amenable to quick accurate spectrophotometric assay, so useful in setting up enzyme purification regimes. Our hope that, once purified, the NADH dehydrogenase component in plentiful supply would enable us to purify the oxygen-inserting protein(s) by reconstituting the system for assay purposes was not fulfilled. Reassociation of the pure NADH dehydrogenase with crude oxygenating fractions was inefficient and attempts to purify the separate components of the complex, relying on an inefficient *in vitro* reassociation for assay, made little headway. We were thus driven back to an alternative that had also proved initially unrewarding—purification of the intact complex.

We discovered that a more judicious choice of ammonium sulfate concentration range for fractionation permitted significant progress and that this, in combination with ion exchange chromatography, resulted in significant purification of the complex (Trudgill *et al.*, 1966b). Although by no means homogeneous, the partially purified complex had certain advantages as experimental material: electron transport was very tightly coupled so that reaction stoichiometry could be unequivocally established; flavin remained tightly bound; and, rather interestingly, sensitivity to non-heme iron chelating agents was greatly reduced. Although some progress had been made, the true nature and number of components of the complex still eluded us as did the precise nature of the prosthetic group of the oxygenating component and the nature of the oxygen species involved in the biological Baeyer-Villiger reaction system. At this crucial and fascinating stage, I regrettably had to leave Urbana to take up a post at Aberystwyth. Two years in Illinois with Gunny had opened my eyes to the fascination of alicyclic structures, the exciting and challenging problems which they present, both at the metabolic and enzyme mechanism level, and the importance of microorganisms capable of degrading them in the catabolic phase of the carbon cycle.

III. METABOLISM OF CYCLOHEXANOL AND CYCLOPENTANOL

After overcoming cultural shock and the problem once again of finding suitable accommodations, planning lecture courses, etc., a research area had to be established and confronted. With Gunny's enthusiasm and inspiration still ringing in my ears, it seemed logical and essential that I should continue work in the area of alicyclic molecule degradation. I chose relatively simple alicyclic structures such as cyclohexanol and cyclopentanol for initial study—these seemed to have some characteristics to recommend them. First, microorganisms capable of growth with them were easily isolated from the biosphere; second, we hoped that their greater simplicity would enable us to establish more complete degradative sequences than had, to date, been established for (+)−camphor; and third that any oxygenases catalyzing Beayer-Villiger oxygen insertion reactions might be more easily purified than had been the case of that from the camphor-utilizing strain of *P. putida*.

Our subsequent studies with a strain of *Acinetobacter,* generously donated by Dr. P. J. Chapman, a strain of *Nocardia,* both grown with cyclohexanol, and a strain of *Pseudomonas* grown with cyclopentanol have reinforced the previous studies in Gunny's laboratory which showed the importance of ring oxygen insertion in the degradation of alicyclic ketones. We soon established the pre-

P. W. Trudgill

dicted dehydrogenation of the alicyclic alcohol to the prospective ketone and, to our delight, the involvement of a Bayer-Villiger type of monooxygenation, forming 1-oxa-2-oxocycloheptane (ω-caprolactone) from cyclohexanone. Further degradation steps yielded adipate and, although the degradation of this dicarboxylic acid was not studied in detail, the work of Chapman and Duggleby (1967) made it likely that β-oxidation gives rise to succinyl-CoA and acetyl-CoA entering the central metabolic pathways (Norris and Trudgill, 1971; Griffin and Trudgill, 1972; Donoghue and Trudgill, 1975). The pathway for cyclohexanol metabolism by *Acinetobacter* NCIB 9871 is shown in Fig. 2. Once the metabolic sequences had been established, purification of the ring oxygen-inserting enzymes was undertaken with enthusiasm and interest. As we had hoped, the enzymes involved in the oxygenation of these simpler molecules proved to be

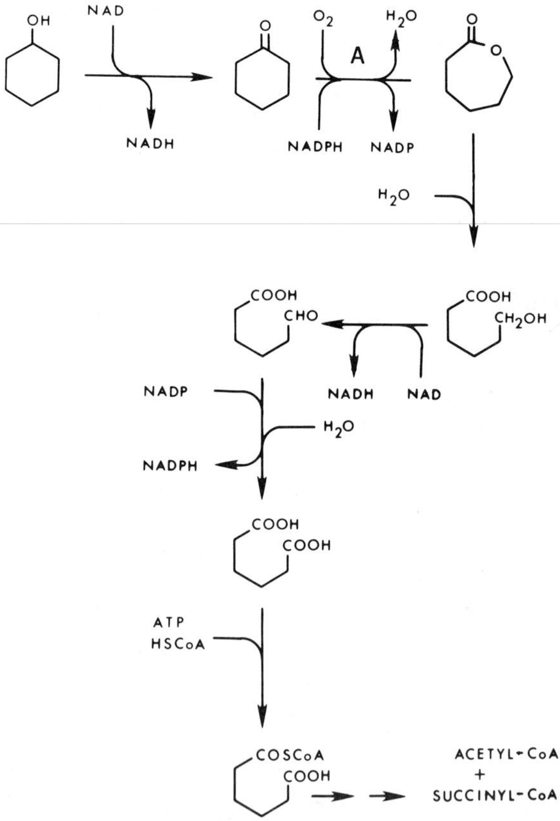

Fig. 2. The pathway of cyclohexanol degradation by *Acinetobacter* NCIB 9871. Some characteristics of the monooxygenase catalyzing the Baeyer-Villiger oxygenation step (reaction A) are given in Table I.

TABLE I

Characteristics of Cyclohexanone Monooxygenases

Characteristic	Source of enzyme		Ketone substrate	K_m (μM)	V_{max}^a (cyclohexanone 100%)
	N. globerula CL 1	Acinetobacter NCIB 9871			
Molecular weight	53000	59000	(structure: 4-methylcyclohexanone)	9	91
Soluble protein of cell (%)	8	3	(structure: 2-methylcyclohexanone)	11	61
Prosthetic group	FAD	FAD	(structure: 3-hydroxycyclohexanone)	12	93
Moles FAD/mole protein	1	1	(structure: bicyclic ketone)	140	63
pH Optimum	8.4	9	(structure: cycloheptanone)	200	58
Electron donor	NADPH	NADPH	(structure: 4-hydroxycyclohexanone)	390	69
Ketone specificity	Broad	Broad →	(structure: menthone-type ketone)	640	83
Group at catalytic center	–SH	–SH	(structure: cyclooctanone)	1800	13
Catalytic center activity	1020	1380	(structure: cyclopentanone)	3600	64
K_m for NADPH (μM)	31	6.9			
K_m for cyclohexanone (μM)	1.5	17.8			
No. of polypeptide chains	1	1			

[a] All at ∞ ketone concentrations, 80 μM NADPH and 260 μM oxygen.

much more amenable to purification than that from the $(+)$−camphor-grown *P. putida* C1B, and all three were obtained in a pure state (Donoghue *et al.*, 1976; Griffin and Trudgill, 1976). They appear to be quite different structurally from the former enzyme. The two cyclohexanone monooxygenases are simple molecules consisting of a single polypeptide chain and carrying a single molecule of FAD. There is no evidence for the presence or catalytic involvement of transition metal ions. It is interesting that they bear a remarkable superficial similarity to aromatic ring hydroxylases such as *p*-hydroxybenzoate hydroxylase (Howell *et al.*, 1972) and salicylate hydroxylase (Yamamoto *et al.*, 1965). Known characteristics of the cyclohexanone monooxygenases from *N. globerula* CL1 and *Acinetobacter* NCIB 9871 are shown in Table I. A possible oxygenation mechanism, involving an oxygenated species of reduced enzyme-bound FAD, had been proposed (Trudgill, 1978) and broadly supported by recent experimental evidence [Ryerson, C., Ballou, D., and Walsh, C. (in preparation)]. Rapid reaction kinetic and spectral studies, so elegantly used to determine the oxygenated flavin species involved in *p*-hydroxybenzoate oxygenation (Entsch *et al.*, 1976) should, in principle, be capable of elucidating the reactive species involved in the biological Baeyer-Villiger reaction to give us complete understanding of this particular type of mixed-function oxygenase.

IV. METABOLISM OF ALICYCLIC ACIDS

A. Metabolism of Cyclohexane Carboxylic Acid

In addition to our own studies with alicyclic alcohols and ketones, a number of workers have been actively involved in a consideration of the mechanisms by which bacteria degrade alicyclic hydrocarbons and molecules with other substituent groups. Of particular interest is the observation that ring oxygen insertion is not obligatory for alicyclic ring cleavage. In the short space available, the compound cyclohexane carboxylic acid affords an excellent illustration of this point. Arising from studies by Evans and co-workers at Bangor in North Wales (Dutton and Evans, 1969) and from work by Guyer and Hegeman (1969), it became evident that many bacteria degrade cyclohexane carboxylic acid by β-oxidation since the position of the ring in relation to the carboxyl group does not preclude this. A recent paper by Blakley (1978) working with a strain of *Alcaligenes* has clearly confirmed this with a detailed exploration at both the whole cell and subcellular level.

In addition, an alternative route for the degradation of this compound involves the action of a hydroxylase that generates *trans*-4-hydroxycyclohexane carboxylic acid which, following dehydrogenation to form 4-oxocyclohexane carboxylic acid, is aromatized to *p*-hydroxybenzoate and degraded by established routes (Blakley, 1975; Kaneda, 1974; Smith and Callely, 1975; Taylor and Trudgill, 1978). An interesting aspect of this metabolic pathway is that the secondary alcohol-generating monooxygenase is reminiscent of the multiprotein (+)−camphor 5-exohydroxylase from *P. putida*. Unfortunately this enzyme is very unstable in all investigated systems. The most stable enzyme, that from our strain of *Alcaligenes* (Taylor and Trudgill, 1978), exhibits concentration/activity characteristics in crude cell extracts which are indicative of it being a multiprotein system. It is thus doubly unfortunate that it has proved to be too unstable for successful purification.

A further extension of a consideration of the degradation of cyclohexane carboxylic acid includes cycloalkyl alkanes. Molecules such as heptadecylcyclohexane are degraded by hydroxylation of the terminal methyl group followed by oxidation of the alcohol to carboxyl followed by β-oxidation. In this case the side chain has an odd number of carbon atoms and β-oxidation can continue unimpeded through cyclohexane carboxyl-CoA (Beam and Perry, 1974a). However, if the hydrocarbon contains an even number of carbon atoms in the side chain, then hydroxylation, oxidation, and β-oxidation will generate cyclohexylacetyl-CoA which, like a fatty acid carrying a methyl group at C-3, is not amenable to β-oxidation. Work by Beam and Perry·(1974b) indicated the recalcitrant nature of cyclohexylacetic acid since it was accumulated by organisms capable of growth with dodecylcyclohexane, only the carbon of acetyl-CoA units cleaved from the side chain being available to the organisms. It is true that α-oxidation of the side chain would yield a molecule in which a β-oxidative ring cleavage could occur, but available evidence suggests that this is not quantitatively important.

B. Metabolism of Cyclohexylacetic Acid

It occurred to us that cyclohexylacetic acid had some characteristics in common with intermediates formed in the degradation of (+)−camphor. A substituted cyclopentylacetic acid and a substituted cyclopentenylacetic acid are produced by *M. rhodochrous* T1 and *P. putida* C1B, respectively (Fig. 1). The fact that these are degradable gave us confidence to investigate the bacterial metabolism of cyclohexylacetic acid. Theoretically one might expect that ring hydroxylation would be a first step in either aromatization of the structure to *p*-hydroxyphenylacetic acid, which is degradable (Sparnins *et al.*, 1974; Hareland *et al.*, 1975), or in formation of the cyclic ketone which could then be attacked by ring oxygen insertion. In the event neither of these predictions proved to be true and the pathway established for cyclohexylacetic acid degradation is inherently interesting by virtue of the involvement of a tertiary alcohol intermediate and the mechanism by which the acetyl side chain is eliminated.

Elective culture, with cyclohexylacetic acid as the carbon source, resulted in the isolation of a strain of *Arthrobacter* capable of growth with cyclohexylacetic acid as the sole source of carbon from a soil sample that was heavily contaminated with aviation fuel. The interesting and rather surprising initial observation that this organism was also capable of growth with cyclohexanone and other intermediates of the described pathway for cyclohexanol degradation (Fig. 2) was explained by the observation that cyclohexanone transiently accumulated during growth of the *Arthrobacter* on cyclohexylacetic acid at some 60% of

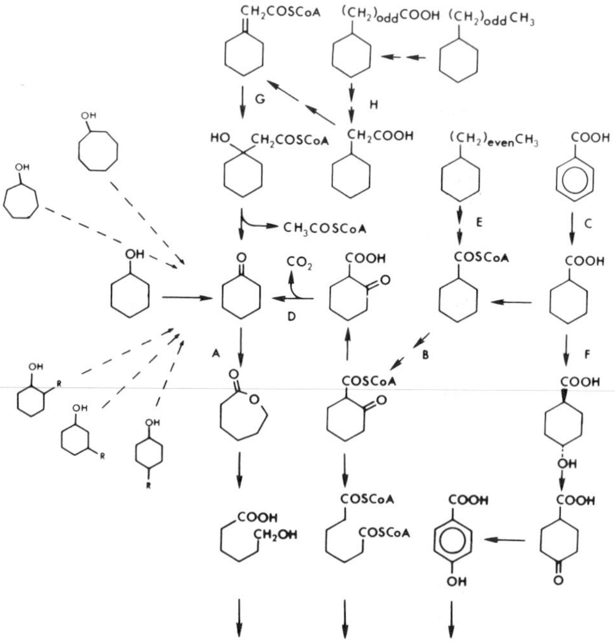

Fig. 3. Metabolic routes involved in the degradation of a variety of cyclohexane derivatives and related alicyclic compounds. Pathway A, the established route for cyclohexanol degradation (Donoghue and Trudgill, 1972), cycloalkanols of varied ring size, and with additional hydroxyl and methyl groups are cleaved by parallel pathways. Pathway B, the β-oxidative route for cyclohexane carboxylic acid degradation (Blakley, 1978) into which benzoate metabolism by *Rhodopseudomonas palustris* (C) is integrated (Dutton and Evans, 1969). The possibility of integrating cyclohexane carboxylic acid metabolism into the pathway for cyclohexanone degradation by a decarboxylation step (reaction D) is suggested by anaerobic studies with a species of *Moraxella* (Williams and Evans, 1975). n-Alkylcycloalkanes with an odd number of carbon atoms in the side chain yield cyclohexane carboxyl-CoA (E) by β-oxidation. Pathway F, the aromatization route for cyclohexane carboxylic acid metabolism (Blakley, 1975; Kaneda, 1974; Smith and Cally, 1975; Taylor and Trudgill, 1978). There is *no* evidence that a combination of reaction sequences C and F leads to the conversion of benzoate into p-hydroxybenzoate. Pathway G, the conversion of cyclohexylacetic acid into cyclohexanone and acetyl-CoA; n-alkylcycloalkanes with an even number of carbon atoms in the side chain are degraded primarily to cyclohexylacetic acid (H) by certain strains of *Mycobacterium* (Beam and Perry, 1974b).

theoretical maximum yield, only to be consumed in the latter stages of growth. Subsequent studies at both the whole cell and subcellular level confirmed the involvement of cyclohexanone as an intermediate in cyclohexylacetic acid degradation. Oxidation by *Arthrobacter* CA1 begins with the initiation of a β-oxidation cycle but, because of the position of the ring in relation to the carboxyl group, this is blocked subsequent to the hydration step. The intervention of an induced (1'-hydroxycyclohex-1'-yl)acetyl-CoA lyase cleaves a carbon-carbon bond with the formation of equimolar amounts of cyclohexanone and acetyl-CoA (Fig. 3, pathways G and A) (Ougham and Trudgill, 1978) and permits the integration of cyclohexylacetic acid degradation into the established pathway for cyclohexanone metabolism.

In addition, we have recently shown that this organism, in conjunction with *Mycobacterium vaccae* 7EIC which is able to partially degrade dodecylcyclohexane and other *n*-alkylcycloalkanes with an even number of carbon atoms in the side chain with formation of cyclohexylacetic acid (Beam and Perry, 1974b), is capable of the complete degradation of these hydrocarbons. The hydrocarbon tolerant nature of *Arthrobacter* CA1 and its ability to utilize the metabolite accumulated by *M. vaccae* 7EIC facilitates the establishment of stable mixed cultures (Feinberg *et al.*, 1980). This overall metabolic sequence (H,G,A) is shown in conjunction with a diagrammatic summary of known and probable metabolic routes for the degradation of a variety of cyclohexyl derivatives in Fig. 3.

Although our own work with relatively simple alicyclic molecules grew from strong seeds sown in Urbana and followed a divergent course, exploring the variety of ring cleavage mechanisms used by microorganisms and the manner in which different substituent groups affect or dictate ring cleavage patterns, it is fun (and Gunny has always said that science should be fun) to look back on the metabolic sequence described for (+)−camphor degradation by *P. putida* C1B with a sense of perspective that accumulated knowledge now allows.

V. CAMPHOR REVISITED

Cyclic metabolites accumulated by *P. putida* C1B grown with (+)−camphor indicated that the progressive cleavage of the bicyclic structure was dependent upon hydroxylation to form 5-*exo*hydroxycamphor, dehydrogenation to yield the 2,5-dioxocamphane and two biological Baeyer-Villiger steps (Bradshaw *et al.*, 1959; Conrad *et al.*, 1965a,b). These and subsequent studies amply confirmed the role of a ring oxygen insertion reaction in the first ring cleavage step, although in retrospect it does have some unusual features. If the order of investigations had been reversed and simple structures like cyclohexanol and cyclopentanol had been studied prior to (+)−camphor, one would have wrongly predicted that cleavage of the first camphor ring would proceed by ring oxygen insertion in the established position and hydrolytic cleavage of the lactone thus formed! The reason why this does not occur may possibly be associated with our recent unpublished observation that *P. putida* C1B does not possess the appropriate inducible lactone hydrolase, a situation reminiscent of *Acinetobacter* 6.3 (Davey and Trudgill, 1977) which, because of a similar lesion, is restricted to growth with alicyclic molecules that upon ring oxygenation give rise to unstable lactones. The broad specificity of the ring oxygen-inserting monooxygenase enables *P. putida* C1B to form lactones from $(+)$−camphor 5-*exo*hydroxycamphor and 5-*endo*hydroxycamphor as well as oxygenating 2,5-dioxocamphane (Gunsalus *et al.,* 1965). However, only in the latter case is ring cleavage confidently reported and it takes place not by hydrolytic cleavage but by a concerted enzyme reaction or spontaneous rearrangement.

An absence of lactone hydrolase activity would also explain another early observation. One of the interesting metabolites accumulated by *P. putida* C1B was the lactone 1-oxa-2-oxo-4,5,5,-trimethyl-6-carboxymethyl -Δ^3-cyclohexene (Fig. 1). We all assumed that this, formed by another Baeyer-Villiger oxygenation step, was the precursor of the first acyclic metabolite. Metabolic studies with this intermediate were, however, thwarted by very low rates of oxidation by whole cells and a failure to obtain cell-free systems capable of catalyzing further metabolic steps. Against this background it is interesting to speculate upon alternative possibilities.

Let us suppose, for the moment, that this lactone is a dead-end metabolite formed by the action of the broad specificity lactone-forming monooxygenase on 3,4,4-trimethyl-5-carboxymethyl-Δ^2-cyclopentenone. This supposition is not without precedent if one considers, for example, the work of another of Gunny's former associates on the degradation of monocyclic terpenes, such as limonene, where a broad spectrum of metabolites is accumulated by whole cells, not all of which are intermediates of the sequence leading to ring cleavage (Dhavalikar and Bhattacharyya, 1966).

In retrospect two alternative lines of attack seem feasible. First, hydration of the double bond to form 2-hydroxy-3,4,4,-trimethyl-5-carboxymethylcyclo pentanone could be followed by ring oxygen insertion between the keto and hydroxyl groups with the formation of an unstable lactone that would undergo spontaneous rearrangement and ring cleavage (Fig. 4, pathway A). Second, the possibility of the initiation of a fatty acid β-oxidation cycle which, as is the case with cyclohexylacetic acid (Fig. 3), will be thwarted at the hydroxyacyl-CoA dehydrogenase step. Removal of the side chain by the action of a lyase would leave a 1,2-dione which is likely to equilibrate in solution between the *enol* form and its hydrate (Bakule and Long, 1963). A biological Baeyer-Villiger oxygenation of the hydrate is metabolically acceptable (Davey and Trudgill, 1977) and would again give rise to an inherently unstable lactone followed by a spontaneous ring opening without the agency of a lactone hydrolase (Fig. 4, pathway B).

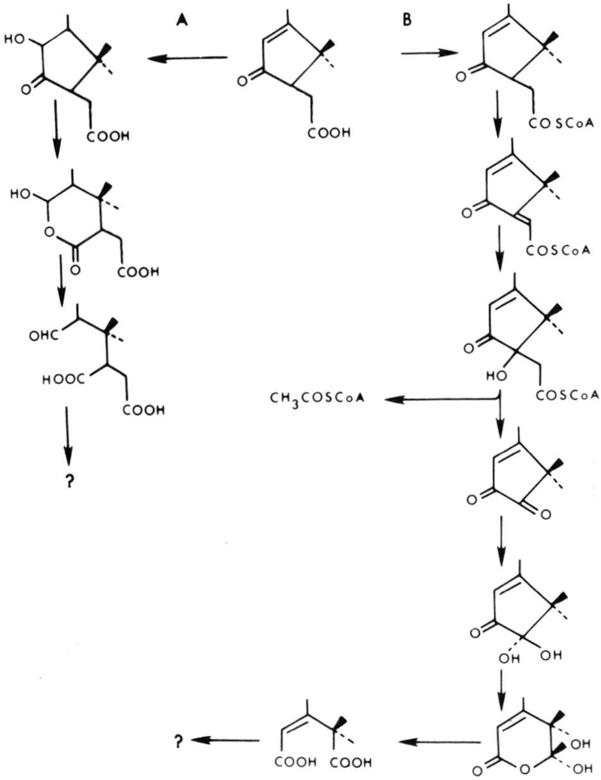

Fig. 4. Two *postulated* alternative routes for the metabolic cleavage of 3,4,4-trimethyl-5-carboxymethyl-Δ^2-cyclopentenone which do not involve the mandatory participation of a lactone hydrolase. Both routes are based upon metabolic transformations known to occur with derivatives of cyclohexane. In route B reduction of the ring double bond could, of course, take place at some point in the sequence of steps displayed.

While I am not suggesting that such metabolic alternatives actually occur in *P. putida* C1B or are in any sense obligatory [the established pathway for (+)−camphor degradation by *M. rhodochrous* T1 (Chapman *et al.*, 1966) demonstrates that this is not so], such alternatives may be forced on an organism by specific lesions in the proportions of the genome-specifying enzymes of degradative sequences and make an interesting departure point for further experimentation.

In writing this contribution for this dedicatory volume to Gunny, it is hoped that I have shown how his perception and inspiration opened up a research area to me, full of surprises and the excitement that goes along with them. In addition, the process of "going away to listen and to learn" which he has so often advocated, coupled with a subsequent divergence of approach to a common research area, allows one to look back on those studies from a different and perhaps helpful viewpoint.

REFERENCES

Bakule, R., and Long, F. A. (1963). Keto–enol transformation of 1,2-cyclohexanedione. I. Hydration and keto–enol equilibria. *J. Am. Chem. Soc.* **85,** 2309–2312.

Beam, H. W., and Perry, J. J. (1974a). Microbial degradation of cycloparaffinic hydrocarbons via co-metabolism and commensalism. *J. Gen. Microbiol.* **82,** 163–169.

Beam, H. W., and Perry, J. J. (1974b). Microbial degradation and assimilation of *n*-alkyl-substituted cycloparaffins. *J. Bacteriol.* **118,** 394–399.

Blakley, E. R. (1975). The microbial degradation of cyclohexanecarboxylic acid: A pathway involving aromatization to form *p*-hydroxybenzoic acid. *Can. J. Microbiol.* **20,** 1297–1306.

Blakley, E. R. (1978). The microbial degradation of cyclohexane carboxylic acid by a β-oxidation pathway with simultaneous induction to the utilization of benzoate. *Can. J. Microbiol.* **24,** 847–855.

Bradshaw, W. H., Conrad, H. E., Corey, E. J., Gunsalus, I. C., and Lednicer, D. (1959). Microbiological degradation of (+)−camphor. *J. Am. Chem. Soc.* **81,** 5507.

Chapman, P. J., and Duggleby, R. G. (1967). Dicarboxylic acid catabolism by bacteria. *Biochem. J.* **103,** 7c.

Chapman, P. J., Meerman, G., Gunsalus, I. C., Srinivasan, R., and Reinhart, K. L. (1966). A new acyclic metabolite in camphor oxidation. *J. Am. Chem. Soc.* **88,** 618–619.

Conrad, H. E., DuBus, R., and Gunsalus, I. C. (1961). An enzyme system for cyclic ketone lactonization. *Biochem. Biophys. Res. Commun.* **6,** 293–297.

Conrad, H. E., DuBus, R., Namtvedt, M. J., and Gunsalus, I. C. (1965a). Mixed function oxidation. II. Separation and properties of the enzymes catalysing camphor lactonization. *J. Biol. Chem.* **240,** 495–503.

Conrad, H. E., Lieb, K., and Gunsalus, I. C. (1965b). Mixed function oxidation. III. An electron transport complex in camphor ketolactonization. *J. Biol. Chem.* **240,** 4029–4037.

Cushman, D. W., Tsai, R. L., and Gunsalus, I. C. (1967). The ferroprotein component of a methylene hydroxylase. *Biochem. Biophys. Res. Commun.* **26,** 577–583.

Dagley, S., and Trudgill, P. W. (1965). The metabolism of galactarate, D-glucarate and various pentoses by a species of *Pseudomonas. Biochem. J.* **95,** 48–58.

Dagley, S., Chapman, P. J., Gibson, D. T., and Wood, J. M. (1964). Degradation of the benzene nucleus by bacteria. *Nature (London)* **202,** 775–778.

Davey, J. F., and Trudgill, P. W. (1977). The metabolism of *trans*-cyclohexan-1,2-diol by an *Acinetobacter* species. *Eur. J. Biochem.* **74,** 115–127.

Dhavalikar, R. S., and Bhattacharyya, P. K. (1966). Microbial transformations of terpenes. Part VIII. Fermentation of limonene by a soil *Pseudomonad. Indian J. Biochem.* **3,** 144–157.

Donoghue, N. A., and Trudgill, P. W. (1975). The metabolism of cyclohexanol by *Acinetobacter* NCIB 9871. *Eur. J. Biochem.* **60,** 1–7.

Donoghue, N. A., Norris, D. B., and Trudgill, P. W. (1976). The purification and properties of cyclohexanone oxygenase from *Nocardia globerula* CL1 and *Acinetobacter* NCIB 9871. *Eur. J. Biochem.* **63,** 175–192.

Dutton, P. L., and Evans, W. C. (1969). The metabolism of aromatic compounds by *Rhodopseudomonas palustris.* A new, reductive, method of aromatic ring metabolism. *Biochem. J.* **113,** 525–536.

Entsch, B., Ballou, D. P., and Massey, V. (1976). Flavin-oxygen derivatives involved in hydroxylation by *p*-hydroxybenzoate hydroxylase. *J. Biol. Chem.* **251,** 2550–2563.

Feinberg, E. L., Ramage, P. I. N., and Trudgill, P. W. (1980). *J. Gen. Microbiol.* **121**, 507–511.

Griffin, M., and Trudgill, P. W. (1972). The metabolism of cyclopentanol by *Pseudomonas* NCIB 9872. *Biochem. J.* **129**, 595–603.

Griffin, M., and Trudgill, P. W. (1976). Purification and properties of cyclopentanone oxygenase of *Pseudomonas* NCIB 9872. *Eur. J. Biochem.* 63, 199–209.

Gunsalus, I. C., Conrad, H. E., Trudgill, P. W., and Jacobson, L. A. (1965). Regulation of catabolic metabolism. *Is. J. Med. Sci.* **1**, 1099–1119.

Gunsalus, I. C., Meeks, J. R., Lipscomb, J. D., Debrunner, P. G., and Münck, E. (1974). Bacterial monooxygenases—The P450 cytochrome system. *In* "Molecular Mechanisms of Oxygen Activation" (O. Hayaishi, ed.), pp. 559–613. Academic Press, New York.

Guyer, M., and Hegeman, G. (1969). Evidence for a reductive pathway for the anaerobic metabolism of benzoate. *J. Bacteriol.* **99**, 906–907.

Hareland, W. A., Crawford, R. L., Chapman, P. J., and Dagley, S. (1975). Metabolic function and properties of 4-hydroxyphenylacetic acid 1-hydroxylase from *Pseudomonas acidivorans*. *J. Bacteriol.* **121**, 272–285.

Howell, L. G., Spector, T., and Massey, V. (1972). Purification and properties of *p*-hydroxybenzoate hydroxylase from *Pseudomonas fluorescens*. *J. Biol. Chem.* **247**, 4340–4350.

Kaneda, T., (1974). Enzymatic aromatization of 4-ketocyclohexanecarboxylic acid to *p*-hydroxybenzoic acid. *Biochem. Biophys. Res. Commun.* **58**, 140–144.

Norris, D. B., and Trudgill, P. W. (1971). The metabolism of cyclohexanol by *Nocardia globerula* CL1. *Biochem. J.* **121**, 363–370.

Ougham, H. J., and Trudgill, P. W. (1978). The microbial metabolism of cyclohexylacetic acid. *Biochem. Soc. Trans.* **6**, 1324–1326.

Ryerson, C., Ballou, D., and Walsh, C. Mechanistic studies on cyclohexanone oxygenase (in preparation).

Smith, D. I., and Callely, A. G. (1975). The microbial degradation of cyclohexanecarboxylic acid. *J. Gen. Microbiol.* **91**, 210–212.

Sparnins, V. L., Chapman, P. J., and Dagley, S. (1974). Bacterial degradation of 4-hydroxyphenylacetic acid and homoprotocatechuic acid. *J. Bacteriol.* **120**, 159–167.

Taylor, D. G., and Trudgill, P. W. (1978). Metabolism of cyclohexane carboxylic acid by *Alcaligenes* strain W1. *J. Bacteriol.* **134**, 401–411.

Trudgill, P. W. (1978). Microbial degradation of alicyclic hydrocarbons. *In* "Developments in Biodegradation of Hydrocarbons" (R. J. Watkinson, ed.), pp. 47–84. Appl. Sci. Publ. Ltd., London.

Trudgill, P. W., DuBus, R., and Gunsalus, I. C. (1966a). Mixed function oxidation. V. Flavin interaction with the reduced diphosphopyridine nucleotide dehydrogenase, one of the enzymes participating in camphor lactonization. *J. Biol. Chem.* **241**, 1194–1205.

Trudgill, P. W., DuBus, R., and Gunsalus, I. C. (1966b). Mixed function oxidation. VI. Purification of a tightly coupled electron transport complex in camphor lactonization. *J. Biol. Chem.* **241**, 4288–4290.

Watson, G. K., Houghton, C., and Cain, R. B. (1974). Microbial metabolism of the pyridine ring. The metabolism of pyridine-3,4-diol (3,4-dihydroxypyridine) by *Agrobacterium* sp. *Biochem. J.* **140**, 277–292.

Williams, R. J., and Evans, W. C. (1975). The metabolism of benzoate by *Moraxella* species through anaerobic nitrate respiration. Evidence for a reductive pathway. *Biochem. J.* **148**, 1–10.

Yamamoto, S., Katagiri, M., Maeno, H., and Hayaishi, O. (1965). Salicylate hydroxylase, a monooxygenase requiring flavin adenine dinucleotide. I. Purification and general properties. *J. Biol. Chem.* **240**, 3408–3413.

8

Microbial Metabolism
of Anthracycline
Antibiotics

Vincent P. Marshall

I. INTRODUCTION

Adriamycin and daunomycin are anthracycline antibiotics which are clinically effective in the treatment of solid tumors and leukemias (Burchenal and Carter, 1972; Weil *et al.*, 1973). Despite the effectiveness of these agents, their use must be limited because of their cardiotoxic properties (Lefrak *et al.*, 1973). In an effort to reduce such toxicity, extensive microbial conversion of anthracycline compounds has been performed in our laboratories. Some of these studies have dealt with adriamycin and daunomycin and now have been extended to other anthracyclines including nogalamycin and the steffimycins. It was hoped that the therapeutic properties of these agents might be improved by this manipulation, and that the resulting data might contribute to our understanding of the metabolic processes involved.

Metabolic routes for the mammalian metabolism of adriamycin and daunomycin have been presented (Bachur, 1975; Takanishi and Bachur, 1975), and have proved to be essentially identical as would be expected due to their chemical similarity (Fig. 1). Other studies have also indicated considerable similarity between the mammalian and microbial metabolism of these compounds (Marshall *et al.*, 1976a, 1978a). In addition, the investigation of analogous metabolic

75

EXPERIENCES IN BIOCHEMICAL PERCEPTION
Copyright © 1982 by Academic Press, Inc.
All rights of reproduction in any form reserved.
ISBN 0-12-528420-9

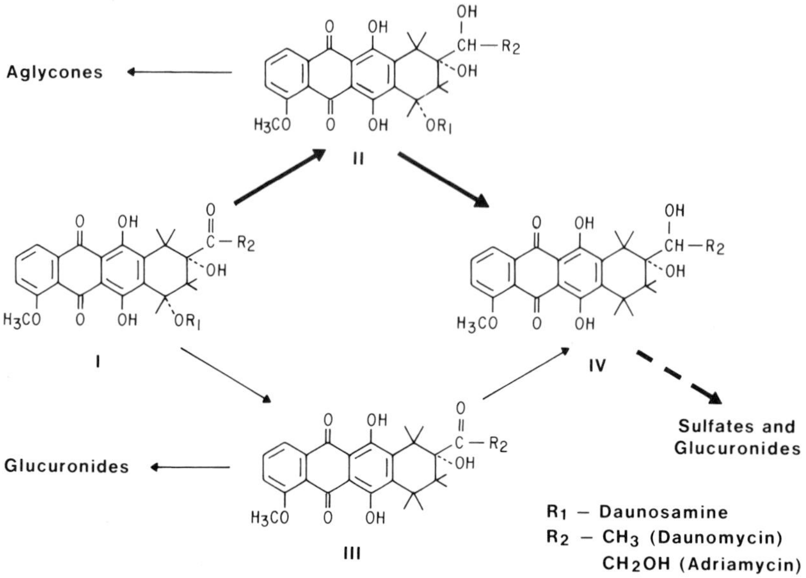

Fig. 1. The proposed pathway for the mammalian metabolism of adriamycin and daunomycin (Bachur, 1975; Takanishi and Bachur, 1975). I, adriamycin/daunomycin; II, adriamycinol/daunomycinol; III, 7-deoxyadriamycinone/7-deoxydaunomycinone; IV, 7-deoxyadriamycinol aglycone/7-deoxydaunomycinol aglycone. The heavy arrows indicate the primary pathway; light arrows indicate minor routes of metabolism.

pathways as such has demonstrated an efficient means for the microbial production of human drug metabolites for pharmacological and toxicological evaluation.

The modes of anthracycline bioconversion reported here include reductive glycosidic cleavage (Fig. 2) and ketonic carbonyl reduction. A current review presents these and other reported anthracycline bioconversions (Marshall and Wiley, 1981). The structures of the polyketide derived anthracycline substrates (Paulick *et al.*, 1976; Wiley *et al.*, 1978) are presented in Table I.

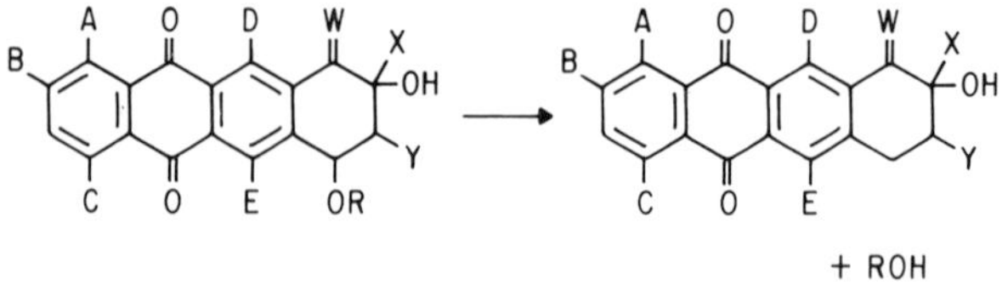

Fig. 2. Reductive cleavage of anthracycline compounds.

TABLE I

Structures of Anthracycline Substrates

Anthracycline	A	B	C	D	E	W	X	Y	R
Daunomycin	H	H	CH_3O	HO	HO	H,H	CH_3CO	H	
Adriamycin	H	H	CH_3O	HO	HO	H,H	CH_2OHCO	H	As above
Nogalamycin	$C_6H_{15}NO_4$		HO	H	HO	$H,COOCH_3$	CH_3	H	
Steffimycin	H	CH_3O	HO	H	HO	$=O$	CH_3	CH_3O	
Steffimycin B	H	CH_3O	HO	H	HO	$=O$	CH_3	CH_3O	
Steffimycinone	H	CH_3O	HO	H	HO	$=O$	CH_3	CH_3O	H
Cinerubin	HO	H	HO	H	HO	$H,COOCH_3$	C_2H_5	H	

II. MICROBIAL METABOLISM OF ANTHRACYCLINE ANTIBIOTICS

A. Reductive Glycosidic Cleavage

Figure 2 shows the conversion of anthracycline compounds to their 7-deoxy aglycones through anaerobically catalyzed, reductive glycosidic cleavage. The anthracycline compounds converted by this means using whole bacteria and their extracts include daunomycin (Marshall *et al.*, 1976a,b, 1978a; Wiley and Marshall, 1975), 13-dihydrodaunomycin (Marshall *et al.*, 1978a), adriamycin (Marshall *et al.*, 1978a; Reuckert *et al.*, 1979), nogalamycin (Marshall *et al.*, 1976b; Reuckert *et al.*, 1979; Wiley and Marshall, 1975), steffimycin (Marshall *et al.*, 1976b; McCarville and Marshall, 1977; Reuckert *et al.*, 1979; Wiley and Marshall, 1975), steffimycin B (Marshall *et al.*, 1976b; Reuckert *et al.*, 1979; Wiley and Marshall, 1975), steffimycinone (Marshall *et al.*, 1976b; McCarville and Marshall, 1977; Wiley and Marshall, 1975; Wiley *et al.*, 1977), 10-dihydrosteffimycinone (Marshall *et al.*, 1978d; Wiley *et al.*, 1977), and cinerubin A (Marshall *et al.*, 1976b). The 7-deoxy aglycone reaction products were purified by extraction and chromatography on silia gel (Marshall *et al.*, 1976a,b, 1978a,d; Reuckert *et al.*, 1979; Wiley and Marshall, 1975; Wiley *et al.*, 1977) and were identified by means of mass spectra (Marshall *et al.*, 1976a,b, and 1978a; Reuckert *et al.*, 1979; Wiley and Marshall, 1975; Wiley *et al.*, 1977), uv-visible spectra (Marshall *et al.*, 1976b; Wiley and Marshall, 1975), infrared spectra (Wiley and Marshall, 1975), NMR (Marshall *et al.*, 1976b; Wiley and Marshall, 1975; Wiley *et al.*, 1977), chromatography against standards (Marshall *et al.*, 1976a,b, 1978a; Reuckert *et al.*, 1979; Wiley and Marshall, 1975; Wiley *et al.*, 1977), and by melting point (Marshall *et al.*, 1976b; Wiley and Marshall, 1975).

The bacteria investigated which perform these conversions include *Aeromonas hydrophila* (Marshall *et al.*, 1976b; McCarville and Marshall, 1977; Wiley and Marshall, 1975; Wiley *et al.*, 1977), *Escherichia coli* (Marshall *et al.*, 1976b; Wiley and Marshall, 1975), *Citrobacter freundii* (Marshall *et al.*, 1976b; Wiley and Marshall, 1975), *Streptomyces nogalater* (Reuckert *et al.*, 1979), and *Streptomyces steffisburgensis* (Marshall *et al.*, 1976a, 1978a). Cell-free conversion of these compounds to their 7-deoxy aglycones using crude enzyme preparations of *A. hydrophila* (Marshall *et al.*, 1976b; McCarville and Marshall, 1977; Wiley and Marshall, 1975), *S. nogalater* (Reuckert *et al.*, 1979), and *S. steffisburgensis* (Marshall *et al.*, 1976a, 1978a) requires reduced pyridine nucleotide with a preference for NADH. The enzyme from *A. hydrophila* was purified ca. 100-fold and was estimated to have a molecular weight of 35,000 (McCarville and Marshall, 1977). Further, the purified enzyme displays absolute requirements for NADH and anaerobic reaction conditions.

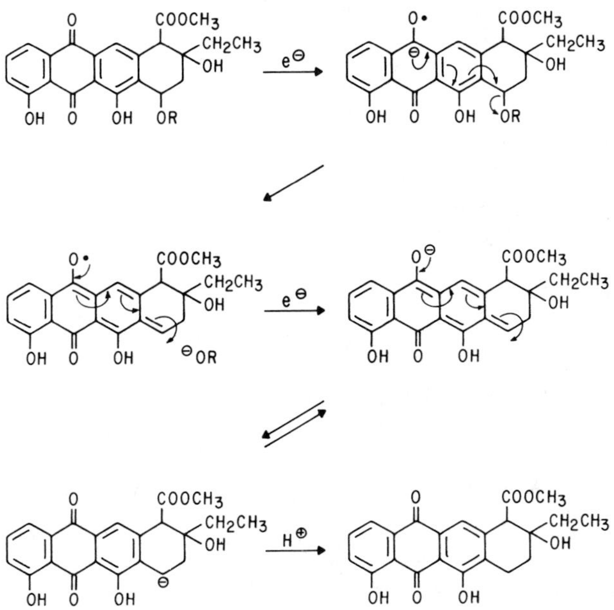

Fig. 3. The proposed reation mechanism for the anaerobically catalyzed, reductive glycosidic cleavage of aclacinomycin A (Komiyama *et al.*, 1979).

Reductive glycosidic cleavage of adriamycin and daunomycin is known to occur as the initial step of the minor mammalian metabolic route for their detoxification and removal (Fig. 1) (Bachur, 1975; Takanishi and Bachur, 1975). In addition, reductive glycosidic cleavage occurs as the second step of their primary mammalian metabolic pathway in which daumonycinol (13-dihydrodaunomycin) and adriamycinol (13-dihydroadriamycin) are converted to their 7-deoxy aglycones (Fig. 1) (Bachur, 1975; Takanishi and Bachur, 1975). All of these reactions catalyzed in mammalian tissue require NADPH (Asbell *et al.*, 1972; and Bachur and Gee, 1976). The mammalian-type enzyme has been purified and was found to be a flavoprotein. In one instance it was designated as cytochrome *c* reductase (Oki *et al.*, 1977) and in another cytochrome P450 reductase (Komiyama *et al.*, 1979). Several closely related reaction mechanisms have been advanced for anthracycline reductive glycosidic cleavage (Komiyama *et al.*, 1979; Wiley *et al.*, 1977; Yesair and McNitt, 1976). Figure 3 shows the proposed mechanism for the reductive glycosidic cleavage of aclacinomycin A (Komiyama *et al.*, 1979). A comparison of the *S. nogalater* and rat liver enzymes indicates that the mammalian enzyme is ca. 20 times more active than the bacterial enzyme with nogalamycin as a substrate and 300 times more active using adriamycin as the substrate (Reuckert *et al.*, 1979).

B. Ketonic Carbonyl Reduction

1. C-13 Ketonic Carbonyl Reduction of Daunomycin-Related Anthracyclines

Both the fungus *Mucor spinosus* and its cell-free extracts reduce the C-13 ketonic carbonyl of daunomycin to yield daunomycinol by a NADPH-dependent reaction (Marshall *et al.*, 1978a). In this study daunomycinol was purified by extraction and chromatography on silica gel and identified by mass spectrum and chromatography against standards (Marshall *et al.*, 1968a). This reaction corresponds to the initial step of daunomycin metabolism in mammals by the primary route of catabolism (Fig. 1) (Takanishi and Bachur, 1975). The mammalian enzyme also requires NADPH (Felsted *et al.*, 1974). Figure 4 demonstrates the C-13 ketonic carbonyl reduction of daunomycin. Interestingly, neither *M. spinosus* nor its extracts catalyze C-13 ketonic carbonyl reduction of adriamycin.

The bacterium *S. steffisburgensis* and its cell-free extracts convert 7-deoxydaunomycinone and 7-deoxyadriamycinone, the 7-deoxy aglycones of daunomycin and adriamycin, to their C-13 dihydro derivatives by ketonic carbonyl reduction (Marshall *et al.*, 1976a, 1978a). These metabolites, 7-deoxydaunomycinol aglycone and 7-deoxyadriamycinol aglycone, were purified and identified in a like manner to daunomycinol (Marshall *et al.*, 1976a, 1978a). When catalyzed by *S. steffisburgensis* this reaction requires NADPH (Marshall *et al.*, 1976a, 1978a). The latter reactions occur in mammals as the NADPH-dependent second step of the minor pathway for the metabolism of adriamycin and daunomycin (Fig. 1) (Bachur, 1975; Takanishi and Bachur, 1975).

2. C-10 Ketonic Carbonyl Reduction of Steffimycin-Related Anthracyclines

Streptomyces nogalater and *Streptomyces peucetius* var. *caesius* catalyze C-10 ketonic carbonyl reduction of steffimycinone (Fig. 5) (Marshall *et al.*,

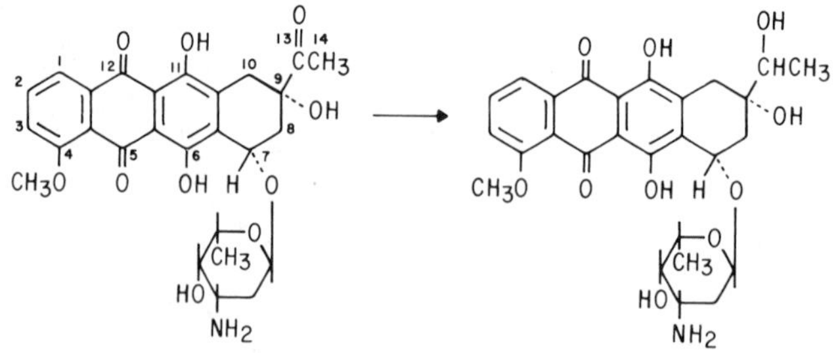

Fig. 4. C-13 ketonic carbonyl reduction of daunomycin.

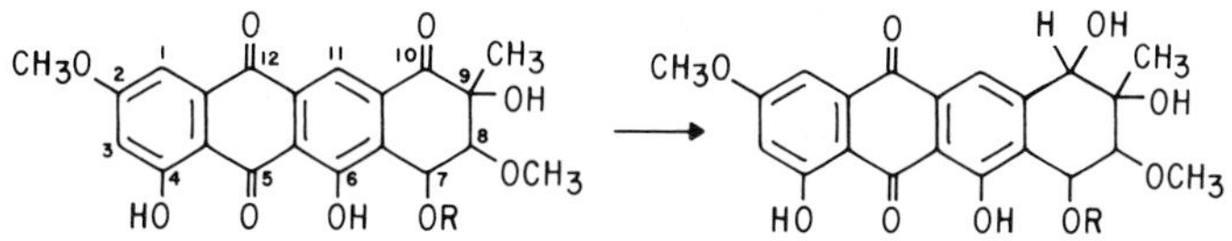

Fig. 5. C-10 ketonic carbonyl reduction of steffimycin related anthracyclines.

1978b,c; Wiley *et al.*, 1977). Using cell-free preparations of *S. nogalater*, the process of carbonyl reduction has been shown to be NADPH linked (Wiley *et al.*, 1977). The reaction product, 10-dihydrosteffimycinone, was isolated by extraction and chromatography on silica gel and was identified by comparison of various physical properties and spectral data with those of anthentic materials obtained by chemical means (Wiley *et al.*, 1977).

Chaetomium, UC 4634, converts steffimycin and steffimycin B to 10-dihydrosteffimycin B by NADPH-linked ketonic carbonyl reduction (Marshall *et al.*, 1980; Wiley *et al.*, 1980). In addition, *Actinoplanes utahensis* performs C-10 ketonic carbonyl reduction of these compounds (Marshall *et al.*, 1980; Wiley *et al.*, 1980). The conversion catalyzed by *Chaetomium* can be performed using cell-free extracts or by mycelia in fermentation while the *Actinoplanes* process has been shown to occur only in fermentation (Marshall *et al.*, 1981; Wiley *et al.*, 1980). The 10-dihydro derivatives formed in this study were purified by extraction and chromatography on silica gel and were identified by chemical analysis, PMR, CMR, and mass spectra (Wiley *et al.*, 1980). Figure 5 demonstrates the C-10 ketonic carbonyl reduction of steffimycin and steffimycin B.

III. CONCLUSION

Improvement of the therapeutic value of an antitumor agent could be achieved through modifications resulting in increased potency or reduced toxicity. Although many of the transformation products reported here are less toxic than their parent substrates, they lack the potency to be clinically useful antitumor agents. Other transformation reactions which might be expected to improve the therapeutic properties of an anthracycline compound could include glycosidation of a-glycones, transglycosylations, N-demethylations, and hydroxylations.

In addition to our primary goal of obtaining antitumor agents with improved therapeutic properties, these studies have demonstrated microbial models of human adriamycin and daunomycin metabolism. Such models are of potential value for the efficient production of drug metabolites for use in various aspects of pharmacological testing.

In summary, the microbial model of human adriamycin and daunomycin metabolism (Fig. 1) includes the following reactions. The model of the minor pathway for the metabolism of these compounds is initiated by NADH-linked reductive glycosidic cleavage catalyzed by *A. hydrophila* and *S. steffisburgensis*. The second step of the model, C-13 ketonic carbonyl reduction of 7-deoxyadiamycinone or 7-deoxydaunomycinone, is catalyzed by *S. steffisburgensis* through a NADPH-dependent enzyme. The first reaction of the model of daunomycin metabolism by the primary mammalian route is catalyzed by *M. spinosus* through NADPH-linked ketonic carbonyl reduction. This reaction is followed by the NADH-dependent reductive glycosidic cleavage of daunomycinol catalyzed by *S. steffisburgensis*.

IV. PERSONAL NOTE

As a 22-year-old biology student from Cherokee County, Oklahoma, and a graduate of a college directly descended from the Cherokee Male and Female Seminaries, I approached my appointment at the University of Oklahoma Medical Center with great impatience and expectation. I was to do graduate studies with Professor Sokatch, a Gunsalus colleague of long standing. I was convinced that here was the embodiment of all that was exciting in microbiology and biochemistry. It was indeed my good fortune to become associated with such an able scientist and to unknowingly become a part of the extended Gunsalus scientific family. As my studies progressed, I became aware of the Gunsalus excellence which I hoped to directly experience. Through the efforts of Jack Sokatch, I was able to obtain a postdoctoral appointment with Gunny in Urbana.

At this time, I became associated with Professors Frauenfelder and Debrunner. During our weekly biochemistry–physics discussions, I would witness the transformation of our data into complex spin hamiltonians which, with great surprise, I found to be understood by some of Gunny's undergraduate students. As Gunny would sense my frustration he would tell me, "What one monkey can do another can learn." Through the guidance of Gunny and his more sophisticated students, I was tutored into a state of rudimentary understanding. At this time I began to make myself useful through "low temperature microbiology" and the guidance of *P. putida* in the production of enzymes more amenable to study by physical probes. At the close of my 3-year stay with Gunny, I was ready to approach science with the insights and knowledge that I had obtained from him.

Shortly after joining the research staff at Upjohn, I was approached by Oldrich Sebek who informed me of the possibility of working with my present colleague, Paul Wiley, doing biomodification of antitumor agents. Here again, a good core group was available to enable continuation of the efforts which, for me, were direct extensions of what I had learned from Gunsalus.

ACKNOWLEDGMENT

The author is indebted to Dr. P. F. Wiley for collaboration in these studies. These studies were supported in part by contracts NOI-CM-43753 and NOI-CM-77100, DCT, NIH, HEW.

REFERENCES

Asbell, M. A., Schwartzenback, E., Bullock, F. J., and Yesair, D. W. (1972). Daunomycin and adriamycin metabolism *via* reductive glycosidic cleavage. *J. Pharmacol. Exp. Ther.* **182,** 63–69.

Bachur, N. R. (1975). Adriamycin metabolism in man. *In* "Chemotheraphy" (K. Hellman and T. A. Connors, eds.), pp. 105–111. Plenum, New York.

Bachur, N. R, and Gee, M. V. (1976). Microsomal reductive glycosidase. *J. Pharmacol. Exp. Ther.* **197,** 681–686.

Burchenal, J. H., and Carter, S. K. (1972). New cancer chemotherapeutic agents. *Cancer* **30,** 1639–1646.

Felsted, R. L., Gee, M., and Bachur, N. (1974). Rat liver daunorubicin reductase. *J. Biol. Chem.* **249,** 3672–3679.

Komiyama, T., Oki, T., and Inui, T. (1979). A proposed reaction mechanism for the enzymatic reductive cleavage of glycosidic bond in anthracycline antibiotics. *J. Antibiot.* **32,** 1219–1222.

Lefrak, E. A., Pitha, J., Rosenheim, S., and Gottlieb, J. A. (1973). A clinicopathologic analysis of adriamycin cardiotoxicity. *Cancer* **32,** 302–314.

McCarville, M., and Marshall, V. (1977). Partial purification and characterization of a bacterial enzyme catalyzing reductive cleavage of anthracycline glycosides. *Biochem. Biophys. Res. Commun.* **74,** 331–335.

Marshall, V. P., and Wiley, P. F. (1981). Microbial transformations of antibiotics. *In* "Microbial Transformations of Physiologically Active Compounds" (J. P. N. Rosazza, ed.). CRC Press, West Palm Beach, Florida.

Marshall, V. P., Reisender, E. A., and Wiley, P. F. (1976a). Bacterial metabolism of daunomycin. *J. Antibiot.* **29,** 966–968.

Marshall, V. P., Reisender, E. A., Reineke, L. M., Johnson, J. H., and Wiley, P. F. (1976b). Reductive microbial conversion of anthracycline antibiotics. *Biochemistry* **15,** 4139–4145.

Marshall, V. P., McGovren, J. P., Richard, F. A., Richard, R. E., and Wiley, P. F. (1978a). Microbial metabolism of anthracycline antibiotics daunomycin and adriamycin. *J. Antibiot.* **31,** 336–342.

Marshall, V. P., Elrod, D. W., Koert, J. M., Reisender, E. A., and Wiley, P. F. (1978b). Process for preparing steffimycinol. U.S. Patent 4,077,844.

Marshall, V. P., Elrod, D. W., Koert, J. M., Reisender, E. A., and Wiley, P. F. (1978c). Process for producing steffimycinol. U.S. Patent 4,106,944.

Marshall, V. P., Elrod, D. W., Koert, J. M., Reisender, E. A., and Wiley, P. F. (1978d). Process for preparing 7-deoxysteffimycinol. U.S. Patent 4,116,769.

Marshall, V. P., Elrod, D. W., and Wiley, P. F. (1980). Antibiotics 10-dihydrosteffimycin and 10-dihydrosteffimycin B. U.S. Patent 4,209,611.

Marshall, V. P., Elrod, D. W., and Wiley, P. F. (1981). Process for producing 10-dihydrosteffimycin and 10-dihydrosteffimycin B and microorganisms for producing same. U.S. Patent 4,264,726.

Oki, T., Komiyama, T., Tone, H., Inui, T., Takeuchi, T., and Umezawa, H. (1977). Reductive cleavage of anthracycline glycosides by microsomal NADPH-cytochrome C reductase. *J. Antibiot.* **30,** 613–615.

Paulick, R. C., Casey, M. L., and Whitlock, H. W. (1976). A ^{13}C nuclear magnetic resonance study of the biosynthesis of daunomycin from $^{13}CH_3^{13}CO_2Na$. *J. Am. Chem. Soc.* **98,** 3370–3371.

Reuckert, P. W., Wiley, P. F., McGovren, J. P., and Marshall, V. P. (1979). Mammalian and microbial cell-free conversion of anthracycline antibiotics and analogs. *J. Antibiot.* **32,** 141–147.

Takanishi, S., and Bachur, N. R. (1975). Daunorubicin metabolites in human urine. *J. Pharmacol. Exp. Ther.* **195,** 41–49.

Weil, M., *et al.* (1973). Daunorubicin in the therapy of acute granulocytic leukemia. *Cancer Res.* **33,** 921–928.

Wiley, P. F., and Marshall, V. P. (1975). Microbial conversion of anthracycline antibiotics. *J. Antibiot.* **28,** 838–840.

Wiley, P. F., Koert, J. M., Elrod, D. W., Reisender, E. A., and Marshall, V. P. (1977). Bacterial metabolism of anthracycline antibiotics. Steffimycinone and steffimycinol conversions. *J. Antibiot.* **30,** 649–654.

Wiley, P. F., Elrod, D. W., and Marshall, V. P. (1978). Biosynthesis of the anthracycline antibiotics nogalamycin and steffimycin B. *J. Org. Chem.* **43,** 3457–3461.

Wiley, P. F., Slavicek, J. M., Elrod, D. W., and Marshall, V. P. (1980). Microbial conversion of steffimycin and steffimycin B to 10-dihydrosteffimycin and 10-dihydrosteffimycin B. *J. Antibiot.* **33,** 819–823.

Yesair, D. W., and McNitt, S. (1976). Proposed mechanism for the metabolism of daunorubicin and adriamycin *via* reductive glycosidic cleavage. *Hoppe-Seyler's Z. Physiol. Chem.* **357,** 1066–1067.

9

Fatty Acid and
Electron Transport
in Pseudomonads

Richard A. Hartline
and
William A. Toscano, Jr.

Our professional association with I. C. Gunsalus (Gunny) is difficult to document accurately because to us he is, at times, a difficult person to interpret and evaluate. His personality is endowed with the same characteristics as all humans except that the complexity and magnitude of the characteristics seem several powers greater. At times his attitudes, feelings, and moods are unmistakable whereas at other times they defy interpretation because of his complex nature. However, one aspect of Gunny that we believe is obvious is his dedication to his work and ancillary interests, which is second to none.

Gunny's talent for succinctly and metaphorically stating profound philosophical scientific lessons is legendary. Although it is possible that because of their terseness and occasional stern delivery some of the statements could be interpreted by students as subtle pointed humor or even criticism, we do not consider that their purpose. Instead, we believe that his intention is to have them benefit from his experience by providing advice, with minimal verbiage, on essentials for success in research. Perhaps all of these characteristics are what make him a uniquely interesting individual. In spite of what we view as a seemingly impossible documentary task, we are pleased to have our efforts included in this volume.

Writing this chapter as two generations was prompted by what could be viewed as an academic lineage. In 1968 Dick Hartline left his postdoctoral

EXPERIENCES IN BIOCHEMICAL PERCEPTION
Copyright © 1982 by Academic Press, Inc.
All rights of reproduction in any form reserved.
ISBN 0-12-528420-9

position with Gunny to accept a faculty position in the Department of Chemistry at Indiana University of Pennsylvania. Within a few years, he entered into collaboration with Bill Toscano to study bacterial membrane transport (Toscano and Hartline, 1973; Dubler *et al.*, 1974). After completion of a Master's degree and realizing the need for further training, Toscano moved to the University of Illinois to pursue doctoral studies under the guidance of I. C. Gunsalus.

As with any two generations there were differences in our experiences at Urbana. The people and directions of research changed but, as is true with any dynamic institution, some things transcended time. We both observed that in the schools of chemical and biological sciences an attitude of dedication and excitement for science prevailed. This was complemented by an atmosphere in which one could easily obtain constructive criticism and advice and develop both intellectual and technical skills in a challenging environment. In the research group with which we were associated, there was Gunny, who, in addition to providing the necessary space and equipment, was eager to discuss research and influence professional development so that some day one might have the skills to become an independent investigator.

THE FIRST GENERATION*

Having just obtained my Ph.D. degree at the University of California under the patient and informative direction of Victor Rodwell, I moved to the midwest to initiate postdoctoral studies in Gunny's laboratory at the University of Illinois. Ambivalent is the best way to describe my attitude on arriving in Urbana on a cold January day in 1966. While I admit to a sense of anticipatory excitement toward the forthcoming venture, there was also a sense of hesitation. The hesitation eminated from my interest in teaching which strongly superseded my interest in research and, because of limited experience, an uncertainty of my potential to do independent investigation. Gunny's response to this was, "Don't worry, we'll teach you about research." As with many of his quick phrases, I comprehended the details and value of the comment after I had learned the lessons to which I believe he was referring.

It was a time of meeting many interesting people. Their presence was evidence of Gunny's ability to bring together capable and talented individuals and to provide them with an opportunity to interact, learn, and develop their potential. Lou Jacobson was about to complete his Ph.D. degree and, before moving on to the University of Pittsburgh, introduced me to the local folklore and techniques necessary to initiate my research. Randolf Tsai was an alert and pleasant individual beginning his doctoral studies. Unfortunately, he passed away at an early

*By Richard A. Hartline.

age. It was a personal loss to all who knew him and, I believe, a loss of quality contributions to the scientific community. On a more pleasant note, there was Al Chakrabarty, whose friendly personality and keen sense of humor prevails to this day, as does his productive fascination and curiosity about bacterial plasmids. He alerted me to the importance of the role of these DNA molecules in the metabolic versatility of pseudomonads. There were many others who made this period in my life personally and scientifically interesting, whether or not they realize it (Dick Bartholemous, John Clark, Ed Conrad, Dave Cushman, Carol Gunsalus, Steve and Sherry Queener, Mary Jane Nametvedt, John Niblack, John Tsibis, and Chaing An Yu—a belated thank you to all).

Prior to my arrival in Urbana, Gunny suggested that as a member of his research group I should follow up preliminary studies which indicated that keto steroids may induce the D-camphor (2-bornanone) catabolic enzymes in *Pseudomonas putida* (Gunsalus *et al.,* 1965). Experiments that I performed upon my arrival in Urbana revealed that steriods do not induce these enzymes. Quite suddenly I was without a research problem and uncertain as to what direction my research activities should proceed. For reasons I do not remember, if I ever knew, Gunny and I were having minor communication problems—probably a result of my inexperience in interpretive skills. Nevertheless, as best as I can recall it was Lou Jacobson who mentioned to me that Gunny felt a study of induction specificity analogous to George Hegemans' (1966) investigation of the mandalate degradative enzymes of *P. putida* would be interesting. Since I had no particularly pressing research plans, I took the advice and studied the induction specificity of the camphor catabolic enzymes and their repression by succinate and glucose (Hartline and Gunsalus, 1971). These studies were interesting to me and clearly served to teach me more about research and preparing manuscripts for publication.

Although I have not continued research on camphor metabolism, I have continued to work with pseudomonads. After leaving the University of Illinois I returned to investigating bacterial catabolism of α-aminoadipate (Wood and Hartline, 1971a; Perfetti *et al.,* 1972; Pekala and Hartline, 1973; Kopchick and Hartline, 1979), an extension of earlier work (Hartline and Rodwell, 1971), and have since become involved in studying bacterial membrane transport (Wood and Hartline, 1971; Toscano and Hartline, 1973; Dubler *et al.,* 1974; Pekala *et al.,* 1975; Edwards *et al.,* 1979). In addition, in recent years I have embarked on interdisciplinary research with a psychologist interested in the biochemistry of behavior, specifically in studying the molecular basis for alcohol tolerance in inbred mouse strains (Goldbort *et al.,* 1976; Fioriglio *et al.,* 1979; Duckett *et al.,* 1981). This activity has opened my eyes to the fascination and complexities of neurobiochemistry.

My initial interest in bacterial membrane transport of nonpolar molecules originated from what I consider an experience in biochemical perception which occurred during my tenure in Gunny's lab. For this reason, I have chosen to describe briefly my on-going activity investigating fatty acid transport of *Pseudomonas oleovorans*. It was while I was growing *P. putida* on camphor, a relatively water-insoluble compound, that I first became curious about the transport mechanism of hydrophobic molecules by bacterial cells. It would be later, however, before I would pursue that interest. In fact, 4 years passed and I had moved to my present location before embarking on studies with Bill Toscano on octanoate transport in *P. oleovorans* (Toscano and Hartline, 1973).

Octoanoate was selected because it is relatively hydrophobic but has some degree of water solubility, making it easier to study than a totally apolar molecule. While the initial classical characterization of the process was informative, our continued research activity on this system was prompted by the observation that octanoate is concentrated intracellularly as the free acid (Toscano and Hartline, 1973). This feature of transport attracted our attention because it contrasted with the mechanism of vectorial acylation proposed, but not unequivocally established, for fatty acid transport by *Escherichia coli* (Klein *et al.*, 1971). In this vectorial acylation, transport across the membrane would be driven solely by the activity of acyl-CoA synthetase (acyl thiokinase), the first enzyme in fatty acid catabolism, resulting in the intracellular deposition of the fatty acid exclusively as the CoA derivative.

A vectorial acylation driven by the activity of an acetyl-CoA:butyrate-CoA transferase enzyme rather than of a synthetase has been suggested from studies of butyrate transport in *E. coli* vesicles (Frerman, 1973). However, other interpretations not consistent with vectorial acylation are possible. Moreover, the more recent observation that *E. coli* vesicles transport butyrate as the free acid in the presence of phenazine methosulfate and ascorbate (Ramos *et al.*, 1976) casts serious doubt on butyrate transport by vectorial acylation. While I have not discounted the possible involvement of a transferase enzyme(s) if the mechanism of fatty acid transport in pseudomonads is vectorial acylation, the data presently available indicate that catalysis of fatty acid-CoA formation in these organisms is by synthetase enzymes, not by transferases (Trust and Millis, 1971).

To elucidate the detailed mechanism of fatty acid transport by *P. oleovorans* we first prepared membrane vesicles from cells grown on octanoate plus NH_4Cl and examined transport in the absence of intracellular metabolism. In particular, it was of interest to determine whether transport occurred in the absence of acyl-CoA synthetase activity. Vesicles in the presence of a wide variety of electron donors or preloaded with CoA and ATP to enhance any synthetase activity exhibit no capacity to transport octanoate (VanNess, 1975; Jones, 1980).

It is unlikely that the method of vesicle preparation caused the loss of transport function, since membranes prepared from cells grown on proline are fully capable of proline transport (VanNess, 1975). However, in view of the report that vesicle transport of acetate, propionate, and butyrate can only be assayed by flow dialysis (Ramos *et al.*, 1976), I considered that the filtration method used to measure octanoate transport might be inadequate. Attempts thus far to detect vesicle transport of octanoate by flow dialysis have been unsuccessful.

Vesicles that are unable to generate an electrochemical membrane potential would most likely lack transport function. The electrochemical potential, $\Delta\mu H^+$, consists of two variable components, $\Delta\psi$, the membrane potential, and ΔpH, the difference in pH across the membrane, which are related to $\Delta\mu H^+$ according to the equation $\Delta\mu H^+ = \Delta\psi - (2.3/F)RT \,\Delta$pH. Since membranes prepared from cells grown on octanoate generate an electrochemical force ($\Delta\mu H^+$) of 148 mV at an extracellular pH of 6.6 and an intracellular pH of 7.5 (Jones, 1980),* the absence of octanoate transport could not be equated with the inability of vesicles to generate any electrochemical potential.

The next consideration was that the absence of transport might reflect the loss of the cell wall, the outer membrane, or a periplasmic binding protein during vesicle preparation. To test these possibilities I decided to work with spheroplasts (Jones, 1980). Octanoate uptake by spheroplasts is greater than that by whole cells, eliminating involvement in transport of any extra-inner membrane component(s). Isolation and identification of the radioactive molecules within the spheroplasts following uptake of [1-^{14}C]octanoate revealed that octanoate is concentrated within the spheroplasts 63-fold (1.28 mM) and 50-fold (1.03 mM) relative to the initial extraspheroplast concentration (20.4 μM) at pH 5.5. and 7.5, respectively. Examination of spheroplast uptake in the presence of the ionophores valinomycin and nigericin revealed that the individual components of $\Delta\mu H^+$ represent the driving force for octanoate uptake at extracellular pH values of 5.5 and 7.5. The component of $\Delta\mu H^+$ required for transport at pH 5.5. is ΔpH. At pH 7.5, where there is no ΔpH, only $\Delta\psi$ is required.

Recently, I have examined octanoate uptake by whole cells in phosphate-free buffer following incubation for 1 hour in the presence of arsenate to deplete intracellular ATP (Romano *et al.*, 1980). The rate of uptake is 77% that of cells incubated in the absence of arsenate. Since energy for the synthetase reaction comes from ATP (Weeks *et al.*, 1969; Trust and Millis, 1971), depletion of intracellular ATP should strongly inhibit uptake if the process is a synthetase-driven vectorial acylation.

From the studies carried out thus far, my first, and perhaps naive, approximation of the process of octanoate transport by *P. oleovorans* is as follows:

1. In view of the intracellular and intraspheroplast concentrations of octanoate and lack of significant inhibition of uptake by arsenate, transport solely by vectorial acylation involving a synthetase enzyme seems unlikely.

2. The different involvement of the components of $\Delta\mu H^+$ in transport at

---

*I wish to thank Dr. Dan Robertson for determining the value of $\Delta\psi$, ΔpH, the intracellular pH, and frequent informative discussions.

different pH values may indicate the presence of a carrier system analogous to that described by Ramos and Kaback (1977) for transport of lactate and glucose 6-phosphate in *E. coli*. These systems cotransport protons and substrates with stoichiometries that are 1:1 at pH 5.5 and 2:1 at pH 7.5.

It is obvious that further studies are essential to fully explain the mechanism of transport of fatty acids by pseudomonads. My immediate plans are to determine the underlying influence(s) responsible for the absence of octanoate transport in vesicles, to examine transport in mutants deficient in octanoyl-CoA synthetase and acyl-CoA:octanoate-CoA transferase activities, and to assy for these enzyme activities in mutants unable to transport octanoate. As is often the case, the results of these studies will dictate future experimental direction.

The modest amount of research success I have had the pleasure of experiencing in the past decade has, no doubt, been influenced by Gunny's excitement and fascination for science in general and bacterial systems in particular. Although Gunny's reminder that to learn more I needed to listen more and talk less has been useful in my continuous efforts to become educated and knowledgeable, it is his perceptive lessons on research which I consider the hallmark of his influence. These lessons helped in the development of my confidence to do independent research and, when research seems at an impass, caused me to consider that many apparent obstacles are not so great that they cannot be overcome with careful analytical consideration, intellectual effort, experienced advice, hard work, and, above all, perseverance. It is my hope that Gunny views my attempts at applying these lessons as evidence that I benefited from my stay in his laboratory and considers his efforts worthwhile.

THE SECOND GENERATION*

It is difficult for a neophyte scientist to reflect over a short career and assess the entire impact of experiencing Gunny's laboratory. Gunny's formal training in bacteriology and chemistry dictated the overall direction of the research. There was, however, an attraction for people whose interests ranged from the natural history of microorganisms to physics. An excitement for science was always present, with Gunny providing a challenging environment in which one could expand both intellectual and technical skills. For instance, Gunny, together with Hans Frauenfelder and Peter Debrunner, established weekly interchanges, called "microcolloquia," between collaborating biochemists and physicists. These meetings were attempts to familiarize the two groups with one another's lan-

*By William A. Toscano, Jr.

guage in an effort to bridge the gap between biology and quantum mechanics. They proved to be a fruitful forum for exchange of data and ideas.

It seems appropriate to list a few of the many scientists attracted, for one reason or another, to the laboratory and who *in toto* added to the scientific environment. An all-inclusive list would be impossible; however, a few immediately come to mind. The laboratory was divided into genetics and chemistry sections. A search for the elusive plasmids coding for the metabolism of camphor, octane, and naphthalene was carried on by Monique Hermann, Dvorah Katz, Hank Heath, Miera Shaham, Jim Johnston, and Roberta Farrell (Gunsalus *et al.*, 1975). The chemistry side was manned by John Lipscomb, Ralph Meeks, and Steve Sligar. It was Steve who bridged the gap to physics. It seemed natural from my past experience for Gunny to assign me a desk in the genetics lab so I could learn microbiol physiology.

Govind Garg, a young assistant professor on leave from Pantnagar, India, and I were fortunate to work in the lab side by side with Gunny on the large-scale growth of *Pseudomonas putida* on camphor for rapid and efficient purification of the cytochrome $P450_{cam}$ components. Gunny was a tireless worker with an excellent sense of laboratory techniques undiminished by years of directing research from his office. We would work until two or three in the morning and he would be impatiently waiting for our arrival at nine that same morning to start the day's experiments and plan the direction we should take. Gunny allowed us the freedom to make the decisions but was direct in informing us of disagreements in approach. During those months he tried to impart to us his philosophy for attacking the heart of a problem and for gleaning as much as the data would allow without doing extraneous experiments. Subsequently, Gerald Wagner was instrumental in streamlining our operation into an efficient "purification machine" (Gunsalus and Wagner, 1978).

At Gunny's urging I turned my attention to the three-component cytochrome oxidase system from *Pseudomonas aeruginosa*. Horio *et al.* (1961) had previously observed that *P. aeruginosa* grown anaerobically in the presence of nitrate induces a new cytochrome system containing two hemes, one of the c type and the other of a chlorin or d type. This cytochrome is capable of accepting electrons from either cytochrome c_{551} or the copper-containing protein azurin (Gudat *et al.*, 1973). Even though the enzyme has long been known as *Pseudomonas* cytochrome oxidase, its physiological role is ascribed as a nitrite reductase. We were interested in examining this system as a model to study the four-electron reduction of oxygen because of its similarities to the mammalian cytochrome a-a_3 complex. *Pseudomonas* cytochrome oxidase had been previously purified, but because of the strenuous conditions necessary for extraction and purification as well as for low growth yields, Gunny encouraged us to give this system another look. After examining the growth characteristics of several strains of *P. aeruginosa* with the technical assistance of Leon Goodyear and

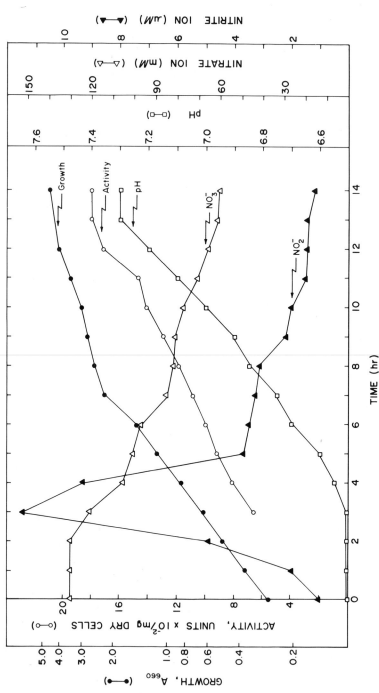

Fig. 1. Growth of *P. aeruginosa* PaG 18 in large culture on citrate and nitrate ion. A 25-liter culture of cells growing with limited aeration on citrate and KNO$_3$ supplemented with Hutner's salts was used as an inoculum for a 250-liter growth of cells. Growth ($\bullet$—$\bullet$) was followed at 660 nm using a Bausch and Lomb Spectronic 20; Activity (○—○) was measured in cell extracts by following the rate of oxidation of reduced cytochrome c_{551} where one unit is equal to 1 μmol cytochrome c_{551} oxidized per minute; pH (□—□) was measured with a Radiometer electrode and was controlled by means of a pH stat. Nitrate ion (△—△) was measured by the chemical method of Cataldo *et al.* (1975); nitrite ion was measured by the method of Taras (1958) (▲—▲).

excellent advice of Ralph Wolfe, we settled on a strain generously donated by David Wharton. A typical growth curve for this strain, which we designated as PaG 18, using citrate as a carbon source and nitrate as the electron acceptor, is given in Fig. 1. We typically obtained yields of 10 gm wet weight of cells per liter of culture.

It was fortuitous that we chose to supplement the growth medium with Hutner mineral salts (Cohen-Bazire *et al.*, 1957) since the cell paste, when subsequently washed with low-ionic-strength buffer, caused autolysis of the organism, which greatly facilitated enzyme extraction. When we used other mineral salts lacking EDTA or nitrilotriacetic acid (NTA), no autolysis was observed. Similar effects of complexing agents on *P. aeruginosa* had been observed by Wilkenson (1970), who noted that treatment of the organism with EDTA or NTA resulted in cells which were "osmotically fragile" and would lyse on exposure to low-ionic-strength buffer. The growth conditions described above allowed us to extract easily large quantities of not only the cytochrome oxidase, but also the attendent electron transfer components, cytochrome c_{551} and azurin. I then set out to purify

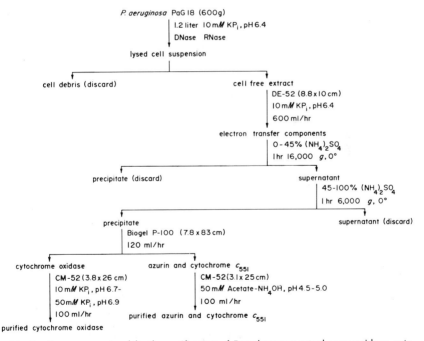

Fig. 2. Summary protocol for the purification of *Pseudomonas* cytochrome oxidase, cytochrome c_{551}, and azurin. The autolysed cell-free extract was applied to a DE-52 column at room temperature. All other steps were performed at 4° and all columns were run in the ascending direction.

the electron transfer system with the capable assistance of Mary Perez and Jon Hinton. A summary of our protocol is given in Fig. 2. We typically obtained 1.6 gm of cytochrome oxidase, 800 mg of azurin, and 300 mg of cytochrome c_{551} per kilogram of cells by using this simplified purification scheme. Some of the chemical properties of the electron transfer components determined with the expert assistance of B. S. Shastry are summarized in Table I. The presence of Steve Sligar in the laboratory made kinetic measurements an easy matter since he applied his physics and computer skills to automating the assays. Some of the parameters that we found for the reduction of either nitrite or oxygen are summarized in Table II. Because of the ease with which we could grow the organism in high yield and the simplified purification procedure, we were able to prepare

TABLE I

Summary of Chemical Properties of Electron Transfer Components from *P. Aeruginosa*

Amino acid	Cytochrome oxidase[a]	Cytochrome c_{551}[a]	Azurin[a]
Lysine	53	8	11
Histidine	15	1	4
Arginine	27	1	1
Aspartic	63	8	1
Threonine	33	2	19
Serine	32	3	10
Glutamic	65	10	10
Proline	40	6	4
Glycine	53	7	11
Alanine	55	13	7
Cysteic acid[b]	2	2	3
Valine	53	7	10
Methionine	9	2	6
Isoleucine	33	3	4
Leucine	43	4	10
Tyrosine	28	1	2
Phenylalanine	18	2	2
Tryptophan[c]	15	2	0
Minimum mol. weight	70,000	8,700	13,900
$\bar{V}_1$	0.74	0.74	0.73
p*I*	5.8	4.7	
Prosthetic group	1 Heme c and 1 heme d per mole protein	1 Heme c per mole protein	1 Cu per mole protein

[a] Data in residues per mole protein.
[b] Cystic acid was determined by performic acid oxidation.
[c] Tryptophan was measured by base hydrolysis.

TABLE II

Kinetic Constants for Nitrite and Oxygen Reduction by *Pseudomonas* Cytochrome Oxidase Using Cytochrome c_{551} and Azurin as Electron Donors

Donor/property	Reduction of	
	Nitrite	Oxygen
Azurin		
Temperature optimum (°C)	38	38
pH optimum	5	5
K_m (μM)	120	39
Ton (μM/min/μmol)	1030	126
E_a (kcal/mol)	11	11
Cytochrome c_{551}		
Temperature optimum (°C)	38	38
pH optimum	6	6
K_m (μM)	97	18
Ton (μM/min/mol)	2900	520
E_a (kcal/mol)	6	8

[57]Fe-enriched samples of the heme-containing components for Mossbauer probes of the system (Dwivedi *et al.*, 1979).

Pursuant to our work with the soluble cytochrome oxidase, Gunny allowed me to investigate along with Irmelin Probst the membrane-bound aerobically induced cytochrome oxidase from *P. aeruginosa*. I feel that this experience with less-soluble systems provided the background necessary to deal with the complexities of adenylate cyclase which I am currently pursuing (Toscano *et al.*, 1979).

It seems appropriate to mention my teaching experience at Urbana. I believe Gunny felt that it coincided in importance to research training. At the time, Gunny was in charge of the graduate laboratory course at Illinois and I was fortunate to be able to assist him as a *major domo* for several years. It was Gunny's philosophy that lectures should be short and handled by experts, with major emphasis on modern up-to-date technology of biochemistry. We were blessed to be able to draw upon Gregorio Weber for fluorescence, Echard Muenck and Paul Schmidt for magnetic resonance, Robert Switzer for kinetics, Ed Voss for immunochemistry, Olke Uhlenbeck for nucleic acids, and Bob Gennis for general physical biochemistry. Gunny was instrumental in introducing the use of video-taped lecture notes so that the students could afford to listen to the lectures rather than being tied to note taking, and he introduced the PLATO concept to biochemists so that the students would not be afraid to explore the potentials of allowing a machine to take care of tedium. I hope the lessons I learned will be of help in the direction I am now taking with students.

Many individuals greatly enriched my time in Urbana both scientifically and personally. Dorothy Gunsalus was an extremely charming hostess whose wit and grace had a profound effect on Gunny and his students. Etha Broom, Gunny's longtime secretary, not only took excellent care of the usual duties, but also served as a calming force with advice and kindness. Gerry Wagner supplied valued scientific criticism and has the finest espresso pot and apartif collection in Urbana which he lent to many a late night discussion of science. And, of course, Gunny was a sort of Don Padrone who expended a great deal of effort and energy to provide us with an atmosphere in which we could grow and mature scientifically and personally. Some of the lessons he tried to impart were not always pleasant, but they were highly educational in preparing us for the world of independent research.

REFERENCES

Cataldo, D. A., Haroon, M., Schrader, L. E., and Youngs, V. L. (1975). Rapid determination of nitrate in plant tissue by nitration of salicylic acid. *Commun. Soil Sci. Plant Anal.* **6,** 71-80.

Cohen-Bazire, G., Sistrom, W. G., and Stanier, R. Y. (1957). Kinetic studies of pigment synthesis by non-sulfur purple bacteria. *J. Cell. Comp. Physiol.* **49,** 25-28.

Dubler, R., Toscano, W. A., and Hartline, R. A. (1974). Transport of succinate by *Pseudomonas putida. Arch. Biochem. Biophys.* **160,** 422-429.

Duckett, S., Schneider, C. W., and Hartline, R. A. (1981). Oxidation of alcohol in free-moving mice from high and low preference strains. *Pharmacol., Biochem. Behav.* **15,** 495-499.

Dwivedi, A., Toscano, W. A., Jr., and Debrunner, P. G. (1979). Mossbauer spectra of cytochrome c_{551}: Intrinsic heterogeneity related to g strain. *Biochim. Biophys. Acta* **576,** 502-508.

Edwards, W. V., Sando, J. J., and Hartline, R. A. (1979). Transport of C_5 dicarboxylic compounds by *Pseudomonas putida. J. Bacteriol.* **139,** 748-754.

Fioriglio, C., Wood, J., Hartline, R. A., and Schneider, C. W. (1979). A quantitative analysis of ethanol and acetaldehyde expired by inbred mouse strains. *Pharmacol., Biochem. Behav.* **12,** 467-469.

Frerman, F. E. (1973). The role of acetyl coenzyme A: Butyrate coenzyme A in the transference uptake of butyrate by isolated membrane vesicles of *Escherchia coli. Arch. Biochem. Biophys.* **159,** 444-452.

Goldbort, R., Schneider, C. W., and Hartline, R. A. (1976). Butanediols: Selection, open field activity, and NAD reduction by liver extracts in inbred mouse strains. *Pharmacol., Biochem. Behav.* **5,** 263-268.

Gudat, J. C., Singh, J., and Wharton, D. C. (1973). Cytochrome oxidase from *Pseudomonas aeruginosa.* I. Purification and properties. *Biochim. Biophys. Acta* **292,** 376-390.

Gunsalus, I. C., and Wagner, G. C. (1978). Cytochrome P450$_{CAM}$. *In* "Methods in Enzymology" (S. Fleischer and L. Packer, eds.), Vol. 52, pp. 166-188. Academic Press, New York.

Gunsalus, I. C., Conrad, H. E., Trudgill, P. W., and Jacobson, L. A. (1965). Regulation of catabolic metabolism. *Isr. J. Med. Sci.* **1,** 1099-1119.

Gunsalus, I. C., Hermann, M., Toscano, W. A., Jr., Katz, D., and Garg, G. K. (1975). Plasmids and metabolic diversity. *In* "Microbiology—1974" (D. Schlessinger, ed.), pp. 207-212. Am. Soc. Microbiol., Washington, D.C.

Hartline, R. A., and Gunsalus, I. C. (1971). Induction specificity and catabolite repression of the early enzymes in camphor degradation. *J. Bacteriol.* **106**, 468–478.

Hartline, R. A., and Rodwell, V. W. (1971). Metabolism of pipecolic acid in a *Pseudomonas* species. VI. Precursors of glutamate. *Arch. Biochem. Biophys.* **142**, 32–39.

Hegeman, G. D. (1966). Synthesis of the enzymes of the mandelate pathway by *Pseudomonas putida*. *J. Bacteriol.* **91**, 1140–1154.

Horio, T., Higashi, T., Yamanaka, T., Matsubara, H., and Okunuki, K. (1961). Purification and properties of cytochrome oxidase from *Pseudomonas aeruginosa*. *J. Biol. Chem.* **236**, 944–951.

Jones, T. (1980). Mechanism of octanoate transport in *Pseudomonas oleovorans*. M.S. Thesis, Department of Biology, Indiana Univ. of Pennsylvania.

Klein, K., Steinberg, R., Fiethen, B., and Overath, P. (1971). An inducible system for the uptake of fatty acids and further characterization of *old* mutants. *Eur. J. Biochem.* **19**, 442–450.

Kopchick, C., and Hartline, R. A. (1979). α-Hydroxyglutarate as an intermediate in the catabolism of α-aminoadipate by *Pseudomonas putida*. *J. Biol. Chem.* **254**, 3259–3263.

Pekala, P., and Hartline, R. A. (1973). Isolation of radioactive D- and L-α-aminoadipate of high specific activity by selective bacterial metabolism. *Anal. Biochem.* **55**, 411–419.

Pekala, P., Perfetti, T., and Hartline, R. A. (1975). Physiological basis for preferential uptake of D-α-aminoadipate over the L-isomer by *Alcaligenes denitrificans*. *Biochim. Biophys. Acta* **394**, 65–75.

Perfetti, R., Campbell, R., Titus, J., and Hartline, R. A. (1972). Catabolism of pipecolate to glutamate in *Pseudomonas putida*. *J. Biol. Chem.* **247**, 4089–4095.

Ramos, S., and Kabak, H. R. (1977). pH-dependent changes in proton:substrate stoichiometries during active transport in *Escherichia coli* membrane vesicles. *Biochemistry* **16**, 4271–4275.

Ramos, S., Schuldiner, S., and Kabak, H. R. (1976). The electrochemical gradient of protons and its relationship to active transport in *Escherichia coli* membrane vesicles. *Proc. Natl. Acad. Sci. U.S.A.* **73**, 1892–1896.

Romano, A. H., Voytek, A., and Brushkin, A. M. (1980). Energization of glucose transport by *Pseudomonas fluorescens*. *J. Bacteriol.* **142**, 755–762.

Taras, M. J. (1958). Nitrogen. *In* "Colorimetric Determination of Non-Metals" (D. F. Boltz, ed.), pp. 75–160. Wiley, New York.

Toscano, W. A., and Hartline, R. A. (1973). Transport of sodium octanoate by *Pseudomonas oleovorans*. *J. Bacteriol.* **116**, 541–547.

Toscano, W. A., Jr., Westcott, K. R., LaPorte, D. C., and Storm, D. R. (1979). Evidence for a dissociable protein subunit required for calmodulin stimulation of brain adenylate cyclase. *Proc. Natl. Acad. Sci. U.S.A.* **76**, 5582–5586.

Trust, T. J., and Millis, N. F. (1971). Activation of the C_2 to C_{19} monocarboxylic acids by *Pseudomonas*. *J. Bacteriol.* **105**, 1216–1218.

VanNess, B. (1975). Investigation of normal octanoate, transport in membrane vesicles of *Pseudomonas oleovorans* and mutants of *Pseudomonas*. M.S. Thesis, Department of Chemistry, Indiana Univ. of Pennsylvania.

Weeks, G., Shapiro, M., Burns, R. O., and Wakil, S. (1969). Control of fatty acid metabolism I. Induction of the enzymes of fatty acid oxidation in *Escherichia coli*. *J. Bacteriol.* **97**, 827–836.

Wilkenson, S. G. (1970). Cell walls of *Pseudomonas* species sensitive to ethylenediaminetetraacetic acid. *J. Bacteriol.* **104**, 1035–1044.

Wood, T., and Hartline, R. A. (1971a). Preferential uptake of D-α-aminoadipate from a racemic mixture by an *Alcaligenes denitrificans*. *Biochim. Biophys. Acta* **230**, 446–450.

Wood, T., and Hartline, R. A. (1971b). A synthesis of DL-α-aminoadipate and its *N*-chloroacetyl derivative. *Anal. Biochem.* **43**, 282–287.

II

Genetics

10

Order and Disorder in Genome Arrangement

Bruce Holloway

INTRODUCTION

The geneticist and the geographer have more in common than a mere proximity of alphabetical arrangement. They both have a fancy for constructing maps. In each discipline, a map provides a firm basis on which further investigations and discoveries can be made. It is an efficient way of assembling information from a variety of sources. Just as geographers can draw maps of a country in different ways, for example, in terms of its physical characteristics, population density, or agricultural production, geneticists can assemble hereditary information by constructing chromosome maps which represent a linear array of marker locations derived from recombination data or the distribution of cutting sites of selected restriction endonucleases as determined by the molecular weights of DNA fragments.

A number of reasons can be offered to explain the high priority that geneticists give to obtaining data that can be used to construct a map. In their simplest form such data can be used to establish the order of genes on the chromosome. Once identified, map locations can be used as the necessary experimental basis for the construction of hybrids which have desired biological properties, a procedure essential for successful plant and animal breeding. The data may also enable the

101

EXPERIENCES IN BIOCHEMICAL PERCEPTION
Copyright © 1982 by Academic Press, Inc.
All rights of reproduction in any form reserved.
ISBN 0-12-528420-9

identification of a functional arrangement of genes; a good example is the operon.

MAPPING THE BACTERIAL GENOME

Bacterial geneticists are fortunate in that there are a number of natural features that help in the mapping of the single bacterial chromosome. There are a variety of techniques that can be used, depending on the bacterium in question. Conjugation, transformation, and transduction all have special advantages and disadvantages. The much studied *Escherichia coli* K12 has one of the best known chromosomal maps of all organisms studied, with over 1000 markers located, which is in excess of 30% of the total number of genes possessed by this organism.

Bacteria have an additional property. With most higher organisms any variation in chromosome number usually results in reduced viability, survival prospects, or fertility. This is not true in the case of bacteria where the discovery of plasmids has introduced an element of disorder into the specification of bacterial genomes. First, it means that genes controlling bacterial function may be on one or another DNA molecule. Second, plasmids may be lost either spontaneously or under particular experimental conditions. Unlike aneuploids of higher organisms, whereas the loss of a plasmid may mean loss of a specific set of functions for bacteria, such as antibiotic resistance or the ability to mobilize bacterial chromosome, it does not usually result in loss of viability for the bacterium. The list of plasmid-coded functions that can be part of the bacterial phenotype grows larger as more and more plasmids are identified in more and more genera. Currently it includes resistance to antibiotics; resistance to metals; bacterial chromosome transfer; synthesis of bacterial toxins; ability to use specific compounds as energy sources; synthesis of bacteriocins; determinants of human, animal, and plant virulence; tumor formation and nitrogen fixation in plants; and ability to synthesize an amino acid (Broda, 1979). There is an additional potential for variation in those cases where the plasmid can become integrated into the continuity of the bacterial chromosome. The best example is that of F in *E. coli*, but other plasmids do have this property of increasing the chromosomal information, at the same time altering the linkage relationship of chromosomal genes.

THE GENETICS OF BACTERIA OTHER THAN *E. Coli* K12

Apart from the pioneering work of Griffith and Avery, MacLeod, and McCarty with the *Pneumococcus,* which established the phenomenon of transformation, the use of bacteria in their own right as subjects for genetic analysis dates from the mid-1940's with the description of conjugation in *E. coli* K12 by Lederberg and Tatum. For the next 15 years most bacterial genetic work was carried out on this one species and on the related organism, *Salmonella typhimurium*. The genetic study of bacteria other than enterobacteria was considered to have minimal interest by most microbial geneticists, with the exception of a few antipodean eccentrics.

It was not long before the advantages of microbial genetics as an experimental approach to the understanding of the biology of microorganisms became obvious. The genus *Pseudomonas* had been a favored subject of bacterial physiologists and biochemists for some years because its species had such diverse metabolic activities. Clearly, there were advantages in knowing something about pseudomonad genetics, and a variety of attempts were made to adapt the techniques of *E. coli* genetics to the fluorescent pseudomonads. From hindsight, the *Pseudomonas* biochemists were unlucky. As subsequent work has shown, lysogeny in this group of organisms is almost unknown (Holloway, 1969; Holloway *et al.*, 1971) and plasmids with chromosome-mobilizing ability occur only rarely (Chakrabarty, 1976).

This author can attest to many hours spent looking for transducing bacteriophages active on selected strains of *Pseudomonas putida* and related species with only very limited success (Holloway and van de Putte, 1968). This is in contrast to the situation with *Pseudomonas aeruginosa* where up to 30% of *P. aeruginosa* strains carry plasmids with chromosomal-mobilizing ability, and where nearly all *P. aeruginosa* strains are lysogenic for at least one bacteriophage and many of these phages are capable of transduction. It is likely that other workers have made similar searches for genetic factors in *P. putida* and related species and have never published the negative results obtained. The reason for the rarity of lysogenic strains of *P. putida* still remains something of a mystery. It was a commonly held view of *Pseudomonas* workers in the late 1960's that *P. putida* looked like a naturally occurring, recombination-deficient organism and that there was no need to search for *recA* mutants as had been done so successfully in *E. coli* (Clark and Margulies, 1965)! Attempts to transfer bacteriophages from *P. aeruginosa* to *P. putida* were unsuccessful, as were attempts to transfer the chromosomal-mobilizing plasmid FP2 of *P. aeruginosa* to *P. putida*.

THE GENETICS OF *P. putida*

The means for genetic analysis of *P. putida* remained in this almost virginal state until the isolation from sewage of a bacteriophage that could transduce *P. putida* (Chakrabarty *et al.*, 1968). It was a fact well known to bacterial geneticists and bacteriophage workers that virulent bacteriophages could be isolated from sewage for almost any species of bacterium. The phage folklore of the day did not predict that a virulent phage would be capable of transduction; indeed quite the opposite.

Subsequently, it has been found that transduction is a property of a number of virulent bacteriophages and is even found in a T phage. The bacteriophage, *pf*16, which was isolated from Illinois sewage, has never been completely described in the literature. Nevertheless, its discovery enabled the first transductional analysis in *P. putida* and subsequently a variant was isolated, *pfdm,* which was able to mobilize the chromosome of *P. putida* (Chakrabarty and Gunsalus, 1969). This latter work introduced the idea that genetic elements such as bacteriophages and plasmids could be genetically modified by passage through bacteria and acquire characteristics that made them efficient chromosome-mobilizing agents. The isolations of *pf*16 and *pfdm* in Gunsalus's laboratory were imaginative excursions outside the tenets of temporary microbial genetics. Their isolation encouraged other workers to seek chromosome-mobilizing agents in a variety of new places; in turn this has led to the establishment of genetic systems in a wide variety of other bacterial genera. It is now possible to carry out joint genetic and biochemical investigations in a range of *Pseudomonas* species and in a number of other bacteria that previously did not have experimental systems of genetic recombination.

THE PROMISCUOUS PLASMID

By the late 1960's much of the basis of the current knowledge of plasmids had been established. From the early days of the characterization in pathogenic bacteria isolated in Japan, it was known that plasmids coding for a variety of antibiotic resistances had only a very limited host range. Plasmids found in enteric bacteria could not be transferred to organisms other than enteric bacteria. It was thus of interest when Lowbury and his colleagues isolated *P. aeruginosa* strains highly resistant to carbenicillin, from patients suffering from burns (Lowbury *et al.*, 1969). Furthermore, the same high levels of resistance were found in strains of *Klebsiella* and *Proteus* present in the same burns (Ayliffe *et al.*, 1972). It was shown that the multiple resistance to carbenicillin, kanamycin, and tetracycline was due to a transmissible plasmid which transferred readily among almost all gram-negative bacteria. This was the first isolation of a wide host-range plasmid and, although the significance of this discovery for the epidemiology of antibiotic resistance in pathogenic bacteria is obvious, these plasmids have acquired an even greater importance in that they can mobilize the bacterial chromosome in a number of gram-negative bacterial genera.

Other plasmids similar to the ones first isolated have been found to fall into the incompatibility group P1 (IncP-1). Their chromosome-mobilizing ability was first demonstrated in *P. aeruginosa* (Stanisich and Holloway, 1971). However, in that genus, this ability was strain specific. Two strains of *P. aeruginosa* have been studied extensively for their genetic characteristics, and whereas IncP-1 plasmids had highly effective Cma in strain PAT, this was almost absent in strain PAO. By selection for plasmid variants among the rare recombinants found in these PAO crosses with IncP-1 plasmids, it was possible to isolate IncP-1 plasmid variants with enhanced chromosome mobilization (ECM plasmids), the first well-characterized member of this group being R68.45 (Haas and Holloway, 1976, 1978). This plasmid has been shown to promote chromosome transfer in the following genera and is contributing extensively to the genetic knowledge of these organisms: *P. aeruginosa, P. putida, P. glycinea, Rhizobium legumino-sarum, Rh. meliloti, Rhodopseudomonas sphaeroides, E. coli, Agrobacterium tumefaciens, Azospirillum brasiliensis,* and *Erwinia chrysanthemi* (Holloway, 1979; Holloway *et al.,* 1979; Hamada *et al.,* 1979; Chatterjee, 1980).

The molecular nature of R68.45 is now being revealed in a series of studies using restriction endonuclease analysis, heteroduplex techniques, and Southern hybridization procedures. It has been shown that R68.45 differs from its parent plasmid R68 by the possession of an additional copy of a 2.1–2.4 Kb sequence of DNA known variously as ISP or IS8. In R68.45 this sequence is present as two tandem copies located near the kanamycin-resistant determinant on the plasmid DNA (Riess *et al.,* 1980; Leemans *et al.,* 1980). The various genetic and physicochemical methods which are being used to determine the molecular basis of the Cma properties of R68.45 provide a good example of the sophisticated techniques now available for mapping in microorganisms and of the value of mapping in providing answers to genetic questions.

ECM plasmids derived from IncP-1 plasmids possess an additional property. This is their ability to generate hybrid plasmids containing a fragment of bacterial chromosome. The entire ECM plasmid genome is retained, including the wide host-range characteristics, and the hybrid plasmid can be transferred between unrelated bacterial genera. The first such hybrids were isolated in *P. aeruginosa;* one such R prime, R′PA1, was shown to carry the entire R68.45 genome plus about 3–4 minutes of the *P. aeruginosa* chromosome including the *argA, argB, argH,* and *lys-12* genes (Holloway, 1978). A similar type of hybrid plasmid has been isolated which carries a segment of the *E. coli* chromosome carrying the *trp* operon and the *cysB* gene. This plasmid, R′EC1, can be transferred to *P. aeruginosa* where it complements mutants of all six *trp* genes at efficiencies which give wild-type growth in the absence of tryptophan for *P. aeruginosa* tryptophan auxotrophs, which also carry this plasmid prime. Preliminary studies by Irving Crawford suggest that the regulation of the tryptophan biosynthetic enzymes in these hybrids is different from that found in *E. coli* (I. Crawford, personal communication).

GENE ARRANGEMENT AND REGULATORY PATTERNS

Indeed the value of a combined genetic and biochemical approach to a further understanding of the evolution of patterns of intermediary metabolism is well illustrated by the studies that have been made with the tryptophan pathway (Crawford, 1975). It has been shown in *E. coli* that all five structural genes of the pathway are contiguous and all are regulated coordinately (Crawford, 1975). Fargie and Holloway (1965), by means of transduction in *P. aeruginosa*, showed that functionally related genes of biosynthetic pathways were not clustered in the manner that had been shown to be the case in *E. coli* and *S. typhimurium*.

Using phage *pf*16, Chakrabarty *et al.* (1968) showed that the genes determining tryptophan biosynthesis in *P. putida* were arranged in three groups on the chromosome: *trpA, B; trpC, D, E;* and *trpF*. Furthermore, unlike *E. coli*, where the regulation of all five genes is coordinately repressed by tryptophan, in *P. putida, trpA, B* are induced by tryptophan; *trpC, D, E* are repressed; and *trpF* is constitutive. This pattern of gene distribution and regulatory pattern has also been shown for *P. aeruginosa* (Calhoun *et al.*, 1973). Differences in gene arrangement and the manner of regulation between the enterobacteria and *Pseudomonas* have been shown in other pathways, including those for the biosynthesis of arginine and pyrimidines. The significance of these differences in gene arrangement and regulation has yet to be determined, but it is clear that repression is not the predominant mode of regulation for biosynthetic genes in pseudomonads.

Much remains to be achieved in this area of gene arrangement and gene regulation in the pseudomonads. Development of work on this topic has been inhibited by the inability to map the chromosome of a variety of species of *Pseudomonas*. Fortunately this problem is being resolved. A variety of plasmids with chromosome-mobilizing ability are now being developed for *P. putida,* and a chromosome map with about 50 genes located has been constructed (Dean and Morgan, manuscript in preparation). Of particular interest from these results is the possibility that the chromosome maps of *P. aeruginosa* and *P. putida* are basically similar but that some regions of the *P. putida* chromosome are inverted relative to the *P. aeruginosa* map.

Furthermore, with continued refinements in the isolation of R primes derived from various species using R68.45 and related plasmids, the development of techniques for complementation mapping may enable comparison of chromosomal regions from a number of *Pseudomonas* species with the more detailed maps of *P. aeruginosa* and *P. putida*. Complementation mapping is accomplished by constructing an R prime plasmid that carries a chromosome fragment of the unmapped species. This plasmid is then transferred to a range of known auxotrophic and other mutants of *P. aeruginosa* or *P. putida*. Complementation of the mutant by the prime plasmid to produce a wild-type phenotype is taken to indicate that a wild-type allele of the complemented gene is present on the chromosome fragment of the prime plasmid. Data accumulated in this way for a variety of species of *Pseudomonas* would provide information essential for the understanding of the evolutionary relationships of the various *Pseudomonas* species. It is difficult to suggest another genus of bacteria for which there is so much potential for the blending of genetic and biochemical information for a study of this nature.

THE PLASMID—NATURE'S WILD CARD

While the future is promising for the chromosomal mapping of a range of *Pseudomonas* species, there is an exciting uncertainty regarding the plasmid component of the genome of these various species. For the genus as a whole, continued examination of strains results in extending the known variety of plasmids. For *P. aeruginosa,* at least 30% of strains carry FP plasmids with chromosome-mobilizing ability. Some of these plasmids have been shown to be capable of transfer to other species. Plasmids carrying antibiotic resistance determinants are being isolated with increasing frequency from *Pseudomonas* species associated with human and animal disease, and some of these can be transferred to other, nonpathogenic species. Plasmids can be readily isolated from phytopathogenic species, although they may not necessarily be associated with the virulence characteristics of these species. In the fluorescent pseudomonads, the range of plasmids that confer the ability to use a variety of substrates as the energy source of growth, is increasing. Plasmids that have similar characteristics with respect to substrate utilization are found to vary in their molecular structure (Duggleby *et al.,* 1977). The interactions of these plasmids with the bacterial chromosome remain to be determined. For example, can such plasmids integrate into the chromosome? Why is the utilization of some substrates determined by chromosomal determinants while others have plasmid-borne determinants? Is there any relationship of this plasmid DNA to chromosomal DNA?

These are only some of the questions to which answers are now possible by application of the techniques of molecular biology, combined with the older, classical techniques of gene mapping.

The development of this combined biochemical and genetic approach for the understanding of the pseudomonads has been achieved by the combined efforts of many workers. It is a privilege to acknowledge the help, the advice, and the encouragement I have received over the years from Gunny.

ACKNOWLEDGMENT

Research work in the author's laboratory is supported by the Australian Research Grants Committee and the National Health and Medical Research Council.

REFERENCES

Ayliffe, G. A., Lowbury, E. J. L., and Roe, E. (1972). Transferable carbenicillin resistance in *Pseudomonas aeruginosa*. *Nature (London), New Biol.* **235,** 141.

Broda, P. (1979). "Plasmids." Freeman, San Francisco, California.

Calhoun, D. H., Pierson, D. L., and Jensen, R. A. (1973). The regulation of tryptophan biosynthesis in *Pseudomonas aeruginosa*. *Mol. Gen. Genet.* **121,** 117–132.

Chakrabarty, A. M. (1976). Plasmids in *Pseudomonas. Annu. Rev. Genet.* **10,** 7–30.

Chakrabarty, A. M., and Gunsalus, I. C. (1969) Defective phage and chromosome mobilization in *Pseudomonas. Proc. Natl. Acad. Sci. U.S.A.* **64,** 1217–1223.

Chakrabarty, A. M., Gunsalus, C. F., and Gunsalus, I. C. (1968). Transduction and the clustering of genes in fluorescent pseudomonads. *Proc. Natl. Acad. Sci. U.S.A.* **60,** 168–175.

Chatterjee, A. K. (1980). Acceptance by *Erwinia* spp. of R plasmid R68.45 and its ability to mobilize the chromosome of *Erwinia chrysanthemi. J. Bacteriol.* **142,** 111–119.

Clark, A. J., and Margulies, A. D. (1965). Isolation and characterization of recombination deficient mutants of *Escherichia coli* K12. *Proc. Natl. Acad. Sci. U.S.A.* **53,** 451–459.

Crawford, I. P. (1975). Gene arrangements in the evolution of the tryptophan synthetic pathway. *Bacteriol. Rev.* **39,** 87–120.

Duggleby, C. J., Bayley, S. A., Worsey, M. J., Williams, P. A., and Broda, P. (1977). Molecular sizes and relationships of TOL plasmids in *Pseudomonas. J. Bacteriol.* **130,** 1274–1280.

Fargie, B., and Holloway, B. W. (1965). Absence of clustering of functionally related genes in *Pseudomonas aeruginosa. Genet. Res.* **6,** 284–299.

Haas, D., and Holloway, B. W. (1976). R factor variants with enhanced sex factor activity in *Pseudomonas aeruginosa. Mol. Gen. Genet.* **144,** 243–251.

Haas, D., and Holloway, B. W. (1978). Chromosome mobilization by the R plasmid R68.45: A tool in *Pseudomonas* genetics. *Mol. Gen. Genet.* **158,** 229–237.

Hamada, S. E., Luckey, J. P., and Farrand, S. K. (1979). R-plasmid-mediated chromosomal gene transfer in *Agrobacterium tumefaciens. J. Bacteriol.* **139,** 280–286.

Holloway, B. W. (1969). Genetics of *Pseudomonas. Bacteriol. Rev.* **33,** 419–443.

Holloway, B. W. (1978). Isolation and characterization of an R′ plasmid in *Pseudomonas aeruginosa. J. Bacteriol.* **133,** 1078–1082.

Holloway, B. W. (1979). Plasmids that mobilize bacterial chromosome. *Plasmid* **2,** 1–19.

Holloway, B. W., and van de Putte, P. (1968). Transducing phage for *Pseudomonas putida. Nature (London)* **217,** 459–460.

Holloway, B. W., Krishnapillai, V., and Stanisich, V. (1971). *Pseudomonas* genetics. *Annu. Rev. Genet.* **5,** 425–446.

Holloway, B. W., Krishnapillai, V., and Morgan, A. F. (1979). Chromosomal genetics of *Pseudomonas. Microbiol. Rev.* **43,** 73–102.

Leemans, J., Villaroel, R., Silva, B., van Montagu, M., and Schell, J. (1980). Direct repetition of a 1.2 md DNA sequence is involved in site-specific recombination by the P1 plasmid R68. *Gene* **10,** 319–328.

Lowbury, E. J. L., Kidson, A., Lilly, H. A., Ayliffe, G. A. J., and Jones, R. J. (1969). Sensitivity of *Pseudomonas aeruginosa* to antibiotics: Emergence of strains highly resistant to carbenicillin. *Lancet* **2,** 448–452.

Riess, G., Holloway, B. W., and Pühler, A. (1980). R68.45, a plasmid with chromosome mobilizing ability, carries a tandem duplication. *Genet. Res.* **36,** 99–109.

Stanisich, V. A., and Holloway, B. W. (1971). Chromosome transfer in *Pseudomonas aeruginosa* mediated by R factors. *Genet. Res.* **17,** 169–172.

11

Plasmids and Nutritional Diversity

A. M. Chakrabarty

The time frame during which bacterial plasmids specifying catabolic functions against various exotic organic compounds started evolving is difficult to assess, and remains speculative. However, the time and place when the concept that microorganisms may have evolved plasmids for coping with a changing nutritional environment, is still quite fresh in my memory. It was late 1967/early 1968 when Caroline (Gunny's late wife) and myself in Gunny's laboratory at Urbana were trying to map the camphor-degradative genes on the chromosome of *Pseudomonas putida*. We had previously observed that a tryptophan marker and a fluorophenylalanine resistance marker were quite close, and in some of our transductional experiments involving Cam⁻ recipients, selection of Cam⁺ cells appeared to produce tiny fragments of colonies on fluorophenylalanine plates, when this resistance was used as a nonselected outside marker. The question before us, and it seemed very profound at that time, was whether four tiny partially formed colonies, that could perhaps also arise by mutations, might be considered one whole colony and could perhaps indicate linkage between *cam* genes and *fpa* genes. Caroline and I argued constantly about this interpretation, both basically agreeing at the end that it was some kind of a linkage. Since it seemed to be an interesting observation, Caroline asked for an appointment with Gunny for discussion of our data. The meeting was total chaos, since once

111

EXPERIENCES IN BIOCHEMICAL PERCEPTION
Copyright © 1982 by Academic Press, Inc.
All rights of reproduction in any form reserved.
ISBN 0-12-528420-9

Gunny started laughing after hearing about our new linkage theory, he never really stopped, except for taking a few deep breaths once in a while. This offended Caroline a great deal, not so much because she thought highly of the theory, but because she felt that she was about to lose her poise in front of one of her newly arrived foreign admirers. Be that as it may, she tried to convince Gunny that the *cam* genes must be near the *fpa* genes since she had mapped most of the other genetic regions, and could not detect any linkage and, of course, the genes *had* to be somewhere (on the chromosome)! Quite innocently, Gunny asked her if she ever thought it could be outside the chromosome, if indeed she failed to detect linkage with all other markers. That thought never crept in our minds, mainly because we were accustomed to think of metabolic pathways as integral parts of the chromosome. Gunny then asked one of his graduate students, Jim Rheinwald, to look into the genetics of camphor degradation, and it was Caroline's suggestions and insights and Jim's superb experimental skills and a keen sense of observation that established the camphor genes as part of a plasmid (Chakrabarty *et al.,* 1968; Rheinwald *et al.,* 1973). Since then, many plasmids, each specifying a separate degradative pathway, have been characterized in the laboratory of Gunny and others. In this chapter, I will simply attempt to describe the regulatory mode and the evolutionary characteristics of some of the plasmids, including the CAM plasmid.

REGULATION OF PLASMID-CODED ENZYMES

The plasmid-coded degradative enzymes show interesting differences from chromosomal enzymes in their mode of regulation. Thus, while chromosomal enzymes may be either inducible or constitutive, the plasmid-coded enzymes studied so far invariably appear to be inducible. This is well illustrated by the case of oxidation of aliphatic alcohols such as octanol. Octanol can be oxidized by a variety of *Pseudomonas* species either through chromosomally coded enzymes or in *P. putida* via OCT-plasmid-coded enzymes (Grund *et al.,* 1975). The chromosomal enzymes for octanol utilization are produced at low constitutive levels, while the OCT-coded octane hydroxylase as well as the redundant octanol dehydrogenase are inducible (Benson and Shapiro, 1976). A second mode of difference appears to be the presence of genetic clustering units corresponding to operons on the plasmid, but a lack of extensive genetic clusterings of functionally related genes on the chromosome. Thus the catechol degradative pathway genes, as well as benzoate, *p*-hydroxybenzoate, or shikimate degradative genes in *P. putida,* while mapping on one portion of the chromosome, do not show tight linkages among themselves (Wheelis and Stanier, 1970), while plasmids such as CAM, TOL, and NAH, demonstrate tight clustering among segments of genes involved in specific segments of the pathway, i.e., camphor to compound XI (Rheinwald *et al.*, 1973), naphthalene to salicylate, etc. The presence of clusters of such genes specifying coordinated synthesis of a group of functionally related enzymes on plasmid, and sometimes on chromosomes such as the amidase or the mandelate gene clusters (Betz *et al.*, 1974; Chakrabarty *et al.*, 1968), raises the interesting question if many of the chromosomal gene clusters may have been derived by transpositional events from plasmids and vice versa. Evidence is gradually accumulating which suggests that many of the chromosomal and plasmid-coded enzymes are regulated as a positively controlled system, i.e., the regulatory gene produces a protein product which in the presence of the primary inducer activates the transcriptional machinary of the operon. For plasmid-coded pathways, the mode of regulation under positive control has been demonstrated for toluene degradation coded by genes on the TOL plasmid (Franklin and Williams, 1980) and a similar situation appears to be operative for octane dissimilation encoded by the OCT plasmid (Shapiro *et al.*, 1980). The xylene degradative enzymes encoded by the plasmid XYL in *Pseudomonas* Pxy are inducible, the block of enzymes converting xylene to toluate are induced by xylene, methylbenzyl alcohol, or the corresponding aldehyde, but not by toluate (Friello *et al.*, 1976). The *meta* pathway enzymes for toluate degradation were demonstrated to be induced by toluates and presumably by xylenes as well. The presence of strongly polar Xyl$^-$ Tol$^+$ mutants indicates the presence of two separate regulatory units corresponding to xylene to toluate step and subsequent steps for toluate oxidation via the *meta* pathway (Friello *et al.*, 1976). The induction of both xylene and toluate degradative pathways by the common inducer xylene suggests that bifunctional regulatory molecules are involved in the simultaneous derepression of both the operons. This mode of regulation has subsequently been confirmed for the TOL plasmid which also specifies xylene degradation (Worsey *et al.*, 1978). Similar to XYL, TOL harbors two sets of operons corresponding to the xylene to toluate and toluate to pyruvate/acetate steps. The two operons are under the control of two regulator genes *xylR* and *xylS*. *XylR* appears to control both the units by specifying an activator protein (xylR$^+$ being trans dominant to xylR$^-$) that in combination with any of the inducers (xylene, methylbenzyl alcohol, etc.) triggers "on" the two units. *XylS*, on the other hand, appears to regulate only the genes for the *meta* pathway enzymes, presumably also by a positive control mechanism.

The nature of positive control of the alkane oxidation as specified by the OCT plasmid is less direct. The *alkA*, *alkB*, and *alkE* genes coding for the inducible soluble and membrane components of alkane hydroxylase and alcohol dehydrogenase activities have been shown to be clustered together to form an operon which is transcribed in the order B-A-E (Shapiro *et al.*, 1980). A regulatory gene *alkR* has been identified which affects the regulation of both alkane hydroxylase components and of alcohol dehydrogenase. There are alleles of *alkR* which specify noninducible, constitutive, and altered induction specificity phenotypes

(Fennewald *et al.*, 1979). Insertion of transposons such as Tn7 into the *alkR* region produces pleiotropic mutants which appear not to be inducible for either alkane hydroxylase components or for alcohol dehydrogenase, suggesting that the gene encodes a positive regulator protein. Trans dominance of *alkR⁺* over *alkR⁻* has so far not been demonstrated.

The clustering of genes encoding portions of a complete pathway and bifunctional nature of the regulatory protein is also evident in the case of camphor degradation as specified by the CAM plasmid. The contribution of the Gunsalus laboratory in this regard is phenomenal. The regulation of the enzymes of the pathway, the organization of genes, and the chemistry, physics, and mechanism of oxygenase action, have all been demonstrated in a series of most elegant publications from the laboratory of Dr. Gunsalus (Gunsalus and Marshall, 1971). Since we are concerned only with the genetic regulation of the degradative enzymes, and other former colleagues of Dr. Gunsalus will deal with many of the other aspects, I will briefly mention some of the interesting facets of the regulation of the CAM-coded enzymes. The genes specifying the first few enzymes of the pathway are tightly linked and regulated in a coordinate manner (Rheinwald *et al.*, 1973). The genes governing the biodegradation of an intermediate, compound XI to isobutyrate stage, appear to be clustered on another part of the plasmid. Since the camphor plasmid is very large (nearly 300 million daltons), the distance among blocks of genes is reminiscent of another similar large plasmid OCT, belonging to the same incompatibility group *inc*P2. The CAM plasmid appears to contain only a few, but not all, isobutyrate degradative genes. The *P. putida* chromosome, however, has a full complement of the isobutyrate degradative genes.

Both the camphor to XI and the XI to isobutyrate blocks of enzymes are induced by camphor (Gunsalus *et al.*, 1967). Unlike the TOL plasmid, where toluate cannot induce xylene oxidase group of enzymes, compound XI not only induces its own catabolic enzymes, but appears to induce the camphor hydroxylase, F dehydrogenase, and the ketolactonase activities as well. Thus the early enzymes of the camphor pathway are product induced by compound XI. One of the most interesting features of the regulation of the camphor pathway is the regulation of some isobutyrate degradative (*ibu*) genes associated with the CAM plasmid. As can be seen from the results in Table I, it is possible to isolate two types of Ibu⁻ chromosomal mutants in *P. putida* PpG1. One group, illustrated by *ibu*-1 and *ibu*-3 cannot accept the CAM plasmid and are incapable of supporting growth with camphor, even on receipt of the CAM plasmid as part of CAM-OCT. It seems that functional forms of these genes are missing in the CAM plasmid. Mutants such as *ibu*-7 or *ibu*-11, on the other hand, accept the CAM plasmid and grow well with camphor, but not with isobutyrate. Since camphor is metabolized via isobutyrate, the *ibu*-7 or *ibu*-11 mutations are fully

TABLE I

Transfer of the CAM Plasmid to Several Isobutyrate-Negative Mutants of *P. putida*

Donor	Recipient	Select	Transfer frequency	Exconjugant phenotype[a]
AC61 Trp⁻ CAM⁺ *P. putida*	AC64 (*ibu*-1)	Cam⁺	$< 10^{-8}$	
	AC65 (*ibu*-3)	Cam⁺	$< 10^{-8}$	
	AC66 (*ibu*-7)	Cam⁺	1×10^{-3}	ibu± Cam⁺
	AC67 (*ibu*-11)	Cam⁺	3×10^{-3}	ibu± Cam⁺
AC59 Trp⁻ CAM-OCT⁺ *P. putida*	AC64	Oct⁺	2×10^{-3}	ibu⁻ Cam⁻ Oct⁺
	AC65	Oct⁺	1×10^{-3}	ibu⁻ Cam⁻Oct⁺

[a] ibu±, Extremely slow growth with isobutyrate as a sole source of carbon.

complemented by the corresponding functional genes present on the CAM plasmid, but an interesting mode of regulation prevents such cells from utilizing isobutyrate. This is seen more clearly from the results in Fig. 1. Chromosomal isobutyrate pathway is inducible and is fully induced with isobutyrate. The wild type thus grows well with isobutyrate after an initial lag. The CAM⁺ *ibu*-7 grows well with 10 mM camphor, to a lesser extent with 2 mM camphor, but exceedingly slowly with 10 mM isobutyrate. Inclusion of 2 mM camphor, which induces the camphor pathway, allows good growth with isobutyrate. It appears that the isobutyrate enzymes coded by the CAM plasmid are not inducible by isobutyrate, but are induced only by camphor. The presence of small amount of camphor therefore allows induction and rapid utilization of isobutyrate by the CAM⁺ *ibu*-7 cells.

Many interpretations are possible regarding the presence of some *ibu* degradative genes on the CAM plasmid, under the inductive control of camphor. We have previously hypothesized that during evolution of a degradative plasmid, a lack of clustering of chromosomal genes facilitates the recruitment of many such genes under plasmid regulatory controls (Farrell and Chakrabarty, 1979). It is tempting to speculate that from an evolutionary point of view, the formation of the CAM plasmid is not complete, and further recombinational events leading to insertion of the missing *ibu* genes are presumably occurring in nature. An insight into the physical arrangement of the genes and the role of insertion sequences responsible for transfer of blocks of genes will be very valuable in studying the mode of regulation and evolution of CAM and other degradative plasmids.

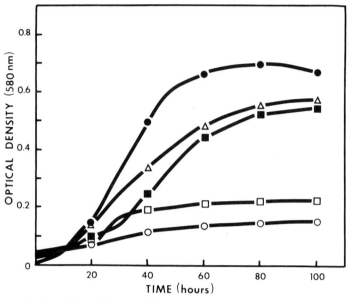

Fig. 1. Induction of the CAM-plasmid-borne *ibu* genes by camphor. CAM⁺ *ibu*-7 (CAM⁺ AC66) was inoculated into minimal media containing 10 mM isobutyrate alone (O—O); 2 mM camphor alone (□—□); 10 mM camphor alone (△—△); and 10 mM isobutyrate + 2 mM camphor (■—■). A wild type (AC30) was also inoculated in minimal +10 mM isobutyrate medium (●—●).

EVOLUTION OF DEGRADATIVE PLASMIDS

The emergence of a group of genes in the form of a plasmid encoding total or partial biodegradation of a hydrocarbon or a synthetic chlorinated compound has important implications in the rapid removal of that compound from the environment. Similar to plasmid-encoded antibiotic resistance, whose rapid spread in nature has posed enormous problems for clinicians, it is likely that the plasmid nature of the degradative genes allows ready dissemination of this property to various microorganisms in soil, thereby greatly increasing the nutritional versatility of soil microorganisms. The lack of persistence of herbicides such as 2,4-D and the emergence of 2,4-D type of degradative plasmids in nature is believed to be interrelated (Fisher *et al.*, 1978), and the persistence of many synthetic compounds such as DDT, 2,4,5-T, etc., appears to be due to a lack of assembly of appropriate degradative genes in the form of a plasmid. Thus 2,4,5-T is known to be cometabolized in nature (Rosenberg and Alexander, 1980), but the inherently slow rate of such metabolism does not allow rapid removal of this compound from the environment. Yet, such compounds are toxic, particularly when accumulation leads to high localized concentrations in nature, so that there is strong selective pressure on the microorganisms to detoxify such compounds. There are two examples of such pressure that I would like to cite, stressing particularly the problems microorganisms had in order to biodegrade man-made compounds. The first example involves the biodegradation of chlorinated biphenyls by microorganisms isolated from the Hudson river sediment. There is an estimated 500,000 pounds of PCB's (polychlorinated biphenyls) that have accumulated over last 30 years in a section of the Hudson river. Because PCB-type of compounds tend to accumulate in the river sediment, where the environment is basically anaerobic or semi-anaerobic, we have been interested in looking at facultatively anaerobic microorganisms that might have developed the capability to dissimilate chlorinated biphenyls. Indeed we have been able to characterize a transmissible plasmid (pAC2I) in a strain of *Klebsiella pneumoniae* (Kamp and Chakrabarty, 1979) that allows conversion of *p*-chlorobiphenyl (pCB) to *p*-chlorobenzoic acid (4 Cba). The evolution of this plasmid in this enteric bacterium is believed to aid in the removal of PCB's from the sediment due to bioconversion of the insoluble PCB's to the water-soluble chlorobenzoates, which can be washed away by the river water. The other interesting feature of the pCB-degradative plasmid pAC21 is that the presence of this plasmid allows expression of other *Pseudomonas* degradative plasmids in this strain. Normally enteric bacteria are not only incapable of utilizing hydrocarbons, but are deficient in expressing hydrocarbon-degradative genes, when such genes are transferred to these strains as part of the broad host range antibiotic resistance plasmid RP4 (Chakrabarty *et al.*, 1978). It is therefore interesting to note that members of the enteric bacteria are evolving specialized hydrocarbon degradative plasmids that allow them to functionally express such genes and utilize hydrocarbons. A rapid spread of this capability may in the future allow other enteric bacteria to utilize a variety of natural or synthetic hydrocarbon pollutants.

The second example of microbial adaptability to withstand high toxic concentrations of synthetic compounds is the evolution of plasmids that allow dechlorination and complete oxidation of simple chlorinated aromatic compounds such as 3-chloro- or 4-chlorobenzoic acids. Although plasmids against other chlorinated compounds such as *p*-chlorobiphenyl as mentioned above, or 2,4-D, have been described (Table II), such plasmids have been shown to specify an incomplete pathway that does not involve dechlorination. We have recently, however, characterized a plasmid, pAC25, that allows dechlorination and complete oxidation of 3-chlorobenzoic acid (Chatterjee and Chakrabarty, 1981). There are several interesting features of this plasmid-specified pathway. The dechlorination occurs only after the aromaticity of the ring has been broken, similar to *Pseudomonas* B13 described by Knackmuss and his colleagues (Reineke and Knackmuss, 1980). Transfer of pAC25 plasmid to *cat*B mutants of *P. putida*

TABLE II

Degradative Plasmids

Plasmid	Degradative pathway	Nature[a]	Size (million daltons)
CAM	Camphor	Con	~300
OCT	n-Octane	Non-con	~250
SAL	Salicylate	Con	55, 48, 42
NAH	Naphthalene	Con	46
TOL	Xylene/toluene	Con	76
XYL-K	Xylene/toluene	Con	90
2-HP	2-Hydroxypyridine	?	63
NIC	Nicotine/nicotinate	Con	ND[b]
pOAD2	6-Aminohexanoic acid cyclic dimer	Non-con	29
pJP1	2,4-Dichlorophenoxy-acetic acid	Con	58
pAC8 (RP4-TOL)	Xylene/toluene	Con	76
pAC21	p-Chlorobiphenyl	Con	65
pAC25	3-Chlorobenzoate	Con	68
pAC27	3- and 4-Chloro-benzoate	Con	59

[a] Con, conjugative; Non-con, nonconjugative.
[b] ND, not determined.

strains PRS1 allows them to utilize catechol, suggesting that dechlorination occurs at this stage, and furthermore an enzyme, similar to muconate-lactonizing enzyme, may be involved in the lactonization of the chloromuconic acid (Chatterjee and Chakrabarty, 1981). Interestingly, the product of this lactonization reaction is not metabolized *via* β-ketoadipate, but is oxidized via maleylacetate as an intermediate. The plasmid, therefore, encodes several novel enzymes that are specifically involved in the oxidation of 3-chlorobenzoate.

The involvement of maleylacetate as an intermediate in the oxidation of 4-chlorocatechol derived from 4-chlorophenoxyacetic acid was reported previously by Evans *et al.* (1971). It is likely that *Pseudomonas* B13 may oxidize 3-chlorobenzoate also by the maleylacetate pathway (Reineke and Knackmuss, 1980). Since these two pseudomonads were isolated in England and Germany between the 1950's and 1970's, while pAC25-harboring pseudomonad was isolated in the United States, in the late 1970's, it is interesting to question if all such strains may harbor plasmids with homologous DNA sequences corresponding to the maleylacetate pathway, thus having a common ancestry. To what extent such DNA sequences may have been translocated onto plasmids and transferred to microorganisms in nature remains an open question. What is apparent, however, is the evolution of various plasmids that appear to endow on the microbial hosts not only the capability to attack chlorinated compounds and release the chlorine, but also extend this capability to members of other bacterial genera, that have never been known to oxidize any hydrocarbons. The first indication of the involvement of plasmids in determining nutritional versatility in microorganisms came from the laboratory of Dr. Gunsalus. It was his insight, enthusiasm, and brilliant mind that encouraged many of us to explore some of these areas more fully. The contribution of the Gunsalus laboratory in delineating the various facets of microbial nutrition and diversity is mind-boggling, and this volume represents only a fraction of the overall attempts that were initiated and pursued at various times by various colleagues of Gunny. His overall contribution in biology remains too large to be measured in conventional terms.

REFERENCES

Benson, S., and Shapiro, J. (1976). *J. Bacteriol.* **126**, 794-798.

Betz, J. L., Brown, J. E., Clarke, P. H., and Dray, M. (1974). *Genet. Res.* **23**, 335-339.

Chakrabarty, A. M., Gunsalus, C. F., and Gunsalus, I. C. (1968). *Proc. Natl. Acad. Sci. U.S.A.* **60**, 168-175.

Chakrabarty, A. M., Friello, D. A., and Bopp, L. H. (1978). *Proc. Natl. Acad. Sci. U.S.A.* **75**, 3109-3112.

Chatterjee, D. K., and Chakrabarty, A. M. (1981). *In* "Microbial Degradation of Xenobiotics and Recalcitrant Compounds" (T. Leisinger, A. M. Cook, J. Nuesch, and R. Hutter, eds.). Academic Press, New York, pp. 213-219.

Evans, W. C., Smith, B. S. W., Moss, P., and Fernley, H. N. (1971). *Biochem. J.* **122**, 509-517.

Farrel, R., and Chakrabarty, A. M. (1979). *In* "Plasmids of Medical, Environmental and Commercial Importance" (K. N. Timmis and A. Puhler, eds.), pp. 97-109. Elsevier/North-Holland Biomedical Press, Amsterdam.

Fennewald, M., Benson, S., Oppici, M., and Shapiro, J. (1979). *J. Bacteriol.* **139**, 940-952.

Fisher, P. R., Appleton, J., and Pemberton, J. M. (1978). *J. Bacteriol.* **135**, 798-804.

Franklin, F. C. H., and Williams, P. A. (1980). *Mol. Gen. Genet.* **177**, 321-328.

Friello, D. A., Mylroie, J. R., Gibson, D. T., Rogers, J. E., and Chakrabarty, A. M. (1976). *J. Bacteriol.* **127**, 1217-1224.

Grund, A., Shapiro, J., Fennewald, M., Bacha, P., Leahy, J., Markbreiter, K., Nieder, M., and Toepfer, M. (1975). *J. Bacteriol.* **123**, 546-556.

Gunsalus, I. C., and Marshall, V. P. (1971). *CRC Crit. Rev. Microbiol.* **1**, 291-310.

Gunsalus, I. C., Bertland, A. M., and Jacobson, L. A. (1967). *Arch. Mikrobiol.* **59**, 113-122.

Kamp, P. F., and Chakrabarty, A. M. (1979). *In* "Plasmids of Medical, Environmental and Commercial Importance" (K. N. Timmis and A. Puhler, eds.), pp. 275-285. Elsevier/North-Holland Biomedical Press, Amsterdam.

Reineke, W., and Knackmuss, H.-J. (1980). *J. Bacteriol.* **142**, 467-473.

Rheinwald, J. G., Chakrabarty, A. M., and Gunsalus, I. C. (1973). *Proc. Natl. Acad. Sci. U.S.A.* **70**, 885-889.

Rosenberg, A., and Alexander, M. (1980). *J. Agric. Food Chem.* **28,** 297–302.
Shapiro, J. A., Benson, S., and Fennewald, M. (1980). *In* ''Plasmids and Transposons' (C. Stuttard and K. R. Rozee, eds.), pp. 1–19. Academic Press, New York.
Wheelis, M. L., and Stanier, R. Y. (1970). *Genetics* **66,** 245–266.
Worsey, M. J., Franklin, F. C. H., and Williams, P. A. (1978). *J. Bacteriol.* **134,** 757–764.

12

Communication among Coevolving Genes

L. Nicholas Ornston

Memory is a flexible instrument, and truth would not be served if I were to describe how I came to be a graduate student in Roger Stanier's laboratory in the early 1960's. Suffice it to say I was lucky—lucky in the topics being explored and lucky in the people who were exploring them. Stanier was my Doctor-Father in a diverse scientific family. It took some time to sort out all that occurred during Gunny's stimulating visits to Berkeley but, as time passed, I came to realize that in Gunsalus I had acquired a Doctor-Godfather.

At that time Gunsalus and Stanier were starting separate investigations into the metabolic diversity of *Pseudomonas*. Gunsalus' group had begun to elucidate the complex biochemistry underlying a single metabolic process, the utilization of camphor as a growth substrate. The diverse nutritional properties of *Pseudomonas* can serve as a basis for their classification, and Stanier had initiated an extensive survey of their metabolic potential (Stanier *et al.*, 1966). A question implicit in both studies was the evolutionary origin of metabolic diversity. What set of genetic and selective events gave rise to the extraordinary nutritional diversity found in *Pseudomonas?* One hunch, expressed by Gunsalus in 1963, was that bacteria were in communication with each other. He felt that plasmids were involved in the acquisition and exchange of metabolic information; research from his laboratory (Rheinwald *et al.*, 1973) was to prove him

EXPERIENCES IN BIOCHEMICAL PERCEPTION
Copyright © 1982 by Academic Press, Inc.
All rights of reproduction in any form reserved.
ISBN 0-12-528420-9

correct. Ensuing enthusiasm about the role of plasmids in metabolic evolution is justified, but it should be remembered that the nutritional classification of *Pseudomonas* works: many growth properties are genetically stable characteristics that help to define clearly circumscribed subgroups within the genus. This probably would not be the case if genetic information for most catabolic traits was carried on plasmids that were transferred freely among different *Pseudomonas* species. Whether they experienced a wanderjahr or not, genes for many catabolic pathways appear to have settled down as components of established genomes.

The inference that evolution was the abiding concern of that era illustrates the power of retrospection. Actually much of the research was directed to understanding the physiological controls that allowed representatives of *Pseudomonas* to express rapidly genes for multienzyme catabolic pathways. Investigations in Stanier's laboratory (Palleroni and Stanier, 1964; Hegeman, 1966; Ornston, 1966) led to the conclusion that blocks of enzymes were induced semi-sequentially by a few metabolites produced in the dissimilation of a primary growth substrate.

My own study was directed to mechanisms that govern induction of the β-ketoadipate pathway. The work was hampered by the fact that we did not know what all of the enzymes did, and hence it was necessary to determine metabolic intermediates that had not been previously identified. Stanier's thorough studies of simultaneous adaptation had given him his fill of metabolic pathways, and he felt that I should get the ''boring biochemistry'' out of the way so that I could get on with the physiology. I shared Stanier's desire for haste on the metabolic work, but the biochemistry involved a detailed net of seeming contradictions that did not dispel simply. It was during Gunny's visits to Berkeley that I learned that he, a man who spoke knowledgeably on so many topics, also had a willing ear. It was later that I came to appreciate that Gunny's mind operates simultaneously on several circuits: he listened responsively to my sad tales of anomolous mutants and, no doubt at the same time, he kept his intellect stimulated by privately pondering problems of greater significance.

Once unraveled, the β-ketoadipate pathway (Ornston and Stanier, 1966; Stanier and Ornston, 1973) posed some immediate evolutionary questions, many of which remain to be answered. As shown in Fig. 1, the two branches of the pathway are chemically analogous and, as shown by Canovas and Stanier (1967), the later steps in the pathway are mediated by isofunctional enzymes in *Acinetobacter*. These findings suggested a common evolutionary origin for enzymes mediating parallel steps in the protocatechuate and catechol branches of the pathway (Fig. 1.). Fungi employ a metabolic variant of the pathway (Cain *et al.*, 1968), and this implied that the pathway evolved independently in eukaryotes and prokaryotes (Ornston and Stanier, 1966). Diverse transcriptional controls were found in bacteria (Ornston, 1966; Canovas and Stanier, 1967;

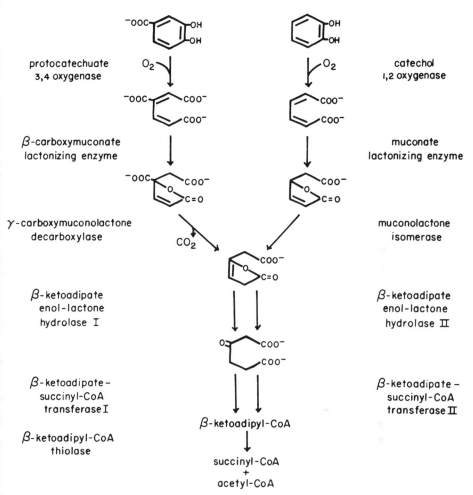

Fig. 1. Central steps of the β-ketoadipate pathway in bacteria. Analogous metabolic transformations convert protocatechuate and catechol to β-ketoadipate enol-lactone. Induction patterns used in *Acinetobacter* require the synthesis of isofunctional enzymes for the steps that follow metabolic convergence of the two branches of the pathway at β-ketoadipate enol-lactone.

Johnson and Stanier 1971; Ornston and Ornston, 1972). These discoveries suggested that some regulatory genes for the β-ketoadipate pathway arose from separate evolutionary origins and raised the possibility that the β-ketoadipate pathway evolved independently in different procaryotic groups (Canovas *et al.*, 1967).

There were two general approaches to the evolutionary questions. One, the descriptive approach, was to determine the primary structures of the gene products and, on the basis of this evidence, to deduce evolutionary relationships. The second approach was directed evolution (Clarke, 1974): what had happened once might be expected to happen again, and it might be possible to obtain mutant strains in which enzymes coding for reactions in one branch of the β-ketoadipate pathway had assumed activities associated with the other branch.

Directed evolution was on my mind when I enjoyed the hospitality of Gunny's laboratory in 1968–1969. I planned to delete structural genes for the catechol branch and to select mutant strains in which the deleted activities were taken over by enzymes of the protocatechuate branch. The first step was to isolate mutants carrying the required deletions. Gunny noted that many spontaneous mutations are deletions, so we developed a procedure for isolating spontaneous mutants (Ornston et al., 1969) and showed that a large fraction of them carried deletion mutations (Wheelis and Ornston, 1972). The second step, the selection of mutant strains forming enzymes with altered specificity, went less smoothly. A reason we can now offer for our lack of success is that genes for the two branches of the β-ketoadipate pathway have diverged widely from each other. Numerous mutations may be required to convert the catalytic properties of one enzyme to the properties of a homologous but widely divergent enzyme with an analogous activity.

Our results forced us to emphasize the descriptive approach to evolution. This necessity turned out to be fortunate because comparison of protein structures has given us insights that we would not have enjoyed had our attention been diverted by successful experiments in directed evolution. Due largely to the efforts of Dr. Wu-Kuang Yeh, automated techniques have yielded the NH_2-terminal amino acid sequences of many enzymes of the β-ketoadipate pathway. The results favor the following interpretations regarding communication among coevolving genes.

REARRANGEMENTS AMONG STRUCTURAL AND REGULATORY GENES

The NH_2-terminal amino acid sequences of *Acinetobacter* and *Pseudomonas* carboxymuconolactone decarboxylase are identical in about 50% of the positions (Yeh et al., 1980b). The decarboxylase is induced by protocatechuate in *Acinetobacter* (Canovas and Stanier, 1967) and by β-ketoadipate in fluorescent *Pseudomonas* species (Ornston, 1966). Thus it appears that, as described by Crawford (1975) for the tryptophan biosynthetic pathway, genetic rearrangements have placed homologous structural genes under control exerted by different regulatory genes. This is in accord with the hypothesis that major evolutionary steps are achieved by mutations that alter the regulation of gene expression (Wilson *et al.*, 1977).

EXTENSIVE DIVERGENCE OF HOMOLOGOUS GENES AS THEY COEVOLVE WITHIN A CELL LINE

Isofunctional enol–lactone hydrolases I and II are found in *Acinetobacter:* enol–lactone hydrolase I is induced with the protocatechuate suite of enzymes and enol–lactone hydrolases II is induced with the catechol enzymes (Patel *et al.*, 1975). The enol–lactone hydrolases do not appear to be regulated at the level of their activity, and selective pressures for the binding of different chemical ligands is unlikely to have contributed to their divergence. Nevertheless, the NH_2-terminal amino acid sequences of the enzymes have diverged widely; identical residues are found in only 6 of the 30 positions (Yeh *et al.*, 1980a). Therefore it appears likely that the enol–lactone hydrolase genes accumulated a large number of nucleotide substitutions as they became established within *Acinetobacter* (Ornston and Yeh, 1981).

SIMILAR AMINO ACID SEQUENCES IN ENZYMES WITH DIFFERENT CATALYTIC ACTIVITIES

The NH_2-terminal amino acid sequences of muconolactone isomerases and ketoadipate enol–lactone hydrolases, enzymes that mediate consecutive reactions (Fig. 1), resemble each other (Yeh *et al.*, 1978, 1980a). The appearance of similar amino acid sequences in enzymes with different activities may be interpreted three ways.

1. Duplication of a gene gave rise to the ancestors of genes for enzymes mediating consecutive reactions. This interpretation would be in accord with Horowitz' (1945) suggestion that selection for similar binding sites (rather than catalytic sites) could serve as a basis for the evolution of new enzymes. Three lines of evidence indicate that this interpretation is not applicable to the observations we have made. First, it is difficult to imagine how the similar isomerase–hydrolase sequences could have been conserved against the wide background of sequence divergence observed within the respective isomerase and hydrolase gene families (Yeh and Ornston, 1980; Ornston and Yeh, 1981). Second, optimal sequence identity in pairing of different isomerases and hydrolases requires shifts in the overall alignment of the sequences (Yeh *et al.*, 1980a). It therefore appears that more than one genetic event gave rise to the totality of observed

isomerase–hydrolase sequence similarities. Third, additional sequence similarities are observed in comparison of enzymes mediating reactions that are separated by several metabolic steps. For example, similar amino acid sequences are found in protocatechuate oxygenase and ketoadipate enol–lactone hydrolase, enzymes that subject chemically dissimilar substrates to entirely different catalytic processes (Fig. 1; Yeh and Ornston, 1980).

2. Similar amino acid sequences could have arisen from separate genetic origins as a result of convergent evolution of similar primary structures in different enzymes. On the basis of available evidence, this proposal cannot be excluded, but it is difficult to reconcile with the fact that the putatively convergent isomerase–hydrolase sequences have not been conserved within the respective isomerase and hydrolase enzyme families (Yeh and Ornston, 1980; Ornston and Yeh, 1981).

3. Mutations caused the substitution of oligonucleotide sequences from one segment of DNA into another. As noted above, selective pressures may favor the rapid divergence of homologous genes as they become established within a genome. In principle, rapid genetic divergence could be achieved by a swift succession of mononucleotide substitutions. We suggest an alternative mechanism, a novel form of mutation causing the substitution of oligonucleotide sequences from one region of DNA into another. If the oligonucleotide substitutions were intragenic, repeated sequences would appear within the mutated gene (Ornston and Yeh, 1979; McCorkle et al., 1980). If the oligonucleotide substitutions were intergenic, similar amino acid sequences would appear in genes with different evolutionary origins (Yeh and Ornston, 1980).

In sum, comparison of enzymes of the β-ketoadipate pathway calls attention to genetic processes that altered the transcriptional control of genes and, in some instances, may have caused novel oligonucleotide substitution mutations. Thus, as a derivative of Stanier and Gunsalus, I conclude that a gene, like an idea, may represent a combination of influences derived from quite different ancestors.

REFERENCES

Cain, R. B., Bilton, R. F., and Darrah, J. A. (1968). The metabolism of aromatic acids by microorganisms. Metabolic pathways in the fungi. *Biochem. J.* **108,** 797–828.
Canovas, J. L., and Stanier, R. Y. (1967). Regulation of the enzymes of the β-ketoadipate pathway in *Moraxella calcoacetica. Eur. J. Biochem.* **1,** 289–300.
Canovas, J. L., Ornston, L. N., and Stanier, R. Y. (1976). Evolutionary significance of metabolic control systems. *Science* **156,** 1695–1699.
Clarke, P. H. (1974). The evolution of enzymes for the utilization of novel substrates. *Symp. Soc. Gen. Microbiol.* **24,** 183–217.
Crawford, I. P. (1975). Gene rearrangements in the evolution of the tryptophan synthetic pathway. *Bacteriol. Rev.* **39,** 87–120.

Hegemen, G. D. (1966). Synthesis of the enzymes of the mandelate pathway by *Pseudomonas putida*. I. Synthesis of enzymes of the wild type. *J. Bacteriol.* **91**, 1140–1154.

Horowitz, N. H. (1945). On the evolution of biochemical syntheses. *Proc. Natl. Acad. Sci. U.S.A.* **31**, 153–157.

Johnson, B. F., and Stanier, R. Y. (1971). Regulation of the β-ketoadipate pathway in *Alcaligenes eutrophus*. *J. Bacteriol.* **107**, 476–485.

McCorkle, G. M., Yeh, W. K., Fletcher, P., and Ornston, L. N. (1980). Repetitions in the NH₂-terminal amino acid sequence of β-ketoadipate enol-lactone hydrolase from *Pseudomonas putida*. *J. Biol. Chem.* **255**, 6335–6341.

Ornston, L. N. (1966). The conversion of protacatechuate and catechol to β-ketoadipate by *Pseudomonas putida*. IV. Regulation. *J. Biol. Chem.* **241**, 3800–3810.

Ornston, L. N., and Stanier, R. Y. (1966). The conversion of catechol and protocatechuate to β-ketoadipate by *Pseudomonas putida*. I. Biochemistry. *J. Biol. Chem.* **241**, 3776–3786.

Ornston, L. N., and Yeh, W. K. (1979). Origins of metabolic diversity: Evolutionary divergence by sequence substitution. *Proc. Natl. Acad. Sci. U.S.A.* **76**, 3996–4000.

Ornston, L. N., and Yeh, W. K. (1981). Toward molecular natural history. *Microbiology* **1981**, 140–143.

Ornston, L. N., Ornston, M. K., and Chou, G. (1969). Isolation of spontaneous mutants of *Pseudomonas putida*. *Biochem. Biophys. Res. Commun.* **36**, 179–184.

Ornston, M. K., and Ornston, L. N. (1966). The regulation of the β-ketoadipate pathway in *Pseudomonas acidovorans* and *Pseudomonas testosteroni*. *J. Gen. Microbiol.* **73**, 455–464.

Palleroni, N. J., and Stanier, R. Y. (1964). Regulatory mechanisms governing synthesis of the enzymes for tryptophan oxidation by *Pseudomonas fluorescens*. *J. Gen. Microbiol.* **35**, 319–334.

Patel, R. N., Mazumdar, S., and Ornston, L. N. (1975). β-Ketoadipate enol-lactone hydrolases I and II from *Acinetobacter calcoacetius*. *J. Biol. Chem.* **250**, 6567–6577.

Rheinwald, J. G., Chakrabarty, A. M., and Gunsalus, I. C. (1973). A transmissible plasmid controlling camphor oxidation in *Pseudomonas putida*. *Proc. Natl. Acad. Sci. U.S.A.* **70**, 885–889.

Stanier, R. Y., and Ornston, L. N. (1973). The β-ketoadipate pathway. *Adv. Microb. Physiol.* **9**, 89–151.

Stanier, R. Y., Palleroni, N. J., and Doudosoff, M. (1966). The aerobic pseudomonads: A taxonomic study. *J. Gen. Microbiol.* **43**, 159–271.

Wheelis, M. L., and Ornston, L. N. (1972). Genetic control of enzyme induction in the β-ketoadipate pathway of *Pseudomonas putida*: Deletion mapping of *cat* mutations. *J. Bacteriol.* **109**, 790–795.

Wilson, A. C., Carlson, S. S., and White, T. J. (1977). Biochemical evolution. *Annu. Rev. Biochem.* **46**, 573–639.

Yeh, W. K., and Ornston, L. N. (1980). Origins of metabolic diversity: Substitution of homologous sequences into genes for enzymes with different activities. *Proc. Natl. Acad. Sci. U.S.A.* **77**, 5365–5369.

Yeh, W. K., Davis, G., Fletcher, P., and Ornston, L. N. (1978). Homologous amino acid sequences in enzymes mediating sequential metabolic reactions. *J. Biol. Chem.* **253**, 4920–4923.

Yeh, W. K., Fletcher, P., and Ornston, L. N. (1980a). Evolutionary divergence of co-selected β-ketoadipate enol-lactone hydrolases in *Acinetobacter calcoaceticus*. *J. Biol. Chem.* **255**, 6342–6346.

Yeh, W. K., Fletcher, P., and Ornston, L. N. (1980b). Homologies in the NH₂-terminal aminc acid sequences of γ-carboxymuconolactone decarboxylases and muconolactone isomerases. *J. Biol. Chem.* **255**, 6347–6354.

13

Mixed Regulation in a Biosynthetic Pathway: Learning How to Listen

Irving P. Crawford

I. DISCOVERY

A. Introduction—Why Tryptophan?

Late in 1965, following a plan we had previously agreed on, I. C. Gunsalus brought a collection of recently isolated *Pseudomonas putida* amino acid auxotrophs to my laboratory in La Jolla. We had hoped to use them to explore and extend the embryonic genetic system available for that organism, a species of great interest to my collaborator because of its camphor-degrading ability. We chose to focus on mutants affecting the tryptophan synthetic pathway. This pathway from chorismate to tryptophan (Fig. 1) is relatively short, unbranched, and in both prokaryotic groups that had been studied up until then, several enteric bacteria and a bacillus, all of its structural genes were clustered on the chromosome and regulated in unison.

B. Comparison of *P. putida* with Other Bacteria

The information available on the genetics and biochemistry of the tryptophan pathway in prokaryotes has been reviewed recently (Crawford, 1975, 1980). The

129

EXPERIENCES IN BIOCHEMICAL PERCEPTION
Copyright © 1982 by Academic Press, Inc.
All rights of reproduction in any form reserved.
ISBN 0-12-528420-9

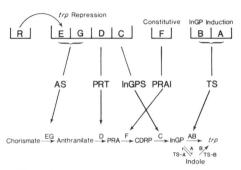

Fig. 1. Tryptophan biosynthetic pathway and gene arrangement in *P. aeruginosa*. Gene symbols: R, gene for a repressor acting on the *trpEGDC* cluster; E, G, D, C, B, and A, *trp* genes whose products catalyze the reaction indicated by the arrow. Enzyme designations: AS, anthranilate synthase; PRT, anthranilate–phosphoribosyl transferase; PRAI, N-phosphoribosylanthranilate isomerase; InGPS, indoleglycerol phosphate synthase; TS, tryptophan synthase. Pathway intermediates: PRA, phosphoribosylanthranilate; CDRP, 1-(o-carboxyphenylamino)-1-deoxyribulose phosphate; InGP, indoleglycerol phosphate (Manch and Crawford, 1981).

reactions of the pathway are identical in all species examined, but we now know that the number of structural genes employed, their chromosomal arrangement, and the regulatory mechanisms used vary widely. The first hint of surprises in store came with our investigation of the *P. putida* mutants isolated in the Gunsalus laboratory (Crawford and Gunsalus, 1966). Enzyme assays in extracts of the wild type and its auxotrophic mutants failed to show the "lock step" response of all the activities of the pathway to tryptophan availability expected from the extensive work on the enteric bacteria. Adding excess tryptophan to the medium in which the wild type was growing repressed tryptophan synthase levels about sevenfold but had little effect on the rest of the enzymes of the pathway. Conversely, when an auxotroph was starved for tryptophan it was seen to derepress the first, second, and fourth enzymes while levels of the third enzyme, an isomerase, and tryptophan synthase remained fixed. At that time we had mutants deficient in every enzyme activity except one, the A reaction of tryptophan synthase. (More precisely, the only mutants lacking this activity also lacked the B reaction so there was no tryptophan synthase activity to measure when they were starved for tryptophan.) One mutant in the *trpB* gene whose tryptophan synthase A reaction was preserved proved to be the exception to the regulatory rules just described, for its tryptophan synthase activity did increase very significantly upon depriving the cell of tryptophan.

These results proved quite incomprehensible at first, but my collaborator insisted that *P. putida* was trying to tell us something interesting and that we should ask more questions and keep an open mind.

C. Unusual Reluctance of *P. putida* Auxotrophs to Grow on Indole

One advantage in studying the tryptophan synthetic pathway is that two of the intermediates can be taken up readily by most bacterial cells, thus allowing characterization of most *trp* auxotrophs by a few rapid growth and accumulation tests. When the intermediates in question were brought into play with our collection of *P. putida* tryptophan auxotrophs, it was immediately obvious that one mutant class, blocked in the first enzyme, which should have been able to accept either anthranilate or indole in place of tryptophan, in fact grew well on anthranilate but very poorly on indole (Crawford and Gunsalus, 1966). It later became apparent that indole at higher concentrations could be utilized much better, but we were employing concentrations of 5–10 μg/ml, an amount more than adequate for the growth of tryptophan auxotrophs of *Bacillus subtilis* and the enteric bacteria. *Pseudomonas putida* mutants blocked between anthranilate and indoleglycerol phosphate also grew very slowly on low levels of indole. The one class of *trp* auxotroph able to use indole well was not present in our first collection, but we learned later that *trpA* mutants having lost the A reaction while retaining the B reaction of tryptophan synthase grow very well on minimal amounts of indole.

D. Tryptophan Synthase Assays of *P. putida* Mutants Grown under Various Conditions

When we examined the enzyme levels of various *trp* mutants grown on limiting tryptophan or, in the case of *trpE* mutants, on anthranilate, only the anthranilate-grown cells had levels of activity in the tryptophan synthase B reaction approaching that seen in the wild type growing on minimal medium. All tryptophan-grown cells had much less, approximately the levels seen in wild type grown with excess tryptophan. Suspecting that the slow growth of auxotrophs on indole might be due to those repressed enzyme levels, we selected spontaneous variants of *trpE* and *trpD* strains able to grow well on low indole levels. After prototrophs due to reversion of the preexisting mutation were identified and disposed of, two classes of indole-utilizers remained. These were most easily differentiated in the *trpE* case where one class could grow on anthranilate while the other had lost this ability concurrent with gaining the ability to use indole. The former proved to have a high, constitutive level of tryptophan synthase production, though the regulation of the first four enzymes remained normal for *P. putida*. The latter quite unexpectedly proved to be entirely lacking activity in the tryptophan synthase A reaction. Enzyme assays of such cells grown on indole showed higher tryptophan synthase B activity levels than tryptophan grown cells, approaching the level of wild type growing in minimal medium. When these cells were presented with anthranilate, which they could carry only as far as indole-glycerol phosphate in the pathway, along with tryptophan at any level, an extraordinarily high level of tryptophan synthase was seen, some 40-fold higher than with indole grown cells and 200-fold above the basal level in tryptophan grown cells.

With these results we became convinced that the sole factor regulating tryptophan synthase in *P. putida* was the level of the substrate, indoleglycerol phosphate. Subsequent experience confirmed this, and later the same mechanism was shown to be operative in *Pseudomonas aeruginosa* (Calhoun *et al.*, 1973). Our first sortie into the tryptophan pathway of *P. putida* had left us with the tentative conclusion that the genes of this short, specific branch of the aromatic acid synthetic scheme had three strikingly different regulatory modes (Fig. 1). *TrpF*, the gene for PRA isomerase, appeared to lack regulation in the usual sense and to be fixed, regardless of the availability of pathway intermediates or the end product. The genes for the first, second, and fourth enzymes, which eventually turned out to be four in number, did show tryptophan repression, but interestingly the activity of the first enzyme had a much wider range of derepression than *trpD* and *trpC*. The tryptophan synthase gene pair, in sharp contrast, was unresponsive to the amount of tryptophan in the cell but was induced by its substrate, indoleglycerol phospate.

E. *trp* Gene Mapping in *P. putida*

Using pf16, the *P. putida* lytic bacteriophage they had developed as a transducing agent, Chakrabarty *et al.* (1968) showed that the *trp* genes are dispersed to three chromosomal locations. Genes for the first, second, and fourth enzymes are cotransduced, the *trpA* and *trpB* genes are closely linked to each other but unlinked to the first group, and *trpF*, the gene for the unregulated enzyme, is not linked to either cluster (Fig. 1). A similar dispersion of the *trp* genes of *P. aeruginosa* to three chromosomal locations has been reported (Calhoun *et al.*, 1973; Holloway *et al.*, 1979). A fine structure map of three of the four genes in the early enzyme cluster of *P. putida* was developed by Gunsalus *et al.* (1968). In this map the order of the genes is *trpE-trpD-trpC*, but there is a gene-sized gap between *trpE* and *trpD*. There is an unlinked *trpR* gene encoding a negative repressor for this four-gene cluster (Maurer and Crawford, 1971). The possibility exists that there is additional regulation by attenuation between the promoter and *trpE*, in a manner similar to the regulation of the enteric bacterial *trp* operon (Yanofsky, 1981). There should also be some regulatory mechanism responsible for the disproportionate synthesis of the *trpEG* and the *trpDC* components of this gene cluster.

There are no published fine structure maps of the *trpAB* region of *P. putida*, nor does one exist for the *trpAB* genes of *P. aeruginosa*. The approximate position on the chromosome of the three sites bearing *trp* genes is known for *P. aeruginosa* (Holloway *et al.*, 1979).

F. Other Examples of Induction in Biosynthetic Pathways

Although there are no other proved examples of inducible enzymes in the tryptophan pathway of microorganisms, occasional instances of it have been seen in other pathways. Isopropylmalate isomerase and dehydrogenase in the leucine pathway in *Neurospora* (Gross, 1965) and acetolactate isomeroreductase, product of the *ilvC* gene in the isoleucine–valine pathway of *E. coli* (Watson *et al.*, 1979), are both induced by their substrates rather than repressed by the end products of the pathway. Doubtless other examples of inducible biosynthetic enzymes will be found as investigations continue.

II. ATTEMPT TO CHARACTERIZE TRYPTOPHAN SYNTHASE REGULATION IN *P. putida* BY GENETIC ANALYSIS

A. Further Characterization of Indole-Utilizing Secondary Mutants

The most interesting class of indole-utilizing variants of *P. putida* auxotrophs blocked early in the pathway was the one having lost the ability to convert indoleglycerol phosphate to indole (see Section I,D). Even in those cases where the variant was selected after nitrosoguanidine mutagenesis, spontaneous reversions were found to have regained normal regulation along with the ability to use indoleglycerol phosphate as a substrate, implying that a single point mutation was involved (Proctor and Crawford, 1975). This mutation was shown to be a missense change in *trpA;* particular care was taken to determine whether it allowed, or even augmented, the reversal of the tryptophan synthase A reaction, the conversion of indole and glyceraldehyde 3-phosphate to indoleglycerol phosphate. No evidence for this reverse reaction was observed when whole cells were exposed to radioactive indole or when the purified missense α subunit, combined with normal β_2 subunit, was examined enzymologically *in vitro* (Proctor and Crawford, 1975).

In view of more recent results (to be described in Section III,C and D), it seems that these matters should be reopened. Certainly the simplest explanation for the *trpA* mutant's effect on regulation would be that it still allows indoleglycerol phosphate to be formed from indole but blocks its utilization in the forward reaction. We did find a few "revertants" of the double mutant that gained the ability to grow on anthranilate without losing the ability to grown on low levels of indole (Proctor and Crawford, 1975). These were not explained. Work with two different types of tryptophan synthase mutants in which all three reactions were abolished showed that, in these cases at least, indole could not serve at all as an inducer in place of indoleglycerol phosphate. One type was a missense trpA mutation that destroyed the ability of the α subunit to combine with the β_2 subunit; the other was a trpB nonsense mutation.

The most tempting hypothesis in 1975 to explain the results just described was that tryptophan synthase in P. putida was autogenously regulated. Specifically, it was hypothesized that the trpA gene product was, or was part of, a repressor that interacted with the operator in the absence of inducer molecules to block transcription of the trpA-trpB gene pair (Proctor and Crawford, 1975). (Negative rather than positive regulation, i.e., repression in the absence of the inducer rather than facilitation in its presence, was chosen arbitrarily for the model. Only its autogenous character was suggested by the data, we believed.)

Unfortunately no direct tests of the autogenous induction model were feasible at the time it was proposed. No nonsense mutations or deletions of trpA were found, despite diligent searching. One additional suggestive finding was the discovery that one missense mutation in trpA first obtained as an indole utilizer in a trpC background (Crawford and Gunsalus, 1966) resulted in loss of the tryptophan synthase A reaction and partial constitutivity, i.e., a sevenfold elevation in the basal tryptophan synthase level. Revertants to trpA+ obtained spontaneously reverted to the normal basal activity (Proctor and Crawford, 1976). We concluded that this particular trpA mutation had affected both the enzymatic activity of the α subunit and its efficiency as a repressor, i.e., its ability to bind to DNA.

Thus the results of a strenuous attempt to isolate and characterize indole-utilizing variants of P. putida gave suggestive evidence that the same subunit of the enzyme that binds indoleglycerol phosphate as a substrate is involved in its recognition as an inducer. No direct test of this hypothesis could be formulated at the time, however.

B. Fine Structure of the trpAB Region

Having a number of mutants possessing selectable phenotypes affecting the trpA and trpB genes of P. putida, it seemed logical to attempt to construct a fine structure map by transduction, as had been accomplished for the trpE, D, and C genes (see Section I,E). Unfortunately, recombination values among these mutants were so low that very little information was obtained beyond the fact that all mutations affecting tryptophan synthase or its regulation are tightly clustered. It could not even be ascertained whether the operator–promoter region was on the trpB side or the trpA side of the structural genes.

C. The Autogenous Regulation Hypothesis

The hypothesis that the *trpA* gene product plays a role in its own regulation had a certain aesthetic appeal. *Escherichia coli* and other enteric bacteria synthesize only a single regulatory protein to control the production of all the tryptophan enzymes *en bloc,* as well as the tryptophan-sensitive isozyme of 3-deoxy-D-arabino-heptulosonate-7-phosphate synthase, the first enzyme in the common aromatic acid pathway (Gibson and Pittard, 1968). By dispersing the *trp* genes to three chromosomal locations and allotting a different regulatory scheme to each cluster, the fluorescent pseudomonads might have had to devote more genetic material to regulation of the pathway and thereby appreciably increased the chance that things might go awry. For an organism that survives because of its nutritional versatility, finding it necessary to "park" many blocks of degradative genes on extrachromosomal elements, this might seem to be an unwise course. If the isolated *trpF* gene requires no regulatory protein, having a fixed level of expression adequate for all contingencies, and if the *trpA* and *trpB* genes use the *trpA* gene product as the regulatory protein, one can see how the organism might acquire regulatory versatility in the pathway without sacrificing much of its presumably precious genetic space to unnecessary regulatory machinery. As instances multiplied of confirmed autogenous regulation in other systems, such as the *araC* (Casadaban, 1976) and *trpR* (Gunsalus and Yanofsky, 1980) genes of *E. coli*, it became more comfortable to accept the indirect evidence supporting the autoregulatory hypothesis, yet there was one uncomfortable fact that would not disappear. The *trpA* gene product of *P. putida* is similar in size, physical properties, amino acid composition, and the sequence of the first 24 amino acids to the analogous protein in *E. coli* (Enatsu and Crawford, 1971; Crawford and Yanofsky, 1971). Although not able to form complexes with heterologous β_2 subunits and form an active enzyme, the considerable similarities in the two α subunits made one skeptical that the *Pseudomonas* one had evolved an additional function, the ability to bind DNA and serve as a repressor or activator. Therefore, when the opportunity arrived to make a direct test of the autogenous induction hypothesis through the use of recombinant DNA methods, we welcomed it eagerly.

III. CLONING CERTAIN *P. aeruginosa trp* GENES IN *E. coli*

A. Rate of Gene Expression in Foreign Cytoplasm

Early in 1976, Robert Hedges, working in Naomi Datta's department at the Royal Postgraduate Medical School at Hammersmith Hospital in London, succeeded in producing two R prime plasmids bearing different *Pseudomonas trp* genes. He mated *P. aeruginosa* carrying the "improved" (for chromosome mobilizing ability) P incompatibility class plasmid R68.44 (Haas and Holloway, 1976) with an *E. coli trpA* or *trpE* mutant. One R prime carried *trpA* and *trpB*, the other carried *trpE* and *trpG*. When these were proffered by mail they presented a new way to approach the analysis of the regulation of *Pseudomonas trp* genes, one that could make use of the extensive repertory of genetic techniques available in *E. coli*.

First it should be noted that the source of the chromosomal segment in these R prime plasmids was *P. aeruginosa*, not *P. putida* in which most of our previous work had been done. The evidence available, however, including analyses of enzyme levels in various auxotrophs grown with limiting and excess tryptophan (Calhoun *et al.*, 1973), intimates that these two related species use identical means to regulate their *trp* genes.

The first surprise these R prime strains provided was the faint-hearted way their *Pseudomonas trp* genes were expressed in *E. coli*. Several days were required to develop respectable colonies on minimal agar plates when growth was dependent on the plasmid-borne foreign chromosmal segment. Not surprisingly, the plasmids' enzyme activities, anthranilate synthase and tryptophan synthase, respectively, were at the limits of detectability in the assays normally employed. We were unable to find cells with improved function arising either spontaneously or following mutagenesis. We did obtain such variants after long-term selection for improved growth rate through iterative passages in liquid minimal medium. This suggests that multiple mutations, each with a small individual effect, might be required to overcome the original impediment to expression. When the variants with improved function were analyzed, the changes proved to be on the plasmid rather than the *E. coli* chromosome, but no significant deletions, insertions, or other major DNA rearrangements could be detected by restriction enzyme analysis (Hedges *et al.*, 1977; additional unpublished results). Assays of an intermediate version of the tryptophan synthase plasmid, termed p*trpAB*-1, and the most active version, p*trpAB*-2, in a suitably mutant *E. coli* host showed a very significant, about 70-fold, induction by indoleglycerol phosphate. In the absence of the inducer the cells failed to grow on indole, confirming that regulation of the plasmid-borne *trpA* and *trpB* genes is "normal" for *Pseudomonas* and that indole is not an inducer. Indole-utilizing variants were selected. Two classes were found; in one the plasmid-borne *trp* genes were expressed constitutively at a high rate, and in the other indole proved to be nearly as effective an inducer as indoleglycerol phosphate but activity in the indoleglycerol phosphate to indole reaction was missing. These results paralleled perfectly the ones obtained earlier with *P. putida*, giving confidence that the entire regulatory apparatus for the tryptophan synthase genes is present on the plasmid and gives normal *Pseudomonas* behavior in *E. coli*, once the expressional impediment is overcome.

B. Gene Order as Determined by Deletion Analysis

The chromosomal segment in the series of p*trpAB* plasmids is 75 Mdaltons in size, much larger than the 1.3 Mdaltons of DNA required to encode the α and β polypeptides. Subcloning into the multicopy vehicle pBR322 through several steps reduced the size of the active chromosomal segment to 3.4 Mdaltons without affecting the mode of regulation (Manch and Crawford, 1981). A restriction site map of this plasmid is shown in Fig. 2. A crucially located pair of *Eco*RI sites in this plasmid allowed the construction *in vitro* of a deletion that proved able to produce only the β chain of the enzyme but to have retained inducible regulation. Near the middle of the cloned segment there are two *Bgl*II sites separated by 0.31 Mdaltons of DNA. Deleting the intervening segment results in loss of expression of both *trpB* and *trpA*, yet the *trpA* gene remains intact, shown by the recovery of α subunit activity on subcloning the remaining insert into a site distal to the strong λ promoter in pHUB4 (Manch and Crawford, 1982). These and other results indicate the gene order to be promoter-*trpB*-*trpA*.

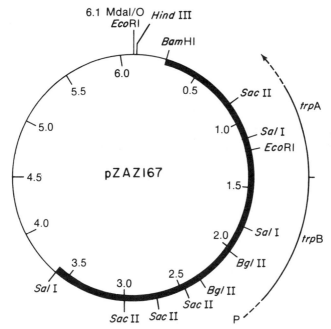

Fig. 2. Deduced map of the plasmid pZAZ167. Cloned *P. aeruginosa* chromosomal DNA is indicated by the heavy line; vector (pBR322) DNA is indicated by the light line. Distances are in Mdaltons. The approximate positions of the *trpB* gene, *trpA* gene, and their promoter are shown outside the circle, with the direction of transcription indicated by the arrowhead. The dashed line indicates uncertainty about where transcription may start and end.

It is worth noting that *trpA* lies distal to *trpB* in all other bacteria where the direction of transcription is known, including three enteric bacterial genera and *B. subtilis*. In *Neurospora* and *Saccharomyces*, however, where the *trpA* and *trpB* functions are fused to produce a single polypeptide, the order is reversed (Manney *et al.*, 1969).

C. Evidence against Autogenous Regulation

The fact that the *Eco*RI deletion described in the preceding section retains normal regulation of the *trpB* gene is antithetical to the hypothesis of autogenous regulation. It still seemed possible that only an N-terminal segment or domain of the α subunit might be needed for the regulatory function, however. Therefore, a collection of longer deletions was constructed through the agency of the double-stranded DNA exonuclease BAL31. The chromosomal insert from pZAZ167 was first inserted into pACYC184 to make a plasmid compatible with the TrpB$^-$TrpA$^+$ plasmid needed as a source of α subunits. This pACYC184 derivative was termed pZAZ125. It exhibited typical *Pseudomonas* inducibility. Deletions originating at its unique *Bam*HI site were constructed *in vitro* and transformed into the usual *E. coli trpEBA* recipient. Those that had lost the ability to produce normal tryptophan synthase were examined by restriction enzyme digestion to ascertain the extent of the deleted area. The subset whose deletion extended beyond the *Eco*RI site in the *trpA* gene was tested for the ability to produce β_2 subunit by complementation *in vivo* with the α subunit-producing plasmid. Three plasmids in this subset were examined in detail; each of them showed normal regulation of *trpB* (Manch and Crawford, 1982). We conclude that the α subunit is *not* involved in the induction of the *trpBA* gene pair, and earlier results interpreted as evidence for autogenous regulation must have a different explanation.

D. Evidence for a Positive Regulator, the *trpI* Gene Product

The result in the previous section posed a paradox. All the information required for an inducible enzyme system is borne on the chromosomal segment of pZAZ167, yet deletion of *trpA* and all the DNA downstream from it is without regulatory consequences. Investigation of the region upstream from the promoter, the approximately 1.3 Mdaltons of DNA between the *Sal*I end of the insert and the first *Bgl*II site, was facilitated by the occurrence within it of three *Sac*II sites whose location is indicated in Fig. 2. *In vitro* deletion of either or both of the small *Sac*II-bounded segments within this region was relatively easily accomplished. These deleted plasmids all exhibit the same phenotype. They confer upon *E. coli trpEBA* the ability to grow on indole or anthranilate, but growth is very slow and is equivalent with either supplement. Examination of enzyme levels showed a low, fixed level of tryptophan synthase regardless of the presence or absence of the inducer. These results are not readily explainable as alteration of the promoter–operator region, as that is thought to lie between the two *Bgl* II sites some distance away. Moreover, identical phenotypes are seen with deletion of either small *Sac*II segment. The results are most compatible with the existence of a structural gene producing a positive regulatory protein that facilitates transcription at the *trpBA* promoter when inducer is present. This positive regulatory element would then join a growing list of such proteins in microbial genetics, including the *araC* gene product (Englesberg *et al.*, 1965), the catabolite activator protein (Zubay *et al.*, 1970), the *ilvY* gene product (Watson *et al.*, 1979) and elements concerned with the regulation of genes involved in nitrogen catabolism (Tyler, 1978; Kustu *et al.*, 1979), nitrogen fixation (Ausubel *et al.*, 1979), and alkaline phosphatase (Wanner and Latterell, 1980). This gene, if its existence is confirmed, will be termed *trpI* (Manch and Crawford, 1982).

IV. UNSOLVED PROBLEMS AND FUTURE EXPERIMENTS

A. The *trpEGDC* Region and Its Regulation

The R prime plasmid that Hedges isolated bearing the *trpE* and *trpG* genes deserves attention as much as the p*trpAB* plasmid. In this case the known repressor gene, *trpR*, is unlinked to the structural genes so one would expect a fixed, high level of expression of the anthranilate synthase genes. Instead, in all the experiments performed so far we have seen relatively low levels of activity with about a fivefold "repression" by growth in excess tryptophan. These results suggest the possibility that the *Pseudomonas trpEGDC* cluster, like the enteric bacterial *trp* operon (Crawford and Stauffer, 1980), may be regulated by both repression and attenuation. From the detailed knowledge of the mechanism of attenuation in *E. coli* (Yanofsky, 1981), it is conceivable that a segment of DNA between the promoter–operator and the *trpE* gene that functions as an optional transcription termination device in one species might preserve this function during expression in the cytoplasm of another species. This is our present hypothesis for the mechanism of regulation of the plasmid-borne *Pseudomonas trpE* and *trpG* genes in *E. coli*. DNA sequence studies may or may not bear this out.

There is also a need to clarify the disparity in the range of derepression of the *trpEG* and the *trpDC* gene segments. If these four genes are in fact a single transcription unit with a variable transcription termination site between the *trpG* and *trpD* genes, this represents a new kind of regulation for genes functioning in the tryptophan synthetic pathway. An alternative hypothesis, that there is a second promoter for the *trpDC* gene pair with an independent operator and/or attenuator site for its regulation, is equally compatible with present data. Possibly some additional cloning of *Pseudomonas* chromosomal segments in this vicinity will be necessary to solve this problem.

B. *trpF*, a "Fixed" Gene in a Regulated Pathway

The gene for this 39,000 dalton enzyme, the functional counterpart of the C-terminal half of the enteric bacterial *trpC* gene, has not yet been cloned. Suitable *E. coli* mutants lacking only the phosphoribosyl–anthranilate isomerase activity do exist, however, and there is some justification for the undertaking. The sum of the molecular weights of the *trpC* and *trpF* gene products in *P. putida* is 71,000 daltons (Crawford, 1975), considerably larger than the 45,000 dalton *E. coli* fused gene product. It would be interesting to ascertain the nature and location of the "extra" amino acids associated with having discrete rather than fused enzymes.

It is known that a form of "metabolic" regulation of the expression of the tryptophan operon occurs in *E. coli*. Under conditions where the growth rate of the organism is slow, the rate of expression of the *trp* operon is reduced, even in the absence of *trp* repressor and attenuator function. It is not known whether this kind of modulation of *trpF* gene function occurs in *Pseudomonas*. The recent demonstration of a minature attenuator effecting metabolic regulation of the *E. coli* chromosomal β-lactamase gene (Jaurin *et al.*, 1981) prompts the suggestion that search for similar modulators for such ostensibly "uncontrolled" genes as *trpF* in *P. putida* and *P. aeruginosa* might be worthwhile.

C. *trpBA*, an Independent Genetic Unit

When and if the *trpI* regulatory gene is firmly ensconced in its position upstream from the promoter–operator region, there will be a new group of questions to be answered concerning this inducible segment of the biosynthetic pathway. Is the *trpI* gene product a repressor in the absence of inducer as well as an activator in its presence, resembling the *araC* gene product in this respect? Perhaps this is true in its own cytoplasm, though the very low level of activity of the *Sac*II deletion-containing plasmids in *E. coli* suggests it may not be true in this "foreign" cytoplasm. It would be interesting to examine the function of *Sac*II deleted mutants when returned to *Pseudomonas*. The vectors used in the *E. coli* experiments cannot be maintained in *Pseudomonas* cytoplasm, of course, but the appropriate segment might be transferred to a P class plasmid or to an RSF1010 derivative (Wood *et al.*, 1981) which can. It might be appropriate to use *P. putida* or a *P. aeruginosa rec-2* mutant (Chandler and Krishnapillai, 1974) for these studies to forestall recombination between the cloned segment and the chromosome. These studies might also include the unmodified chromosomal segment from p*trpAB*-O which functions poorly in *E. coli*. DNA sequence studies are needed to define the nature of the mutations in p*trpAB*-1 and p*trpAB*-2 and to define the promoter and any regulatory sequence for *trpI*.

It will soon be necessary to return to the *P. putida* and *P. aeruginosa* trpA mutations with their now unexplained effect on the induction mechanism. Certainly recombinant DNA methodology could be used to attack this puzzling problem. The most logical hypothesis, that the modified α-subunit retains activity in the reverse reaction though it has lost it in the forward reaction, thus allowing indoleglycerol phosphate to be formed from indole, remains unsupported. Past experience indicates the desirability of bringing new techniques to bear on unresolved problems in *Pseudomonas* rather than relying too heavily on inappropriate models based on better-studied paradigms in *E. coli*.

V. ENVOI

The patient reader has now retraced along with me the rather devious path we have traveled since the winter of 1966 when *P. putida* presented I. C. Gunsalus and me with some unexpected results. Not surprisingly, when the bacterium (or a segment of its chromosome) was challenged with sensible questions it delivered credible answers. Though we sometimes wandered astray, it was usually because we had developed preconceived notions about the answers we wanted to hear. The great generalization summarized as "the unity of biochemistry" by A. J. Kluyver and his disciples in the Delft school of microbiology means only that the principles and general plan of metabolism are similar for all living forms. Nothing shows more clearly than the variations uncovered in the regulatory mechanisms of the tryptophan pathway that organisms in general and microbes in particular have found a wide variety of means to achieve their metabolic goals. If I may attempt a Gunsalus-like aphorism, they are all making music, but each one has its own instrument and song. That, to me, is why we must keep trying to learn to listen.

Grateful appreciation is extended all those who helped in the investigation of *Pseudomonas* and its *trp* genes during the past 15 years. The names of most, but not all, are discernable in the references; Ananda Chakrabarty, Carol Gunsalus, and Susan Sikes played differing but invaluable roles in the exposition; Toshio Enatsu, Richard Maurer, and Alan Proctor carried the first part of the development section; while Bob Hedges, Barbara Wang, Elizabeth M. Yelverton, Annelie James, and Jean Manch have been invaluable during the introduction and development of the second theme. To I. C. Gunsalus, without whom the piece would not even have been conceived, no expression of gratitude would be adequate.

REFERENCES

Ausubel, F. M., Bird, S. C., Durbin, K. J., Janssen, K. A., Margolskee, R. F., and Peskin, A. P. (1979). Glutamine synthase mutations which affect expression of nitrogen fixation genes in *Klebsiella pneumoniae*. *J. Bacteriol.* **140**, 597–606.

Calhoun, D. H., Pierson, D. L., and Jensen, R. A. (1973). The regulation of tryptophan biosynthesis in *Pseudomonas aeruginosa*. *Mol. Gen. Genet.* **121**, 117–132.

Casadaban, M. J. (1976). Regulation of the regulatory gene for the arabinose pathway, *araC*. *J. Mol. Biol.* **104**, 557–566.

Chakrabarty, A. M., Gunsalus, C. F., and Gunsalus, I. C. (1968). Transduction and the clustering of genes in fluorescent pseudomonads. *Proc. Natl. Acad. Sci. U.S.A.* **60**, 168–175.

Chandler, P. M., and Krishnapillai, V. (1974). Isolation and properties of recombination deficient mutants of *Pseudomonas aeruginosa*. *Mutat. Res.* **23**, 15–23.

Crawford, I. P. (1975). Gene rearrangements in the evolution of the tryptophan synthetic pathway. *Bacteriol. Rev.* **39**, 87–120.

Crawford, I. P. (1980). Comparative studies on the regulation of tryptophan synthesis. *CRC Crit. Rev. Biochem.* **8**, 175–189.

Crawford, I. P., and Gunsalus, I. C. (1966). Inducibility of tryptophan synthetase in *Pseudomonas putida*. *Proc. Natl. Acad. Sci. U.S.A.* **56**, 717–724.

Crawford, I. P., and Stauffer, G. V. (1980). Regulation of tryptophan biosynthesis. *Annu. Rev. Biochem.* **49**, 163–195.

Crawford, I. P., and Yanofsky, C. (1971). *Pseudomonas putida* tryptophan synthetase: Partial sequence of the α subunit. *J. Bacteriol.* **108**, 248–253.

Enatsu, T., and Crawford, I. P. (1971). *Pseudomonas putida* tryptophan synthetase. *J. Bacteriol.* **108**, 431–438.

Englesberg, E., Irr, J., Power, J., and Lee, N. (1965). Positive control of enzyme synthesis by gene C in the L-arabinose system. *J. Bacteriol.* **90**, 946–957.

Gibson, F., and Pittard, J. (1968). Pathways of biosynthesis of aromatic amino acids and vitamins and their control in microorganisms. *Bacteriol. Rev.* **32**, 465–494.

Gross, S. R. (1965). The regulation of synthesis of leucine biosynthetic enzymes in *Neurospora*. *Proc. Natl. Acad. Sci. U.S.A.* **54**, 1538–1546.

Gunsalus, I. C., Gunsalus, C. F., Chakrabarty, A. M., Sikes, S., and Crawford, I. P. (1968). Fine structure of the tryptophan genes in *Pseudomonas putida*. *Genetics* **60**, 419–435.

Gunsalus, R. P., and Yanofsky, C. (1980). Nucleotide sequence and expression of *Escherichia coli trpR*, the structural gene for the *trp* aporepressor. *Proc. Natl. Acad. Sci. U.S.A.* **77**, 7117–7121.

Haas, D., and Holloway, B. W. (1976). R factor variants with enhanced sex factor activity in *Pseudomonas aeruginosa*. *Mol. Gen. Genet.* **144**, 243–251.

Hedges, R. W., Jacob, A. E., and Crawford, I. P. (1977). Wide ranging plasmid bearing the *Pseudomonas aeruginosa* tryptophan synthase genes. *Nature (London)* **267**, 283–284.

Holloway, B. W., Krishnapillai, V., and Morgan, A. F. (1979). Chromosomal genetics of *Pseudomonas*. *Microbiol. Rev.* **43**, 73–102.

Jaurin, B., Grundström, T., Edlund, T., and Normark, S. (1981). The *E. coli* β-lactamase attenuator mediates growth rate dependent regulation. *Nature (London)* **290**, 221–225.

Kustu, S., Burton, D., Garcia, E., McCarter, L., and McFarland, N. (1979). Nitrogen control in *Salmonella*: Regulation by the *glnR* and *glnF* gene products. *Proc. Natl. Acad. Sci. U.S.A.* **76**, 4576–4580.

Manch, J. N., and Crawford, I. P. (1981). Ordering the tryptophan synthase genes of *Pseudomonas aeruginosa* by cloning in *Escherichia coli*. *J. Bacteriol.* **146**, 102–107.

Manch, J. N., and Crawford, I. P. (1982). Genetic evidence for a positive-acting regulatory factor mediating induction in the tryptophan pathway of *Pseudomonas aeruginosa. J. Mol. Biol.* (in press).

Manney, T. E., Duntze, W., Janosko, N., and Salazar, J. (1969). Genetic and biochemical studies of partially active tryptophan synthetase mutants of *Saccharomyces cerevisiae. J. Bacteriol.* **99,** 590–596.

Maurer, R., and Crawford, I. P. (1971). New regulatory mutant affecting some of the tryptophan genes in *Pseudomonas putida. J. Bacteriol.* **106,** 331–338.

Proctor, A. R., and Crawford, I. P. (1975). Autogenous regulation of the inducible tryptophan synthase of *Pseudomonas putida. Proc. Natl. Acad. Sci. U.S.A.* **72,** 1249–1253.

Proctor, A. R., and Crawford, I. P. (1976). Evidence for autogenous regulation of *Pseudomonas putida* tryptophan synthase. *J. Bacteriol.* **126,** 547–549.

Tyler, B. (1978). Regulation of the assimilation of nitrogen compounds. *Annu. Rev. Biochem.* **47,** 1127–1162.

Wanner, B. L., and Latterell, P. (1980). Mutants affected in alkaline phosphatase expression: Evidence for multiple positive regulators of the phosphate regulon in *Escherichia coli. Genetics* **96,** 353–366.

Watson, M. D., Wild, J., and Umbarger, H. E. (1979). Positive control of *ilvC* expression in *Escherichia coli* K12: Identification and mapping of regulatory gene *ilvY. J. Bacteriol.* **139,** 1014–1020.

Wood, D. O., Hollinger, M. F., and Tindol, M. B. (1981). Versatile cloning vector for *Pseudomonas aeruginosa. J. Bacteriol.* **145,** 1448–1451.

Yanofsky, C. (1981). Attenuation in the control of expression of bacterial operons. *Nature (London)* **289,** 751–758.

Zubay, G., Schwartz, D., and Beckwith, J. (1970). Mechanism of activation of catabolite-sensitive genes: A positive control system. *Proc. Natl. Acad. Sci. U.S.A.* **66,** 104–110.

III
Regulation

14

Regulation of
L-Threonine Dehydrase
by Ligand-Induced
Oligomerization:
An Odyssey Born of the
Pyridoxal Phosphate Era

D. J. LeBlond,
R. C. Menson,
and
W. A. Wood

September of 1940 was a fortunate time for me because I (W.A.W.) came under the influence of Gunny as my faculty advisor the day I first registered at Cornell University. First in 1943, and then in 1946–1947 as an undergraduate I began to work in his laboratory which, after the war, was shared with Wayne Umbreit. In that period as well as during my graduate school years at Indiana University, my values and concepts of research were established from daily scientific discussions with and accompanying continual intellectual challenges from Gunny. His admonition to read John Dewey led me to discover the philosophical basis for resolution of indeterminant situations, an experience which has served me well ever since. His rather stern requirements as to what constitutes a good experiment and what standards to apply in making assertions from the data spurred me and many others to a performance level that under other circumstances or in a different environment would not have been attained or aspired to. Accompanying

EXPERIENCES IN BIOCHEMICAL PERCEPTION
Copyright © 1982 by Academic Press, Inc.
All rights of reproduction in any form reserved.
ISBN 0-12-528420-9

these often disturbing encounters was a genuine personal interest in my well being and future, and this concern was especially valuable during the period of wartime military service and postwar uncertainty.

When I returned from military service in 1946, Gunsalus, Umbreit, and their associates had discovered (Bellamy *et al.*, 1945), synthesized (Gunsalus *et al.*, 1944, 1945; Umbreit *et al.*, 1945), and established the structure (Gunsalus and Umbreit, 1947) of the coenzyme for tyrosine decarboxylase, pyridoxal 5'-phosphate. With the then world's supply in hand (about 1 gm of the barium salt), investigation of the numerous roles of vitamin B_6 coenzymes in amino acid metabolism was furiously being investigated. It was an exciting time. Several decarboxylases (Bellamy *et al.*, 1945; Gunsalus *et al.*, 1944; Umbreit and Gunsalus, 1945), glutamic–aspartic transaminase (Lichtstein *et al.*, 1945; Umbreit *et al.*, 1946: O'Kane and Gunsalus, 1947), as well as tryptophan synthetase (Umbreit *et al.*, 1946b) and tryptophanase (Wood *et al.*, 1947) were shown to require the new coenzyme.

With characteristic insight for which he is so well known, Gunny compared the equations for the reactions catalyzed by tryptophanase and by tryptophan synthetase and then suggested to me that serine deaminase should also require pyridoxal phosphate.

$$\text{Indole + serine} \xrightarrow[\text{synthetase}]{\text{tryptophan}} \text{tryptophan} + H_2O$$

$$\underline{\text{Tryptophan} + H_2O \xrightarrow{\text{tryptophanase}} \text{indole + pyruvate} + NH_3}$$

$$\text{Serine} \xrightarrow[\text{deaminase}]{\text{serine}} \text{pyruvate} + NH_3$$

This started me on an investigation which has been full of surprises and challenges and has formed the basis for much of my research as an independent investigator [see reviews by Wood (1969) and Dunne and Wood (1975)].

Properties of L-Serine Deaminase

Contrary to many pyridoxal phosphate-linked enzymes, "serine deaminase" reveals its nature only begrudgingly. Further, because of its only slowly perceived complex nature, a clear picture of its function and regulation has been elusive and in some aspects is still a subject of controversy.

For years AMP was the only "coenzyme" or activator for serine deaminase that could be demonstrated (Wood and Gunsalus, 1949); unfortunately its role in catalysis was far from obvious. In addition, only one other report of AMP as an activator had appeared, namely, for phosphorolysis of glycogen (Cori and Cori, 1936). For the serine deaminase of *Escherichia coli*, resolution of pyridoxal phosphate and reactivation was not accomplished by the typical procedures effective then with decarboxylases, glutamic–aspartic transaminase (O'Kane and Gunsalus, 1947), tryptophan synthetase (Umbreit *et al.*, 1946), and tryptophanase (Wood *et al.*, 1947). Much later a role for pyridoxal phosphate was found by Umbarger and Brown (1957) and confirmed by Phillips and Wood (1965). Now resolution of the holodeaminase by incubation with cysteine is the routine procedure (Whanger *et al.*, 1968). In due course the deaminase was renamed biodegradative L-threonine dehydrase for the following reasons: (1) the deaminase "commits suicide" during the deamination of L-serine whereas the conversion of L-threonine was linear with time (Wood and Gunsalus, 1949); (2) the dehydrase is induced and functions only under "energy-poor" conditions when the generation of ATP is needed; glucose causes severe catabolite repression (Wood and Gunsalus, 1949; Umbarger and Brown, 1957); and (3) the mechanism of pyridoxal phosphate-assisted α-β elimination from the work of Chargaff and Sprinson (1943), Metzler *et al.* (1954), Braunstein and Shemyakin (1953), and Phillips and Wood (1965) showed that the primary enzyme-catalyzed event was the removal of water.

Role of AMP

At the low dehydrase concentrations typical of our coupled assay which uses lactic dehydrogenase and NADH to follow α-ketobutyrate production, the observed activation by AMP results from the large decrease in K_m for L-threonine upon addition of AMP (Table I) (Menson, 1976; LeBlond, 1980); there is also about a twofold increase in V_{max}. Thus the long observed activation does not result as much from an increase in catalytic capability as it does from the fact that pseudo zero-order kinetics are not attainable in the absence of AMP at any achievable L-threonine concentration due to the high K_m. In contrast, this state (L-threonine saturation) can be attained readily in the presence of AMP. At higher dehydrase concentrations and using assays that depend on the accumulation of α-ketobutyrate, the effects of AMP are diminished or are not seen (Tokushige and Nakazawa, 1972; Shizuta *et al.*, 1973). This has been attributed to oligomerization in the absence of AMP. However, the insensitivity to AMP may also result from the known inhibitory effects of α-ketobutyrate (Shizuta *et al.*, 1973).

In addition to the kinetic effect, AMP also causes a major change in protein structure. At low dehydrase concentrations, AMP causes dimerization and tetramerization of the dehydrase with the dimer (at least) having the low K_m value. Increasing the protein concentration in the absence of AMP also causes oligomer formation. Such oligomers have an even higher K_m for L-threonine (Gerlt *et al.*, 1973) as well as the inability to respond to AMP as reported by Shizuta *et al.* (1973).

TABLE I

The Effect of AMP on Behavior of Threonine Dehydrase[a]

Parameter	Without AMP	With AMP
V_{max} (IU $\times$ 10^{-4})	1.88 $\pm$ 0.04	3.51 $\pm$ 0.03
		3.20 $\pm$ 0.02[b]
$S_{0.5}$ (mM)	264 $\pm$ 17	6.75 $\pm$ 0.5
		7.63 $\pm$ 0.2[b]
Hill coefficient, n	1.1 $\pm$ 0.02	1.17 $\pm$ 0.03
		1.08 $\pm$ 0.007[b]
Correlation	0.9924	0.995
coefficient		0.9960[b]
$S_{20,w}$	3.6 S	5.75–6.86 S
Molecular weight,		
gel electrophoresis	36,600	70,500

[a] Initial rate data were processed as described by LeBlond *et al.*, 1980a,b.
[b] Values were averaged from four determinations made by the method of substrate addition (LeBlond *et al.*, 1980b).

The lack of appreciation of the effect of linkage between (1) kinetic behavior and the state of oligomerization, (2) the existence of a mixture of dehydrase oligomers in equilibrium under many conditions, (3) ability of α-ketobutyrate (Shizuta *et al.*, 1973) and pyruvate (Feldman and Datta, 1975) to inhibit and inactivate, respectively, and (4) the different experimental protocols and methodologies and especially the effect of α-ketobutyrate occurring in assays depending on its accumulation, have often resulted in contradictory or inconsistent results both within and between laboratory groups. This has led to proposals of two somewhat different models for the role of oligomerization and AMP in regulation of catalytic activity.

Drs. Shizuta and Hayaishi (1976) have proposed (Fig. 1), largely on the basis of their work, that: dehydrase monomers have catalytic activity but a low affinity for L-threonine (extreme left); AMP causes dimer formation (reaction 1); dimers have a high affinity for L-threonine but are inactive (reaction 2); dimers with L-threonine, or intermediates bound, dissociate to yield active monomers with either L-threonine, intermediates, or products bound (reaction 3); and following conversion to product (reactions 4,5) dissociation of product to yield monomers ready to enter a second catalytic cycle (reaction 6). A more complex version of this scheme by Shizuta and Hayaishi (1976) increases the number of branches and options that apply with and without AMP and at high and low protein concentrations. However, Fig. 1 contains the unique feature which seems to predominate in the model, i.e., association and dissociation in each reaction cycle. This model was devised to accommodate the observed changes in K_m and

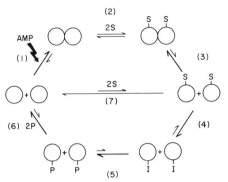

Fig. 1. A hypothetical role of association–dissociation in the enzyme reaction according to Shizuta and Hayaishi (1976). Circles depict monomers, S = L-threonine, I = intermediates, and P = product.

activity caused by AMP at some dehydrase concentrations, as well as the oligomerization observed in the presence and absence of AMP and especially the lack of AMP activation at high dehydrase concentrations. They have assumed that oligomers formed in the absence and presence of AMP are essentially the same.

We have studied the ligand-induced association mostly at low dehydrase concentrations under conditions where the α-ketobutyrate steady state concentration is always about 10^{-6} M (Dunne *et al.*, 1973); the K_i for α-ketobutyrate is reported to be 5×10^{-3} M (Shizuta *et al.*, 1973). Thus, an inhibition by α-ketobutyrate does not occur. This work has led us to propose a simpler model (Fig. 2) (Dunne *et al.*, 1974) in which: (1) the dehydrase, in the absence of AMP, exists as a monomer with a high K_m for L-threonine; (2) AMP binding

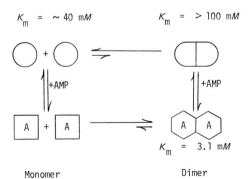

Fig. 2. Model for activation of threonine dehydrase according to Dunne *et al.* (1974). A represents the binding of AMP.

causes a first-order conformational change in monomers; (3) monomers undergo a second-order dimerization; and (4) the dimers undergo a first-order conformational change to yield different dimers which have a low K_m for L-threonine. In our model, the dimer is active rather than being inactive as in the Shizuta–Hayaishi model. Since the K_m for dimers formed at high protein concentration in the absence of AMP is higher rather than lower (Gerlt *et al.*, 1973), it is concluded that such dimers differ materially from those formed in the presence of AMP.

Major attention has been directed to establish firmly the main feature of our model, i.e., that both AMP binding and dimerization are required for the K_m change rather than one of these, for instance oligomerization, being incidental.

RESULTS

Active Enzyme Centrifugation

The sedimentation velocity of the molecular species which are engaged in catalysis was determined essentially as described by Kemper and Everse (1973) and Cohen and Mire (1971). A band of L-threonine dehydrase was layered on a

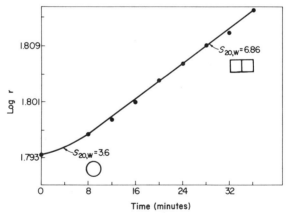

Fig. 3. Association of active threonine dehydrase monomers on addition of AMP. AMP-free dehydrase was layered on an assay column containing AMP. Centrifugation was at 60,000 rpm and 20° in an An-F Ti Rotor. The monochromotor was set at 310 nm to measure α-ketobutyrate. The assay solution consisted of 0.075 M potassium phosphate, pH 8.0, 5 mM DTT, 5 mM AMP, and 100 mM L-threonine. The enzyme was diluted to a concentration of 8 μg/ml in 0.01 M potassium phosphate, pH 8.0, 5 mM DTT and 100 mM D-threonine. The sedimentation coefficient was corrected for viscosity and density.

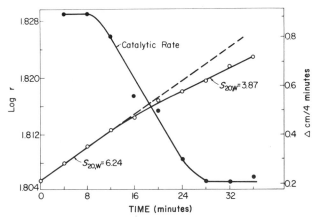

Fig. 4. Dissociation of active threonine dehydrase oligomer on removal of AMP. The dehydrase in an AMP-containing solution was layered on a liquid column containing the catalytic assay components but not AMP. Centrifugation conditions were as in Fig. 3. The assay solution consisted of 0.075 M potassium phosphate, pH 8.0, 5 mM DTT and 100 mM L-threonine. The enzyme was diluted to 12.9 μg/ml in 0.01 M potassium phosphate, pH 8.0, 5 mM DTT, and 5 mM AMP. The open circles represent the sedimentation data and refer to the left-hand axis; the relative activity is represented by the closed circles and refers to the right-hand axis. The sedimentation coefficients were corrected for density and viscosity.

liquid column in an ultracentrifuge rotor containing all components of the assay system. In some instances horseshoe crab lactic dehydrogenase ($S = 3.95$; Long and Kaplan, 1973) and NADH were used in a coupled assay observed at 340 nm (Dunne *et al.*, 1973). Test runs showed that the lactic dehydrogenase concentration across the liquid column was nonlimiting on the measured rate of catalysis. In other experiments, the accumulated α-ketobutyrate was measured directly at 310 nm. Figure 3 shows the behavior of a band of dehydrase (8 μg/ml) in the absence of AMP which was layered on a liquid column containing the components of the assay system and also AMP. As the dehydrase encounters AMP during its migration down the liquid column, the sedimentation velocity increases from 3.6 to 6.86 S. This reflects a conversion of catalytically active monomers to catalytically active dimers. In the inverse situation, shown in Fig. 4, dehydrase diluted to 12.9 μg/ml in the presence of 5 mM AMP and layered on liquid column containing an assay mixture without AMP, decreases from a sedimentation velocity of 6.24 to 3.87 S, which is equivalent to dissociation of dimers into monomers. The catalytic rate, as calculated from the ΔA values from one time scan to the next shows the expected approximately four- to fivefold decrease in catalytic activity which coincides with the decrease in sedimentation velocity. This reflects the 15-fold increase in K_m that occurs on the removal of AMP. These results firmly establish that both K_m and molecular weight changes occur in the catalytic species under the same environmental conditions and protein concentrations. Similar molecular weight changes under catalytic conditions, but assayed separately, were observed by sucrose gradient centrifugation (Whanger *et al.*, 1968).

Shizuta and Hayaishi (1976) have postulated that when AMP is present, both monomeric and dimeric species participate in catalysis in sequential fashion. Under such conditions the observed sedimentation velocity for such a rapidly associating and dissociating system should be intermediate between the sedimentation velocity values for monomer and dimer, with the position depending on the life times of the two forms. Under the conditions of these experiments, i.e., low protein concentrations such an intermediate sedimentation velocity was not observed; in fact, the value in the presence of AMP is somewhat higher than would be expected for a globular dimeric protein of 72,000–80,000 MW.

These and similar data permit the use of changes in activity at constant dehydrase concentration as an indicator of changes in the state of oligomerization due to addition or removal of AMP. This property has been utilized in subsequent investigations of the mechanism of activation.

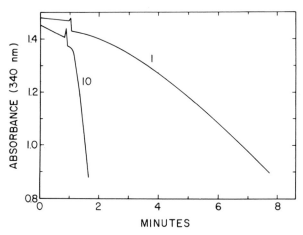

Fig. 5. Hysteresis in the activation of threonine dehydrase by AMP. Changes in the absorbance in a stirred cuvette containing 1 mM DTT, 0.275 mM NADH, 1 mg/ml bovine heart LDH, 0.1 M potassium phosphate, pH 8.0, and either 0.035 or 0.35 IU of dehydrase (designated by 1 or 10 in the figure) were measured before and after the addition of 0.05 ml of 200 mM potassium AMP, pH 8.0 (at the spike). Data were collected and stored as described by LeBlond et al. (1980a,b). The solid lines represent tracings of data plotted using an HP 7200 flat bed plotter interfaced to the HP 9815A programmable calculator.

Protein Concentration Order for Activation

When AMP is added to a low concentration of AMP-free dehydrase (monomers; Menson, 1976) in a complete assay system, there is a hysteretic[1] activation process whose rate is dehydrase concentration dependent (Fig. 5). The increase in activity is equivalent to the increase in the amount of AMP-activated dimers. Numerical differentation of the curve (Gerlt et al., 1973) gives the reaction rate at anytime (a line tangent to the curve at time t). Straight lines representing the rate at various times or stages of activation have slopes that are proportional to the rates of activation at each protein concentration (second derivative of the time course of activation curve). Recent determinations using higher data collection rates (LeBlond et al., 1980a,b) and over a 50-fold greater range of protein concentrations yielded a protein concentration order of 2.01 ± 0.06 (Fig. 6).[2] These data, like those of Gerlt et al. (1973), are most easily interpreted as indicating that the second-order process of dimerization is rate

---

[1]It is assumed that addition of AMP results in instantaneous AMP binding to the monomeric dehydrase. The subsequent slow increase in velocity resulting from protein structure changes fits the terminology of Frieden (1970). For threonine dehydrase, the slow response results from a rate limiting dimerization of AMP-liganded monomers.

[2]In the absence of AMP, unactivated threonine dehydrase displays low activity in the normal assay. Thus, $V_a = L(V_L - V_f) + L_0V_f$, where V_a is the activation rate, L is the dehydrase monomer concentration at any time, L_0 is the initial monomer concentration, V_L and V_f are the unactivated and fully activated rates of dehydration in IU nmol^{-1} corresponding to the rates for monomer and dimer.

$$dV/dt = dL/dt\ (V_L - V_f) \tag{1}$$

also

$$dL/dt = k_2L^2 \tag{2}$$

where k_2 is the second-order monomer association constant.

$$dL/dt = k_2L^2\ (V_f - V_L) \tag{3}$$

$$\log(dV_a/dt) = 2 \log L + \log k_2\ (V_f - V_L) \tag{4}$$

It has been shown (LeBlond, 1980) that $\dfrac{V_f}{V_L} = 20$, therefore $V_f \gg V_L$.

Hence,

$$y \text{ intercept} = \log k_2V_f \tag{5}$$

$$k_2 = \frac{10^{(\text{intercept})}}{V_f} = \frac{10^{14.49}\ ^{\text{IU}}\text{ml}^{-1}\text{ min}^{-1}}{(480\ \text{IU/mg})(40{,}000\ \text{mg/ml})\ 60\ \text{sec min}^{-1}}$$

$$k_2 = 2.7 \pm 0.5 \times 10^5\ M^{-1}\ \text{sec}^{-1}$$

The line in Fig. 6 is derived from a least squares fit to the data
$$y = 2.02 \pm 0.06x + 14.49 \pm 0.5b$$

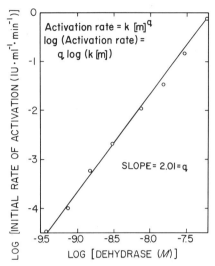

Fig. 6. Determination of the protein order (q) of the initial rate of threonine dehydrase activation by AMP. Initial rates of activation were determined from the data in Fig. 5 by least squares fits of sets of 11 data points to straight lines (LeBlond et al., 1980a,b). The dehydrase monomer concentration was calculated from the amount added (in IU) to the cuvette (from Fig. 5), a monomer MW of 40,000 and a maximum specific activity of 480 IU/mg. The line is a least squares fit through the points.

limiting and is necessary for the observed increase in rate (mostly due to the decreased K_m).

To determine independently the order of the activation process caused by AMP, time–velocity data (Fig. 5) were fit to linear transformations of either the second[3]- or the first[4]-order integrated rate equation.

In this analysis there is uncertainty in the value to use for V_f, the velocity at

[3]Integrated second-order rate equation

$$\frac{V_f}{V_f - V} = \frac{(L_0 k_2 t + 1) V_f}{V_f - V_s} \qquad (6)$$

$$y \text{ intercept} = \frac{V_f}{V_f - V_s}$$

$$\text{slope} = L_0 k_2 \quad \left(\frac{V_f}{V_f - V_s}\right) \quad \div \quad \left(\frac{V_f}{V_f - V_s}\right) \quad = L_0 k_2$$

In a plot of L_0 vs $L_0 k_2$, the slope $= k_2$, where V_f, V_s, and V are rates for dimer, monomer, and that at time t, L_0 is initial concentration of monomer, k_2 is the second-order constant, and t is time.

[4]Integrated first-order rate equation

$$\ln \frac{V_f}{V_f - V} = k_1 t + \ln \frac{V_f}{V_f - V_s} \qquad (7)$$

where the notation is the same as in footnote 3.

maximum activation. This value may be obtained from the amount of enzyme used and a specific activity of 480 IU/mg. However, this assumes no inactivation or inhibition. Alternatively the value of V_f can be adjusted using an iteration routine in the computer program to maximize the strength of the linear fit. Using the best V_f value, the data may be compared to the theoretical line in a differential plot of dehydrase activity vs min^{-1} (Fig. 7).

Although the second-order fit was slightly better, statistically, the data correlated well with either first- or second-order models because the curves were similar in the region where data were available. The V_f value derived for the second-order fit was 0.064 IU compared to 0.0638 IU added, based on the standard activity assay. In contrast, the calculated V_f value for a first-order fit was 0.057 IU, which could occur only with 11% inactivation, and for which there is no experimental evidence.

Using a V_f value of 0.0638 IU, plots of $[V_f$ (AMP activated dimer)$]/[V_f - V$ (at any time)$]$ vs time^3 were linear (Fig. 8), whereas plots of ln $V_f/(V_f - V)$ vs time^4 were curved (not shown). These results are consistent with a second-order process for activation (LeBlond, 1980).

Thus, both active enzyme centrifugation and activation kinetics established that dimerization of monomers and activation due to AMP are linked.

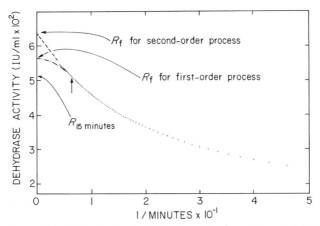

Fig. 7. Approach to full activation by AMP. To a stirred cuvette containing 1 mM DDT, 0.275 mM NADH, 1 mg/ml bovine heart LDH, 0.1 M potassium phosphate, pH 8.0, and 0.12 × 8 IU of threonine dehydrase in a 2 ml volume, was added 0.05 ml of 200 mM potassium AMP, pH 8.0. The catalytic reaction was followed at 340 nm and reaction rates calculated as described in the text for Fig. 5 and by LeBlond et al. (1980a,b). V_f values expected for the first[4]- and second[3]-order processes were estimated by a parabolic search which maximized the strength of linear fits to either Eq. 7 or 6. The V_L value for these fits were obtained from the reaction rates observed prior to the addition of AMP. Dehydrase monomer concentration (L_0) was obtained assuming an MW of 40,000 and a specific activity of 480 IU/mg. Theoretical lines for second-order (---) or first-order (-·-·-) were calculated from the optimized fits of Eq. 6 or 7 to the data.

Rate Constants for Dimerization and Catalysis

A rate constant for dimerization can be calculated from the second-order plot of log inital activation rate vs log of dehydrase concentration[2] (Fig. 6); with a y intercept of 14.49, the rate constant is $2.7 \times 10^5 \ M^{-1} \ sec^{-1}$. Although this value may be in error by an order of magnitude as indicated by the high standard deviation of the intercept (± 0.5), the value is in reasonably good agreement with rate constants derived from second-order plots or calculated from the diffusion equation (see below).

As already shown (Fig. 8), second-order plots using the amount of enzyme added in IU as the maximum activated velocity (V_f) were linear over at least a tenfold range of protein concentration. A plot of the slope/intercept ratios from lines in Fig. 8 vs protein concentration[3] yields a straight line passing near the origin with a correlation coefficient of 0.967 (Fig. 9). This slope gives a better estimate of the second-order rate constant for activation, and yields a value of $8.8 \pm 1.0 \times 10^5 \ M^{-1} \ sec^{-1}$. As indicated above, a first-order plot similar to the second-order plot in Fig. 8 yields curved lines. After adjusting the V_f value to give straight line, first-order plots of the data ($V_f = 0.058$), a plot of slope/intercept ratios vs protein concentrations, similar to that in Fig. 9, shows a dependency on protein concentration. This is inconsistent with a first-order protein concentration dependency; instead, it is characteristic of a second-order process.

The upper limit of the rate constant for dimerization or activation can be

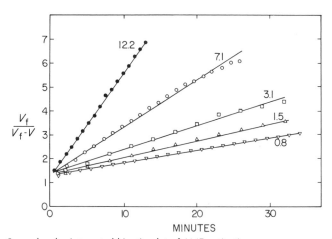

Fig. 8. Second-order integrated kinetic plot of AMP-activation progress curves. Data from activation progress curves similar to those described in Fig. 5 were differentiated as described by LeBlond et al. (1980a,b). The numbers adjacent to the lines give the enzyme concentration during the activation process in IU/ml $\times 10^{-2}$. Catalytic activity was determined at 385.2 nm ($\square$, $\circ$, $\bullet$), 372.5 nm ($\triangle$), and 340 nm ($\triangledown$).

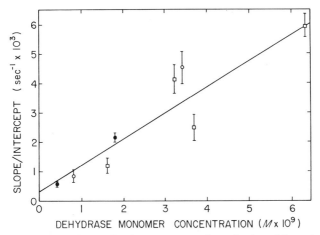

Fig. 9. Determination of second-order rate constant for activation of threonine dehydrase by AMP. Slopes and intercepts were obtained from Fig. 7 (data from two additional experiments are included) and the ratio of slope to intercept plotted vs dehydrase concentration. The catalytic reaction was followed by measuring the absorbance at 340 nm (●), 372.5 nm (○), or 382.5 nm (□). The bars represent the approximate standard deviation of the slope/intercept ratio determined from slope and intercept variances in the least squares fits of Fig. 7. The weighted data were fitted to a least squares line and k_2 was calculated from this slope according to Eq. 5. The value of k_2 and its approximate standard deviation were determined from this analysis.

calculated (with several assumptions) from Koren and Hammes (1976).[5] A rate constant for activation of $9 \times 10^5 \ M^{-1} \ \text{sec}^{-1}$ was obtained in this manner, whereas a value of $7 \times 10^5 \ M^{-1} \ \text{sec}^{-1}$ has also been reported (Shizuta *et al.*, 1969). Thus,

[5]From Koren and Hammes (1976),

$$k_2 = \frac{8\pi N\alpha Des}{1000} \tag{8}$$

where k_2 is the second-order rate constant for conversion of monomers to dimers, N is Avagadro's number, and α is the closest approach distance of two monomers, i.e., two times the monomer radius. D is the diffusion coefficient, e is a factor for electrostatic interaction between monomers, and s is a steric factor to account for the restricted approach of two monomers.

By combining Eq. 8 with Fick's first law of diffusion for spherical particles

$$D = \frac{RT}{hf} \tag{9}$$

where D is the diffusion coefficient, R is the gas constant, T is the temperature in °K, f is the frictional coefficient, and h is the viscosity,

$$k_2 = \frac{8\pi N\alpha RTes}{1000 \ hf} \tag{10}$$

For this calculation the diffusion coefficient determined for tetramers (Shizuta *et al.*, 1969) has

2.5-9 × 10⁵ is a reasonable estimate for this constant and suggests that the dimerization process may be diffusion-limited (Gutfreund, 1972).

For a cyclic process in the presence of AMP as postulated by Shizuta and Hayaishi (1976) in which there is both monomer association and dimer dissociation in each cycle, the observed rate of catalysis cannot exceed the rate of association.

$$[\text{monomer}]k_{\text{cat}} = [\text{monomer}]^2 k_{\text{assoc}}$$
(first order)　　(second order)

The k_{cat} value for threonine dehydration is 3.2×10^{-2} sec^{-1}.[6] Thus, in a calculation[7] of the minimum dehydrase concentration giving the observed velocity, the monomer concentration must equal or exceed 3.55^{-4} M or about 14.2 mg/ml for the rate of association to be non-rate limiting on the known rate of catalysis. Even correcting for the reported diminished catalytic rate at high protein concentrations (> 1 mg/ml), the dehydrase concentration required for association–dissociation to be nonrate limiting would have to be higher than that present.

Effect of Viscosity on the Rate Constants for Association and Catalysis

It can be shown[5] that the rate constant for dimerization is inversely proportional to viscosity (see Eq. 10, footnote 5). Thus, increasing the viscosity of the medium should lower the rate constant for association. In the simplest case, if association is necessary for catalysis as in the Shizuta–Hayaishi model, increasing the viscosity should decrease the association rate and the catalytic rate similarly.

When activation progress curves were run at increasing sucrose concentrations, the second-order activation or association constant decreased as shown in Fig. 10. As predicted by Eq. 10 (footnote 5), the data fit a straight line with a correlation coefficient of 0.935. In interpreting this result it is assumed that sucrose had no effects other than changing the viscosity of the medium. Because oligomer formation has been readily observed even at very low protein concen-

---

been used, α was taken at 80 Å; the electrostatic factor used was that of chymotrypsin, 10^{-2}, although Koren and Hammes (1976) have calculated values as low as 10^{-3} for β-lactoglobulin; s was taken as 2% of the 4π solid angle as used by Koren and Hammes (1976).

[6] $k_{\text{cat}} = \dfrac{(480 \ \mu\text{mol/min/mg})(40{,}000 \ \text{mg}/\mu\text{mol})}{60 \ \text{sec/min}}$

$k_{\text{cat}} = 3.2 \times 10^2$ sec^{-1}

[7] $[\text{monomer}] \ 3.2 \times 10^2$ sec$^{-1} = [\text{monomer}]^2 \ 9 \times 10^5 \ M^{-1}$ sec

$\qquad [\text{monomer}] = 3.5 \times 10^{-4} \ M$

$\qquad\qquad\qquad\quad = 3.5 \times 10^{-4} \times 40{,}000 = 14.2$ mg/ml

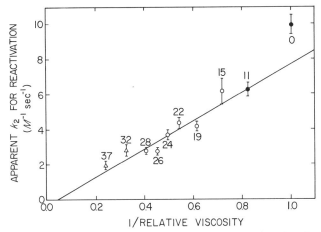

Fig. 10. Dependence of second-order reactivation rate constant on viscosity. The apparent k_2 for reactivation was determined from reactivation progress curve data as described in Fig. 5 and in the text. Either 2 (●), 4 (○), or 6 (△) μg of dehydrase (specific activity 463 IU/ml) were added to the stirred cuvette. Error bars on the data points represent the standard deviations of the determined k_2 values and were used to weight the fit of the data to the least squares line indicated in the figure. The numbers adjacent to each point give the sucrose concentration (%, w/v) in the activation mixture.

trations (ca. 0.02 μg/ml) in sucrose 5–20% gradients (Whanger *et al.*, 1968), a major decrease in association constant seems unlikely at least at the lower sucrose concentrations used. V_f, the velocity at maximum activation used in these calculations, was derived from separate determinations of catalytic rate in the standard assay with the corresponding amount of sucrose added. At the highest sucrose concentration the dehydrase activity decreased twofold; under the same conditions the rate constant for activation of the dehydrase by AMP decreased fivefold. These results seem to indicate that there is a differential effect of sucrose on association and catalytic activity such that the catalytic rate does not depend on association of monomers in each catalytic cycle.

Ultracentrifugation in the Absence of AMP

The possibility that dimerization of monomers occurs under conditions in Fig. 5 before addition of AMP was tested by determining the sedimentation velocity at two dehydrase concentrations (Fig. 11). From $S_{20,w}$ values of 3.6 and 6.6 at 8.4 IU (17.5 μg/ml) and 107 IU (223 μg/ml), the dissociation constant for dimers can be calculated to be between 5 and 50 × 10^{-7} *M*; a value of 117 × 10^{-7} was calculated (Menson, 1976) from active enzyme centrifugation experiments which contained higher concentrations of salt carried in with the high

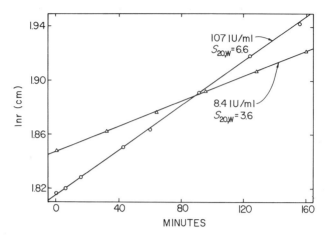

Fig. 11. Boundary sedimentation velocity of threonine dehydrase in the absence of AMP as a function of enzyme concentration. Ultracentrifugation of the dehydrase in the absence of AMP was carried out at 44,000 rpm and at 20°. The photometer was set to either 280 nm (O) or 230 nm (Δ). AMP was removed by filtration through Sephadex G-25 (20 cm). The dehydrase was diluted in 1 mM DTT, 1 mM EDTA, 0.1 M potassium phosphate, pH 8.0, maintained for 5° on ice, centrifuged and assayed before filling the ultracentrifuge cell. Distance to the center of rotation was calculated from the inflection point of scanner tracings. A partial specific volume of 0.738 ml/gm was used for calculation of sedimentation coefficients. The enzyme concentration of the centrifuged solutions are given in the figure. Best fit lines through the points were determined by least squares regression.

levels of lactate dehydrogenase, as well as from the reagents of the catalytic assay. From this it can be calculated (Anderson, 1971; Kirschner and Tanford, 1964)[8] that for 1.1 IU/ml of dehydrase, which is the highest concentration used in activation experiments, that less than 16% of the dehydrase would be in the dimer form before addition of AMP.

Thus, these data do not suggest a prominent role for dimerization in the absence of AMP in the rate limiting activation process. Rather, they suggest an explanation for the very rapid but only fractional activation observed when AMP is added and is followed by the slower protein concentration dependent activation

[8]From Kirshner and Tanford (1964)

$$\alpha = \frac{S_D - S_{obs}}{S_D - S_M} \qquad (11)$$

and Anderson (1971)

$$k_{2,1} = \frac{2\alpha^2 C}{(1 - \alpha)MW} \qquad (12)$$

where α is the degree of dissociation, S_D, S_{obs}, and S_M are sedimentation coefficients for dimer, observed sample, and monomer, $k_{2,1}$ is the dimer to monomer dissociation constant, C is the dehydrase concentration in mg/ml, and MW is the molecular weight of the protomer.

(Fig. 5). This rapid activation on AMP binding would result from a very rapid conformational isomerization of a small amount of preexistent dimers and would be expected if such dimers did not dissociate and reassociate before activation occurred. This process would be rapid because it is first order and not diffusion-limited.

SUMMARY

New data are presented to demonstrate that the activation of L-threonine dehydratase of *E. coli* by AMP requires dimerization of the monomeric dehydrase. Active enzyme centrifugation demonstrated a large increase in sedimentation velocity, consistent with a dimerization process on encountering AMP, and a similar spontaneous decrease in sedimentation velocity on removal of AMP. Analysis of the hysteretic activation process showed the rate limiting step to be second order in protein concentration and gave usable estimates of the rate constant for dimerization. From k_{cat} and the rate constant for association, it was shown that the model for AMP activation proposed by Shizuta and Hayaishi (1976) involving dimer–monomer dissociation and monomer–dimer association in each catalytic cycle could not occur at rates consistent with observed catalytic rates unless the monomer concentration was much in excess of 1 mg/ml. Therefore, a model for the activation process involving binding of AMP to high K_m monomers, a first-order conformational change in AMP-liganded monomers, second-order dimerization of monomers with AMP, and first-order conformational changes in AMP dimers to give low K_m dimers with AMP seems to be favored.

ACKNOWLEDGMENT

Supported by a National Science Foundation Grant PCM 77-08586. Contribution No. 9771, Michigan Agricultural Experiment Station.

REFERENCES

Anderson, M. E. (1971). Sedimentation equilibrium experiments on the self-association of hemoglobin from the lamprey *Petromyzon marinus*. *J. Biol. Chem.* **246**, 4800–4806.

Bellamy, W. D., Umbreit, W. W., and Gunsalus, I. C. (1945). The function of pyridoxine: Conversion of members of the vitamin B_6 group into codecarboxylase. *J. Biol. Chem.* **160**, 461–472.

Braunstein, A. E., and Shemyakin, M. M. (1953). A theory of amino acid metabolic processes catalyzed by pyridoxal-dependent enzymes. *Biokhimiya* **18**, 393–411.

Chargaff, E., and Sprinson, D. B. (1943). The mechanism of deamination of serine by *Bacterium coli*. *J. Biol. Chem.* **148**, 249–250.

Cohen, R., and Mire, M. (1971). Analytical-band centrifugation of an active enzyme–substrate complex. 1. Principle and practice of the centrifugation. *Eur. J. Biochem.* **23**, 267–275.

Cori, G. T., and Cori, C. F. (1936). The formation of hexosephosphate esters in frog muscle. *J. Biol. Chem.* **116**, 119–128.

Dunne, C. P., and Wood, W. A. (1975). L-Threonine dehydrase as a model of allosteric control involving ligand-induced oligomerization. *Curr. Top. Cell. Regul.* **9**, 65–101.

Dunne, C. P., Gerlt, J. A., Rabinowitz, K. W., and Wood, W. A. (1973). The mechanism of action of 5′ adenylic acid-activated threonine dehydrase. IV. Characterization of kinetic effect of adenosine monophosphate. *J. Biol. Chem.* **248**, 8189–8199.

Dunne, C. P., Menson, R. C., Gerlt, J. A., and Wood, W. A. (1974). Regulation of L-threonine dehydrase via ligand-induced oligomerization. *In* "Metabolic Interconversion of Enzymes 1973" (E. H. Fischer, E. G. Krebs, H. Neurath, and E. R. Stadtman, eds.), pp. 349–360. Springer-Verlag, Berlin and New York.

Feldman, D. A., and Datta, P. (1975). Catabolite inactivation of biodegradative threonine dehydratase of *Escherichia coli. Biochemistry* **14**, 1760–1767.

Frieden, C. (1970). Kinetic aspects of regulation of metabolic processes: The hysteretic effect. *J. Biol. Chem.*. **245**, 5788–5799.

Gerlt, J. A., Rabinowitz, K. W., Dunne, C. P., and Wood, W. A. (1973). The mechanism of action of 5′-adenylic acid-activated threonine dehydrase. V. Relation between ligand-induced allosteric activation and protomer–oligomer interconversion. *J. Biol. Chem.* **248**, 8200–8206.

Gunsalus, I. C., and Umbreit, W. W. (1947). Codecarboxylase not the 3-phosphate of pyridoxal. *J. Biol. Chem.* **170**, 415–416.

Gunsalus, I. C., Bellamy, W. D., and Umbreit, W. W. (1944). A phosphorylated derivative of pyridoxal as the coenzyme of tyrosine decarboxylase. *J. Biol. Chem.* **155**, 685–686.

Gunsalus, I. C., Umbreit, W. W., Bellamy, W. D., and Foust, C. E. (1945). Some properties of synthetic codecarboxylase. *J. Biol. Chem.* **161**, 743–744.

Gutfreund, H. (1972). "Enzymes; Physical Principles," pp. 159–160. Wiley (Interscience), New York.

Kemper, D. L., and Everse, J. (1973). Active enzyme centrifugation. *In* "Methods in Enzymology" (C. H. W. Hirs and S. N. Timasheff, eds.), Vol. 27, pp. 67–82. Academic Press, New York.

Kirshner, A. G., and Tanford, C. (1964). The dissociation of hemoglobin by inorganic salts. *Biochemistry* **3**, 291–296.

Koren, R., and Hammes, G. (1976). A kinetic study of protein–protein interactions. *Biochemistry* **15**, 1165–1170.

LeBlond, D. J. (1980). Importance of dimerization in the adenosine 5′ monophosphate activation of biodegradative L-threonine dehydrase from *Escherichia coli*. Ph.D. Thesis, Michigan State Univ., East Lansing.

LeBlond, D. J., Ashendel, C. L., and Wood, W. A. (1980a). Determination of enzyme kinetic parameters by continuous addition of substrate to a single reaction mixture and analysis by a tangent–slope procedure. I. Analysis of the method using computed progress curves. *Anal. Biochem.* **104**, 355–369.

LeBlond, D. J., Ashendel, C. L., and Wood, W. A. (1980b). Determination of enzyme kinetic parameters by continuous addition of substrate to a single reaction mixture and analysis by a tangent–slope procedure. II. Application of the method of soluble and immobilized enzymes. *Anal. Biochem.* **104**, 370–385.

Lichstein, H. C., Gunsalus, I. C., and Umbreit, W. W. (1945). Function of the vitamin B_6 group: Pyridoxal phosphate (codecarboxylase) in transamination. *J. Biol. Chem.* **161**, 311–320.

Long, G. L., and Kaplan, N. O. (1973). Diphosphopyridine nucleotide linked D-lactate dehydrogenases from the horseshoe crab, *Limulus polyphemus* and the seaworm *Nereis virens. Arch. Biochem. Biophys.* **154**, 696–710.

Menson, R. C. (1976). Active species and quaternary structure of biodegradative L-threonine dehydrase from *Escherichia coli*. Ph.D. Thesis, Michigan State Univ., East Lansing.

Metzler, D. E., Ikawa, M., and Snell, E. E. (1954). A general mechanism of vitamin B_6-catalyzed reactions. *J. Am. Chem. Soc.* **76**, 648-652.

O'Kane, D. E., and Gunsalus, I. C. (1947). The resolution and purification of glutamic-aspartic transaminase. *J. Biol. Chem.* **170**, 425-432.

Phillips, A. T., and Wood, W. A. (1965). The mechanism of action of 5'-adenylic acid-activated threonine dehydrase. *J. Biol. Chem.* **240**, 4703-4709.

Shizuta, Y., and Hayaishi, O. (1976). Regulation of biodegradative threonine deaminase. *Curr. Top. Cell. Regul.* **11**, 99-146.

Shizuta, Y., Nakazawa, A., Tokushige, M., and Hayaishi, O. (1969). Studies on the interaction between regulatory enzymes and effectors. III. Crystallization and characterization of adenosine 5'-monophosphate-dependent threonine deaminase from *Escherichia coli*. *J. Biol. Chem.* **244**, 1883-1889.

Shizuta, Y., Kurosawa, A., Inoue, K., Tanabe, T., and Hayaishi, O. (1973). Regulation of biodegradative threonine deaminase. I. Allosteric inhibition of the enzyme by a reaction product and its reversal by adenosine 5'-monophosphate. *J. Biol. Chem.* **248**, 512-520.

Tokushige, M., and Nakazawa, A. (1972). Spectral and regulatory properties of biodegradative threonine deaminase. *J. Biochem. (Tokyo)* **72**, 713-722.

Umbarger, H. E., and Brown, B. (1957). Threonine deamination in *Escherichia coli*. II. Evidence for two L-threonine deaminases. *J. Bacteriol.* **73**, 105-112.

Umbreit, W. W., and Gunsalus, I. C. (1945). The function of pyridoxine derivatives: Arginine and glutamic acid decarboxylases. *J. Biol. Chem.* **159**, 333-341.

Umbreit, W. W., Bellamy, W. D., and Gunsalus, I. C. (1945). The function of pyridoxine derivatives: A comparison of natural and synthetic codecarboxylase. *Arch. Biochem.* **7**, 185-199.

Umbreit, W. W., O'Kane, D. J., and Gunsalus, I. C. (1946a). Mechanism of pyridoxial phosphate function in bacterial transamination. *J. Bacteriol.* **51**, 576.

Umbreit, W. W., Wood, W. A., and Gunsalus, I. C. (1946b). The activity of pyridoxal phosphate in tryptophane formation by cell-free enzyme preparations. *J. Biol. Chem.* **165**, 731-732.

Whanger, P. D., Phillips, A. T., Rabinowitz, K. W., Piperno, J. R., Shada, J. D., and Wood, W. A. (1968). Mechanism of action of 5'-adenylic acid-activated threonine dehydrase. II. Protomer-oligomer interconversions and related properties. *J. Biol. Chem.* **243**, 167-173.

Wood, W. A. (1969). Allosteric L-threonine dehydrases of microorganisms. *Curr. Top. Cell. Regul.* **1**, 161-182.

Wood, W. A., and Gunsalus, I. C. (1949). Serine and threonine deaminases of *Escherichia coli*: Activators for a cell-free enzyme. *J. Biol. Chem.* **181**, 171-182.

Wood, W. A., Gunsalus, I. C., and Umbreit, W. W. (1947). Function of pyridoxal phosphate: Resolution and purification of the tryptophanase enzyme of *Escherichia coli*. *J. Biol. Chem.* **170**, 313-321.

15

Organization
and Expression
of an *E. coli* Cluster
of Genes Involved in
the Translation Process

Marianne Grunberg-Manago

When I first started research, I was interested in the mechanism of intermediary metabolism and attracted by the main area of Gunny's interest—but the discovery of polynucleotide phosphorylase switched my work toward gene expression and our field of research diverged until recently when our interests converged again with the progress of recombinant DNA.

However, I feel that my 9-month stay in Gunny's lab in 1953 had a tremendous impact on my scientific activity. More important than picking up new facts or new techniques was learning Gunny's way of approaching a scientific problem.

His extremely critical mind and uncompromising scientific honesty which does not tolerate the slightest departure from the facts is accompanied by a rich imagination and an intuition enabling his research to escape from beaten tracks. Discussing experimental results with Gunny and hearing him give seminars (far from classically didactic but revealing the way his mind works) was a fascinating experience for me.

With his knowledge in microbiology and biochemistry, as well as organic chemistry and physics, Gunny can easily assert that ''The technique does not determine the problem, but the problem defines the technique.''

After leaving Gunny's group, when I came to Severo Ochoa's lab, I had not

EXPERIENCES IN BIOCHEMICAL PERCEPTION
Copyright © 1982 by Academic Press, Inc.
All rights of reproduction in any form reserved.
ISBN 0-12-528420-9

only acquired a good training as an enzymologist but, more important, had gained self-confidence and complete reliance in my experiments, and was not afraid to pursue them even when the results did not come as expected or did not fit with the generally accepted concepts.

I first met Gunny in Paris during the International Congress of Biochemistry in July, 1952, at a small café near the Sorbonne. It had been agreed with Severo Ochoa that I would join his group in New York by the fall of 1953 after first spending some time with I. C. Gunsalus. I believe Severo was quite happy with the idea of getting a "Gunny-trained" enzymologist. The meeting with Gunny would, hopefully, formulate my plans.

It did not turn out at all as expected, however. I could not understand a single word of his rapid verbal flow and was so confused that I forgot any English I knew. Although I was reassured by his benevolent smile, I could not make out whether or not he agreed to my joining his group. I asked G. Cohen who had been present what Dr. Gunsalus had said and George answered "it was not important." I guess he had not understood Gunny either. I then awaited a letter—when it finally came it was nice, but vague, with a handwritten postscript that I felt was important but that neither I nor anybody else in the lab could decipher. This did not discourage me and in February, 1953, my husband and I came to Urbana after a boat trip during a winter storm and hours of riding a train from New York. We were both amazed at the size of the United States and how much Urbana differed from New York. Since then, we have learned to understand Gunny (albeit not always his scrawl) and to like Urbana both in winter and in summer, and a solid friendship has arisen which only grew deeper as the years have passed.

The enzyme we studied in Urbana, citritase (Grunberg-Manago and Gunsalus, 1953), not only introduced me to enzymology but also to the United States as well, because it gave us the opportunity for a wonderful drive to San Francisco where I presented the work.

From citritase (Grunberg-Manago and Gunsalus, 1953) and acetokinase (Rose *et al.,* 1954), which completed my training as an enzymologist in New York, the discovery of polynucleotide phosphorylase (Grunberg-Manago and Ochoa, 1955) switched my interest to gene expression, but I never forgot my training as an enzymologist and always tried to approach problems with that frame of mind.

ORGANIZATION AND EXPRESSION OF THE INITIATION FACTOR IF3 *E. coli* GENE CLUSTER

One of the central problems in understanding the dynamics of cellular growth is to know how the enzymes required for protein synthesis are regulated. Under conditions of rapid growth, the rate of synthesis of these enzymes is increased in a coordinate manner over the rate found in slowly growing cells (Maalhe, 1979), but the levels of the different components of the synthesizing machinery vary by two orders of magnitude. The components (protein and RNA) of the translational machinery are coded by more than 100 genes found scattered throughout the *E. coli* chromosome (Nomura *et al.*, 1977). Some regions of the chromosome, however, code for clusters of genes involved at different stages of translation (Nomura and Post, 1980). The mechanism of a coordinate expression of the different genes in the different transcriptional units as well as within the individual transcriptional units is unclear.

We were interested in the regulation of the synthesis of protein components involved in the initiation of translation. The three protein factors (IF1, IF2, and IF3) specifically involved in the positioning of initiator tRNA and in the selection of mRNA initiation sites are regulated in response to cell growth rate in parallel with ribosomes (J. Hershey, personal communication).

The aim of our work was to identify and map the structural genes for the initiation factors and to study their expressions together with some of the other translational components. I hope that these studies, in addition to providing results on the regulation of expression of initiation factors, will permit understanding of the role of these proteins *in vivo* which, particularly for IF3 and IF1, is still unknown.

Initiation would appear to be an obvious translational control (Lodish, 1976) and, in fact, there is strong indication that the control of ribosomal protein synthesis occurs precisely at this step (Yates *et al.*, 1980; Dean and Nomura, 1980) as does that of gene 32 protein (Lemaire *et al.*, 1978).

TRANSLATIONAL INITIATION PATHWAYS

Initiation of protein synthesis is the process whereby the ribosomes bind both mRNA and initiator tRNA, fMet-tRNA^{fMet} (Grunberg-Manago *et al.*, 1978; Grunberg-Manago, 1980). This tRNA is specific for the first amino acid which will start the polypeptide chain at its N terminus; initiator tRNA is positioned at a specific "P site" in such a way that it can start the elongation phase of protein synthesis.

The procaryotic process is complex and includes numerous steps; it is catalyzed by the three initiation factors, IF1, IF2, and IF3. These proteins are transitorily associated with the ribosomes from which they can be removed by high salt wash. The different components involved in the initiation process have been identified and purified, and the primary structure of many of them is known. We also have a broad picture of the pathways where they are involved and interact as well as of their location on the ribosome during the different initiation steps.

A brief summary of the initiation sequence is shown below:

$$70 \text{ S} \rightleftharpoons 50 \text{ S} + 30 \text{ S} \tag{1}$$

$$30 \text{ S} + \text{fMet-tRNA}^{\text{fMet}} + \text{mRNA} + \text{GTP} \rightleftharpoons 30 \text{ S fMet-tRNA}^{\text{fMet}} \text{ mRNA GTP} \tag{2}$$

$$50 \text{ S} + 30 \text{ S fMet-tRNA}^{\text{fMet}} \text{ mRNA GTP} \rightleftharpoons 70 \text{ S fMet-tRNA}^{\text{fMet}} \text{ (P) mRNA} + \text{GDP} + \text{P}_i \tag{3}$$

First the 70 S ribosomal couple dissociates into its two subunits, 30 S and 50 S. Under physiological ionic conditions, the equilibrium is toward association and requires the two initiation factors, IF1 and IF3, to dissociate the ribosome into its subunits: IF1 increases the rates of subunit association and dissociation whereas IF3 binds to the 30 S particle, which then becomes unable to find to the 50 S subunit (Godefroy-Colburn *et al.*, 1975). This could be due entirely to a steric hindrance, IF3 being located at the contact region between the subunits (Cooperman *et al.*, 1981), or to a conformational change of the 30 S subunit caused by IF3 binding as has been reported.

In the second step the 30 S subunit forms a preinitiation complex with formyl methionine-tRNA and mRNA. IF3 is required for mRNA binding, whereas IF2, the third initiation factor, is required for initiator tRNA binding; GTP is also required at this step.

IF3 leaves the complex upon fMet-tRNA and mRNA binding; as soon as the factor is released, the 30 S subunit again becomes capable of associating with the 50 S subunit. IF1 is released during association of the two subunits, while IF2 is released from the 70 S complex and requires GTP hydrolysis for this release. The final initiation complex consists of 70 S ribosome, mRNA, and initiator tRNA.

During these steps two critical events take place:

1. The ribosome selects a specific mRNA for translation; our knowledge is scarce in that respect and several regulatory mechanisms have been suggested for IF3 during that process (Lee-Huang and Ochoa, 1971; Revel, 1972).

2. The ribosome selects the region of mRNA containing the proper initiation codon, AUG or GUG. These triplets are not specific for fMet-tRNA coding and discrimination should occur among the numerous triplets coding for Met-tRNA^{Met} or Val-tRNA, AUG or GUG, respectively, and those coding for initiator tRNA (Grunberg-Manago, 1980; Steitz, 1980).

Our understanding of the mechanism of selection of the proper initiation triplet has made considerable progress due to the hypothesis by Shine and Dalgarno (Shine and Dalgarno, 1974). They attributed the selection specificity to the interaction taking place between a polypurine region, located in the vicinity of the 5' end of the initiator triplet, and the 3' terminal sequence of the RNA of the small ribosomal subunit. It has been found that all known initiation regions contain a common purine-rich sequence (Shine and Dalgarno sequence) with a GGAG stretch complementary to the CUCC sequence of the 16 S RNA (Steitz and Steege, 1977; Steitz, 1980). Biochemical and genetic evidence (Steitz, 1980; Steitz and Steege, 1977; Dunn *et al.*, 1978) support this mechanism of selection of the initiation region of mRNA. The Shine and Dalgarno sequence is undoubtedly important for the selection of the mRNA initiation region. A decrease in the homology with the Shine and Dalgarno sequence or a change of position bringing the homologous sequence into a less optimal position markedly reduces the translation efficiency (Roberts *et al.*, 1979; Chang *et al.*, 1980). However, the detailed molecular mechanism is still not understood. For example, a single substitution in the Shine and Dalgarno sequence from GGAGGC to GGGGG considerably decreases the initiation efficiency, whereas thermodynamic calculations suggest that the interaction of these two regions with the complementary segment on the 16 S RNA should not be considerably different (Chang *et al.*, 1980). Furthermore, not all the potential initiator codons approximately juxtaposed to the region with a Shine and Dalgarno sequence are recognized as starting triplets. Finally, we do not understand how protein factors, in particular IF3, affect this interaction.

Isolation of possible lethal mutants for initiation components and particularly for IF3 is necessary to allow a clear demonstration of whether the different elements found *in vitro* are required for protein synthesis *in vivo*.

ISOLATION OF A THERMOSENSITIVE STRAIN CONTAINING A THERMOLABILE IF3

A thermosensitive mutant with a thermolabile IF3 was isolated from a collection of mutants obtained after nitrosoguanidine mutagenesis and enrichment for thermosensitivity by using the tritiated amino acid "suicide" method (Springer *et al.*, 1977a). Cell-free extracts of the thermosensitive mutants were then screened *in vitro* for thermolabile initiation factors. The effect of preincubating the extracts at 40°C was compared for two tests; one, dependent on initiation factor activity, and another, which is not. The first test measured the incorporation, into TCA-precipitable products, of [^{14}C]valine in response to poly(U,G) at 5 mM Mg^{2+}, using precharged aminoacyl-tRNA's; the second measured [^{14}C]phenylalanine incorporation in response to poly(U) at 10 mM Mg^{2+}, using precharged phenylalanyl-tRNA. Both tests are supposed to be insensitive to aminoacyl-tRNA ligase modifications in the extracts. Some mutants did not behave like the parental strain D1 in these tests, and one of them, C18, was studied further (Table I).

When preincubated at 43°C, a 1.5 M ammonium chloride ribosomal wash (crude IF fraction) of C18 shows inactivation kinetics different from those of the wild-type strain. The fMet-tRNA^{fMet} binding capacity of the mutant crude IF fraction is only 36% of its original value after 2 hours of preincubation, whereas

TABLE I

Screening of Thermosensitive Mutants[a]

Strains	% Activity after preincubation		
	[¹⁴C]Phenyl incorporated (2)	[¹⁴C]Val incorporated (1)	½
C18	158	71	0.44
C90	135	72	0.53
C259	77	40	0.51
C38	70	37	0.52
C178	82	96	1.17
D1	102	74	0.72

[a] Effect of preincubation 10 minutes at 40°C on crude extracts (from Springer et al., 1981).

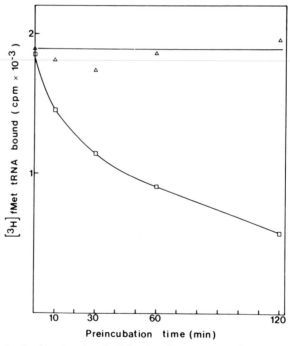

Fig. 1. Inactivation kinetics of crude IF fractions from mutant and parental strains (Springer et al., 1977a). Preincubation was carried out at 43°C. The preincubation mixture contained Tris-HCl (pH 7.5) 50 mM; NH$_4$Cl, 50 mM; Mg acetate, 5 mM. (□) Crude IF fraction from C18 (0.49 mg/ml); (△) crude IF fraction from D1 (0.32 mg/ml).

the activity of the parental strain is stable (Fig. 1). Addition of pure wild-type IF3 prior to preincubation of the mixture eliminated the thermolability of the crude IF fraction from the mutant strain. Subsequently, it was rigorously proved, by comparing different tests, that the defect occurs in the activity of initiation factor IF3. The study of initiation factor IF3 was particularly interesting since, as previously mentioned, it has multiple functions.

The mutation is located near 38 minutes on the *E. coli* genetic map and is 68% cotransducible with the *aroD* marker. The otherwise isogenic strains, AB 1361 and AB 1365, were isolated as thermosensitive and thermoresistant transductants of AB 1360, respectively. This was done by selecting for *aroD*$^+$ transductants of AB 1360 using phage P1virus grown on the thermosensitive strain C18.

Unfortunately, the mutants C18 and AB 1361 were not only modified in the IF3 gene but also in the small subunit of phenylalanyl-tRNA synthetase (Springer *et al.*, 1977a; Hennecke *et al.*, 1977a), and it proved difficult to separate genetically the two defects. However, this mutant enabled isolation of λ-transducing phages complementing its thermosensitivity (Springer *et al.*, 1977b). Such phages integrated in the mutant chromosome, reversing both the mutant thermolability of IF3 (Table II) and its low phenylalanyl-tRNA synthetase activity. One of these phages (λp2) was shown to carry the following structural genes: *infC* for initiation factor IF3 (22,000), *pheS* and *pheT* for the α and β subunits of phenylalanyl-tRNA synthetase (38,000 and 94,000), *thrS* for threonyl-tRNA synthetase (78,000), and *P12* for a 12,000-dalton protein of unidentified function.

The evidence that λp2 phage carries the structural genes for these proteins

TABLE II

Thermolability of Formylmethionyl-tRNA^{fMet} Binding Activity in the Mutant, Lysogen, and Wild-Type Extracts^a

	Preincubation temperature				
	0°C	50°C		55°C	
	cpm	cpm	Activity left (%)	cpm	Activity left (%)
Mutant (AB 1361)	3053	645	21.1	417	13.6
Mutant + λp2 phage	4030	2262	56.1	972	24.1
Mutant + λp7 phage	4891	2853	58.3	1149	23.5
Wild-type (AB 1365)	3726	2529	67.9	864	23.2

^{a} The 55% to 75% saturated (NH$_4$)$_2$ SO$_4$ fractions of the 1.5 *M* NH$_4$Cl ribosome wash were preincubated 30 minutes in 50 m*M* Tris HCl (pH 7.5), 50 m*M* NH$_4$Cl, 5 m*M* Mg acetate (from Springer *et al.*, 1977b).

comes from genetic complementation data and an SDS–polyacrylamide gel electrophoretic analysis of labeled proteins synthesized in uv irradiated cells. After infection of lysogenic strains with λp2, five protein bands appear on polyacrylamide gel electrophoresis, corresponding to genes not repressible by λ repressor and thus transcribed from *E. coli* promoters (Fig. 2, sample 5). The

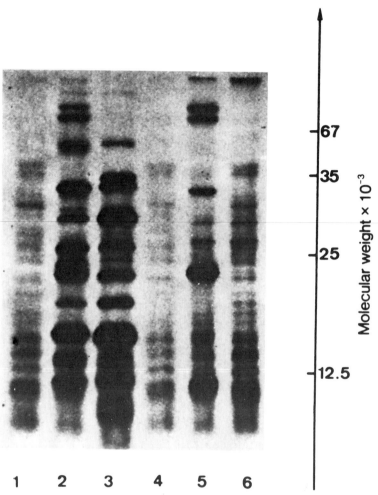

Fig. 2. Analysis of the sonicated extracts of infected cells in the presence and absence of repressor (Springer *et al.*, 1977b). Samples: 1, uninfected 159 *E. coli* strain; 2, 159 infected with λp2; 3, 159 infected with Y199 (phage carrying several deletions in the λb2 region where *E. coli* DNA was inserted); 4, uninfected 159 (λind⁻); 5, 159 (λind⁻) infected with λp2; 6, 159 (λ ind⁻) infected with Y199.

molecular weight of these proteins, their fingerprints, and their cross reaction with specific antibodies allowed their identification (Hennecke *et al.*, 1977a,b; Springer *et al.*, 1977b).

Some transcription units containing genes involved in different aspects of translation have been described, e.g., in the Str-Spc region, ribosomal proteins S12 and S7 are cotranscribed with EF-G and EF-Tu (Nomura and Post, 1980). This cotranscription would suggest that there are some common features in the regulation of ribosomal proteins and the two factors involved in elongation. For the cluster of genes containing the two aminoacyl-tRNA synthetases and the gene for initiation factor IF3, the same possibility of cotranscription exists and hence of a specific regulatory link between initiation of protein synthesis and aminoacylation of tRNA. Since aminoacylation itself is involved in the regulation of the expression of many amino acid operons, there might be some control mechanism connecting the initiation of protein synthesis and the expression of some operons involved in the synthesis of the protein constituents. The potential importance of such a control led us to investigate how these genes are expressed from the *E. coli* chromosome, and first to a thorough study of their localization on the *E. coli* chromosome.

ORDER OF THE GENES IN λp2 AS STUDIED BY THEIR SEGREGATION PATTERN IN DELETED PHAGES

Starting from the original phage (λp2) carrying the whole cluster of genes, a set of phages, deleted for some of the genes in the cluster (Springer *et al.*, 1979a), was isolated. The original λp2 transducing phage was ideal for this purpose because almost all of the nonessential parts of λ were absent or replaced by *E. coli* DNA. Thus, selecting for deletions that did not affect the phage viability yielded phages where *E. coli* DNA was deleted. The deleted phages were selected by their resistance to a chelating agent—pyrophosphate. It is known that such resistance depends on the size of the DNA packed in the head of the bacteriophage. Under specific conditions phages with shorter-sized DNA are pyrophosphate resistant, whereas phages with longer DNA are sensitive to that chelating agent.

This set of phages was studied genetically by complementation of *pheS, pheT,* and *thrS* mutants (Table III). The phages were also characterized biochemically by SDS–polyacrylamide gel analysis of the proteins synthesized in infected uv irradiated cells. As seen in Table III, the biochemical and genetic data coincide. Deletions should appear in a phage stock as single spontaneous mutational events implying that the resistant phages each carry a single deletion (although in one instance a double deletion has been detected, see p. 176). For a single deletion

TABLE III

Coding Content of the Pyrophosphate-Resistant Phages Derived from λp2[a]

	A: Genetic complementation[b]			B: Genes expressed in the uv irradiated cells[a]				
	pheT	pheS	thrS	β	α	P12	IF3	TRS
λp2	+	+	+	+	+	+	+	+
λpp1–4	+	−	−	+	−	−	−	−
λpp1–9	−	−	+	−	−	+	+	+
λpp1–16	−	−	−	−	−	−	−	−
λpp1–46	−	+	+	−	+	+	+	+
λpp1–103	+	+	−	+	+	+	+	−
λpp1–104	+	+	+	+	+	+	+	+
λpp1–125	−	−	+	−	−	−	+	+
λpp1–141	−	−	−	−	−	+	+	−
λpp2–3	+	+	−	+	+	−	−	−
λpp2–34	−	−	+	−	−	+	+	+
λpp3–1	−	−	−	−	−	−	−	−
λpp3–3	+	−	−	+	−	−	−	−
λpp3–6	−	−	+	−	−	−	+	+

[a] From Springer et al., 1979a.

[b] Experiment A: (+) continuous growth on the spot; (−) discontinuous growth (varying between <10 to >100 colonies).

[c] Experiment B: (+) the corresponding band is present on the gel; (−) the corresponding band is absent from the gel.

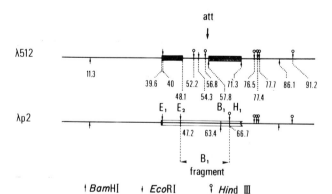

Fig. 3. Restriction endonuclease map of λ512 and λp2 (Plumbridge et al., 1980). Restriction sites are represented by ↑ BamHI; ↓ EcoRI; ♂ HindIII. The numbers are in % λ units. The EcoRI site (E1) in lac is located at 40%. EcoRI₂ (E2), BamHI (B1), and HindIII₁ (H1) are restriction sites within the E. coli DNA insert of λp2. These sites are named consistently in all the figures. (■) lac DNA; (▨) deleted DNA; (□) inserted DNA.

which eliminates the expression of two genes, no expressed gene can be located in the interval between the two missing one.

This mapping rationale was applied to the data of Table III: the existence of λpp1-4 shows that *pheT* is external to the other genes. The existence of λpp1-9 shows that *pheS* and *pheT* are external to the other three genes while that of λpp1-125 indicates that P12 is not located between *thrS* and *infC* but is adjacent to *pheS* and *pheT*. Thus, the order found was (*thrS, infC*) *P12, pheS, pheT,* the order of *thrS* and *infC* not being determined.

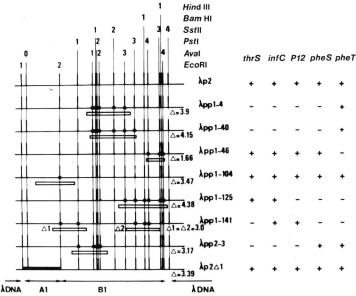

Fig. 4. Correlation of the restriction endonuclease maps of the λp2 DNA, the derived deleted phages, and the pattern of expression of the genes carried by these phages (Plumbridge *et al.*, 1980). The left-hand side shows the restriction maps of the central part of the phages corresponding to the region of *E. coli* DNA insert. Cleavage sites for each restriction enzyme are represented by vertical lines of unique length, corresponding to the position of the name of the restriction enzyme listed on the right. The sites for each enzyme within the *E. coli* DNA insert are numbered from left to right. The restriction sites of λp2 eliminated by deletions in the derived phages are indicated by black dots. The lengths of the deletions (Δ) are indicated in Kb and are drawn to scale. However, the precise end points of these deletions are not known unless the deletion is closely bracketed by restriction sites. In λp2Δ1, A1 is deleted and so both the length and the end points of the deletion are accurately defined. A1 designates the DNA fragment between *Eco*RI₁ and *Eco*RI₂, and B1 the fragment between *Eco*RI₂ and *Hind*III₁. Between λDNA and A1 is a small piece of lac DNA retained from λ512. The right *E. coli* DNA-DNA junction is not precisely defined but is located to the right of *Sst*II₄. The right-hand side shows the pattern of expression of the different phages. (+) The gene is expressed from the corresponding phage; (−) the gene is not expressed.

To further order the genes, the genetic content of the phages was compared to the structure of their DNA studied with restriction endonucleases (Springer *et al.*, 1979a,b; Plumbridge *et al.*, 1980). The structure of the original phage λp2 DNA is shown in Fig. 3. λp2 was derived by insertion of *Eco*RI digested *E. coli* DNA within the two *Eco*RI external fragments of λ512 (Fig. 3). The *E. coli* DNA in λp2 was thus expected to be located within two *Eco*RI sites. However, this is not the case, and we believe that the actual structure of λp2 is explained by the appearance of a deletion which eliminated the right-hand side *E. coli*–DNA junction, i.e. causing the loss of the extreme *Eco*RI right site of *E. coli* DNA and also the reconstituted *Bam*HI site at 58.1/71.3% λ of *Bam*.

Restriction enzymes were also used to compare the DNA of some of the derived deleted phages with that of λp2 (Fig. 4). Since in λpp1-46 (Fig. 4) *pheT* is the only gene not expressed and since the *Hnd*dIII site is deleted, *pheT* is the right-hand terminal gene. Similarly in λpp1-141 the *Eco*RI₂* site is deleted and *thrS* is not expressed, so *thrS* must be the left-hand terminal gene. Because *infC* is expressed from this phage, the order of the genes on λp2 is λ structural genes A → J, *thrS*, *infC*, "*P12*," *pheS*, *pheT*, λ immunity region.

PHYSICAL LOCATION OF THE GENES ON λp2

1. All the Characterized Genes of λp2 Are Located within Fragment B1

The *E. coli* insert of λp2 can be divided into three fragments (Fig. 3): the *Eco*RI₁-*Eco*RI₂, the *Eco*RI₂-*Hin*dIII (B1 fragment), and the *Hin*dIII to *E. coli* DNA junction. The B1 fragment was cloned within the *Eco*RI and *Hin*dIII sites of pBR322 to yield the plasmid pB1 (Fig. 5) which was shown by genetic complementation to carry *pheS*, *pheT*, and *thrS*. Plasmid pB1 was also shown to carry *infC* because strains carrying this plasmid overproduce a protein with the same proteolytic fingerprints as IF3. Fragment B1 was also cloned within a λ integration proficient vector. This phage was shown to express *thrS*, *pheS*, and *pheT* under conditions where λ promoters are nonfunctional (in lysogens). This means that all these genes (and also *infC* and *P12* which are between *thrS* and *pheT*) and their promoters must be located between the sites *Eco*RI₂ and *Hin*dIII.

2. Physical Location of *infC* within the B1 Fragment

Since *Pst*I cuts pB1 into several fragments (Fig. 5), subcloning the *Pst*1 fragments of pB1 into the *Pst*I site of pBR322 seemed a convenient method for

---

*Subscripts after restriction enzyme sites indicate the number of the site.

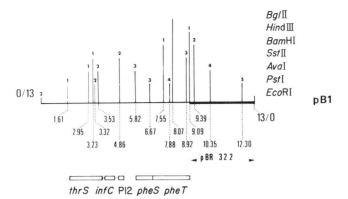

Fig. 5. Restriction endonuclease map of pB1 (Plumbridge *et al.*, 1980). The restriction sites are represented by vertical lines as in Fig. 4 and individual sites are numbered as in the preceding figures. The numbers in the bottom half of the figure give the distance in Kb of each site from *Eco*RI₁ site. The *Ava*I recognition sequence is CPyCGPuG. The *Ava*I₁ site is also a XhoI site (recognition sequence CTCGAG). The *Ava*I₂ and *Ava*I₃ sites are also *Sma*I (recognition sequence CCCGGG). The DNA derived from pBR322 is indicated with a heavy line. The length of DNA required to code for a protein of the sizes observed for phenylalanyl-tRNA synthetase, threonyl-tRNA synthetase, and IF3 are indicated by the boxes. The genes for *pheS* and *pheT* are precisely located between *Ava*I₃ and *Hind*III₁ while for *thrS* and *infC* the freedom of location of the genes is indicated by the horizontal dotted line.

further analyzing the DNA of pB1. The structure of the DNA of some of these plasmids is shown in Fig. 6. Since *infC* is expressed by pB5-57 (Fig. 6), the gene is located between the sites *Pst*I₂ and *Pst*I₃. This fragment of 3.34 kb is considerably longer than the expected size of the *infC* gene, 0.55 kb, based on the molecular weight of IF3. The position of *infC* within the *Pst*I₂ to *Pst*I₃ fragment, however, can be more precisely located; since removal of the *Ava*I₂ to *Ava*I₃ fragment eliminates *infC* expression (pB8-7 and pB9-1) but its reinsertion in the opposite orientation (pB8-9) allows *infC* expression, *infC* must be entirely located within the *Ava*I₂-*Ava*I₃ fragment (2.3 kb). Although these arguments only apply strictly to the structural gene, it is very probable that the *infC* promoter is also contained within the fragment. The level of overproduction of IF3 produced by all the plasmids is about the same, irrespective of fragment orientation (data not shown). This would be expected if IF3 were transcribed from its own promoter in every case, and not result from a readthrough from a plasmid promoter, in some orientations, and be its own promoter, in others. Phage λpp2-3 (Fig. 4) restricts even more *infC* position. Since the deletion here covers *thrS*, *infC*, and "*P12*," the whole of *infC* must be deleted. Since the deletion stops to the left of *Sst*II₂ it implies that all of *infC* and at least part of "*P12*" must be to the left of the *Sst*II₂ site. However this argument does not hold if "*P12*" is expressed from

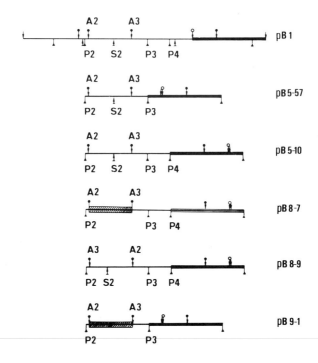

‡ EcoR] ⸮ HindⅢ ⸮ Ava] ↓ PstI ⸱ SstⅡ

Fig. 6. Structure of several plasmids derived from different fragments of B1 cloned in pBR322 (Plumbridge et al., 1980). Restriction enzyme sites are represented by arrows (as indicated on figure) and the sites are numbered as in Fig. 3. DNA derived from pBR322 is indicated by the heavy line. DNA which has been deleted by in vitro recombination between AvaI sites is indicated by a cross-hatched line.

infC promoter (for which we have no information) since deletion of the promoter proximal part of infC would also eliminate "P12" expression.

By cloning SstII₁-SstII₂ and SstII₂-SstII₃ fragments in the unique SstII site of λY199, it has been shown that infC gene is not expressed by either one of the fragments. The only possible solution is that the SstII₂ site cuts the infC gene. As infC is only 0.54 Kb long (corresponding to 20,700 molecular weight), this result located the gene within 0.54 Kb (Springer et al., 1982).   The nucleotide sequence of infC shows that the structural part of the gene is 540 bp long and that the SstII cut is at nucleotide 393 (in collaboration with G. Fayat, C. Sacerdot, S. Blanquet, personal communication). It also suggests that P12 is under the infC promoter.

3. Localization of Other Genes within the B1 Fragment

pheS is not expressed by pB5-57 nor by a plasmid-carrying fragment $PstI_3$-$PstI_4$ as assayed by genetic complementation, but by pB5-10 so that the gene covers the site $PstI_3$. Since *pheS* is expressed regardless of the orientation of the fragment between sites $AvaI_2$ and $AvaI_3$ (pB8-9 and pB5-10), *pheS* must be entirely to the right of the $AvaI_3$ site (Fig. 6). Since the plasmid corresponding to the $PstI_3$-$PstI_5$ fragment of pB1 (pB6-33) expresses *pheT*, all the *pheT* structural gene must be between $PstI_3$ and *Hin*dIII. Based on the published molecular weights for α and β PRS (38,000 and 94,000, respectively), the genes for α and β PRS should require 3.47 kb of DNA. Since there is 3.26 kd of DNA between $AvaI_3$ and *Hin*dIII, this suggests that *pheS* and *pheT* occupy all the DNA in this region.

λpp1-104 expresses *thrS* and is deleted between the $AvaI$ site in A1 (called $AvaI_0$) and $PstI_1$ (which are 4.55 kb apart). The deletion in λpp1-104 is about 3.5 kb long and thus covers only part of this stretch of DNA. Therefore, a limitation to *thrS* on the left is that it must start after this deletion. In subsequent experiments no transcription unit was found to cross the $PstI_1$ site (J. A. Plumbridge, unpublished results) implying that *thrS* must be located entirely to the left or right of this site. Between $AvaI_0$ and $PstI_1$ there is 4.54 kb DNA; the deletion in λpp1-104 removes 3.5 kb. A protein of the size of threonyl-tRNA synthetase requires 2 kb DNA and thus *thrS* cannot be located to the left of $PstI_1$ but must be between $PstI_1$ and *infC* as shown in Fig. 4. It has recently been shown that the start of *thrS* is located at 0.83 Kb to the left of $PstI_2$ (Springer *et al.*, 1982).

TRANSCRIPTION OF THE GENES AROUND *infC*

In order to find out whether cotranscription occurred within this group of genes, mRNAs were isolated. [³H]Uracil-labeled mRNA's were isolated from a strain carrying pB1 to increase the cellular yield of mRNA corresponding to the B1 region (Plumbridge and Springer, 1980). This labeled mRNA was found to hybridize exclusively to the heavy strand of the separated strands of λp2 DNA (Fig. 7). At the plateau 11% of the total input cpm hybridized to the heavy strand, whereas hybridization to the light strand was less than 1% of that to the heavy strand (i.e., less than 0.1% of the input cpm). In λ^+ the heavy strand gives rise to the rightward transcripts starting from the promoters p_r and p_Q, allowing expression of the late genes in the direction A to J. In λp2 the *E. coli* DNA is inserted so that the order of genes is A → J, *thrS, infC, pheS, pheT*, N. If, as is found for most plaque-forming λ-transducing phages, the heavy strand of λp2 corresponds to that of λ^+, then the *E. coli* genes are expressed from the same strands as A to J and thus in the direction *thrS* to *pheT*.

Since the background hybridization to the light strand of λp2 was so low, it was

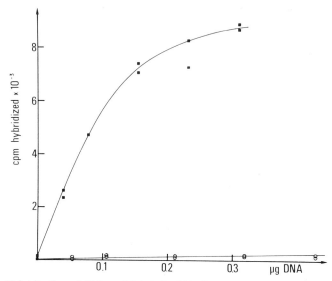

Fig. 7. Hybridization of [³H]uracil-labeled mRNA from IBPC 1365 pB1 to the separated strands of λp2 DNA (Plumbridge and Springer, 1980). Phage particles of λp2 were purified and used for DNA strand separation. After separation, the strands were dialyzed into 2XSSC buffer (SSC is 0.15 M NaCl, 0.015 M Na₃ citrate). IBPC 1365 pB1 was grown in minimal glucose medium containing 50 μg/ml arginine, proline, histidine, uracil, and cytidine at 37°C. At OD of 0.4 at 650 nm the cells were spun down, washed, and resuspended in the same medium without uracil and cytidine. After 10 minutes of incubation the cells were labeled for 2 minutes with [5-³H]uracil (0.1 mCi ml⁻¹ culture, specific activity 30 Ci mmol⁻¹) and then immediately lysed by the boiling SDS method, and mRNA extracted. The mRNA was treated with iodoacetate treated DNase to remove any plasmid DNA which might have been extracted with the mRNA. After ethanol precipitation the RNA was dissolved in sterile H₂O. The yield was 17.5 μg RNA (3.4 × 10⁶ cpm) per ml of culture. Liquid hybridization was carried out in 250 μl 2 X SSC for 4 hours at 67°C using a fixed amount (75,000 cpm) of [³H]uracil mRNA and increasing amounts of heavy (■) and light (○) strand λp2 DNA.

checked that this strand competed with mRNA for the heavy strand and was hybridized to a complementary strand in particular. In addition it was checked that mRNA prepared from the plasmid-bearing strain was equally representative of all the genes on the B1 fragment. Hybridization of this preparation to plasmid probes for *thrS*, *pheS*, and *pheT* showed that about 12%, 8%, and 18% of the mRNA corresponded to *thrS*, *pheS*, and *pheT*, respectively (the genes themselves occupy about 22.3, 11.4, and ·28.2% of the DNA of the B1 fragment). This shows that *thrS*, *pheS*, or *pheT* cannot possibly be expressed from a weak promoter in the opposite direction at such a low level that it is lost in the 1% background hybridization to the light strand. Thus, it was concluded that *thrS*, *pheS*, and *pheT* are all transcribed in the same direction.

The method developed by An and Friesen (1979) for locating promoters on

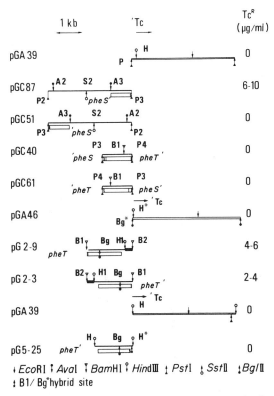

Fig. 8. Structure of plasmids derived from pGA39 and pGA46 (Plumbridge and Springer, 1980). pGA39 and pGA46 (An and Friesen, 1979) are identical except for a short region in front of tetracycline resistance genes (*Tc*, indicated by an arrow) which permit the cloning of different fragments. The plasmids also carry one gene for resistance to chloramphenicol. pGC87, pGC51, pGC40, and pGC61 were isolated from an experiment where *Pst*I fragments from pB1 were cloned into the *Pst*I site of pGA39 selecting for chloramphenicol resistance and subsequently screening for tetracycline resistance. The vector after *Pst*I digestion was treated with calf thymus alkaline phosphatase before ligation with pB1 fragments to reduce the yield of vector pGA39 upon ligation. pG2-3 and pG2-9 were isolated from a similar experiment where pB1 digested with *Bam*HI was ligated with pGA46, digested with *Bgl*II (which gives the same cohesive ends as *Bam*HI). pG5-25 was obtained by inserting the *Hind*III$_1$-*Hind*III* fragment of pG2-3 into the *Hind*III site of pGA39. Restriction sites in *E. coli* DNA are designated as in pB1. H* and Bg* denote *Hind*III and *Bgl*II sites of pGA46. The orientation of the inserted fragment within the plasmid was determined by digestion with an enzyme which cuts the insert and the vector assymmetrically, e.g., to distinguish pGC87 and pGC51 *Ava*I was used (*Ava*I cuts the *Sma*I site of pGA39). The blocked areas of pG2-3 and pG2-9 indicate DNA derived from pBR322. The level of resistance to tetracycline (*Tc*^{R}) that the various plasmids confer to IBPC 1365 is given in the right column. The boxes indicate the position of genes *pheS* and *pheT* within the restriction fragment. The serrated edge shows where a gene is cut out by a restriction site. The primes attached to *pheS* and *pheT* indicate that the gene is incomplete on that side.

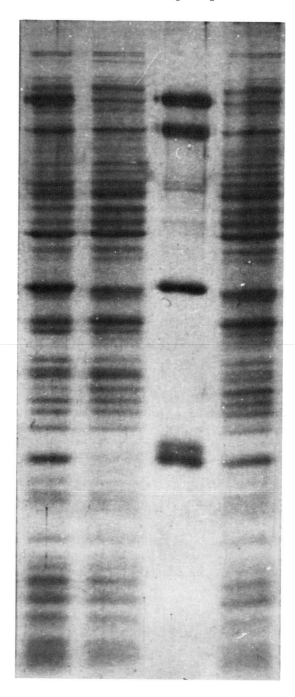

restriction fragments was used to further study the expression of *pheS* and *pheT*. Plasmids have been constructed to allow the insertion of various restriction fragments in front of the gene for tetracycline resistance whose own promoter has been inactivated (Plumbridge and Springer, 1980). If the inserted fragment contains a promoter whose transcript traverses the restriction site immediately before the tetracycline resistance genes (*Tc*) and if the hybrid gene has a correct structure to be expressed, then resistance to tetracycline is observed. Various restriction fragments were analyzed in these plasmids and are described in Fig. 8. In particular the $PstI_2$-$PstI_3$ and the $PstI_3$-$PstI_4$ fragments were inserted in both orientations in pGA39. $PstI_3$-$PstI_4$ contains the end of *pheS* and the beginning of *pheT*. The only plasmid to express resistance to tetracycline is pGC87 with the orientation $PstI_2$-$PstI_3$ → *Tc*. The expression of tetracycline resistance must be due to the *pheS* promoter since *pheS* straddles the site $PstI_3$. $PstI_3$-$PstI_4$ does not activate *Tc* in pGC40, which means either that there is no promoter in $PstI_3$-$PstI_4$ or that the hybrid gene starting in $PstI_3$-$PstI_4$, crossing the *E. coli*–plasmid junction at $PstI_4$ and covering *Tc*, has not a structure allowing expression. However, it was shown that insertion of the fragment $PstI_2$-$PstI_4$ in pGA39 produces a plasmid that does confer tetracycline resistance. This means that the junction between $PstI_3$-$PstI_4$ and pGA39 has indeed a structure allowing expression of *Tc*. Thus, the lack of tetracycline resistance in pGC40 is really due to the absence of a promoter in the fragment where *pheT* starts, and since *pheT* is expressed in the same direction as *pheS*, it must be transcribed from the *pheS* promoter.

To completely exclude the possibility of the transcription of *pheT* in the opposite direction to *pheS*, the fragment $BamHI_1$-$HindIII_1$ was also analyzed. This was done in two steps as described in Fig. 8. The resulting plasmid pG5-25 containing $HindIII_1$-$BamHI_1$ → *Tc* was tetracycline sensitive.

Thus it was concluded that *pheS* and *pheT* are transcribed from one promoter which is carried by the $PstI_2$-$PstI_3$ fragment. This fragment cloned in pBR322

Fig. 9. SDS gel analysis of the total protein content of lysates from cells carrying pB1 and pB5-57 (Plumbridge *et al.,* 1980). A 1-ml aliquot of overnight cultures of the strains in LB medium supplemented with 10 μg/ml tetracycline were spun down and resuspended in 0.1 ml of 10 mM Tris·HCl, pH 6.8, 10 mM MgCl$_2$. The cells were frozen and thawed three times then DNase was added to a final concentration of 0.1 mg/ml. After 20 minutes at 4°C, 0.1 ml of two times concentrated sample buffer was added to the treated cells. A volume equivalent to 0.04 A$_{650}$ units of the original culture was denatured at 100° for 2 minutes and then layered on a 1 mm thick 12.5% polyacrylamide–SDS slab gel. Electrophoresis was performed for 2.5 hours at 100 V, then 2 hours at 150 V. The bromophenol blue left the gel after 4 hours electrophoresis; the gel was then stained. Lane 1, IBPC 1671 pB1; lane 2, IBPC 1671 pBR322; lane 4, IBPC 1671 pB5-57; lane 3, purified proteins from top to bottom, β subunit phenylalanyl-tRNA synthetase, threonyl-tRNA synthetase, α subunit phenylalanyl-tRNA synthetase IF3. Purified IF3 corresponds to two bands (IF3a and IF3b) (Grunberg-Manago *et al.,* 1978).

(pB5-57) expresses *infC,* and the possibility of *pheS* and *pheT* being expressed from *infC* promoter is currently under investigation.

THE EXPRESSION OF THE GENES AROUND *infC* IS DIFFERENTLY REGULATED

Since pB1 is a high-copy-number plasmid, strains carrying pB1 contain multiple copies of *thrS, infC, pheS,* and *pheT.* The products of these genes respond in a very different way to gene dosage. Plasmids (pB1 in particular) carrying *infC* cause the overproduction of a protein of the same molecular weight as IF3, as shown in Fig. 9. This overproduced protein was shown to have the same one-dimensional proteolytic fingerprint pattenr (using *Staphylococcus aureus* V8 protease and papain) as IF3. pB1 causes an overproduction of about 100-fold of both subunits of phenylalanyl-tRNA synthetase whereas threonyl-tRNA synthetase is overproduced only fivefold. This was tested both by protein determination and activities (in collaboration with G. Fayat and S. Blanquet, unpublished experiment). Using specific *pheS, pheT,* and *thrS* hybridization probes, we were able to show that mRNA's corresponding to these genes are present in the cell in about equal amounts. This indicates that phenylalanyl- and threonyl-tRNA synthetases are not regulated in the same way.

pB1 carrying strains grow slowly and fast-growing mutants are easily selected. The great majority of these mutants no longer overproduce phenylalanyl-tRNA synthetase. Invariably the genetic defect was located in the plasmid and not on the chromosome. We were thus able to isolate many kinds of mutant plasmids (deletions, insertions, point mutations) which no longer overproduce phenylalanyl-tRNA synthetase. All the plasmids isolated carrying insertions or point mutations still complement *pheS⁻* and *pheT⁻* strains and thus mainly define genetic loci important for level (and not activity) of phenylalanyl-tRNA synthetase. We are presently studying a number of these mutant plasmids to localize the regulatory regions of *pheS* and *pheT.*

The regulation of phenylalanyl-tRNA synthetase expression shows some other interesting aspects: under the conditions where pB1 causes overproduction of α and β subunits, plasmids carrying *pheS* and a part of *pheT* only overproduce α when the part of *pheT* on the plasmid is long enough.

CONCLUSION

A new approach to study the physiology and the role of initiation factor IF3 has been started. The analysis of the chromosome region near the structural gene for IF3 indicates that it is surrounded by genes for proteins involved in the process of translation: threonyl-tRNA and phenylalanyl-tRNA synthetases. The genes for IF1 and IF2 are not adjacent to that for IF3. If the three genes were adjacent and coordinately regulated, then under conditions where overproduction of IF3 is observed, IF1 and IF2 should be overproduced as well. Since we do not see proteins of the molecular weight of IF1 and IF2 on gels of the plasmid-bearing strains, we assume that IF1 and IF2 are either located elsewhere on the chromosome or subjected to a completely different regulation.

The expression of the genes belonging to this part of the chromosome appears to be under different controls. IF3 and the two subunits of phenylalanyl-tRNA synthetase are overproduced while threonyl-tRNA synthetase is only slightly overproduced. The fact that the presence of a multicopy plasmid carrying the *infC* gene causes the overproduction of IF3 indicates a quantitative dependence of IF3 levels on gene dosage. The synthesis of ribosomal proteins in the cell is not dependent on gene dosage (Yates *et al.*, 1980; Dean and Nomura, 1980). This suggests that IF3 synthesis is not subject to the type of autogenous regulation shown by some ribosomal protein operons (P. Lestienne *et al.*, 1982).

ACKNOWLEDGMENTS

This manuscript was written during my stay at N.I.H. (Bethesda) as a Fogarty Fellow. I wish to heartily thank Dr. Thressa and Earl Stadtman for their warm hospitality.

I thank M. Springer for critically reading the manuscript and M. Jouannaud for preparing it.

This work was supported by the following grants: Centre National de la Recherche Scientifique (Groupe de Recherche 18), DGRST (Convention 78.7.1087), INSERM (ATP No. 52.77.84), Ligue Française Contre le Cancer (Comité de la Seine), and Commissariat à l'Energie Atomique.

REFERENCES

An, G., and Friesen, J. D. (1979). Plasmid vehicles for direct cloning of *Escherichia coli* promoters. *J. Bacteriol.* **140**, 400–407.

Chang, A. C. Y., Erlich, H. A., Gunsalus, R. P., Nunberg, A. C. J. H., Kaufman, R. J., Shimke, R. T., and Cohen, S. N. (1980). Initiation of protein synthesis in bacteria at a translational start codon of mammalian cDNA: Effects of the preceding nucleotide sequence. *Proc. Natl. Acad. Sci. U.S.A.* **77**, 1442–1446.

Cooperman, B. S., Expert-Bezancon, A., Kahan, L., Dondon, J., and Grunberg-Manago, M. (1981). IF3 crosslinking to *Escherichia coli* ribosomal 30S subunits by three different light dependent procedures. Identification of 30S proteins crosslinked to IF3. Utilization of a new two stage crosslinking reagent: ρ Nitrobenzylmaleimide. *Arch. Biochem. Biophys.* **208**, 554–562.

Dean, D., and Nomura, M. (1980). Feedback regulation of ribosomal protein gene expression in *Escherichia coli*. *Proc. Natl. Acad. Sci. U.S.A.* **77**, 3590–3594.

Dunn, J. J., Buzash-Pollert, E., and Studier, F. W. (1978). Mutations of bacteriophage T7 that affect initiation of synthesis of the gene 0,3 protein. *Proc. Natl. Acad. Sci. U.S.A.* **75**, 2741–2745.

Godefroy-Colburn, T., Wolfe, A. D., Dondon, J., Grunberg-Manago, M., Dessen, D., and Pantaloni, D. (1975). Light-scattering studies showing the effect of initiation factors on the reversible dissociation of *Escherichia coli* ribosomes. *J. Mol. Biol.* **94,** 461–478.

Grunberg-Manago, M. (1980). Initiation of protein synthesis as seen in 1979. *In* "Ribosomes: Structure, Function and Genetics" (G. Chambliss, G. R. Craven, J. Davies, K. Davis, L. Kahan, and M. Nomura, eds.), pp. 445–477. University Park Press, Baltimore, Maryland.

Grunberg-Manago, M., and Gunsalus, I. C. (1953). Aerobic and anaerobic citric acid metabolism of *Escherichia coli*. *Bacteriol. Proc.* p. 73.

Grunberg-Manago, M., and Ochoa, S. (1955). Enzymatic synthesis and breakdown of polynucleotides; polynucleotide phosphorylase. *J. Am. Chem. Soc.* **77,** 3165–3166.

Grunberg-Manago, M., Buckingham, R. H., Cooperman, B. S., and Hershey, J. W. B. (1978). Structure and function of the translation machinery. *In* "Relation Between Structure and Function in the Prokaryotic Cell" (R. Y. Stanier, H. J. Rogers, and J. B. Ward, eds.), pp. 27–110. Cambridge Univ. Press, London and New York.

Gualerzi, C., and Pon, C. L. (1981). Protein biosynthesis in prokaryotic cells, mechanism of 30S initiation complex formation in *Escherichia coli*. *In* "Proceedings of the Seventh Aharon Katzi-Katchalsky Conference on Structural Aspects of Recognition and Assembly in Biological Macromolecules" (M. Balaban, J. Sussman, A. Yonath, and W. Traub, eds.), pp. 805–826. ISS Press, Rehovot and Philadelphia.

Hennecke, H., Springer, M., and Böck, A. (1977a). A specialized transducing λ phage carrying the *Escherichia coli* genes for phenylalanyl-tRNA synthetase. *Mol. Gen. Genet.* **152,** 205–210.

Hennecke, H., Böck, A., Thomale, J., and Nass, G. (1977b). Threonyl-transfer ribonucleic acid synthetase from *Escherichia coli:* Subunit structure and genetic analysis of the structural gene by means of a mutated enzyme of a specialized transducing lambda bacteriophage. *J. Bacteriol.* **131,** 943–950.

Lee-Huang, S., and Ochoa, S. (1971). Messenger discriminating species of initiation factor F3. *Nature (London), New Biol.* **234,** 236–239.

Lemaire, G., Gold, L., and Yarus, M. (1978). Autogenous translational repression of bacteriophage T4 gene 32 expression *in vitro*. *J. Mol. Biol.* **126,** 78–90.

Lestienne, P., Dondon, J., Plumbridge, J. A., Howe, J. G., Mayaux, J. F., Springer, M., Blanquet, S., Hershey, J. W. B., and Grunberg-Manago, M. (1982). *Eur. J. Biochem.* (in press).

Lodish, H. F. (1976). Translational control of protein synthesis. *Annu. Rev. Biochem.* **45,** 39–72.

Maalhe, O. (1979). Regulation of the protein synthesizing machinery. Ribosomes, tRNA, factors and so on. *Biol. Regul. Dev.* **1,** 487–542.

Nomura, M., and Post, L. (1980). Organisation of ribosomal genes and regulation of their expression in *Escherichia coli*. *In* "Ribosomes: Structure, Function and Genetics" (G. Chambliss, G. R. Craven, J. Davies, K. Davis, L. Kahan, and M. Nomura, eds.), pp. 671–691. University Park Press, Baltimore, Maryland.

Nomura, M., Morgan, E. A., and Jaskunas, S. R. (1977). Genetics of bacterial ribosomes. *Annu. Rev. Genet.* **11,** 297–347.

Plumbridge, J. A., and Springer, M. (1980). Genes for the two subunits of phenylalanyl-tRNA synthetase of *Escherichia coli* are transcribed from the same promoter. *J. Mol. Biol.* **144,** 595–600.

Plumbridge, J. A., Springer, M., Graffe, M., Goursot, R., and Grunberg-Manago, M. (1980). Physical localization and cloning of the structural gene for *E. coli*. Initiation factor IF3 from a group of genes concerned with translation. *Gene* **11,** 33–42.

Revel, M. (1972). Polypeptide chain initiation: The role of ribosomal proteins factors and ribosomal subunits. *In* "The Mechanism of Protein Synthesis and its Regulation" (L. Bosch, ed.), pp. 87–131. North-Holland Publ., Amsterdam.

Roberts, T. M., Kachich, R., and Ptashne, M. (1979). A general method for maximizing the expression of a cloned gene. *Proc. Natl. Acad. Sci. U.S.A.* **76,** 760–764.

Rose, I., Grunberg-Manago, M., Korey, S. R., and Ochoa, S. (1954). Enzymatic phosphorylation of acetate. *J. Biol. Chem.* **211,** 737–756.

Shine, J., and Dalgarno, L. (1974). The 3′ terminal sequence of *Escherichia coli* 16S ribosomal RNA: Complementarity to nonsense triplets and ribosome binding sites. *Proc. Natl. Acad. Sci. U.S.A.* **71,** 1342–1346.

Springer, M., Graffe, M., and Grunberg-Manago, M. (1977a). Characterization of an *E. coli* mutant with a thermolabile initiation factor IF3 activity. *Mol. Gen. Genet.* **151,** 17–26.

Springer, M., Graffe, M., and Hennecke, H. (1977b). Specialized transducing phage for the initiation factor 3 gene in *Escherichia coli*. *Proc. Natl. Acad. Sci. U.S.A.* **74,** 3970–3974.

Springer, M., Graffe, M., and Grunberg-Manago, M. (1979a). Genetic organization of the *E. coli* chromosome around the structural gene for initiation factor IF3 (infc). *Mol. Gen. Genet.* **169,** 337–343.

Springer, M., Graffe, M., Plumbridge, J. A., and Grunberg-Manago, M. (1979b). The structure of a cluster of *Escherichia coli* genes involved in translation. *Abstr. Int. Congr. Biochem. 11th, 1979* p. 126.

Springer, M., Plumbridge, J. A., Graffe, M., and Grunberg-Manago, M. (1981). *In* "New Horizons in Biological Chemistry" (M. Koike, T. Nagatsu, Y. Okuda, and T. Ozawa, eds.), pp. 43–54. Japan Scientific Societies Press, Nagoya, Japan.

Springer, M., Plumbridge, J. A., Trudel, M., Graffe, M., and Grunberg-Manago, M. (1982). *Molec. Gen. Genet.* (submitted for publication).

Steitz, J. A. (1980). RNA–RNA interactions during polypeptide chain initiation. *In* "Ribosomes: Structure, Function and Genetics" (G. Chambliss, G. R. Craven, J. Davies, K. Davis, L. Kahan, and M. Nomura, eds.), pp. 479–495. University Park Press, Baltimore, Maryland.

Steitz, J. A., and Steege, D. A. (1977). Characterization of two mRNA rRNA complexes implicated in the initiation of protein biosynthesis. *J. Mol. Biol.* **144,** 545–558.

Yates, J. L., Arfsten, A. E., and Nomura, M. (1980). *In vitro* expression of *Escherichia coli* ribosomal protein genes: Autogenous inhibition of translation. *Proc. Natl. Acad. Sci. U.S.A.* **77,** 1837–1841.

16

Posttranscriptional Control of Protein Synthesis during Substrate Adaptation

Lewis A. Jacobson
and
Linda Jen-Jacobson

As a graduate student in the laboratory of I. C. Gunsalus, one of us (L.A.J.) was taught how research often required heuristic rather than simple deduction or induction. On being presented with data, Gunny would first consider, logically enough, the experimental procedures and consistency of the data. But then, almost invariably, he would ask if the conclusions "made sense." Nature he required to be sensible, and its sense comprehensible.

Often, the method was reversed. What "made sense" was first defined, and an experiment then designed to see if "sense" happened to correspond to the facts. One usually learned something about either nature or one's own comprehension of it. Those frequent instances where fact and "sense" were noncongruent were the most informative.

Some years later, we set out to search for regulatory mechanisms which controlled not single genes, or even groups of genes, but the common processes of gene expression. Specifically, we wished to reopen the question of whether gene expression in bacteria could be controlled posttranscriptionally; that is, not

*Dedicated with respect and affection to I. C. Gunsalus, whose unique qualities have enabled him to be a friend to his students and a teacher of his friends.

EXPERIENCES IN BIOCHEMICAL PERCEPTION
Copyright © 1982 by Academic Press, Inc.
All rights of reproduction in any form reserved.
ISBN 0-12-528420-9

at the level of the gene but at the steps which led from messenger RNA (mRNA) to the proteins which were the functional expression of the genetic potential.

The possibility of posttranscriptional controls had been carefully considered, and as thoroughly rejected, during the archetypal investigations of control of expression of the *lac* operon of *Escherichia coli* (Jacob and Monod, 1961). Indeed, a simple view of the energetic economy of bacteria suggested that post-transcriptional controls would be wasteful, in that the prior investment in mRNA synthesis would be discarded without productive use. The mitigating possibility that unused mRNA might be preserved against future need seemed to be pre-cluded by the marked metabolic instability of bacterial mRNA. [The much greater stability of mRNA in eucaryotes is accompanied by a greater prevalence of posttranscriptional controls (Lodish, 1976).]

Under what physiological circumstances might one expect that posttranscrip-tional controls could be reconciled with the logic of energetic investment? When would they, in Gunny's phrase, "make sense"?

We supposed that the need to decrease the rate of protein production would be greatest when the demand for protein products was reduced and when the supply of energy and/or monomers became limiting. Posttranscriptional controls would be most useful when such a situation occurred after investment had already been made in mRNA and in the formation of the translational apparatus (ribosomes, tRNA's, aminoacyl-tRNA synthetases, translation factors).

It had been established that the cellular content of ribosomes in *E. coli* is proportional to the growth rate (Maaloe and Kjeldgaard, 1966) and subsequent work has shown this to be true for aminoacyl-tRNA synthetases and translational factors as well (Neidhardt *et al.*, 1977; Krauss and Leder, 1975). We reasoned that if rapidly growing *E. coli* were forced to undergo a sudden transition to a lower growth rate through the imposition of a temporary carbon source limita-tion, the cells would be faced with an excess of synthetic capacity and, simul-taneously, a pressing need to conserve resources. This protocol is known as an "energy source shift-down" and Koch (1971) has pointed out its pertinence to the natural history of *E. coli*.

When *E. coli* is shifted from a glucose-iminimal to a succinate-minimal medium, no growth is observed turbidimetrically for about 60 minutes, where-upon growth recommences at the lower rate characteristic of the succinate medium (Fig. 1). Adaptation to the new substrate, as measured by succinate oxidation, occurs gradually during the lag phase (Jacobson and Jen-Jacobson, 1980a). The postshift adjustment in the rate of protein synthesis is surprisingly rapid: within less than 30 seconds, the rate of amino acid incorporation into protein drops to about 13% of the preshift rate (Fig. 2).

This downward adjustment in the rate of protein synthesis is far too rapid to be attributable solely to transcriptional control, for even if transcription were *totally* inhibited, which it is not (Westover and Jacobson, 1974b), the rate of protein synthesis could decline no faster than the preexisting mRNA became inactivated. In an exponentially growing culture the functional half-life of total *E. coli* mRNA is about 150 seconds, and in down-shifted cells it is appreciably longer. A seven- to eight-fold reduction in the rate of protein synthesis would require about three half-lives, or a minimum of 20 times longer than we observed. Thus, it follows that the rapid adjustment in the rate of protein synthesis after a sudden shift-down must be accomplished by a posttranscriptional control mechanism.

A clue to the nature of this control was provided by Friesen (1968), who observed that shift-down caused a rapid disappearance of polyribosomes. Polyribosome loss, however, might result from one or more of several causes: loss of cellular mRNA, premature termination of translation, failure of ribosomes to bind to mRNA, or failure of bound ribosomes to begin translation.

The first key to distinguishing these possibilities was the fate of the ribosomes which leave the polysome fraction. Ruscetti and Jacobson (1972) showed that down-shifted cells accumulated not free single ribosomes, but "complexed" single ribosomes. The two kinds of single ribosomes were readily distinguished in sucrose gradients containing NaCl: free ribosomes dissociated into 50 S and 30 S subunits, whereas the "complexed" ribosomes from down-shifted cells did not (Fig. 3).

The inference that the 70 S ribosomes from down-shifted cells were "com-

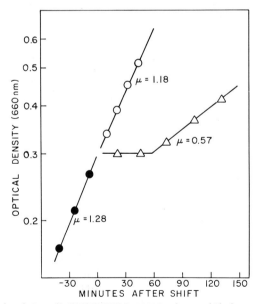

Fig. 1 Growth of *E. coli* K12(λ) ATCC 10798 after a shift from glucose-minimal to succinate-minimal medium. Growth rates (μ) are given in mass doublings per hour.

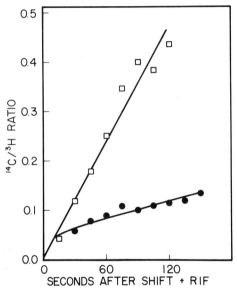

Fig. 2. Early time course of protein labeling in strain K12(λ) treated with rifampin. Cells were labeled before the shift with ^{3}H-labeled amino acid mixture and after the shift with [^{14}C]leucine. (□), Glucose to glucose shift; (●), glucose to succinate shift. The two data points at $t = 15$ seconds were exactly coincident. (Jacobson and Jen-Jacobson, 1980a).

plexed'' was supported by their association with a substantial fraction of the pulse-labeled mRNA in such cells (Ruscetti and Jacobson, 1972), by the detection of *lac* operon mRNA in the 70S ''monosome'' fraction (Westover and Jacobson, 1974b) and by direct observation of the mRNA–ribosome complexes by electron microscopy (Jacobson and Baldassare, 1976). The electron micrographs showed that the 70 S monosomes consisted of single ribosomes bound at the 5'-ends of mRNA strands.

These observations led us to the hypothesis that down-shifted cells control protein synthesis at the level of polypeptide chain initiation. Specifically, we envisioned a rate-limiting step in translation subsequent to the formation of the mRNA–ribosome complex, but prior to the commencement of polypeptide bond synthesis. We imagined that the assembly of the 70 S ribosome–mRNA initiation complex was rapid, with the ribosome then ''dwelling'' at the initiation site for a relatively long time before the relatively rapid steps of translocation and polypeptide chain synthesis (Jacobson and Baldassare, 1976). If polypeptide chain initiation were inhibited while polypeptide chain elongation proceeded at a normal rate, the density of translating ribosomes on mRNA would decrease, producing smaller polyribosomes and, in the limit, an accumulation of 70 S monosomes.

We therefore set out to measure the kinetic parameters of protein synthesis *in vivo*. To study posttranscriptional events in isolation, we have used a protocol in which a glucose-grown culture is divided, half into glucose and half into succinate medium. At the same time we inhibit further transcription. In the case of global mRNA, we inhibited transcription with rifampin, whereas to study β-galactosidase mRNA we have inhibited new transcription by inducer removal and rifampin. We were therefore able to measure the quantity of protein (by labeled amino acid incorporation or enzyme activity) synthesized from a preexisting mRNA population.

As shown in Fig. 4, the amount of protein synthesized from a preexisting mRNA population is markedly reduced in down-shifted cells. The ratio of the protein-forming capacities (ratio of plateau values in Fig. 4) is called the "relative translational yield." In the experiment shown, the relative translational yield was 64%.

Jacquet and Kepes (1971) had identified the individual parameters that contribute to such a translational yield. These include the functional lifetime of the mRNA, the polypeptide chain propagation rate, and the polypeptide chain initiation frequency.

The data of Fig. 4 may be transformed to show the exponential functional inactivation of mRNA (Fig. 5). It is evident that mRNA is inactivated more

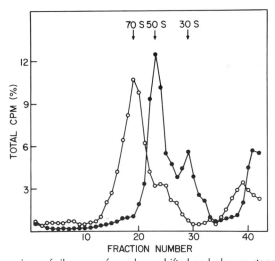

Fig. 3. Comparison of ribosomes from down-shifted and glucose-starved cells. Cultures were labeled during exponential growth with [^{14}C]uracil and harvested 30 minutes after a shift to succinate medium (O) or to carbon-free medium (●). Lysates were sedimented in 15–30% linear sucrose gradients containing 10 mM Tris-HCl, pH 7.4, 5 mM Mg^{2+} and 60 mM Na$^+$. The positions of ^{3}H-labeled markers (ribosomal subunits) are indicated. Further experimental details are in Ruscetti and Jacobson (1972).

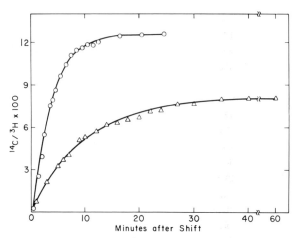

Fig. 4. Synthesis of total protein by strain K12(λ) after rifampin treatment. Cells were labeled before the shift with [³H]leucine and after the shift with [¹⁴C]leucine. Data for cultures shifted to glucose medium (○) or to succinate medium (△) from Westover and Jacobson (1974a).

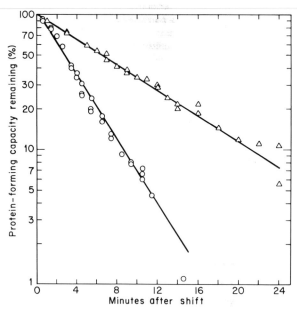

Fig. 5. Decay of protein-forming capacity after rifampin treatment. Data for cells shifted to glucose medium (○) or to succinate medium (△) derived from three independent experiments like that of Fig. 4. (Westover and Jacobson, 1974a).

slowly in the down-shifted cells than in the cells returned to fresh glucose medium. If all other things were equal, this more stable mRNA should support the synthesis of more, not less, protein. The fact that it does not indicates that the number of translating ribosomes traversing the mRNA per unit time must be much less in the down-shifted cells.

We have adduced a number of kinds of evidence to show that the polypeptide chain propagation rate is unaltered in down-shifted cells (Westover and Jacobson, 1974a; Leschine and Jacobson, 1979; Jacobson and Jen-Jacobson, 1980a). The simplest demonstration of this fact comes from the initial kinetics of β-galactosidase induction. Schleif *et al.* (1973) pointed out that if measurements are made at very early times after induction, such that turnover of newly synthesized mRNA is negligible, the amount of mRNA present is linearly proportional to time ($M = k_1 t$) and the amount of enzyme synthesized is proportional to the amount of mRNA present and the time available for its translation ($E = k_2 M t$). Thus, $E = k t^2$ and the amount of enzyme rises quadratically with time, but only after a time T_p which represents the minimum time for translation of the first polypeptide chain. This analysis obviates the need to detect the "first increase" in enzyme activity and, as shown in Fig. 6, indicates that the 1021 amino acids of the β-galactosidase polypeptide are assembled in the same time (95–100 seconds) in both exponential (glucose) and down-shifted (succinate) cultures. The resulting estimate of a polypeptide chain growth rate of 10–11 amino acids per second is very close to estimates by other techniques (Westover and Jacobson,

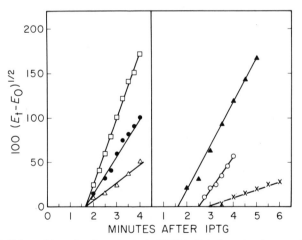

Fig. 6. β-Galactosidase rise times in strain K12(λ). Data from Jacobson and Jen-Jacobson (1980a). $\square$, Glucose to glucose shift, IPTG $t = 0$; $\bullet$, glucose to succinate shift, IPTG $t = 0$ or $\triangle$, IPTG $t = 10$ min; $\bigcirc$, glucose to glucose + α-methylglucoside (1:10) shift, IPTG $t = 0$ or $\blacktriangle$, IPTG $t = 10$ minutes; X, glucose to no carbon shift, IPTG $t = 0$.

TABLE I

Parameters of Protein Synthesis[a]

Protein measured	Relative translational yield (Y) (glucose = 1)	mRNA Lifetime[b] (sec)		Polypeptide completion time, T_p (sec)	Relative initiation frequency[c] (f) (glucose = 1)
		Succinate	Glucose		
Global protein	0.64	550	212	18	0.24
β-Galactosidase[d]	0.67	83	83	100	0.27

[a] Data for *E. coli* K12(λ) strain ATCC 10798 adapted from Jacobson and Jen-Jacobson (1980a).

[b] Mean mRNA lifetime (τ) = $t_{\frac{1}{2}}$/ln2.

[c] Calculated by $Y = (T_{pS} + f\tau_s)/(T_{pG} + \tau_G)$, where subscripts S and G refer to succinate and glucose cultures, respectively.

[d] Measurements made after 5 minutes induction to produce steady-state population of β-galactosidase mRNA (Westover and Jacobson, 1974a), followed by inducer removal.

1974a; Schleif *et al.*, 1973; Johnsen *et al.*, 1977). Thus, there is no decrease in the rate of polypeptide chain propagation in cells subjected to a glucose-to-succinate shift-down. Fig. 6 also shows, however, that other forms of stress on energy metabolism (carbon source starvation or inhibition with α-methylglucoside) may reduce the rate of chain propagation (cf. Johnsen *et al.*, 1977).

With knowledge of the relative translational yield, the rate of polypeptide chain propagation, and the functional lifetime of mRNA, the equations of Jacquet and Kepes (1971) may be adapted to calculate the translational initiation frequency (Westover and Jacobson, 1974a; Jacobson and Jen-Jacobson, 1980a). As shown in Table I, these calculations show that f, the relative translational initiation frequency, is reduced four- to fivefold in down-shifted cells. Furthermore, the degree of reduction is very nearly the same whether measured for global protein by amino acid incorporation, or for β-galactosidase by measurement of enzyme activity.

Although this calculation shows that a reduction in the translational initiation frequency can quantitatively account for the reduced translational yield in down-shifted cells, it gives no further information about the detailed mechanism by which the initiation frequency is reduced. It is clear, however, that the accumulation of ribosome–mRNA complexes in down-shifted cells is not consistent with a mechanism which inhibits the binding of 30 S and 50 S ribosomal subunits to mRNA. Furthermore, the accumulated complexes are apparently devoid of nascent peptide chains (Ruscetti and Jacobson, 1972), so the inhibition must be exerted on a step in the initiation sequence subsequent to the addition of the 50 S subunit to the 30 S–mRNA complex, but prior to the initiation of peptide bond synthesis. Preliminary studies in our laboratory (G. P. Owens and L. A. Jacobson, unpublished data) indicate that the "initiation monosomes" contain significant quantities of initiation factor IF2. The ejection of IF2 from the initiation complex, a reaction which requires GTP hydrolysis (Dubnoff *et al.*, 1972), is therefore the best candidate for the rate-limiting reaction.

To aid in further analysis of this mechanism, we tried for some years to isolate mutants which were defective in the ability to control translational initiation after a shift-down. A number of selection and screening procedures were attempted without success. Then, quite by accident, we discovered that such mutants existed, previously undetected.

As shown in Table II, we were able to distinguish three groups of strains with varying abilities to control translational initiation. We named the pertinent phenotype Tic, for *T*ranslational *I*nitiation *C*ontrol. Tic$^+$ strains, by lucky accident the subjects of our earlier work, have strong control over translational initiation ($f \simeq 0.2$). Tic$^-$ strains apparently lack this ability entirely and translational initiation is unaffected by the shift-down. A third group of strains, designated Tic^{int}, have intermediate degree of control ($f \simeq 0.5$).

TABLE II

Comparison of Tic Phenotypes[a]

Strain	Genotype	Relative translational yield (glucose = 1)	Relative mRNA lifetime (τ_S/τ_G)	Relative initiation frequency (glucose = 1)
Tic$^+$				
K12(λ)	$relA^+spoT^+$	0.64	2.6	0.24
NF162	$relA\ spoT$	0.42	1.9	0.20
Tic$^-$				
W1	$relA^+spoT^+$	0.97	1.0	0.93
W2	$relA^+spoT$	1.02	1.0	1.02
Tic^{int}				
CP78	$relA^+spoT^+$	0.76	1.5	0.49
NF161	$relA^+spoT$	0.70	1.4	0.49
NF859	$relA^+spoT^+$	0.65	1.4	0.45
NF1035	$relA\ spoT^+\ relX$	0.71	1.5	0.47

[a] Data taken from Jacobson and Jen-Jacobson (1980a).

The failure of Tic$^-$ strains to control translation does not represent physiological immunity to the effects of the down-shift, since they are able to inhibit RNA synthesis to approximately the same extent as Tic$^+$ strains (Jacobson and Jen-Jacobson, 1980a). Furthermore, the differences between Tic$^+$ and Tic$^-$ strains are not specific to a down-shift to succinate medium; distinctions are maintained when acetate, lactate, glycerol, or glutamate serve as secondary carbon sources (L. A. Jacobson, unpublished data).

At present, we do not know the genetic basis for these differences in Tic phenotype. This problem is presently under investigation. The data in Table II, however, indicate clearly that the Tic phenotype is not dependent on the genotypes of these strains at the *relA* or *spoT* loci, which govern the metabolism of ppGpp and pppGpp. By comparisons of appropriate strains under differing physiological conditions, we have shown that ppGpp is not an effector of translational initiation in down-shifted cells (Jacobson and Jen-Jacobson, 1980b).

The existence of strains with different Tic phenotypes has also allowed us to assess the role of intracellular ATP and GTP pools in control of translational initiation (Jacobson and Jen-Jacobson, 1980b). Since the physiological stress we apply to elicit such control involves energy limitation, it is hardly surprising that the ATP and GTP pools contract in down-shifted cells. Inasmuch as protein synthesis requires both ATP (for ligation of amino acids to tRNA) and GTP (for initiation and elongation reactions), it seemed possible that contraction of the nucleoside triphosphate pools might place a direct energetic limitation upon one or more of the reactions of protein biosynthesis.

A detailed kinetic analysis of changes in the ATP and GTP pools after shift-down (Fig. 7) shows that this simple hypothesis is incorrect. The ATP and GTP pools contract after shift-down in both Tic$^+$ and Tic$^-$ strains, showing that contraction of the pools is insufficient to elicit control of translational initiation. Furthermore, the postshift contraction in the ATP and GTP pools is far slower than the inhibition of protein synthesis (compare Fig. 7 to Fig. 2). Both pools remain at normal levels at a time when protein synthesis is already maximally inhibited, showing that pool contraction is not necessary to elicit control of translational initiation.

It thus appears that the nucleoside triphosphates, the most direct products of energy metabolism, are neither themselves limiting for protein synthesis nor serving as signals for the inhibition of translational initiation. We have also presented evidence to eliminate ppGpp and pppGpp as candidate effectors (Jacobson and Jen-Jacobson, 1980b) and at present the identity of the hypothetical effector(s) is unknown.

A somewhat more surprising conclusion emerges from the data of Fig. 7. It is apparent that the postshift contractions in the ATP and GTP pools are more rapid and more pronounced in the Tic$^-$ strain, which fails to inhibit translational initiation, than in the Tic$^+$ strain which does. It follows that the ability of Tic$^+$

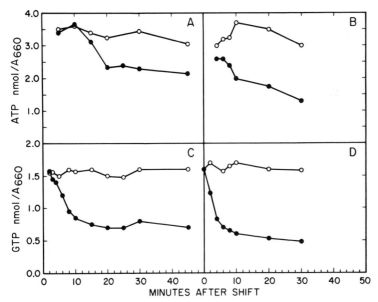

Fig. 7. Intracellular pools of ATP and GTP after shift to glucose medium (○) or to succinate medium (●). A, ATP, strain K12(λ) Tic$^+$; B, ATP, strain W1 Tic$^-$; C, GTP, strain K12(λ) Tic$^+$; D, GTP, strain W1 Tic$^-$. (Jacobson and Jen-Jacobson, 1980b).

strains to control translational initiation improves the ability to maintain homeostasis in these important pools under conditions of energetic stress.

The dynamics of changes in the nucleoside triphosphate pools and in the interrelated kinetic parameters of protein synthesis illustrate the sophistication with which *E. coli* copes with limited energy supply. The data of Table II show a rough correspondence between the degree of inhibition of translational initiation and the degree to which the functional stability of mRNA is increased in downshifted cells. By varying the physiological conditions, we have been able to measure translational initiation and mRNA inactivation rates over a 12-fold range of initiation frequencies (Jacobson and Jen-Jacobson, 1982). Over this entire range, the rate of functional inactivation of mRNA is linearly proportional to the initiation frequency, leading us to postulate that mRNA is protected from functional inactivation when a ribosome "dwells" at its point of attachment to mRNA.

What this means in physiological terms is that Tic$^+$ strains of *E. coli*, by inhibiting both translational initiation and, consequently, mRNA inactivation, are able to extend protein production from an initial mRNA population over a much longer period of time than their Tic$^-$ counterparts (Jacobson and Jen-Jacobson, 1980a). The net effect of this is to reduce the *rate* at which ATP and GTP are consumed in protein biosynthesis, enabling Tic$^+$ cells to maintain better homeostasis when the rate of generation of ATP and GTP is presumably reduced. It remains to be seen, of course, whether this degree of improvement in homeostasis leads to appreciable selective advantage.

We also regard as open the more general question of the true physiological significance of translational control in bacteria. G. P. Owens in our laboratory has shown (unpublished data) that control of translational initiation makes little or no contribution to the limitation of protein synthesis during steady-state growth at very slow rates (doubling times about 7 hours); the rate of protein synthesis in such cells is governed entirely by transcriptional controls. The control of translational initiation observed after a sudden shift-down is therefore most probably a transient regulation for use in emergencies. Translational control, being intrinsically more rapid of effect, bears the same relationship to transcriptional control that control of enzyme activity does to control of enzyme synthesis.

It may be significant that all *E. coli* strains we have examined which have been subject to little historic genetic manipulation show the Tic$^+$ phenotype, whereas strains with a previous history of heavy and repeated mutagenesis often have Tic$^-$ or Tic^{int} phenotype. We suppose that such regulatory variants were under no selective disadvantage under the rather artificial conditions of laboratory cultivation.

We strongly suspect that so sophisticated a regulatory mechanism must have some physiologically important role, and the fact that we do not understand it fully may reflect nothing more than the possibility that we have not yet reproduced in the laboratory the conditions under which *E. coli* evolved this mechanism. Nature undoubtedly "makes sense," but we do not yet comprehend it.

As Gunsalus and Stanier (1962) wrote in their preface to Vol. IV of "The Bacteria," "The terms of the definition have changed, the depth of understanding expanded, but the 'physiology of growth' still remains a sharp tool—a method—providing clues and insight."

ACKNOWLEDGMENTS

These studies were supported by grant GM-20114 from the National Institutes of Health. We are grateful to the American Society for Microbiology and to the Society of Biological Chemists for permission to reprint published materials.

REFERENCES

Dubnoff, J. S., Lockwood, A. H., and Maitra, U. (1972). Studies on the role of guanosine triphosphate in polypeptide chain initiation in *Escherichia coli*. *J. Biol. Chem.* **247,** 2884–2894.

Friesen, J. D. (1968). A study of the relationship between polyribosomes and messenger RNA in *Escherichia coli*. *J. Mol. Biol.* **32,** 183–200.

Gunsalus, I. C., and Stanier R. Y. (1962). "The Bacteria: A Treatise on Structure and Function," Vol. 4. Academic Press, New York.

Jacob, F., and Monod, J. (1961). Genetic regulatory mechanisms in the synthesis of proteins. *J. Mol. Biol.* **3,** 318–356.

Jacobson, L. A., and Baldassare, J. C. (1976). Association of messenger ribonucleic acid with 70S monosomes from down-shifted *Escherichia coli*. *J. Bacteriol.* **127,** 637–643.

Jacobson, L. A., and Jen-Jacobson, L. (1980a). Control of protein synthesis in *Escherichia coli*: Strain differences in control of translational initiation after energy source shift-down. *J. Bacteriol.* **142,** 888–898.

Jacobson, L. A., and Jen-Jacobson, L. (1980b). Control of protein synthesis in *Escherichia coli*: Lack of correlation with changes in intracellular pools of ATP, GTP, and ppGpp. *Arch. Biochem. Biophys.* **203,** 691–696.

Jacobson, L. A., and Jen-Jacobson, L. (1982). In preparation.

Jacquet, M., and Kepes, A. (1971). Initiation, elongation and inactivation of lac messenger RNA in *E. coli* studied by measurement of its β-galactosidase synthesizing capacity *in vivo*. *J. Mol. Biol.* **60,** 453–472.

Johnsen, K., Molin, S., Karlstrom, O., and Maaloe, O. (1977). Control of protein synthesis in *Escherichia coli*: Analysis of an energy source shift-down. *J. Bacteriol.* **131,** 18–29.

Koch, A. L. (1971). The adaptive responses of *Escherichia coli* to a feast and famine existence. *Adv. Microbial Physiol.* **6,** 147–217.

Krauss, S. W., and Leder, P. (1975). Regulation of initiation and elongation factor levels in *Escherichia coli* as assessed by a quantitative immunoassay. *J. Biol. Chem.* **250,** 3752–3758.

Leschine, S. B., and Jacobson, L. A. (1979). Control of protein synthesis in *Escherichia coli*:

Control of bacteriophage Qβ coat protein synthesis after energy source shift-down. *J. Virol.* **30,** 267–278.

Lodish, H. F. (1976). Translational control of protein synthesis. *Annu. Rev. Biochem.* **45,** 39–72.

Maaløe, O., and Kjeldgaard, N. O. (1966). "Control of Macromolecular Synthesis: A Study of DNA, RNA, and Protein Synthesis in Bacteria," p. 71. Benjamin, New York.

Neidhardt, F. C., Bloch, P. L., Pedersen, S., and Reeh, S. (1977). Chemical measurement of steady-state levels of ten aminoacyl-transfer RNA synthetases in *Escherichia coli. J. Bacteriol.* **129,** 378–387.

Ruscetti, F. W., and Jacobson, L. A. (1972). Accumulation of 70S monoribosomes in *Escherichia coli* after energy source shift-down. *J. Bacteriol.* **111,** 142–151.

Schleif, R., Hess, W., Finkelstein, S., and Ellis, D. (1973). Induction kinetics of the L-arabinose operon of *Escherichia coli. J. Bacteriol.* **115,** 9–14.

Westover, K. C., and Jacobson, L. A. (1974a). Control of protein synthesis in *E. coli.* I. Translation and functional inactivation of messenger ribonucleic acid after energy source shift down. *J. Biol. Chem.* **249,** 6272–6279.

Westover, K. C., and Jacobson, L. A. (1974b). Control of protein synthesis in *Escherichia coli.* II. Translation and degradation of lactose operon messenger ribonucleic acid after energy source shift down. *J. Biol. Chem.* **249,** 6280–6287.

17

From Bacterial Camphor Metabolism to Mammalian Protein Kinase Systems Regulated by Cyclic AMP, Cyclic GMP, and Calcium

J. F. Kuo

I. INTRODUCTION

Research had never been my serious preoccupation until I entered the laboratory of Professor I. C. Gunsalus in 1961 as a graduate student with an M.S. degree. By the time I left his laboratory in 1964 (gladly with a Ph.D.), I was fully convinced that scientific investigations, basic or applied, would be my career. In retrospect, aside from a variety of techniques and subjects, the most important training I received from him during that period was to learn how to listen and think when experiments seemed to go nowhere, and to remain objective and open-minded when experiments produced "expected" results. In spite of his many other responsibilities, Professor Gunsalus was never too busy for discussion, providing penetrating insights into the problems encountered and kindling one's imagination far beyond the immediate topics. It has been many years since I left Illinois and the research project of bacterial camphor metabolism; nevertheless, he has remained a constant source of inspiration. He is an individual who

EXPERIENCES IN BIOCHEMICAL PERCEPTION
Copyright © 1982 by Academic Press, Inc.
All rights of reproduction in any form reserved.
ISBN 0-12-528420-9

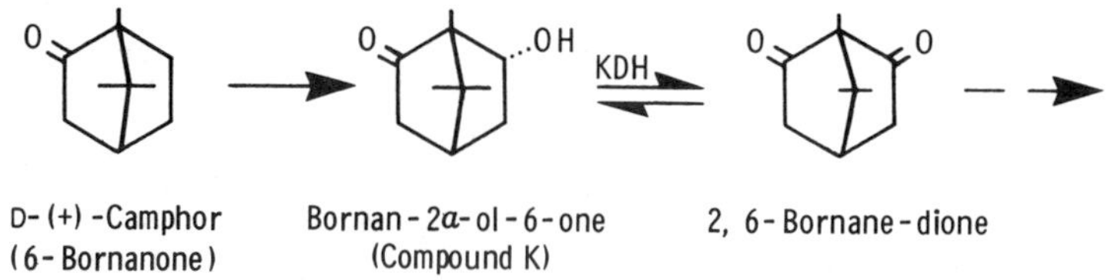

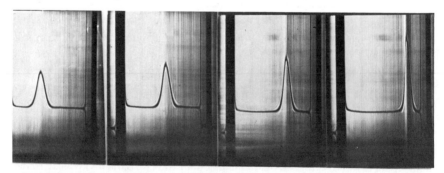

D-(+)-Camphor
(6-Bornanone)

Bornan-2α-ol-6-one
(Compound K)

2, 6-Bornane-dione

Fig. 1. Oxidative metabolism of camphor by *Corynebacterium* sp. strain T_1.

has profoundly influenced my career. It is only fitting that I dedicate this chapter in this book to my mentor Professor Gunsalus, honoring the occasion of his seventieth birthday. I dedicate it to him with deep admiration and affection.

II. A BACTERIAL DEHYDROGENASE IN CAMPHOR OXIDATION

As part of a project attempting to elucidate biochemical and genetic regulations of metabolism of bicyclic monoterpenoids (sources of substrates with a diversity of chemical structures), oxidative catabolism of (D)-(+)−camphor by *Corynebacterium* sp., strain T_1 was being actively investigated by Professor Gunsalus and his associates when I arrived in Illinois. I was immediately given the assignment, as a potential dissertation topic, to establish the occurrence, optimize the induction conditions, and to purify and study the properties and regulatory mechanism, of the then hypothetical bornan-2α-ol-6-one dehydrogenase (KDH), the enzyme involved in the second step of camphor oxidation pathway (Fig. 1). The enzyme was eventually purified to apparent homogeneity (Kuo, 1965), as indicated by the symmetry and nondiffusion of a single Schlieren peak in ultracentrifugation (Fig. 2) and by a single protein band in elec-

Fig. 2. Schlieren pattern of ultracentrifugation of purified KDH. Centrifugation times, from right to left, were 32, 64, 96, and 128 minutes. The $S_{20,w}$ was determined to be 6.04 (Kuo, 1965).

trophoresis. Some notable characteristics of KDH (Kuo, 1965; Gunsalus *et al.*, 1965) include an acidic protein (pI = 5.1) with a $S_{20,w}$ of 6.04 and a molecular weight of 101,000; consists of four nonidentical subunits; an A-type dehydrogenase with four NADH binding sites per mole of enzyme; possesses multiple active sites, thus likely conferring the enzyme with a broad substrate specificity capable of oxidizing a number of enantiomeric as well as epimeric pairs of bornane and non-bornane secondary alcohols.

III. MAMMALIAN PROTEIN KINASE SYSTEMS

A. Cyclic Nucleotide-Dependent Protein Kinases

Following the discovery of cyclic AMP-dependent protein kinase (A-PK) in the skeletal muscle by Walsh *et al.* (1968), we reported a widespread occurrence of the enzyme in a number of species and phyla of the Animal Kingdom (Kuo and Greengard, 1969). Subsequently, we found a separate class of protein kinase preferentially activated by the then new cyclic nucleotide, cyclic GMP, in arthropod (Kuo and Greengard, 1970; Kuo *et al.*, 1971) and mammalian tissues (Greengard and Kuo, 1970; Kuo, 1974). As a unifying hypothesis, we have suggested that the diversity of effects of cyclic AMP and cyclic GMP are mediated through activation of their respective target enzymes, i.e., A-PK and cyclic GMP-dependent protein kinase (G-PK) (Kuo and Greengard, 1969, 1970; Kuo, 1974). This hypothesis has been well supported by experimental evidence accumulated to date, although with a few exceptions in which cyclic nucleotides have been shown to bind to certain proteins unrelated to protein kinases. In addition to cyclic nucleotides, protein kinases are differentially regulated by endogenous proteins. Protein inhibitor inhibits A-PK (Walsh *et al.*, 1971) by interacting with the catalytic subunit of A-PK (Ashby and Walsh, 1972). We have identified the presence of another acidic protein, stimulatory modulator, which augments phosphorylation of histone subfractions (used as "general" substrate proteins for assaying protein kinases) by interacting with substrate proteins rather than with the enzyme (Donnelly *et al.*, 1973; Shoji *et al.*, 1978a). The effects of the two modulators are specific for the two classes of protein kinases, i.e., inhibitory modulator has no effect on G-PK, whereas stimulatory modulator has no effect on A-PK (Kuo and Kuo, 1976). The differential effects of cyclic nucleotides and modulators on the two classes of protein kinases are summarily illustrated in Fig. 3. The modulators are present ubiquitously in tissues with varying ratios (W. N. Kuo *et al.*, 1976). For example, while most rat tissues, such as the liver and lung, contain about equal parts of each factor, the skeletal muscle contains almost exclusively inhibitory modulator and, conversely, the small intestine contains predominantly stimulatory modulator (Fig. 4).

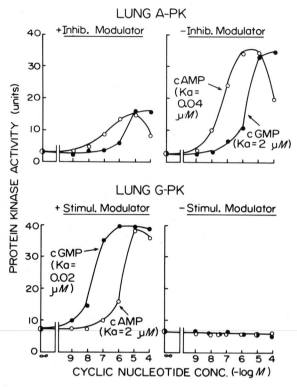

Fig. 3. Differential effects of stimulatory modulator and inhibitory modulator isolated from the rat lung on the phosphorylating activities of G-PK and A-PK, both from the guinea pig fetal lung (from W. N. Kuo *et al.*, 1976, with permission).

B. Calcium-Dependent Protein Kinase

Calcium is another key intracellular mediator for a variety of biological processes. Involvements of Ca^{2+} in protein phosphorylation have been demonstrated, as in the cases of phosphorylase (Cohen *et al.*, 1978), myosin light chain (Walsh *et al.*, 1979), and membrane proteins (Schulam and Greegard, 1978). In all cases, however, the activation of the responsible protein kinases by Ca^{2+} requires the presence of calmodulin, a Ca^{2+} binding protein playing a pivotal role in regulating Ca^{2+}-dependent systems (Cheung, 1980). Recently, Takai *et al.* (1979) reported the presence in the brain of another species of Ca^{2+}-dependent protein kinase (Ca-PK) stimulated by phospholipid rather than by calmodulin. We have confirmed their observations and demonstrated its widespread occurrence in the Animal Kingdom (Kuo *et al.*, 1980). The tissue levels of phospholipid-sensitive Ca-PK, compared to those of A-PK, G-PK, and calmodulin-sensitive Ca-PK, are exceedingly high in certain tissues (such as the brain and spleen) and exhibit a greater disparity among tissues (Kuo *et al.*, 1980), suggesting its discrete and predominant roles in certain processes. As stated earlier, the enzyme is stimulated by phospholipid (such as phosphatidylserine), but not by calmodulin, for its Ca^{2+}-dependent phosphotransferase activity (Table I). Interestingly, its stimulated activity is inhibited by trifluoperazine, an antipsychotic drug shown to inhibit calmodulin-sensitive Ca^{2+}-dependent processes (Weiss and Levin, 1978). This new protein kinase not only provides hitherto unknown mechanisms of actions for Ca^{2+} and phospholipid, but also expands conceptually the possibility of interactions of Ca^{2+} with cyclic nucleotides at the step of protein phosphorylation. The enzyme is now being purified from the extracts of the heart, spleen, and brain in our laboratory. Detailed studies dealing with its catalytic properties and regulatory mechanism are now in progress.

C. Phosphorylation of Endogenous Proteins

Protein phosphorylation is a common final pathway for the diverse effects of cyclic AMP, cyclic GMP, and Ca^{2+}. Demonstrations and identification of en-

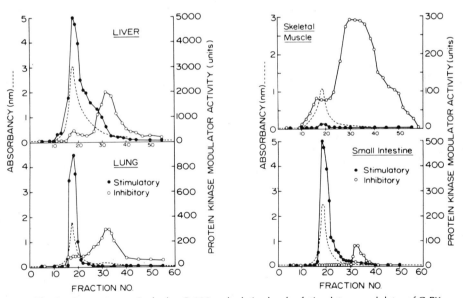

Fig. 4. Separation on Sephadex G-100 and relative levels of stimulatory modulator of G-PK and inhibitory modulator of A-PK in the rat liver, lung, skeletal muscle, and small intestine (from W. N. Kuo et al., 1976, with permission).

TABLE I

Comparative Effects of Phosphatidylserine (PS), Calmodulin, and Trifluoperazine (TFP) on the Activity of Phospholipid-Sensitive Ca-PK[a]

	Enzyme activity (pmol ^{32}P/min)	
Addition	Basal	$+Ca^{2+}$ (0.5 mM)
Rat spleen extract (22 μg protein)		
None	1.9	2.2
PS (5 μg/0.2 ml)	3.2	9.8
Calmodulin (2 μg/0.2 ml)	1.9	2.5
Purified bovine heart enzyme (0.2 μg protein)		
None	2.5	2.8
PS (5 μg/0.2 ml)	3.5	18.2
Calmodulin (2 μg/0.2 ml)	2.6	3.2
TFP (100 μM)	2.4	2.6
PS + TFP	3.2	12.0

[a] Ca-PK activity was assayed as described in Kuo et al. (1980), using lysine-rich histone (40 μg/0.2 ml) as substrate.

dogenous substrate proteins for protein kinases stimulated by these intracellular mediators, therefore, are of special interest. Phosphorylation of endogenous proteins in tissues stimulated by cyclic nucleotides has been a focus of recent investigations (for reviews, see Greengard, 1978; Glass and Krebs, 1980). The Ca^{2+}-dependent phosphorylation of endogenous proteins stimulated by calmodulin has also been demonstrated (for example, see Schulman and Greengard, 1978). In light of the presence of phospholipid-sensitive Ca-PK (Takai et al., 1979; Kuo et al., 1980), we suspected the presence of endogenous proteins whose Ca^{2+}-dependent phosphorylation is specifically augmented by phospholipid. We found that this is indeed the case (Wrenn et al., 1980). As shown in Fig. 5, in the cytosol of the rat cerebral cortex, the Ca^{2+}-dependent protein phosphorylation stimulated by phosphatidylserine is far more numerous and pronounced than that stimulated by calmodulin. In the particulate fraction of the same tissues, however, we noted that phospholipid and calmodulin both effectively stimulate the Ca^{2+}-dependent phosphorylation of specific proteins (Fig. 6). In the heart cytosol, we observed the presence of proteins whose phosphorylation is specifically stimulated by either Ca^{2+} plus phospholipid or Ca^{2+} plus calmodulin; in the particulate fractions (plasma membrane, mitochondria, microsome, and nuclei), however, phosphorylation of proteins is stimulated exclusively by Ca^{2+} plus calmodulin (Katoh et al., 1981). The functional significance of the two putative Ca^{2+}-dependent protein phosphorylation systems is unclear at present. It appears that phospholipid has a major role in regulating Ca^{2+}-dependent

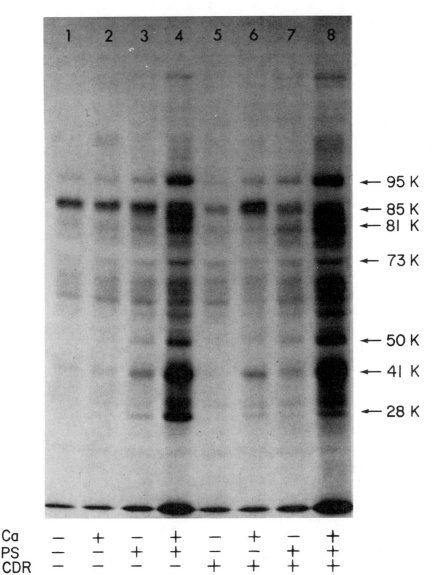

Fig. 5. Effects of Ca^{2+}, phosphatidylserine, and calmodulin on phosphorylation of substrate proteins from the rat cerebral cortex cytosol. The phosphorylation was carried out at 30° for 5 minutes in a reaction mixture (0.2 ml) containing Tris-Cl, pH 7.5, 4 μmol; $MgCl_2$, 0.2 μmol; EGTA, 0.05 μmol; cytosolic proteins, 150–200 μg; [γ-^{32}P]ATP, 0.75 nmol, containing about 2 × 10^7 cpm; in the presence or absence of $CaCl_2$ (0.1 μmol), phosphatidylserine (5 μg), or calmodulin (2 μg) as indicated. The reaction was initiated by addition of [γ-^{32}P]ATP. The sodium dodecyl sulfate–polyacrylamide gel electrophoresis (SDS–PAGE) and autoradiography of the phosphoproteins were performed as described by Rudolph and Krueger (1979). The cytosol used was rendered deficient in calmodulin by treating it with DEAE-cellulose (Wrenn et al., 1980, with permission).

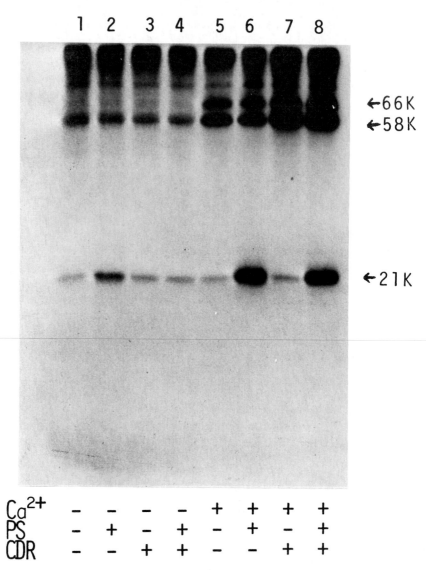

Fig. 6. Effects of Ca²⁺, phosphatidylserine, and calmodulin on phosphorylation of substrate proteins from the guinea pig cerebral cortex total (unfractionated) particulate. The experimental procedures were the same as in Fig. 5, except that the particulate was used as the source of endogenous proteins (Wrenn et al., 1980, with permission).

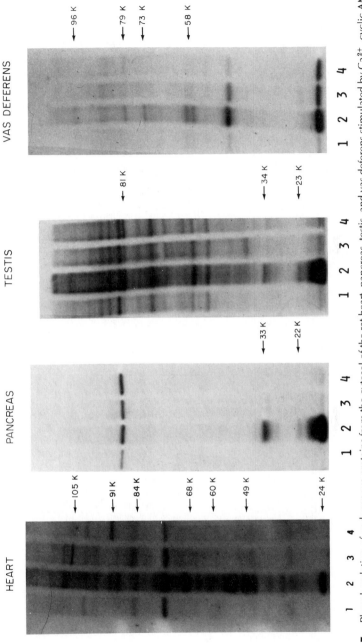

Fig. 7. Phosphorylation of endogenous proteins from the cytosol of the rat heart, pancreas, testis, and vas deferens stimulated by Ca²⁺, cyclic AMP, or cyclic GMP. The experimental procedures were as described in Fig. 5, except for the following variations: lane 1, control; lane 2, phosphatidylserine (5 μg) plus CaCl₂ (0.1 μmol); lane 3, cyclic AMP (0.2 nmol); lane 4, cyclic GMP (0.2 nmol).

phosphorylation in the cytosol, whereas calmodulin is more intimately involved in that process in the membranes.

Phosphorylation of proteins in extracts of the rat heart, pancreas, testis, and vas deferens by different protein kinase systems were compared (R. W. Wrenn and J. F. Kuo, unpublished). It is apparent that Ca^{2+} plus phosphatidylserine augments endogenous protein phosphorylation, which is more numerous and pronounced than that augmented (if demonstrable under the experimental conditions) by cyclic AMP or cyclic GMP (Fig. 7). The biological significance of Ca^{2+}-dependent protein phosphorylation remains largely undefined. Given the rapidly growing realization of Ca^{2+} as a central intracellular mediator, further investigation into this area is clearly in order. Possible interactions of protein phosphorylation systems dependent upon cyclic nucleotides and Ca^{2+} with respect to regulation of biological processes are depicted in Fig. 8. It may be suggested that phosphorylation of different substrate proteins (intermolecular specificity), or specific sites within common proteins (intramolecular specificity), catalyzed by the individual protein kinases may be a basis for the specific responses elicited by physiologic stimuli or pharmacologic agents.

D. Physiopathologic Aspects

Maintenance of normal physiologic processes requires a delicate balance of diverse reactions, including those involving cyclic nucleotides and Ca^{2+} illus-

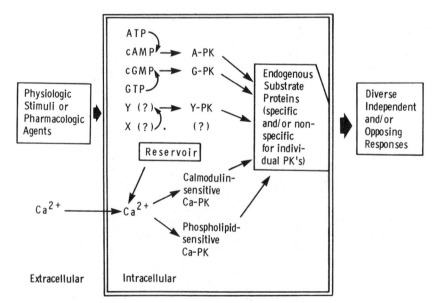

Fig. 8. A postulated scheme depicting biological responses regulated by Ca^{2+}-, cyclic AMP-, and cyclic GMP-dependent protein phosphorylation systems.

TABLE II

Developmental Changes in Levels of A-PK, G-PK, and Phospholipid-Sensitive Ca-PK in Extracts of Guinea Pig Tissues[a]

Tissue	Age	Tissue level (pmol ^{32}P/min/gm tissue)		
		A-PK	G-PK	Ca-PK
Lung	Fetus	960 ± 110	4,700 ± 310	3,200 ± 210
	Adult	2,400 ± 250[b]	1,200 ± 130[b]	2,960 ± 330
Brain	Fetus	4,650 ± 320	650 ± 110	4,200 ± 500
	Adult	4,250 ± 250	1,550 ± 250[b]	21,500 ± 2,100[b]
Liver	Fetus	1,450 ± 100	250 ± 50	1,650 ± 200
	Adult	1,250 ± 150	200 ± 50	3,500 ± 360[b]
Heart	Fetus	1,460 ± 140	410 ± 50	910 ± 50
	Heart	1,970 ± 220	230 ± 50[b]	880 ± 40

[a] The fetus was 20 days before birth, and the adult (pregnant female) was about 300 days old. The data (means ± SE, $n = 3$-5) shown are the net activity stimulated by added cyclic AMP (0.1 μM), cyclic GMP (0.1 μM), or Ca^{2+} (0.5 mM) for the respective classes of protein kinases.

[b] Significantly different from the fetus ($p < .001$ to $p < .05$).

trated in Fig. 8. It is conceivable that alterations or defects in any one site, or combinations of multiple sites, would theoretically result in an imbalance in these interplaying systems, leading to manifestations of special physiologic conditions or pathologic states. We have been actively pursuing this line of research. We have found that virtually all steps in the cyclic nucleotide systems (e.g., hormone receptors, cyclases, protein kinases and their modulators, and phosphodiesterases) are specifically and differentially modified in certain physiopathologic states of tissues, including ontogeny (Kuo, 1975; Helfman *et al.,* 1978), neoplasm (Shoji *et al.,* 1977), liver regeneration (Shoji *et al.,* 1978b), arteriovenous anastomosis and arterial occlusion (Kuo *et al.,* 1977), hypertension (J. F. Kuo *et al.,* 1976), and hormone-induced catecholamine supersensitivity and subsensitivity in the heart (Tse *et al.,* 1978, 1979, 1980). Some of the above observations have been reviewed (Kuo *et al.,* 1978). Ca^{2+}-dependent protein phosphorylation systems are also likely to be the potential sites of bioregulation. We noted recently (Wise *et al.,* 1981) that tissue levels of phospholipid-sensitive Ca-PK in the brain and liver from the fetal guinea pig are lower than those in the corresponding tissues from the adult animal (Table II). The ontogenetic change in the enzyme levels, however, is not detectable in the lung and heart. In comparison, the developmental-related changes in levels of A-PK and G-PK in some of these tissues are different from each other and from Ca-PK (Table II). These observations clearly demonstrate that changes in levels of protein kinases associated with ontogeny are specific not only for the tissues but also for the types of enzymes involved.

Investigations are now underway in our laboratory to determine whether or not the substrate proteins for protein kinases are also qualitatively or quantitatively altered in certain physiopathology of tissues.

IV. CONCLUDING REMARKS

The enzymology of A-PK and G-PK is well understood. A number of endogenous substrate proteins for A-PK have been identified, many of which are physiologic substrates whose properties or activities have been shown to alter upon phosphorylation (and dephosphorylation). Several endogenous proteins phosphorylated by G-PK have been demonstrated. Their identities and changes in properties upon phosphorylation, however, remain obscure. As for phospholipid-sensitive Ca-PK, neither the enzymology nor the identities of its substrate proteins are known. It is apparent, therefore, that the future direction of research in this area is to fill the gap of knowledge that now exists, and to elucidate the precise modes of interaction among different protein kinase systems, especially at the level of phosphorylation of a diversity of substrate proteins, leading to complex and yet well-defined biological processes.

ACKNOWLEDGMENTS

The original work done in the author's laboratory was supported by NIH grants HL-15696, CA-23391, NS-17608, T32-GM-07594, and T32-AM-07298. Some unpublished data included in this chapter are taken from experiments conducted by Robert W. Wrenn, Norio Katoh, and Bradley C. Wise.

REFERENCES

Ashby, C. D., and Walsh, D. A. (1972). Characterization of the interaction of a protein inhibitor with adenosine 3':5'-monophosphate-dependent protein kinase. Interaction with the catalytic subunit of the protein kinase. *J. Biol. Chem.* **247**, 6637–6642.

Cheung, W. Y. (1980). Calmodulin plays a pivotal role in cellular regulation. *Science* **207**, 19–27.

Cohen, P., Burchell, A., Foulkes, J. G., Cohen, P. T. W., Vanaman, T. C., and Nairn, A. C. (1978). Identification of the Ca^{2+}-dependent modulator protein as the fourth subunit of rabbit skeletal muscle phosphorylase kinase. *FEBS Lett.* **97**, 287–292.

Donnelly, T. E., Jr., Kuo, J. F., Reyes, P. L., Liu, Y. P., and Greengard, P. (1973). Protein kinase modulator from lobster muscle. I. Stimulatory and inhibitory effects of the modulator on the phosphorylation of substrate proteins by guanosine 3':5'-monophosphate-dependent and adenosine 3':5'-monophosphate-dependent protein kinases. *J. Biol. Chem.* **248**, 190–198.

Glass, D. B., and Krebs, E. G. (1980). Protein phosphorylation catalyzed by cyclic AMP-dependent and cyclic GMP-dependent protein kinases. *Annu. Rev. Pharmacol. Toxicol.* **20**, 363–388.

Greengard, P. (1978). Phosphorylated proteins as physiological effectors. *Science* **199**, 146–152.

Greengard, P., and Kuo, J. F. (1970). On the mechanism of action of cyclic AMP. *Adv. Biochem. Psychopharmacol.* **3**, 287–306.

Gunsalus, I. C., Chapman, P. J., and Kuo, J. F. (1965). Control of catalytic specificity and metabolism. *Biochem. Biophys. Res. Commun.* **18**, 924–931.

Helfman, D. M., Brackett, N. L., and Kuo, J. F. (1978). Depression of cytidine 3':5'-monophosphate phosphodiesterase in developing tissues of guinea pig. *Proc. Natl. Acad. Sci. U.S.A.* **75**, 4422–4425.

Katoh, N., Wrenn, R. W., Wise, B. C., Shoji, M., and Kuo, J. F. (1981). Substrate proteins for calmodulin-sensitive and phospholipid-sensitive Ca^{2+}-dependent protein kinases in heart, and inhibition of their phosphorylation by palmitoylcarnitine. *Proc. Natl. Acad. Sci. U.S.A.* **78**, 4813–4817.

Kuo, J. F. (1965). Camphor oxidation. A DPN-linked bornan-2α-ol-6-one dehydrogenase. Ph.D. Thesis, Univ. of Illinois, Urbana.

Kuo, J. F. (1974). Guanosine 3':5'-monophosphate-dependent protein kinase in mammalian tissues. *Proc. Natl. Acad. Sci. U.S.A.* **71**, 4037–4041.

Kuo, J. F. (1975). Changes in relative levels of cyclic GMP-dependent and cyclic AMP-dependent protein kinases in lung, heart and brain of developing guinea pigs. *Proc. Natl. Acad. Sci. U.S.A.* **72**, 2256–2259.

Kuo, J. F., and Greengard, P. (1969). Cyclic nucleotide-dependent protein kinases. IV. Widespread occurrence of adenosine 3':5'-monophosphate-dependent protein kinase in various tissues and phyla of the animal kingdom. *Proc. Natl. Acad. Sci. U.S.A.* **64**, 1349–1355.

Kuo, J. F., and Greengard, P. (1970). Cyclic nucleotide-dependent protein kinases. VI. Isolation and partial purification of a protein kinase activated by guanosine 3':5'-monophosphate. *J. Biol. Chem.* **245**, 2493–2498.

Kuo, J. F., Wyatt, G. R., and Greengard, P. (1971). Cyclic nucleotide-dependent protein kinases. IX. Partial purification and some properties of guanosine 3':5'-monophosphate-dependent and adenosine 3':5'-monophosphate-dependent protein kinases from various tissues and species of arthropoda. *J. Biol. Chem.* **246**, 7159–7167.

Kuo, J. F., Davis, C. W., and Tse, J. (1976). Depressed cardiac cyclic GMP-dependent protein kinase in spontaneously hypertensive rats and its further depression by guanethidine. *Nature (London)* **261**, 335–336.

Kuo, J. F., Malveaux, E. J., Patrick, J. G., Davis, C. W., Kuo, W. N., and Pruitt, A. W. (1977). Cyclic GMP-dependent and cyclic AMP-dependent protein kinases, protein kinase modulators and phosphodiesterases in arteries and veins of dogs. Distribution and effects of arteriovenous fistula and arterial occlusion. *Biochim. Biophys. Acta* **497**, 785–796.

Kuo, J. F., Shoji, M., and Kuo, W. N. (1978). Molecular and physiopathologic aspects of mammalian cyclic GMP-dependent protein kinase. *Annu. Rev. Pharmacol. Toxicol.* **18**, 341–355.

Kuo, J. F., Andersson, R. G. G., Wise, B. C., Mackerlova, L., Solomosson, I., Brackett, N. L., Katoh, N., Shoji, M., and Wrenn, R. W. (1980). Calcium-dependent protein kinase: Widespread occurrence in various tissues and phyla of the animal kingdom, and comparison of effects of phospholipid, calmodulin and trifluoperazine. *Proc. Natl. Acad. Sci. U.S.A.* **77**, 7039–7043.

Kuo, W. N., and Kuo, J. F. (1976). Isolation of stimulatory modulator of cyclic GMP-dependent protein kinase from mammalian heart devoid of inhibitory modulator of cyclic AMP-dependent protein kinase. *J. Biol. Chem.* **251**, 4283–4286.

Kuo, W. N., Shoji, M., and Kuo, J. F. (1976). Stimulatory modulator of guanosine 3':5'-monophosphate-dependent protein kinase from the mammalian tissues. *Biochim. Biophys. Acta* **437**, 142–149.

Rudolph, S. A., and Krueger, B. K. (1979). Endogenous protein phosphorylation and dephosphorylation. *Adv. Cyclic Nucleotide Res.* **10**, 107–133.

Schulman, H., and Greengard, P. (1978). Ca^{2+}-dependent protein phosphorylation system in membranes from various tissues and its activation by "calcium-dependent regulator." *Proc. Natl. Acad. Sci. U.S.A.* **75**, 5432–5436.

Shoji, M., Morris, H. P., Davis, C. W., Brackett, N. L., and Kuo, J. F. (1977). Modified cyclic nucleotide systems in Morris hepatoma 3924A favoring expression of cyclic GMP effect. *Biochim. Biophys. Acta* **500**, 419–424.

Shoji, M., Brackett, N. L., Tse, J., Shapira, R., and Kuo, J. F. (1978a). Molecular properties and mode of action of homogeneous preparation of stimulatory modulator of cyclic GMP-dependent protein kinase from heart. *J. Biol. Chem.* **253**, 3427–3434.

Shoji, M., Brackett, N. L., and Kuo, J. F. (1978b). Cytidine 3′:5′-monophosphate phosphodiesterase. Decreased activity in the regenerating and developing liver. *Science* **202**, 826–828.

Takai, Y., Kishimoto, A., Iwasa, Y., Kawahara, Y., Mori, T., and Nishizuka, Y. (1979). Calcium-dependent activation of a multifunctional protein kinase by membrane phospholipids. *J. Biol. Chem.* **254**, 3692–3695.

Tse, J., Brackett, N. L., and Kuo, J. F. (1978). Alterations in characteristics of cyclic nucleotide systems and in β-adrenergic receptor-mediated activation of cyclic AMP-dependent protein kinase during progression and regression of isoproterenol-induced cardiac hypertrophy. *Biochim. Biophys. Acta* **542**, 399–411.

Tse, J., Powell, J. R., Baste, C. A., Priest, R. E., and Kuo, J. F. (1979). Isoproterenol-induced cardiac hypertrophy. Modifications in characteristics of β-adrenergic receptors, adenylate cyclase and ventricular contraction. *Endocrinology* **105**, 246–255.

Tse, J., Wrenn, R. W., and Kuo, J. F. (1980). Thyroxine-induced changes in characteristics and activities of β-adrenergic receptors and cyclic AMP and cyclic GMP systems in the heart may be related to reputed catecholamine supersensitivity in hyperthyroidism. *Endocrinology* **107**, 6–16.

Walsh, D. A., Perkins, J. P., and Krebs, E. G. (1968). An adenosine 3′:5′-monophosphate-dependent protein kinase from rabbit skeletal muscle. *J. Biol. Chem.* **243**, 3763–3765.

Walsh, D. A., Ashby, C. D., Gonzalez, C., Calkins, D., Fischer, E. H., and Krebs, E. G. (1971). Purification and characterization of a protein inhibitor of adenosine 3′:5′-monophosphate-dependent protein kinase. *J. Biol. Chem.* **246**, 1977–1985.

Walsh, M. P., Vallet, B., Autrics, F., and Demaille, J. G. (1979). Purification and characterization of bovine cardiac calmodulin-dependent myosin light chain kinase. *J. Biol. Chem.* **254**, 12136–12144.

Weiss, B., and Levin, R. M. (1978). Mechanism for selectively inhibiting the activation of cyclic nucleotide phosphodiesterase and adenylate cyclase by antipsychotic agents. *Adv. Cyclic Nucleotide Res.* **9**, 285–304.

Wise, B. C., Andersson, R. G. G., Mackerlova, L., Raynor, R. L., Salomonsson, I., and Kuo, J. F. (1981). Ontogenetic aspects of phospholipid-sensitive calcium-dependent protein kinase in guinea pig tissues. *Biochem. Biophys. Res. Commun.* **99**, 407–413.

Wrenn, R. W., Katoh, N., Wise, B. C., and Kuo, J. F. (1980). Stimulation by phosphatidylserine and calmodulin of calcium-dependent phosphorylation of endogenous proteins from cerebral cortex. *J. Biol. Chem.* **255**, 12042–12046.

18

Phosphorus–Nitrogen Bonds in Proteins

Roberts A. Smith

A good teacher never knows how far his influence may be felt. I first felt Gunny's influence before I even met him, and now more than 20 years after leaving his laboratory, I still feel his influence on my own teaching and research. It is, in fact, because of Gunny's influence that I am now in the Division of Biochemistry in the Chemistry Department at UCLA rather than a dairy farmer on Vancouver Island.

In 1947, I enrolled at the University of British Columbia in the Faculty of Agriculture planning to learn how to run the farm that I hoped eventually to buy. By chance, my undergraduate adviser was Jack Campbell who had been Gunny's first graduate student at Cornell several years earlier. As I took classes from Jack and began to know him better, I eagerly listened to his stories of life at Cornell in Gunny's laboratory. What intrigued me most was that Jack's experience had been not only intellectually rewarding, but also had been exciting. The excitement resulted not merely from pleasant social interaction with a congenial group, but was mainly due to the rewards and fun of scientific experimentation under Gunny's direction. I was enjoying science, and feeling that I would respond to the challenge of research, began to veer from thoughts of a career as a farmer and to consider life as a scientist. I decided to work with Jack Campbell for a Master's degree in Bacteriology and see where things developed from there.

EXPERIENCES IN BIOCHEMICAL PERCEPTION
Copyright © 1982 by Academic Press, Inc.
All rights of reproduction in any form reserved.
ISBN 0-12-528420-9

Under Jack's excellent guidance I became intensely interested in the question of how obligately aerobic bacteria could grow utilizing acetate as their sole source of carbon; and I further decided to continue work on the problem and pursue a Ph.D. When a decision had to be made where to study, I, of course, chose to go to Urbana to work with Gunny. Happily, Gunny accepted me and my problem with me.

Gunny, in 1953, was in the Department of Bacteriology at the University of Illinois where he occupied a marvelously well-equipped L-shaped laboratory in Noyes Hall. The diversity of problems and the breadth of research undertaken there astonished me until I realized that Gunny's passion and energy seemed to be particularly challenged by the stimulation of new facts and novel ideas. He cautioned his students never to be content with one success, but to consider each success as only a step toward examining new questions and solving new problems. At the same time, Gunny imparted another tenet of his type of science— that is, not only should it be new, but it should be excellent.

In many ways, working with Gunny was not always easy. He required excellence in science, and was demanding and critical. His demands on his students, however, were no greater than the demands he placed on himself. Although he was critical, he was not demeaning, but used his criticism to force students to look at problems analytically and to develop critical thinking of their own. Because he was not bound by accepted ideas, he allowed his students to question and doubt. He did not discourage students from disagreeing with him knowing that the true value of a teacher lies in stimulating the natural curiosity of students and encouraging them toward independent thought.

While Gunny was directing students in their scientific experiments, he also took responsibility for their development in other areas. I remember his placing three glasses of white wine before me and demanding that I tell him which was the best and why. In the cultured atmosphere of Gunny's home, we were exposed to good food, good music, fine wine, and stimulating discussions. When his friends in the scientific community came to visit, and almost all the well-known biochemists came, he generally invited students to share dinner and evenings of conversation with them. Thus we had the opportunity of hearing some of the most important scientists in the country discuss their own research and respond to our questions in a more intimate atmosphere than students are generally able to enjoy.

The problem that I had brought from British Columbia piqued Gunny's interest and curiosity, and we were able to make a contribution (Smith and Gunsalus, 1957) to the development of ideas that ultimately led Kornberg and Krebs (1957) to formulate the glyoxylate bypass which provides a metabolic means for certain bacteria and some plant seeds to convert fatty acids into carbohydrates. Although that work had begun with Jack Campbell (Campbell *et al.*, 1953), it matured in

Gunny's laboratory and was ultimately explored and expanded in still other laboratories.

Having done what we thought we could with the isocitric lyase problem, I then became interested in the characterization and formation of succinyl lipoate. Will Gruber, an excellent Austrian-trained organic chemist whom I had known in British Columbia, joined Gunny's laboratory during that period and provided the chemical evidence that enzymatically formed succinyl lipoate was the secondary ester 6-S-succinyl lipoate (Gunsalus and Smith, 1958). My job was to accumulate the succinylated lipoate and to investigate the succinylation process.

In those days, before the general acceptance of column chromatographic methods of protein purification, we dealt with relatively nonsensitive enzyme assays and quite impure enzyme preparations. This led me to a mistaken interpretation of our data, suggesting a thiophosphate of CoA as an intermediate in the succinyl-CoA generating system used in the overall succinylation of lipoate (reactions I and II). Of course the reaction turned out to be much more complex than I had first imagined, but the idea of a reactive phosphorylated intermediate stimulated me to pursue an investigation of other such possibilities later. Despite my false start

$$\text{Succinate} + \text{ATP} + \text{CoA} \rightleftarrows \text{succinyl-CoA} + \text{ADP} + \text{P}_i \tag{1}$$

$$\text{Succinyl-CoA} + \text{lipoate} \rightleftarrows 6\text{-}S\text{-succinyl lipoate} + \text{CoA} \tag{2}$$

with succinyl-CoA synthetase, later colleagues in Gunny's laboratory, employing more purified enzyme preparations, made the critical and exciting observation that succinyl-CoA synthetase is phosphorylated during catalysis and that the phosphoryl group is acid-labile (Upper, 1964). Indeed, the concept of a thiophosphate intermediate, while quite incorrect in the succinyl-CoA synthetase reaction, cysteine-S-phosphate, has subsequently been shown to occur (Pigiet and Conley, 1978) in the bacterial thioredoxin system. Chris Upper's exciting observation (1964) showing that succinyl-CoA synthetase contained a covalently bound phosphoryl group was ultimately extended in Paul Boyer's laboratory (Hultguist *et al.*, 1966) with the first demonstration of the formation of a phosphoryl histidine at the catalytic site of succinyl-CoA synthetase. Although I had one further association with this complex enzyme later in my career (Moyer and Smith, 1966), it remained for others to ultimately elucidate its mechanism of action (Bridger, 1971).

Stimulated by the succinylation work, I began, when I arrived at UCLA, an examination of P–N-containing compounds as possible phosphagens, and for this work I selected phosphoramidate as a model substance. Although others had examined its biological hydrolysis previously, I was, in part, stimulated and encouraged in this work by the success Khorana and his associates (Moffatt and Khorana, 1958) had in chemically synthesizing nucleoside polyphosphates from

P–N-containing substances and their considerable expansion of the chemistry of these compounds.

We were very quickly able to show that extracts of *E. coli* contain at least two enzymes capable of hydrolyzing the P–N bond in phosphoramidate. But more significantly, it was possible to show the direct enzymatic phosphoryl transfer from phosphoramidate to glucose yielding glucose 6-phosphate (Fujimoto and Smith, 1962). Subsequent purification to homogeneity of this enzyme showed that it was a protein of approximately 10,000 daltons (Stevens-Clark *et al.*, 1968a) very rich in basic amino acids. This mystifying enzyme was capable of catalyzing the formation of glucose 6-phosphate as well as glucose 1-phosphate from phosphoramidate and glucose, and, in addition, acted as a phosphoramidase, producing inorganic phosphate and ammonia from phosphoramidate, It also acted as a phosphatase for both glucose 1-phosphate and glucose 6-phosphate and further had the capacity to act as a phosphoglucomutase, since it was capable of transferring the phosphoryl group from glucose 1-phosphate to another molecule of glucose forming glucose 6-phosphate. All of the reactions catalyzed by this enzyme are summarized in Eqs. (3–8).

$$P\text{-}NH_2 + H_2O \rightarrow P_i + NH_3 \tag{3}$$

$$P\text{-}NH_2 + glucose \rightarrow glucose\text{-}6\text{-}P + NH_3 \tag{4}$$

$$P\text{-}NH_2 + glucose \rightarrow glucose\text{-}1\text{-}P + NH_3 \tag{5}$$

$$Glucose\text{-}1\text{-}P + H_2O \rightarrow glucose + P_i \tag{6}$$

$$Glucose\text{-}6\text{-}P + H_2O \rightarrow glucose + P_i \tag{7}$$

$$Glucose\text{-}1\text{-}P + glucose \rightarrow glucose\text{-}6\text{-}P + glucose \tag{8}$$

Subsequent studies demonstrated that the enzyme could use a wide variety of other P–N-containing compounds equally well as phosphoryl donor. Evidence was finally obtained showing that the several transfer processes catalyzed by this enzyme were mediated by a common phosphoryl intermediate. That phosphoryl enzyme intermediate, shown in Scheme 1, was acid-labile and subsequently characterized (Stevens-Clark *et al.*, 1968a,b) as τ-phosphohistidine. Because of its wide specificity with respect to carbohydrate receptor and its apparent constitutive nature, we thought this enzyme might have to do with carbohydrate transport in a manner similar to the system described by Kundig and Roseman (Kundig *et al.*, 1966). However, later experiments ruled this possibility out, and the physiological function of this enzyme remains unknown to date. There is no evidence presently for the occurrence of inorganic phosphoramidate in biological systems, although Correll (1966) has shown the occurrence in certain fungi of imido phosphate polymers which are active phosphoryl donors with the purified enzyme from *E. coli*. The P–N-containing proteins later described in this chapter have not been assayed as substrates for this enzyme.

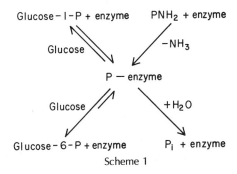

Scheme 1

Experiments employing rat liver microsomal enzyme sources have demonstrated the occurrence of a partially similar system in animal tissue. The careful analysis of this system revealed its probable identity with glucose-6-phosphate phosphatase (Parvin and Smith, 1969) since the phosphoramidate hexose transferase, glucose-6-phosphatase, and the pyrophosphate phosphotransferase system all respond in the same manner to a wide variety of manipulations. By hindsight, a much more likely interpretation of the results obtained with these enzyme systems suggests that phosphoramidate in dilute neutral aqueous solution is capable of chemically phosphorylating a histidine at the active site of these enzymes sufficiently fast to account for the formation of the catalytically active form of the enzyme. Indeed, the synthesis of phosphohistidine first reported by Wagner-Jauregg (Wagner-Jauregg and Hackley, 1953), and more carefully detailed by Hultquist (1968), depends upon precisely this phosphoryl transfer.

At a somewhat later date, and for very different reasons, my interests returned to P–N compounds, particularly their occurrence in proteins. So much attention has been paid to regulation of enzyme activity and conformational changes that take place in structural proteins as a result of phosphorylation that one can hardly help picking up a journal today without seeing at least two or three papers dealing with protein phosphorylation. Unfortunately, almost all such investigations reported involve phosphorylation on hydroxyamino acids with the resultant formation of acid-stable phosphomonoesters in proteins. We became interested in the possibility of chromosomal protein modification by phosphorylation on basic amino acids (Smith et al., 1973) and subsequently described nuclear enzymes obtained from either regenerating rat liver or Walker-256 carcinosarcoma which are capable of phosphorylating both histidines in histone H4 and lysine in histone H1. Perhaps the reason these acid-labile modifications have gone almost ignored is their extreme acid lability; for example, at pH values below 5, in a matter of minutes the P–N bonds are destroyed, and it is common knowledge that basic proteins such as histones behave much more predictably and are less readily degraded under acidic conditions than under neutral or basic conditions. As a result, biochemists, almost universally employing acid conditions, have examined phosphorylation on hydroxyamino acids with great care and have missed the phosphorylation of basic amino acids. We have shown (Chen *et al.*, 1977) that, dependent upon the particular phase of the cell cycle in regenerating rat liver, the ratio of acid-labile to acid-stable phosphoproteins is just about equal and, indeed, in a more recent report, Ringer *et al.* (1980) claim that over 90% of the phosphoryl bonds in chromosomal proteins are acid-labile. Ringer also shows that approximately 40% of the protein phosphorylations taking place in ribosomes are acid-labile.

After describing the formation of phosphohistidine in histone H4, further study revealed (Smith *et al.*, 1974) that both of its histidines occupying positions 18 and 75 (DeLange *et al.*, 1969) were biologically phosphorylated. Chen *et al.* (1974) showed that the H4 kinase appeared to peak in its activity coincident with DNA synthesis in regenerating rat liver, and in a double label experiment employing [32P]-labeled inorganic phosphate and [3H]histidine, he was able to demonstrate that it is strictly old H4 which is phosphorylated on its histidines while new H4 remains unmodified on those residues (Chen *et al.*, 1977). Chen *et al.* (1977) also demonstrated the relatively rapid turnover of H4 phosphate in regenerating liver showing a half-life of approximately 2 hours.

Isolation of this phosphorylated H4 from chromosomal preparations is difficult due to rapid enzymic hydrolysis and general overall lability. Employing phosphoramidate as a specific histidine phosphorylating agent, however, Fujitaki (Fujitaki and Smith, 1981) has easily generated larger quantities of phosphorylated H4. This technique not only frees us from the tedious task of isolating the highly labile H4 kinase, but allows us to investigate the effects on H4 conformation and function solely due to this acid-labile modification. Many years earlier, Rathlev and Rosenberg (1956) described the phosphorylation of the single histidine residue of insulin using phosphoramidate. Such phosphorylation of insulin has not been shown to occur enzymatically nor did their study conclusively show that the histidine residue was the actual phosphate acceptor. In addition, we now have more sensitive probes to characterize these P–N linkages in greater detail.

Employing [32P]-labeled phosphoramidate, we demonstrated the covalent nature of the phosphorylation of H4 as shown in Fig. 1; the product was acid-hydrolyzable and on either enzymatic or basic (3 M KOH) hydrolysis of [32P]-labeled phosphorylated H4 we were able to isolate [32P]phosphohistidine as the only phosphorylated species. Since H4 has only two histidines, each in a different region of the protein (DeLange *et al.*, 1969), we used [31P]-nmr to study the conformation of chemically phosphorylated H4 as any change in environment about the phosphoramidate linkage is indicated by chemical shifts, and relaxation times can be used to detect immobilization. When chemically phosphorylated H4 is placed in a structure-inducing solution, the [31P]-nmr spectrum (Fig. 2) reveals peaks at ≈4.8 ppm and 7.3 ppm (relative to 85% orthophosphoric acid). The former resonance is sharp, corresponds well with standard τ-phosphohistidine,

COOMASSIE BLUE   AUTORADIOGRAPHY

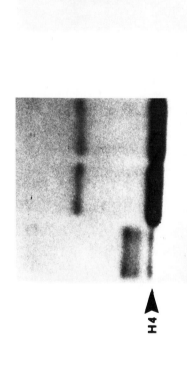

CORE
HISTONES **A**   **N**   **A**   **N**

Fig. 1. Demonstration of the acid lability of chemically phosphorylated histone H4. Histone H4 (10 mg) and ^{32}P-labeled dipotassium phosphoramidate (10 mg) were dissolved in 1 ml H_2O. The solution was allowed to sit overnight at room temperature and was subsequently dialyzed against several changes of H_2O. After dialysis, 40 μl of the phosphorylated H4 mixture was added to 40 μl of a solution containing 4% SDS, 20% glycerol, 10% 2-mercaptoethanol, 0.24 M Tris-HCl pH 8 (neutral loading buffer, N) and another 40 μl of the reaction mixture was added to 40 μl of 4% SDS, 20% glycerol, 10% 2-mercaptoethanol, 1 N HCl (acid loading buffer, A). After incubating 10 minutes at 37°C, the acid-treated sample was neutralized and 30 μl of each was applied to a neutral SDS 15% polyacrylamide gel. Standard core histones are shown on the left. Gels were stained in 0.1% Coomassie blue in 25% isopropanol made slightly alkaline with $NaHCO_3$ and destained in 10% isopropanol, pH also adjusted to 8 with $NaHCO_3$. Gels were dried on Whatman 3MM paper and autoradiography was done with the aid of intensifying screens. Decrease of H4 phosphorylation in acid-treated samples is clearly shown. Slower migrating protein band in the reaction mixtures is a contaminant.

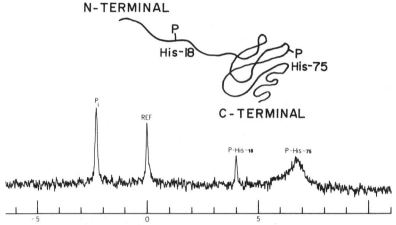

Fig. 2. ^{31}P nmr of chemically phosphorylated histone H4. The nmr spectra were obtained on a Bruker WP-200 nmr spectrometer operating in the Fourier transform mode at 81.02 MH$_z$ for ^{31}P resonance and equipped with a field-frequency lock on the deuterium resonance. The sample tubes used are 10 mm OD. Sample volumes are 2 to 5 ml with at least 20% D$_2$O. Data collected were not proton decoupled. Typical parameters used were spectrometer width 3 kHz, 70° pulse angle, dwell time 166 μsec, 8000 data points in free induction decay, relaxation delay 1.0 sec. pH was measured before and after scanning and was uncorrected for deuterium isotope effect. The reference peak shown is obtained from 85% orthophosporic acid contained in a coaxial capillary tube. Chemical shifts have been corrected with 0 ppm positioned at the corrected value for 85% orthophosphoric acid. The above spectrum is representative of chemically phosphorylated H4 in < 0.1 M NaCl. Higher salt concentrations caused aggregation making nmr analysis difficult. The sample pH is 7 and scanning temperature is 300° K. Number of scans is 17,000.

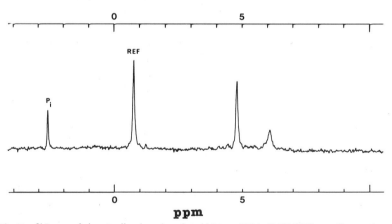

Fig. 3. ^{31}P nmr of chemically phosphorylated histone H4 in 0.1% SDS. nmr Parameters are as described in Fig. 5 except number of scans is 13,000 and pH is 9.3.

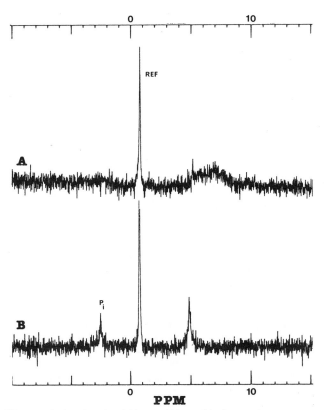

Fig. 4. ^{31}P nmr of phosphorylated histone H4 peptide fragments. nmr parameters are as described in Fig. 5 except number of scans is 16,000. Spectrum A shows chemically phosphorylated chymotryptic H4 fragment H4 (38–102) scanned under conditions described in Fig. 5. Spectrum B shows chemically phosphorylated acetic acid hydrolyzed H4 fragment H4(1–23) scanned under conditions described in Fig. 5.

and has been assigned to phosphorylation of histidine 18. The latter peak is broad suggesting less mobility and has been assigned to phosphorylation on histidine 75. Upon denaturation of phosphorylated H4, the characteristics of the latter resonance change drastically (Fig. 3). In more recent experiments (Fujitaki and Smith, 1981) we have been able to demonstrate by ^{31}P nmr analysis of phosphorylated peptide fragments of H4, that indeed the peak assignments are correct; our interpretations suggesting that the amino terminal end of H4 is mobile in solution while the carboxyl terminal end containing histidine 75 is immobilized (Fig. 4) coincides with an interpretation of H4 conformation arrived at independently through high resolution proton nmr and low angle neutron scattering by Bradbury and his associates (Lewis *et al.*, 1975). We have employed ^{31}P nmr spectroscopy to demonstrate the formation of phosphohistidine in H4 in nuclear extracts obtained from Walker-256 and also from regenerating rat liver. As showin in Fig. 5, the results confirm earlier observations by Bruegger *et al.* (1979) that regenerating rat liver nuclei preparations yield π-histidine phosphorylation in H4 while Walker-256 nuclei yield τ-histidine phosphorylation in H4.

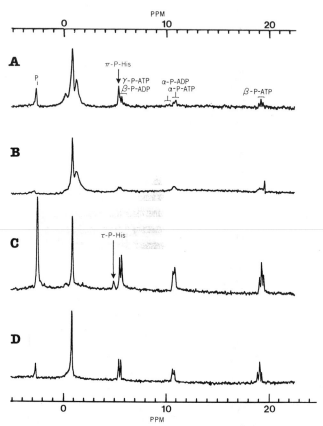

Fig. 5. ^{31}P nmr of *in vitro* enzymatically phosphorylated histone H4. The reaction was done using crude nuclear preparations from either 19-hour regenerating rat liver, A, or Walker-256 carcinsoarcoma, C, as source of kinase under the following conditions: reaction volume, 40 ml; ATP, 400 *M* (two separate additions to make this final concentration); MgCl$_2$, 10 m*M*; glycine–HCl buffer pH 9.5, 50 m*M*; H4, 40 mg; incubation for 10 minutes at 37°C. The reaction was quenched with 4 ml 10% SDS and then dialyzed against several changes of 0.1–1% SDS pH 7 (NaHCO$_3$), 5°C. Samples were then lyophilized and redissolved in H$_2$O/D$_2$O solution and run on ^{31}P nmr under parameters described in Fig. 2. Number of scans is 17,000. Note samples contain SDS and have a pH of 10. Spectra B and D are controls (no added H4) to A and C, respectively.

The chemical shifts obtained match well with those of standard preparations of π-phosphohistidine and τ-phosphohistidine.

In contrast to the work with H4, our studies on the phosphorylation on lysine residues of H1 have not been investigated beyond the demonstration of the phenomenon. An examination employing appropriate double labeling of the histone molecule with [³H]lysine and ³²P-labeled inorganic phosphate has shown that a mixture of both old and new H1 molecules are phosphorylated. Over the course of at least one wave of cell division in regenerating rat liver, there appears to be no increase in the H1 kinase activity in contrast to that seen with H4 kinase (Chen *et al.*, 1974).

Our current thrust with chromosomal proteins is to investigate their phosphorylation on basic amino acids employing the ATP analog, adenosine 5'-O-(3-thiotriphosphate). The P–O linkage of the thiophosphoryl group is known to be generally more stable than its phosphate analog against hydrolysis by phosphatases; thus we are investigating thiophosphoramidate stability on basic amino acids. ³¹P-nmr techniques appear to be a powerful probe for investigating the thiophosphoramidate linkage. Perhaps if these substances appear more stable both biologically and chemically, other laboratories will also recognize the important nature of P–N bonds in proteins, and we may begin to look at phosphorylation in total rather than simply on hydroxyamino acids.

We have also probed the occurrence of P–N bonds in brain proteins, particularly in myelin basic protein. An earlier observation demonstrated the formation both of phosphohistidine and phospholysine in this very basic protein component of myelin (Smith *et al.*, 1976). More recent studies (Steiner, 1980) have also confirmed the occurrence of these very acid and biologically labile linkages in brain proteins and, in a sense, have brought us back to succinyl-CoA synthase which is an important component of both liver and brain mitochondria. A very major difference exists between the brain and liver enzyme. As shown in Fig. 6, the very acid-labile major protein found in rat brain mitochondria is, as demonstrated immunologically, succinyl-CoA synthase (Steiner, 1980). In contrast to the enzyme found in liver mitoplasts, Steiner (1980) finds it is specifically phosphorylated with ATP and appears not to be phosphorylated with GTP. In addition, as shown in Fig. 6, a major acid-stable phosphorylated protein of 40,000 to 42,000 daltons appears within 10 seconds in the brain mitochondria and is not seen in rat liver mitoplasts or rat liver mitochondria unless incubated for much longer periods (½ to 1 hour). Preliminary investigations suggest this latter phosphoprotein is pyruvate dehydrogenase.

Why succinyl-CoA synthase in rat brain mitochondria should be so different from that in rat liver mitochondria in its nucleotide specificity is certainly obscure at this point. One can revert to teleological explanations such as a need in rat liver mitochondria for substrate levels of GTP for fatty acid activation, or GTP, AMP

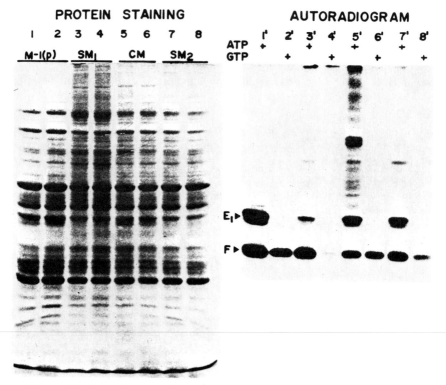

Fig. 6. Phosphorylation of rat brain mitochondrial proteins. Brain mitochondrial fractions (190 μg) were incubated for 20 seconds with [γ-^{32}P]ATP or [γ-^{32}P]GTP as indicated by (+). Samples were quenched with 50 μl of "neutral SDS" consisting of 9% SDS in a solution containing Tris-HCl (30 mM, pH 8.0), 2 mercaptoethanol, 9%; EDTA, 3 mM; and glycerol, 15%. Samples were resolved on 28 cm 10% acrylamide slab gels. Gels were stained in 0.03% Coomassie blue in 25% isopropanol and destained in 10% isopropanol adjusted to pH 8.0 with 2 M Tris-HCl buffer. Gels were dried onto Whatman 3MM paper and placed in contact with X-ray film employing intensifying screens. Lanes 1 and 2, free and synaptic mitochondria; lanes 3 and 4, light synaptic mitochondria; lanes 5 and 6, neuronal cell body-glial mitochondria; lanes 7 and 8, heavy synaptic mitochondria. Note that GTP only slightly phosphorylates the succinyl-CoA synthase (protein F) of heavy synaptic mitochondria and is virtually inactive with the light synaptic mitochondrial enzyme. In contrast (not shown in this figure), ATP is virtually inactive with liver mitochondrial enzyme while GTP is required by that enzyme (Steiner, 1980).

pyrophosphate transphosphorylase and the possible lack of these necessities in brain mitochondria, but such possibilities at this point remain only speculations.

Clearly, P–N bonds occur in proteins both as participants in catalytic transformations as well as in proteins of other function such as the chromosomal proteins and proteins of myelin. The P–N bonds are extremely labile both biologically and chemically and thus their investigation has not been widely popular. However, their occurrence is clearly demonstrated and thus their investigation should move from purely phenomenological to attempts at understanding their biological function.

REFERENCES

Bridger, W. A. (1971). *In* "The Enzymes" (P. D. Boyer, ed.), 3rd ed., Vol. 10, pp. 581–606. Academic Press, New York.

Bruegger, B. B., DeLange, R. J., Smith, R. A., and Lin, Y. C. (1979). *J. Chin. Chem. Soc.* **26**, 5–10.

Campbell, J. J. R., Smith, R. A., and Eagles, B. A. (1953). *Biochim. Biophys. Acta* **11**, 594.

Chen, C.-C., Smith, D. L., Bruegger, B. B., Halpern, R. M., and Smith, R. A. (1974). *Biochemistry* **13**, 3785–3789.

Chen, C.-C., Bruegger, B. B., Kern, C. W., Lin, Y. C., Halpern, R. M., and Smith, R. A. (1977). *Biochemistry* **16**, 4852–4855.

Correll, D. L. (1966). *Science* **151**, 819–820.

DeLange, R. J., Fambrough, D. M., Smith, E. L., and Bonner, J. (1969). *J. Biol. Chem.* **244**, 319–334.

Fujimoto, A., and Smith, R. A. (1962). *Biochim. Biophys. Acta* **56**, 501–511.

Fujitaki, J., and Smith, R. A. (1981). In preparation.

Gunsalus, I. C., and Smith, R. A. (1958). *In* "Proceedings of the International Symposium on Enzyme Chemistry, Tokyo and Kyoto, 1957" (K. Ichibara, ed.), pp. 77–86. Academic Press, New York.

Hultquist, D. E. (1968). *Biochim. Biophys. Acta* **153**, 329–340.

Hultquist, D. E., Moyer, R. W., and Boyer, P. D. (1966). *Biochemistry* **5**, 322–331.

Kornberg, H. L., and Krebs, H. A. (1957). *Nature (London)* **179**, 988–991.

Kundig, W., Kundig, F. D., Anderson, B., and Roseman, S. (1966). *J. Biol. Chem.* **241**, 3243–3246.

Lewis, P. N., Bradbury, E. M., and Crane-Robinson, C. (1975). *Biochemistry* **14**, 3391–3395.

Moffatt, J. G., and Khorana, H. G. (1958). *J. Am. Chem. Soc.* **80**, 3756–3761.

Moyer, R. H., and Smith, R. A. (1966). *Biochem. Biophys. Res. Commun.* **22**, 603–609.

Parvin, R., and Smith, R. A. (1969). *Biochemistry* **8**, 1748–1755.

Pigiet, V., and Conley, R. R. (1978). *J. Biol. Chem.* **253**, 1910–1920.

Rathlev, T., and Rosenberg, T. (1956). *Arch. Biochem. Biophys.* **65**, 319–339.

Ringer, D. P., King, R. L., and Kizer, D. E. (1980). *Fed. Proc., Fed. Am. Soc. Exp. Biol.* **39**, Abstr. 735, 1742.

Smith, D. L., Bruegger, B. B., Halpern, R. M., and Smith, R. A. (1973). *Nature (London)* **246**, 103–104.

Smith, D. L., Chen, C. C., Bruegger, B. B., Holtz, S. L., Halpern, R. M., and Smith, R. A. (1974) *Biochemistry* **13**, 3780–3785.

Smith, L. S., Kern, C. W., Halpern, R. M., and Smith, R. A. (1976). *Biochem. Biophys. Res. Commun.* **71**, 459–465.

Smith, R. A., and Gunsalus, I. C. (1957). *J. Biol. Chem.* **229**, 305–319.

Steiner, A. W. (1980). Thesis, Univ. of California, Los Angeles.

Stevens-Clark, J. R., Theisen, M. C., Conklin, K. A., and Smith, R. A. (1968a) *J. Biol. Chem.* **243,** 4468–4473.
Stevens-Clark, J. R., Conklin, K. A., Fujimoto, A., and Smith, R. A. (1968b) *J. Biol. Chem.* **243,** 4474–4478.
Upper, C. D. (1964). Thesis, Univ. of Illinois, Urbana.
Wagner-Jauregg, T., and Hackley, B. E. (1953). *J. Am. Chem. Soc.* **75,** 2125–2130.

19

Regulation
of Glutamine Synthetase
Degradation

C. N. Oliver,
R. L. Levine,
and
E. R. Stadtman

I. INTRODUCTION

The regulation of cellular metabolism is achieved by mechanisms that modulate the catalytic activities and the concentrations of key enzymes. Regulation of enzyme activities involves reversible alterations of enzyme conformations through allosteric interactions, covalent modification, or by mass action effects of substrates, whose concentrations are subject to both kinetic and thermodynamic constraints (Stadtman, 1970). Regulation of enzyme levels involves modulation of the rates of enzyme synthesis, on the one hand, and the rates of enzyme degradation, on the other (Schimke, 1969). Whereas much is known about the mechanisms utilized in the regulation of enzyme synthesis, comparatively little is known about the mechanisms involved in the regulation of enzyme degradation. The available evidence does show that protein degradation is a dynamic process and that it is a property of all living organisms. The likelihood that all organisms utilize similar if not identical mechanisms is suggested by the generality of several characteristics, most important of which are the dependence of protein degradation on an energy supply (presumably in the form of ATP) and the highly selective nature of the degradation process (Goldberg and St. John, 1976; Holzer and Heinrich, 1980). Since proteolysis is a highly exergonic pro-

EXPERIENCES IN BIOCHEMICAL PERCEPTION
Copyright © 1982 by Academic Press, Inc.
ISBN 0-12-528420-9

cess, the requirement for ATP is not explicable on thermodynamic grounds. The possibility that ATP has a regulatory role finds support in the recent studies of Hershko *et al.* (1980) and Wilkinson *et al.* (1980) showing that the degradation of denatured proteins in reticulocyte lysates is initiated by the ATP-dependent conjugation of a small peptide, ubiquitin, to lysine residues of the protein. Whether or not a similar mechanism can explain the ATP requirement for proteolysis in other biological systems remains to be investigated. The high selectivity of the degradation process is evident from the fact that there are great differences in the degradation rates of normal enzymes, and these are subject to nonsynchronous changes in response to changes in the metabolic state of the cell. Moreover, abnormal proteins (i.e., denatured proteins and defective proteins arising from posttranslational modifications, random errors in protein synthesis, and missense and nonsense mutations) are preferentially degraded (Goldberg and St. John, 1976; Holzer and Heinrich, 1980). Thus, protein degradation serves as a ''garbage disposal system'' that protects cells from the accumulation of excessive amounts of useless waste materials, and at the same time it functions as a recycling system for the conversion of waste materials to free amino acids that can be utilized once again for the synthesis of essential proteins or as a source of energy.

Whereas the characteristics of protein degradation are well defined at the phenomenological level, there is little insight to the underlying mechanism involved. With regard to the degradation of normal enzymes (proteins), two questions remain unanswered: (1) What determines whether a given enzyme will be spared or degraded? (2) When an enzyme is selected for degradation, how is it made susceptible to proteolytic attack? Both are clearly problems of regulation, and because of a commitment of our laboratory to elucidate basic mechanisms of cellular regulation, we have been trying for some years now to develop an *in vitro* system that could be used to investigate these problems. In an effort to identify some enzymes whose rates of degradation are affected by nutritional factors, the effects of nitrogen and carbon starvation on the levels of normal enzymes in *Escherichia coli* and *Klebsiella aerogenes* were examined.

Of the 22 enzymes examined in *E. coli,* the activities of about one-half decreased during starvation, whereas the activities of the others either increased or remained unchanged (Maurizi, 1980; M. Pehlke and E. R. Stadtman, unpublished data). Of particular significance, however, was the finding that variations in enzyme levels elicited by nitrogen starvation were both qualitatively and quantitatively different from those accompanying carbon starvation. Glutamate dehydrogenase, aspartokinase III, and glutamine synthetase are among the enzymes whose activities decreased most rapidly (8–35% per hour) under starvation conditions. In these cases, it was demonstrated that the loss of activity is associated with a loss of enzyme protein, i.e., the loss reflects protein degradation (Maurizi, 1980). It is therefore presumed that decreases in the other enzyme levels are due also to protein degradation. These results demonstrate that nutritional factors are among those that govern enzyme levels. It appears likely, therefore, that nutritional factors are involved in both the selection of those enzymes to be degraded and also in the preparation of marked enzymes for proteolytic attack.

In a series of similar experiments, it was found that nitrogen starvation of *K. aerogenes* MK-53 is accompanied by an accelerated rate of glutamine synthetase degradation, which was inhibited by dinitrophenol and was enhanced by chloramphenicol (Fulks, 1977). Subsequent efforts to observe glutamine synthetase degradation in cell-free extracts of nitrogen-starved *K. aerogenes* failed; however, the cell-free extracts did catalyze rapid inactivation of endogeneous glutamine synthetase, as well as of added highly purified glutamine synthetase from *E. coli*. This inactivation was dependent on the presence of Fe(III), O_2, and NADPH or NADH, and was inhibited by either *o*-phenanthroline, Mn(II) or EDTA, and by catalase (R. M. Fulks and R. L. Levine, unpublished data). Curiously, the inhibition by *o*-phenanthroline was reversed by an excess of Fe(III), whereas the inhibition by EDTA was not; moreover, the requirement for O_2 could not be replaced by H_2O_2, or by H_2O_2-generating systems, either in the presence or absence of added catalase.

In retrospect, it is fortuitous that extracts of the *K. aerogenes* used in these experiments catalyzed the inactivation of glutamine synthetase, because this strain produces little or no catalase, and as noted above, catalase inhibits the inactivation reaction.

In light of the catalase effect, it was possible that the inability of *E. coli* extracts to catalyze glutamine synthetase inactivation is due to the high concentration of catalase in these extracts. This possibility was supported by the fact that addition of *E. coli* extracts to the *K. aerogenes* extracts inhibited the inactivation reaction. Based on its catalase content, the *E. coli* extract was slightly more inhibitory than an equivalent amount of bovine catalase, suggesting either that the *E. coli* catalase is a more potent inhibitor than bovine catalase or that, in addition to catalase, the *E. coli* extracts contain other inhibitory components (i.e., peroxidases).

Prompted by these results, further studies (Oliver and Stadtman, 1980) led to the demonstration that glutamine synthetase inactivation is catalyzed by partially purified enzyme preparations of *E. coli* and *Pseudomonas putida* from which catalase has been removed.

We report here the results obtained with these catalase-free extracts, showing that glutamine synthetase inactivation shows properties in common with the inactivation reaction in *K. aerogenes,* and that a similar inactivation is catalyzed by purified components of a rabbit microsomal P450-cytochrome *c* reductase mixed-function oxidase system, as well as by purified components of a putidaredoxin-dependent mixed-function oxidase system from *P. putida*. Similar inactivation of glutamine synthetase is catalyzed by any one of several nonenzymic model systems. Furthermore, it was demonstrated that the inactivation reaction is dependent on the state of adenylylation of glutamine synthetase and is modulated by the concentrations of glutamate and ATP. Finally, it was found that following inactivation by the mixed-function oxidation reaction, the glutamine synthetase is susceptible to proteolytic degradation. Based on these observations, we propose that the degradation of glutamine synthetase may be a prototype for regulation of the degradation of some normal enzymes.

TABLE I

Glutamine Synthetase (GS) Inactivation by Catalase-Free Enzyme Preparations[a]

	Source of Inactivation System		
Conditions	K. aerogenes (GS lost/10 minutes) (%)	P. putida (GS lost/10 minutes) (%)	E. coli (GS lost/15 minutes) (%)
Complete system	53	28	61
− ATP	—	19	42
− FeCl₃	3	11	—
− NADPH	3	1	1
− O₂	0	0	—
+ Catalase	2	1	3
− Enzyme preparation	—	3	1

[a] The *Klebsiella* extract from strain MK-9000 was obtained by French pressure cell disruption followed by two centrifugation steps. The resulting supernatant fraction contained 15–18 mg/ml protein as determined by the Coomassie blue method (Bradford, 1976) and contained less than 1 unit/ml of catalase (Beers and Sizer, 1952). Similarly prepared *E. coli* extracts possess 350 units/ml of catalase. To measure inactivation of endogenous glutamine synthetase in the *Klebsiella* extract, reaction mixtures (0.250 ml) contained 20 mM 2-methylimidazole buffer (pH 8.0), 10 mM MgCl$_2$, 0.1 mM FeCl$_3$, 1.0 mM NADPH, up to 0.2 ml extract, and where indicated, 0.57 μM catalase. Reactions were started by the addition of nucleotide, incubated at 37°C in a shaking water bath, and at various times aliquots were removed, diluted into cold 10 mM imidazole buffer (pH 7.0), 1 mM MnCl$_2$, 100 mM KCl, and assayed for glutamine synthetase activity by the pH 7.57 γ-glutamyltransferase assay (Stadtman *et al.*, 1979).

Escherichia coli and *P. putida* extracts were prepared by French pressure cell disruption or sonication. The *E. coli* strain used in these studies was a heme-deficient mutant obtained by neomycin selection (Sasarman *et al.*, 1968), which possessed tenfold less catalase activity than wild type. The *P. putida* cells used in this study were not grown in the presence of camphor. Partial purification of the extracts to remove residual catalase activity involved streptomycin sulfate treatment, mercaptoethanol treatment, ammonium sulfate fractionation, DEAE chromatography, followed by concentration to 1–6 mg/ml protein by Coomassie blue assay (Bradford, 1976; details will be published elsewhere). These *E. coli* and *P. putida* preparations were assayed for the capacity to inactivate exogenous purified *E. coli* glutamine synthetase. Reaction mixtures contained 200 μg glutamine synthetase, 1 mM ATP, 1 mM NADPH, 50 mM Tris buffer (pH 7.4), 50 μM FeCl$_3$, 10 mM MgCl$_2$, 80 μg *E. coli* extract, or 53 μg of *P. putida* extract, and where indicated, 0.10 μM bovine catalase. Reaction conditions and sampling were the same as described above, except the sampling buffer was 50 mM Tris (pH 7.4) 10 mM MnCl$_2$.

II. RESULTS

A. Inactivation of Glutamine Synthetase by Catalase-Free Enzyme Preparations

The data in Table I show that partially purified (catalase-free) preparations of *P. putida*, *E. coli*, and *K. aerogenes* catalyze the inactivation of glutamine synthetase. Where tested, inactivation is dependent on NADPH, Fe(III), and O_2, is stimulated by ATP, and is inhibited by catalase.

B. Inactivation of Glutamine Synthetase by P450-Linked Mixed-Function Oxidation Systems

The requirement for NADPH, O_2, and Fe(III) in the above glutamine synthetase inactivation systems suggested that a mixed-function oxidation type of reaction is involved. We therefore examined the ability of two well-defined mixed-function oxidase systems to catalyze inactivation of glutamine synthetase. One of these consisted of highly purified preparations of cytochrome c reductase and phenobarbital-induced P450 (LM$_2$) from rabbit liver microsomes. The other

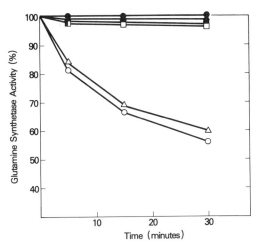

Fig. 1. Inactivation of glutamine synthetase by rabbit liver microsomal P450 and cytochrome c reductase in the presence of NADPH. The complete inactivation mixture (0.2 ml) contained 200 μg of glutamine synthetase, 0.3 μM cytochrome c reductase, 0.15 μM P450 (LM$_2$), 20 μg dilauroylphosphatidylcholine, 1 mM NADPH, 50 mM Tris buffer (pH 7.4), 50 μM FeCl$_3$, 10 mM MgCl$_2$; components were deleted as follows: ○—○, none; ▲—▲, cytochrome c reductase; ■—■, NADPH; □—□, P450; △—△, dilauroylphosphatidylcholine; ●—●, cytochrome c reductase, NADPH, P450, dilauroylphosphatidylcholine. Reaction conditions were the same as those described in *E. coli* extract in Table I.

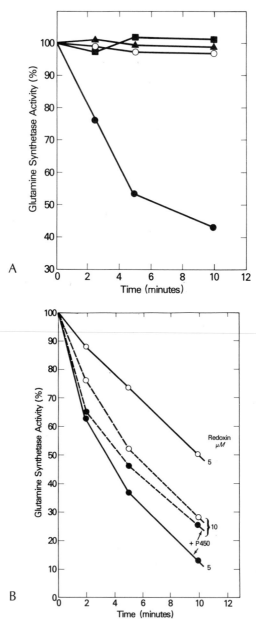

Fig. 2. Inactivation of glutamine synthetase by *Pseudomonas* mixed-function oxidase components. (A) Inactivation of glutamine synthetase by *Pseudomonas* reductase-redoxin in the presence of NADH. The complete inactivation mixture was the same as that described for Table II. Components were deleted as follows: ●—●, none; ■—■, redoxin; ▲—▲, reductase;

consisted of purified preparations of redoxin reductase, redoxin, and $P450_{cam}$ from *P. putida*.

Data summarized in Figs. 1 and 2 show that both of these P450-linked oxidation systems catalyze the inactivation of glutamine synthetase. Inactivation by the microsomal system (Fig. 1) is dependent on cytochrome *c* reductase, P450 (LM_2), and NADPH (Fig. 1), and also on molecular oxygen (Table II). With the rabbit liver microsomal mixed-function oxidation system, there was little, if any, stimulation of the inactivation reaction by the phospholipid, dilauroylphosphatidylcholine (Fig. 1); however, phospholipid was required when another preparation of the rabbit liver cytochrome *c* reductase was used (data not shown).

Results of experiments with the enzymes from *P. putida* are shown in Fig. 2. Surprisingly, high concentrations of redoxin (20 μM) catalyze the inactivation of glutamine synthetase in the absence of added $P450_{cam}$. This inactivation is absolutely dependent on redoxin, redoxin reductase, and NADPH (Fig. 2A), and also on O_2 (Table II). At this high level of redoxin, the further addition of $P450_{cam}$ is without effect (data not shown). However, as shown in Fig. 2B, the rate of inactivation catalyzed by 5 μM redoxin is enhanced considerably by addition of $P450_{cam}$ and less so with 10 μM redoxin.

C. Properties of Various Glutamine Synthetase Inactivation Systems

Other properties of the P450-linked inactivation reactions are summarized in Table II. For comparison, Table II also summarizes the results obtained with a catalase-deficient extract of *K. aerogenes,* as well as those obtained with an artificial system consisting of ascorbate, Fe(III), and O_2. The artificial system was examined because it has been shown to catalyze nonenzymically several reactions that are catalyzed by P450 mixed-function oxidase systems (Udenfriend *et al.,* 1954). From the data in Table II, it is evident that all five inactivation systems share many properties in common. In every case, the inactivation of glutamine synthetase is dependent on O_2 (i.e., it does not occur in either N_2 or argon); it is prevented by catalase, by horseradish peroxidase, and by $MnCl_2$ and is augmented by Fe(III). Sodium azide, an inhibitor of catalase, stimulates the inactivation catalyzed by *K. aerogenes* extract but is without effect on all other systems. Furthermore, the metal ion chelators, *o*-phenanthroline and

---

○—○, NADH. Reaction mixtures were incubated and assayed for glutamine synthetase activity as described in Table I. (B) Effect of redoxin concentration on the stimulation of *Pseudomonas* reductase-redoxin inactivation of glutamine synthetase by $P450_{cam}$. Dashed lines represent mixtures containing 10 μM redoxin, solid lines designate 5 μM redoxin, and closed circles indicate the addition of $P450_{cam}$. Otherwise the reaction mixtures were as described in Table II. Incubations and assays for glutamine synthetase activity were as described in Table I.

TABLE II

Properties of the Glutamine Synthetase Inactivation Systems[a]

		Inactivation System			
				Pseudomonas	
Additions	Klebsiella	Ascorbate	Microsomal	$- P450_{cam}$	$+ P450_{cam}$
None[b]	100	100	100	100	100
Inert gas	0	2	3	20	8
Catalase	19	0	0	4	3
Peroxidase	11	0	14	—	—
NaN_3	168	—	100	106	95
$MnCl_2$	2	29	0	0	0
$FeCl_3$	126	240	135	122	114
EDTA	0	0	0	2	0
EDTA + $FeCl_3$	0	15	0	160	22
o-Phenanthroline	9	0	7	0	5
o-Phenanthroline + $FeCl_3$	75	154	178	88	98

[a] Preparation of the Klebsiella extract was the same as that described in Table I. The Klebsiella inactivation system was the same as in Table I, except that 1 mM NADPH was replaced by 6.5 mM NADH and $FeCl_3$ was not added. Other additions, where indicated, were 0.57 μM catalase, 0.078 μM peroxidase (horseradish), 2 μM superoxide dismutase, 1 mM $MnCl_2$, 100 μM $FeCl_3$, 1 mM EDTA, 1 mM EDTA plus 1.5 mM $FeCl_3$, 180 μM o-phenanthroline, 180 μM o-phenanthroline plus 270 μM $FeCl_3$, 500 μM NaN_3, and 500 μM NaCN. The ascorbate inactivation mixtures contained 0.48 μM glutamine synthetase, 15 mM ascorbate, 100 mM 2-methyl imidazole (pH 7.2), 10 mM $MgCl_2$. Other additions, where indicated, were 0.610 μM catalase, 0.560 μM peroxidase, 5 μM superoxide dismutase, 400 μM $MnCl_2$, 4 mM $MnCl_2$, 100 μM o-phenanthroline, and 100 μM o-phenanthroline plus 500 μM $FeCl_3$. The concentrations of EDTA, $FeCl_3$, and NaN_3 were the same as above. The microsomal inactivation mixture was the same as described for Fig. 1, except that $FeCl_3$ was not added, and the concentrations of other substances, where indicated, were the same as described for the ascorbate system, except that 140 μM superoxide dismutase was used in this experiment. Inactivation mixtures of the Pseudomonas reductase–redoxin contained 130 μg glutamine synthetase, 0.5 μM reductase, 10 μM redoxin, 1 mM NADH, 50 mM Hepes buffer (pH 7.4), and 5 mM $MgCl_2$. The Pseudomonas reductase-redoxin–P450 inactivation mixture was the same as that just described, except that 5 μM redoxin and 0.5 μM P450 were used. Where indicated, the concentrations of other substances were the same as described for the microsomal system, except that 200 μM $FeCl_3$ and 700 μM EDTA plus 900 μM $FeCl_3$ were used. Sampling and assay were described in Table I.

[b] For each system, the extent of inactivation without additions is assumed to be 100.

EDTA, inhibit the inactivation reactions in all systems. In all cases, the inhibitory effect of o-phenanthroline is reversed by the addition of 1.2 to 1.5 times as much Fe(III) as o-phenanthroline; whereas with one exception (i.e., the non-P450-dependent redoxin system), an excess of Fe(III) fails to reverse the inhibition by EDTA. The ability of Fe(III) to reverse the effect of EDTA in the non-P450-linked putidaredoxin system is the only characteristic that is not shared by all of the inactivation systems investigated (the stimulation by NaN_3 of the inactivating activity in *K. aerogenes* extracts might be attributed to the presence of trace amounts of catalase). Curiously, this distinguishing characteristic is lost when P450$_{cam}$ is added to the reductase–redoxin system. Different mechanisms may be involved in the putidaredoxin-catalyzed inactivation of glutamine synthetase in the presence and absence of P450$_{cam}$, since superoxide dismutase, dimethylsulfoxide, and histidine all inhibit the inactivation reaction in the absence of P450 but have little or no effect when P450 is present (Table III). Because an unusually high concentration of superoxide dismutase was used in this experiment, mechanistic implications of its inhibitory effect on the redoxin system are uncertain.

D. Effect of the State of Adenylylation and Substrates of Glutamine Synthetase on Inactivation

Data in Fig. 3 show that in the absence of substrates, ATP and glutamate, the unadenylylated form of glutamine synthetase is more susceptible to inactivation by the microsomal (Fig. 3A) and putidaredoxin (Fig. 3B) mixed-function oxidation systems than is the adenylylated enzyme. However, in the presence of substrates, the susceptibility of the unadenylylated enzyme to inactivation is decreased, while that of the adenylylated enzyme is enhanced. Similar results are obtained also when inactivation is catalyzed by the ascorbate system (Fig. 3C).

TABLE III

Effect of Activated Oxygen Scavengers on the *Pseudomonas* Inactivated Systems[a]

Addition	Concentration (mM)	*Pseudomonas* systems (% of control)	
		Reductase + redoxin	Reductase + redoxin + P450$_{cam}$
None	—	100	100
Superoxide dismutase	0.140	36	90
Dimethyl sulfoxide	94	50	95
Mannitol	100	83	85
Histidine	10	50	85

[a] Conditions for *Pseudomonas* reductase-redoxin and reductase-redoxin–P450$_{cam}$ inactivation reactions were the same as described for Table II. Reaction mixtures were incubated and assayed for glutamine synthetase as described for Table I.

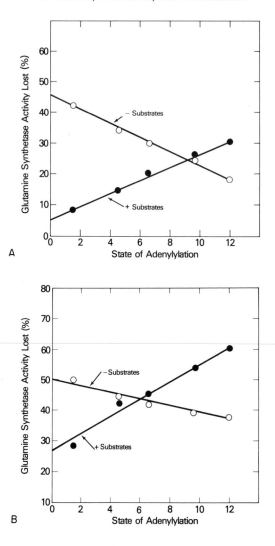

E. Effect of the Inactivation Reaction on the Susceptibility of Glutamine Synthetase to Proteolytic Degradation

Following its inactivation, by any one of several different oxidation systems, glutamine synthetase is susceptible to proteolytic degradation by partially purified enzyme preparations of *E. coli*. Data in Table IV show that in the absence of ATP or NADPH, native glutamine synthetase is not degraded at an appreciable rate, whereas an enzyme that had been inactivated by either the ascorbate system (experiment 1) or the putidaredoxin system (experiment 2) was

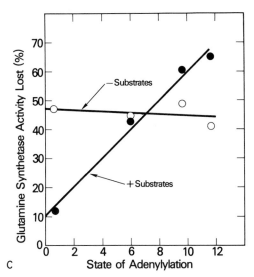

Fig. 3. Effect of substrates and state of adenylylation on the inactivation of glutamine synthetase. (A) Inactivation by the microsomal P450 mixed-function oxidase system. Reaction mixtures contained 200 μg glutamine synthetase of various states of adenylylation, and where indicated, the cosubstrates, 1 mM ATP and 30 mM glutamate, and mixed-function oxidase system. Except for the glutamine synthetase preparations, conditions were as described in Fig. 1. Reaction mixtures were incubated and assayed for glutamine synthetase activity as described in Table I. (B) Inactivation by the *Pseudomonas* reductase-redoxin system. The glutamine synthetase preparations were as in (A); otherwise, conditions were as described for the data in Table II. Reactions mixtures were incubated and assayed for glutamine synthetase as described in Table I. (C) Inactivation by the ascorbate system. Reaction mixtures were incubated and assayed for glutamine synthetase activity as described in Table II.

readily degraded. The partially purified protease preparation used in experiment 1 apparently contained appreciable inactivation activity, since its ability to degrade the native enzyme was greatly stimulated by addition of ATP and NADPH. This stimulation was inhibited by catalase, whereas catalase had little effect on the degradation of the ascorbate-inactivated enzyme. It is noteworthy that ATP stimulated the proteolysis of the enzyme that had been inactivated by either the ascorbate or the putidaredoxin system; the significance of this finding remains to be determined. The data in Table IV are from experiments in which the proteolytic degradation was followed by measuring the loss of glutamine synthetase subunit protein by means of high-pressure liquid chromatography of the reaction mixtures in SDS. In other studies, the proteolytic degradation of native glutamine synthetase and of synthetase that had been inactivated by the microsomal mixed-function oxidation system was followed by SDS slab gel electrophoresis of reaction mixtures. The results are depicted in Fig. 4. Comparison of channel 3

TABLE IV

Proteolysis of Native and Inactivated GS by Partially Purified *E. coli* Extracts[a]

		Proteolysis (%)	
Experiment	Additions	Native GS	Inactivated GS
1	None	0	0
	Extract	9.0	61.3
	Extract + ATP	60.0	73.7
	Extract + NADPH	33.0	63.9
	Extract + ATP + NADPH	72.2	95.8
	Extract (treated 60°C, 5′) + ATP + NADPH	4.4	25.0
	Extract (treated 100°C, 5′) + ATP + NADPH	2.8	1.7
	Extract + ATP + NADPH + catalase	13.9	66.2
2	None	0	0
	Extract	0	24.2
	Extract + ATP	8.9	36.7

[a] Reaction mixtures in experiment 1 contained 200 μg of native or ascorbate-inactivated glutamine synthetase, 23 μg of catalase-free *E. coli* extract similar to preparation described in Table I, 50 mM Tris buffer, (pH 7.4), 50 μM FeCl$_3$, 10 mM MgCl$_2$, and where indicated, 1 mM ATP, 1 mM NADPH, and 0.1 μM bovine catalase. Reaction mixtures in experiment 2 contained 200 μg of native or *Pseudomonas* reductase–redoxin inactivated-reisolated glutamine synthetase, 83 μg of a different preparation of catalase-free *E. coli* extract, 50 mM Tris (pH 7.4), 10 μM FeCl$_3$, 5 mM MgCl$_2$, and where indicated, 1 mM ATP. Experiment 1 was incubated for 30 minutes and experiment 2 for 60 minutes at 37°C. The incubation mixtures were sampled and treated with SDS buffer, as described in Fig. 4. The SDS-treated samples were analyzed by high-pressure liquid chromatography, using a calibrated Toyo Soda SW3000 size exclusion column. The column effluent was monitored at 215 nm in experiment 1 and at 290 nm in experiment 2. Proteolysis was quantitated by determining the loss of glutamine synthetase subunit with time by peak area integration. Appropriate corrections were made for the contribution of the extract protein at each time point under identical incubation conditions.

(untreated GS) with channels 5 and 6 (protease-treated GS) shows that there is little or no loss of native glutamine synthetase subunit during incubation with the *E. coli* protease preparation. However, a comparison of channels 3 and 4 shows that incubation of the microsomal inactivated enzyme with protease leads to a substantial loss of glutamine synthetase subunit protein.

III. DISCUSSION

Any general mechanism for the regulation of enzyme degradation must account for the facts that (1) for a given metabolic state, different enzymes are

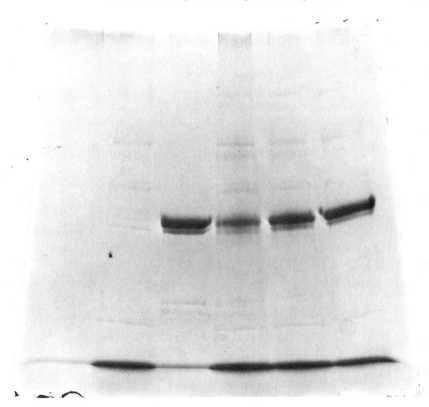

Fig. 4. Sodium dodecyl sulfate (SDS) pore gradient electrophoresis of microsomal P450-inactivated glutamine synthetase treated with an *E. coli* catalase-free protease preparation. Conditions of microsomal P450 inactivation were the same as described in Fig. 1. Protease treatment involved the addition of 80 μg of a partially purified catalase-free *E. coli* extract similar to that described in Table I. This preparation also possessed inactivating activity. Inactivation reactions and protease treatment were carried out at 37°C for 30 minutes each. At the end of incubation, an aliquot of the reaction mixture was removed, diluted twofold into 50 mM Tris buffer (pH 7.4) containing 2% SDS, heated for 3 minutes at 95°C, and loaded on 8–20% acrylamide gradient gels containing 0.1% SDS. Incubation mixtures were as follows: from left to right, lane 1, P450 inactivating system alone; lane 2, *E. coli* protease preparation alone; lane 3, glutamine synthetase alone; lane 4, glutamine synthetase incubated with the microsomal P450 inactivating components followed by treatment with *E. coli* protease preparation; lane 5, same composition as lane 4, except that microsomal P450 inactivation reaction is inhibited by addition of 1 mM EDTA; lane 6, glutamine synthetase incubated with *E. coli* preparation in the presence of 1 mM EDTA to inhibit *E. coli*-dependent inactivation reaction. EDTA does not inhibit proteolysis (data not shown). Inactivation of glutamine synthetase by microsomal P450 components does not lead to loss of subunit protein.

degraded at different rates; and (2) the relative rates of degradation of various enzymes are altered by changes in the nutritional state of the cell. Both criteria could be met if a separate protease were responsible for the degradation of each enzyme; the activity of each protease could then be regulated independently. Such a possibility seems untenable from the standpoint of both cell economy and reason. Much more reasonable is the possibility that only a few proteases are elaborated, and that their abilities to degrade various enzyme substrates is dependent on the exposure of unique recognition (binding) sites on these enzymes. The degradation of a particular enzyme could then be governed by alteration in its conformational state that results in unmasking of the recognition sites. This mechanism is consistent with the data presented here, showing that glutamine synthetase is rapidly inactivated by a mixed-function type oxidase reaction and that this inactivation renders the enzyme susceptible to proteolytic degradation. Regulation of glutamine synthetase degradation occurs at the inactivation step, which is modulated by the state of adenylylation of the enzyme and by its substrates, ATP and glutamate. The synergistic effects of adenylylation and substrates on the inactivation reaction may be rationalized in view of the fact that glutamine is not only a key intermediate in the assimilation of ammonia, but is

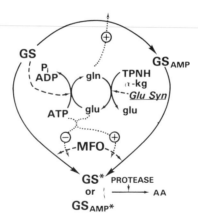

Fig. 5. Relationship between glutamine metabolism and the adenylylation, inactivation, and degradation of glutamine synthetase. The innermost circle illustrates the fact that unadenylylated glutamine synthetase (GS) catalyzes the conversion of ATP, NH_3 (not shown), and glutamate (glu) to glutamine (gln), and that glutamate synthase (*Glu Syn*) catalyzes the conversion of glutamine, TPNH, and α-ketoglutarate (α-kg) to 2 moles of glutamate and TPN (not shown). Conversion of GS and its adenylylated form (GS_{AMP}) to their corresponding inactivated forms, GS^* and GS_{AMP}^*, is catalyzed by the mixed-function oxidase system (MFO). The dotted lines illustrate that MFO inactivation of GS is inhibited by ATP plus glutamate, whereas inactivation of the GS_{AMP} is stimulated by these substrates; the encircled $-$ and $+$ signs indicate inhibition and stimulation, respectively. Moreover, the conversion of GS to GS_{AMP} is stimulated by glutamine.

also a precursor in the biosynthesis of diverse metabolites (Stadtman, 1973). Among these metabolites, glutamate has an unique role because it is not only a substrate for glutamine synthesis, but it is also a major product of glutamine metabolism (see Fig. 5).

It appears significant that unadenylylated (active) glutamine synthetase is protected from irreversible inactivation by ATP and glutamate, whereas these substrates enhance inactivation of the adenylylated enzyme. It might be argued teleologically that as long as there is a demand for glutamine, glutamine synthetase will be present in the unadenylylated (catalytically active) form and that this form of the enzyme will be protected from irreversible inactivation provided there is also an ample supply of ATP and glutamate. However, in the absence of an adequate supply of these substrates, unadenylylated glutamine synthetase is nonfunctional and can therefore be dispensed with. Under these conditions, it is susceptible to irreversible inactivation by the mixed-function oxidase system. Moreover, under conditions where the supplies of ATP and glutamate are not limiting, and the production of glutamine exceeds its demand, glutamine synthetase is no longer needed. Then the enzyme is converted to its catalytically inactive highly adenylylated form, which is further processed for degradation by the mixed-function oxidase system. As noted above, this irreversible inactivation of the adenylylated enzyme is augmented by high concentrations of ATP and glutamate.

Whereas this teleological argument explains the effects of ATP and glutamate in the regulation of glutamine synthetase degradation, it does not explain why under conditions of glutamine excess irreversible inactivation and degradation of glutamine synthetase should be preferred over the reversible inactivation of the enzyme by adenylylation only.

The fact that catalase inhibits the irreversible inactivation of glutamine synthetase raises questions about the physiological significance of the reaction. The concentration of catalase in *E. coli,* when grown under our conditions, is sufficiently high to inhibit completely the inactivation reaction. Therefore, either the mechanism of glutamine synthetase degradation demonstrated here is an artifact of the *in vitro* systems, and has no physiological significance, or else the ability of catalase to inhibit the inactivation step must be under rigorous metabolic control, or possibly catalase has no access to the mixed-function oxidation system because of intracellular compartmentalization. Alternatively, one should consider the possibility that one of the physiological functions of catalase is to protect enzymes such as glutamine synthetase from inadvertant inactivation by mixed-function oxidase-catalyzed reactions. If so, the inactivation reaction would not be a part of the normal mechanism for regulating glutamine synthetase turnover. Proteolytic degradation of the inactivated enzyme would then be regarded as a part of the sanitation system that is used to dispose of abnormal proteins, and only incidentally to dispose of those glutamine synthetase molecules that had escaped the protective influence of catalase and had inadvertently become inactivated by the mixed-function oxidase systems. It should be noted, however, that in the latter postulated roles of catalase and of the proteolytic degradation, there appears to be no rational basis for the regulatory effects of either ATP, glutamate, or adenylylation on the inactivation reaction.

In the absence of more detailed information, it would be presumptive to propose a mechanism for the inactivation reaction. Whatever the mechanism, it must account for the facts that (1) inactivation involves the alteration of no more than 1 of 16 histidine residues per polypeptide chain (R. Levine, unpublished data); and (2) ATP and glutamate stimulate inactivation of adenylylated glutamine synthetase but inhibit inactivation of the unadenylylated enzyme.

Since these enzyme forms differ greatly in their divalent cation requirements (Kingdon *et al.*, 1967), differences in their susceptibilities to inactivation might involve direct interactions of either Fe(II) or Fe(III) at one or both of the divalent cation-binding sites on each of the subunits of the enzyme. Then oxidation and/or reduction of these metal ions *in situ* could lead to the generation of activated oxygen (i.e., hydroxide radical, singlet oxygen, or peroxyderivatives) and subsequently to a specific interaction with histidine at the metal-binding sites. Further speculation at this time is unwarranted.

ACKNOWLEDGMENT

One of the authors (C.N.O.) is a graduate student, John Hopkins University and Foundation for Advanced Education in the Sciences Collaborative Program.

We are indebted to H. Gelboin for highly purified preparations of rabbit liver microsomal cytochrome c reductase, to M. J. Coon for purified preparations of rabbit liver microsomal cytochrome c reductase and the phenobarbital-induced P450 (LM$_2$), to I. C. Gunsalus for the preparations of putidaredoxin, putidaredoxin reductase, and P450$_{cam}$, which had been purified from extracts of *P. putida* that had been grown on camphor as the sole source of carbon and energy, and to M. Magasanik for the culture of *K. aerogenes* strains MK-9000 and MK-53.

REFERENCES

Beers, R. F., Jr., and Sizer, I. W. (1952). A spectrophotometric method for measuring the breakdown of hydrogen peroxide by catalase. *J. Biol. Chem.* **195**, 133–140.

Bradford, M. M. (1976). A rapid and sensitive method for the quantitation of microgram quantities of protein utilizing the principle of protein–dye binding. *Anal. Biochem.* **72**, 248–254.

Fulks, R. M. (1977). Regulation of glutamine synthetase degradation in *Klebsiella aerogenes*. *Fed. Proc., Fed. Am. Soc. Exp. Biol.* **36**, 919 (abstr.).

Goldberg, A. L., and St. John, A. C. (1976). Intracellular protein degradation in mammalian and bacterial cells. *Annu. Rev. Biochem.* **45**, 747–803.

Hershko, A., Ciechanover, A., Heller, H., Haas, A. L., and Rose, I. A. (1980). Proposed role of

ATP in protein breakdown: Conjugation of proteins with multiple chains of the polypeptide of ATP-dependent proteolysis. *Proc. Natl. Acad. Sci. U.S.A.* **77,** 1783-1786.

Holzer, H., and Heinrich, P. C. (1980). Control of proteolysis. *Annu. Rev. Biochem.* **49,** 63-91.

Kingdon, H. S., Shapiro, B. M., and Stadtman, E. R. (1967). Regulation of glutamine synthetase. VIII. ATP:glutamine synthetase adenyltransferase, an enzyme that catalyzes alterations in the regulatory properties of glutamine synthetase. *Proc. Natl. Acad. Sci. U.S.A.* **58,** 1703-1710.

Maurizi, M. R. (1980). Degradation of specific enzymes in *Escherichia coli. Fed. Proc., Fed. Am. Soc. Exp. Biol.* **39,** 403 (abstr.).

Oliver, C. N., and Stadtman, E. R. (1980). Inactivation and proteolysis of glutamine synthetase by *Escherichia coli* extracts. *Fed. Proc., Fed. Am. Soc. Exp. Biol.* **39,** 402 (abstr.).

Sasarman, A., Surcleanu, M., Szégli, G., Horodniceanu, T., Greceanu, V., and Dumitrescu, A. (1968). Hemin-deficient mutants of *Escherichia coli* K-12. *J. Bacteriol.* **96,** 570-572.

Schimke, R. T. (1969). On the roles of synthesis and degradation in regulation of enzyme levels in mammalian tissues. *Curr. Top. Cell. Regul.* **1,** 77-124.

Stadtman, E. R. (1970). Mechanisms of Enzyme Regulation. *In* "The Enzymes" (P. D. Boyer, ed.), 3rd ed., Vol. 1, pp. 397-460. Academic Press, New York.

Stadtman, E. R. (1973). A note on the significance of glutamine in intermediary metabolism. *In* "The Enzymes of Glutamine Metabolism" (S. P. Prusiner and E. R. Stadtman, eds.), pp. 1-6. Academic Press, New York.

Stadtman, E. R., Davis, J. N., Smyrniotis, P. Z., and Wittenberger, M. E. (1979). Enzymatic procedures for determining the average state of adenylylation of *Escherichia coli* glutamine synthetase. *Anal. Biochem.* **95,** 275-285.

Udenfriend, S., Clark, C. T., Axelrod, J., and Brodie, B. B. (1954). Ascorbic acid in aromatic hydroxylation. I. A model system for aromatic hydroxylation. *J. Biol. Chem.* **208,** 731-739.

Wilkinson, K. D., Urban, M. K., and Haas, A. L. (1980). Ubiquitin is the ATP-dependent proteolysis factor 1 of rabbit reticulocytes. *J. Biol. Chem.* **255,** 7529-7532.

IV

Cytochrome P450
and Electron Transport

20

From Stars
to Organic Chemistry
via Cytochrome P450*

Stephen G. Sligar

INTRODUCTION

The celebration of a scientist's seventieth birthday is a memorable occasion and an opportunity to reflect on the man, his contributions to the field of science, and perhaps most importantly, to trace, through the individuals contributing to this volume in his honor, the scientists whose careers he has influenced and aided. This volume has maintained an "open format" of organization. Some contributors have elected to summarize their own work to date in a particular field or present a summary of recent new findings in their laboratory. Others have chosen to describe the particular role that I. C. Gunsalus, or "Gunny," has had in the development of their scientific career. In the next few pages, I have chosen to follow the latter example to a greater extent. One certainly does not need another review of current P450 research, nor do we need a format for presenting a unified though perhaps myopic view of cytochrome P450 reaction chemistry that our research at Yale is leading toward. Rather, I feel it more important to describe in a few pages what life was like as a graduate student in the Gunsalus laboratory. There is always a correct time for a field of research to

*Dedicated to I. C. Gunsalus on his seventieth birthday.

EXPERIENCES IN BIOCHEMICAL PERCEPTION
Copyright © 1982 by Academic Press, Inc.
All rights of reproduction in any form reserved.
ISBN 0-12-528420-9

grow and bear fruit, and it will always be my great fortune to have been in the Gunsalus laboratory during the early to mid-1970's when much of the physical and inorganic characterization of cytochrome P450 was conducted. Additionally, during this period, the "genetics operation" in the Gunsalus group was actively pursuing research endeavors that were clearly far ahead of their time. The molecular characterization of plasmid-coded functions, the restriction mapping of various degradative plasmids, and the elucidation of the molecular biology by which the soil pseudomonads and other organisms exchanged information and thus retained the ability to grow on a wide variety of growth substrates, are still exciting areas of current research in molecular biology. Indeed, the molecular understanding of regulation and control at the level of peripheral metabolism will in all probability provide the model system for the understanding of replicative processes in general. It is interesting to look in retrospective overview at the development of cytochrome P450 research in the Gunsalus laboratory. The close interactions of the Gunsalus laboratory with the laboratories of Debrunner, Frauenfelder, and Munck were key in this research program. Fired by keen friendships and fueled by similar pathological desires for sampling the best wines of the world, this interaction directed the course of P450 investigations in substantial ways. It is interesting, for example, to note that P450 research in the Gunsalus laboratory moved immediately into the physical biochemistry areas and not through the more classical biochemical approaches. Long before a radioactive substrate of the camphor monooxygenase had been documented, the intimate details of the spin Hamiltonian describing the P450 heme iron and the $Fe_2S_2Cys_4$ iron–sulfur center of the redox transport protein, putidaredoxin, had been documented through Mossbauer and epr spectroscopy. A detailed plunge into the organic reaction mechanism of this novel type of alkane hydroxylase was missing in the investigation of the P450 hydroxylase during this period. Again the time was apparently not right, even though we were in some sense "thinking along the right lines." Current research efforts in my laboratory at Yale stress this aspect of oxygenase catalysis through elucidation of the organic chemical mechanisms of the P450-type hydroxylation processes. Thus, it is of interest to examine the environment of the Gunsalus–Debrunner–Frauenfelder interaction which could provide the basic educational opportunity for a biophysicist to travel across the many hills and valleys between elementary particles and transition metal-catalyzed organic reaction mechanisms.

THE ILLINOIS BIOCHEMISTRY/BIOPHYSICS GROUP, 1972–1977

It was a typically cold and bleak January morning in Urbana, Illinois. The second semester at the University had just started, and Peter Deutsch, my teaching assistant in advanced quantum mechanics, and I were discussing the wisdom of voluntarily attending an 8:00 AM class as we trudged the mile across campus to attend Biochemistry I. In some ways we both felt like preschool children stealing access to the cookie jar—what reason did two physics graduate students have for attending a course in the premedical curriculum? Spurred on by the list of physicists who had made key contributions to the field of biological sciences, I had begun to think the newly emerging areas of biophysics represented excellent future opportunities for exciting research. Our first exposure to biochemistry was catching. Over hot coffee in the Union following the lecture, I decided on a career in biochemistry and began to plot the pathways toward attaining the education and research experience needed for this goal. It was simply incredible that a cellular organism could *do* the reactions that were claimed. Although I attended this introductory rendition of biochemistry faithfully, the excitement breeding in the astrophysics group of Professors Lamb, Baym, Pethick, and Pines steered me for the remainder of the semester to the study of the optical properties of white dwarf atmospheres.

Interests in pursuing biological and biochemical studies surfaced again in May when Herb Kubitscheck, the director of the Genetics group at Argonne National Laboratory near Chicago, offered me a fellowship for summer study in the field of radiation biology. This coupled well with a general desire to leave Urbana for a few weeks, and represented the critical educational experience needed to initiate the transition to more biological problems. Herb, a former nuclear physicist with the Manhattan project, knew the experimental and theoretical background that needed reinforcement. From elementary teaching on how to pipette accurately, to design of some detailed phage infection and receptor isolation experiments, the summer of 1972 sank the hook in regard to biochemical research. A month touring England with a visit to Oxford, where my astrophysics mentor, Fred Lamb, was spending the summer, offered the time for reflection and to finalize the decision to initiate the transition from stars to cytochromes. On return to Urbana for the fall semester with perhaps more enthusiasm than concrete ideas, I rushed to Hans Frauenfelder and Peter Debrunner to ascertain the current experimental status of biophysical experiments that were going on in the Physics department. Peter, in what later proved to be a characteristic ability to penetrate, asked what precise experiments I intended to conduct on the enzyme system currently occupying the majority of epr, Mossbauer, and flash photolysis experimental time. Having spent a part of the summer at Argonne studying fluorescence of dye–DNA complexes, and realizing that this was a general spectroscopy not represented in the Debrunner–Frauenfelder group at the time, I decided to utilize the intrinsic and label fluorescence of the P450 monooxygenase proteins to probe multiprotein interactions and dynamics. That day Bob Austin and I began to link photomultiplier tube, power supply, amplifier, xenon lamp, and monochromater to measure the tryptophan fluorescence of cytochrome P450. After a full day in the lab, the late evenings were free for needed background reading at which time two key points emerged. First, we would probably have to do some protein modification to put a long-wavelength fluorophore on the surface of cytochrome P450 to get any useful information on multiprotein dynamics, and second, a spectroscopist named Gregorio Weber had a name which reappeared in the fluorescence literature with amazing frequency. When Peter gently pointed out that Gregorio Weber was in the Biochemistry department only two blocks away, the little homemade fluorimeter that Bob Austin and I had put together looked rather inadequate. Throughout these first few weeks Gunny appeared as the biochemist who was supplying all this lovely brown cytochrome that seemed to have some biological relevance to metabolism. The project began to move when Peter called a joint meeting with Gregorio and Gunny in what was known as "Gunny's outer office," 420 Roger Adams Laboratory. By now I had mastered pretty well the things that could and could not be done with fluorescence, and thus I could present some rational plans for measurement of rotational relaxation rates using fluorescent conjugates of the camphor hydroxylase proteins. Gregorio enjoyed these possibilities but also expressed a keen desire to understand the "red-edge effect" or failure of electronic energy transfer between like chromophores when excited at the long wavelength edge of their absorption spectrum. Though this area of investigation was tabled at the time, history does tend to repeat itself and recently in collaboration with Joe Fruton at Yale we documented the first biological application of the red-edge effect to the study of inter-tryptophan distances in proteins (Hennes *et al.*, 1980). Gunny felt that any physical–chemical studies were exciting and expressed the firm belief that if science "made sense" and was fun, it really did not matter what one worked on as a project. Peter also appeared uncommitted, but gently through questions and feigned misunderstanding, elicited a consensus that to continue studying cytochrome P450 was preferable to moving to a different system. Since it was clear that all future fluorescence investigations were to utilize Gregorio's equipment, Gunny offered a desk down the hall in room 409. Moving all my personal belongings to the hallowed halls of Roger Adams Laboratory, steeped in the history of chemistry, formalized my transfer to biochemistry and related disciplines.

409 Roger Adams Laboratory was shared with John Harrison, and was termed "rebel island" inasmuch as it was physically separated from the remaining Gunsalus laboratories by the Chairman's office. What excitement. The air conditioner never worked, making the summer lab temperatures near 95°, and the snow blew through the window in the winter. But by God there was biochemistry going on. Through the friendships of Dick Spencer, George Mitchell, and Dave Jameson, the Weber fluorescence laboratories, darkened for obvious reasons, took on a magical air with more blinking lights and fancy electronics than most labs in the Physics department. So for the months of October and November, 1972, I began fluorescence experiments on the P450 monoxygenase system. For

this one needed a supply of protein, and this presented the opportunity of dealing with John Lipscomb, a graduate student of Gunny's who has since become a lifelong friend. John was quite frugal with the protein he had so carefully isolated, and would allocate me 1-nmol units. This was fine for fluorescence studies, and I was convinced that perhaps only 10 mg of the protein existed in the world. One night, after a long experimental run, I inadvertently dropped a 0.5-nmol sample of P450 into the ice bucket. The following morning a request to John for another 0.5-nmol unit was met with a long lecture on the scarcity of the protein, the expense and man-years needed to purify it, and the need for all biochemists to be careful and precise. It was only 1 month later that, while browsing late one Saturday night, I found the 8 gm of crystalline cytochrome P450 that was stockpiled from the protein isolation and purification machine that Gunny had created. The First Gunny Rule of Science emerged: *If you want to work on a system, get it isolated in quantity and quality.*

During this first 1 or 2 months time I had little direct contact with Gunny save through participation in the weekly microcolloquia which were held as joint group meetings between the Debrunner, Frauenfelder, and Gunsalus contingencies. My first real exposure was through a "party" Gunny held at his house one Saturday afternoon where the lab, together with the help of hired labor, were directed to the construction of a huge wine cellar in the basement of 1709 Pleasant Circle. Little did I know at that time the number of evenings that would be subsequently spent with Gunny building, cataloging, stocking, and sampling the little quantums of pleasure that came in deep red bottles from the Burgundy region of France.

Most impressive from the start was the easy and open exchange of ideas between members of the biophysics collaboration of Gunsalus, Debrunner, Fraunfelder, Munck, their postdoctorals, graduate students, and support staff. The weekly seminars became almost daily with the "nanocolloquium" series instituted by Hans during the summer and vacation periods, and the luncheons at the Urbana Lincoln Hotel all contributed to an ideal format for the physicists to learn the exciting areas of research in biochemistry, and the biochemists to grasp the language of "spin Hamiltonians" and other spectroscopic terms tossed out idly by the physicists. This interaction between the four groups was one of the most exciting and fruitful examples of interdisciplinary collaboration that I have yet witnessed. Several students emerging from this triumverate have later expressed surprise that most scientific interactions in molecular biochemistry often do not proceed with such openness and enthusiasm. Clear examples of the ease of "crossing the street" offered by this interaction are the separate cases of John Lipscomb and myself. John, the organic chemist by undergraduate training, is now an established resonance spectroscopist at the University of Minnesota, while our research endeavors, though tainted with an undergraduate background in epr spectroscopy, are now in the areas of organic reaction mechanisms. It is precisely the atmosphere created by Gunny, Peter, and Hans that contributed to the mandate to study a scientific problem by any technique that will yield to a mechanistic interpretation. The biophysics collaboration at Illinois in the early 1970's certainly offered the basic training in all the fundamental aspects of molecular studies and thus provided the basis for branching and growing as one's scientific career progressed.

By early December, after 3 months in "rebel island," my fluorescence work had progressed significantly, with documentation of a 1:1 putidaredoxin–P450 binding reaction using fluoresceinisothiocyanate-labeled cytochrome (Sligar *et al.*, 1974a), and the characterization of the putidaredoxin tryptophan fluorescence together with interresidue distance mapping using Forster energy transfer triangulation (Sligar, 1975). Although work was proceeding extremely well, I was totally flabbergasted when Gunny summoned me into his office and decreed that I would present the results of my work at the International Union of Biochemistry (IUB) meeting in Stockholm. Although this was to be my first oral presentation in science, and hence represented a classic "trial by fire," the promise of a trip to Sweden was enough to increase the laboratory work hours to over 16 per day. With this additional effort, progress rose correspondingly. A day or so later Gunny expressed concern that my knowledge of modern biological research might leave something to be desired, and suggested I join the school in Molecular Biology being held that summer in Spetsai, Greece. After all, he said, "It's only a short ride from Copenhagen, where you can chat with Jens Hedegaard and learn some tricks of bacteriology." Such was, and is, Gunny's view of international travel.

The subsequent months passed quickly as we prepared for the upcoming meeting and, in June, Gunny and I met in Copenhagen and enjoyed a lovely drive with Bob Djertoft up the eastern Swedish coastline. An overnight stay at a farmhouse on the island of Oland provided a marvelous exposure to the advantages of Scandanavian living. Gunny is perhaps the most magnificent traveling companion. His desire for sampling life at all turns in the road and his extreme optimism are features of the man that can influence and contribute to the growth of those around him. Practically speaking, when traveling with Gunny one never waits in line at airports, and he always seems to arrange for a four-seat "bed" on overnight international flights. In retrospect, the experience of an international meeting is really quite beneficial to the scientific development of any student, and the scientific content of the Stockholm IUB meeting was exceptional. This was my first exposure to the work of Gilbert and colleagues and the desire for a structural interpretation of nucleic acid–protein interactions. The satellite P450 meeting held after the congress summarized concisely the status of the P450 field in terms of basic biochemistry and biophysics. This time was the high point in a dispute over the role of cytochrome b_5 in hepatic mixed-function oxidation processes, with the organization of 1 full day of alternating pro and con speeches.

With attendence at the Stockholm meetings came the Second and Third Gunny Rules of Science: *Second, if you want financial reimbursement for attending a meeting, you must present a paper at the meeting.* If you have nothing to contribute, stay home and work. *Third, never, never, never give the same data twice.* If there were two meetings held at nearly the same time, as for example the IUB meeting in Stockholm and the satellite P450 at the Karolinska, then two separate and distinct projects must be discussed. Hence at the Karolinska I discussed our work on the chemical modification of putidaredoxin and the kinetic assays of substrate oxygenation (Sligar *et al.*, 1973a), whereas at the main IUB meeting our presentations centered on the fluorescence properties of the P450 hemoprotein (Sligar *et al.*, 1973b).

At the conclusion of the Karolinska meeting we returned to Copenhagen and spent a week with Jens Hedegaard. It was clear that a special relationship existed between Jens and Gunny, beginning with their codiscovery of the P450 camphor hydroxylase in 1968 (Hedegaard and Gunsalus, 1965). A weekend trip to the island of Bjornholm offered the chance to discuss microbiology and experience the excellent seafood that the Danes so easily take for granted. From Copenhagen I flew directly to Athens with Jens, who was also attending the summer school in Greece. With all the excitement of the scientific presentations in Stockholm, I had neglected to plan the next leg of the journey in any great detail. The obvious disaster that was brewing over hotel accommodations in Athens was quietly averted by Peter Debrunner from 5000 miles away. Just as we were preparing to depart from Copenhagen, a telegram magically appeared informing us that a room had been reserved at the King Minos hotel for the period before the boat trip to the island of Spetsai, where the meeting was being held.

Upon return from the overseas pursuit of science, a general letdown ensued. Gunny was quite ready for this, realizing that the time span between the return from 1 year's meetings to the abstract deadline dates for the next does not allow any slack in the experimental pace. Through organization of repeated meetings, microcolloquia, and luncheons to "discuss science," the exploration of new ideas and molecular mechanisms was brought again to full pace. John Lipscomb had initiated a detailed study of protein modification and its effect on the three components of the monoxygenase system. Of particular immediate interest was the role of sulfhydryls at the active site of P450 in dictating substrate binding and catalytic function. In collaboration with John, I began to define the kinetics of mixed-function oxidation in terms of quantifiable rate theory to place on firm ground the qualitative ideas of rate-limiting step and effector function defined previously. This work led us to the definition in molecular terms of the product-forming reaction and the unambiguous requirement for a chemical function associated with the putidaredoxin–P450 interaction and, as such, provided the first bridge into the need to understand the precise chemistry by which a methylene carbon was converted to a secondary alcohol (Lipscomb *et al.*, 1976). Also apparent at this time was increased interaction among the "genetics group" of Bill Toscano, Govind Garg, Jim Johnston, and others. Bill Toscano was instrumental in this regard, having come from a microbiology background with a strong industrial exposure to analytical chemistry; his expertise and broad background were instrumental in developing the purification procedures of the camphor monooxygenase, from the bacteriology of mutant development and culture growth to the isolation and purification of the protein components in high yield. Through Bill's work and that of Gerry Wagner, who joined the laboratory later as a postdoctoral fellow, the normal production of P450, then running at a low of 180 mg P450 per 3000 gm of cell paste through a multicolumn purification that took from 2 to 3 weeks, was reduced to a time period of 3 days with yields approaching 800 mg (Wagner *et al.*, 1978). A central and critical component of the enzymology group was M. J. Namtvedt. M.J., as she is always called, was a principal laboratory technician and worked directly for John Lipscomb and had by far the most seniority in the Gunsalus laboratory. When I "inherited" her abilities on John Lipscomb's graduation, I learned the unique advantage of work with such capable and hard-working technical help.

Our next research efforts focused on dissecting the "wheel," describing qualitatively the reaction cycle of cytochrome P450 (Fig. 1). The first-order autoxidation of the oxygenated intermediate and concomitant production of superoxide ion was documented by chemiluminescence studies (Sligar *et al.*, 1974b), and we began the definition of reaction rates and equilibria, and the necessity for the formation of multiprotein complexes between putidaredoxin and cytochrome P450 for electron transfer and catalytic methylene carbon oxygenation. This period saw work on the primary structure of the P450 macromolecule begun by Karl Dus, then residing on the third floor of Roger Adams Laboratory, with a link to the Gunsalus group through John Harrison, who was beginning to look at the reactivity of the sulfhydryl groups of P450 and their effect on catalysis and electron transfer processes. Following the Stockholm meeting, Kery Yasunobu was brought into the game of sequencing cytochrome P450, and the complete primary structure is now virtually complete (Yasunobu *et al.*, 1980). Of particular interest at the time was the tryptophan content of putidaredoxin and the

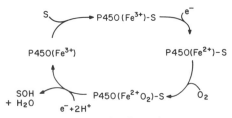

Fig. 1. Reaction cycle of cytochrome P450.

C-terminal sequence of Arg-Gln-Trp-COOH. The fluorescence of this single tryptophan residue indicated that it was in a highly polar environment and was free to move independently of the overall protein tumbling rate, and hence represented a highly unusual environment (Sligar *et al.*, 1974a). Dickerson was proposing at the time a unique electron transfer mechanism for the *c*-type cytochromes using the overlapping π-orbitals of stacked aromatic residues, so we were all thinking aromatics when the unusual environment of the putidaredoxin C-terminus surfaced. It was apparent after studying the putidaredoxin sequence that the glutamine and typtophan residues could be removed with carboxypeptidase, generating a clean modified protein with an arginine C-terminus. This modified putidaredoxin, known as the des-Trp compound, was successfully created, purified, and found to our great excitement to have virtually no activity in the hydroxylase assay (Sligar *et al.*, 1974a). This discovery led me to postulate the involvement of an electrophilic center in P450 hydroxylation chemistry (Sligar *et al.*, 1976a) following theoretical organic suggestions by Hamilton (Hamilton, 1974). Support for the nucleophilic reactivity of oxygenated heme has been obtained by our recent oxygen isotope studies at Yale (Sligar *et al.*, 1980).

The enzymology effort in the Gunsalus group received an injection of new blood and ideas with the arrival of Tom Pederson as a postdoctoral fellow. Tom had received his Ph.D. degree from Michigan State working with Steve Aust on lipid peroxidation, and arrived keen on pursuing physicochemical studies on the camphor monoxygenase. As a resident protein chemist, Tom's talents were initially tapped by the physicists to aid in the purification and characterization of various myoglobin derivatives which were beginning to be extensively explored using laser flash photolysis following Vince Marshall's discovery of the low temperature ligand-binding behavior of hemoproteins. Elucidation of these features formed the basis for the extensive and elegant investigations into macromolecular ligand-binding dynamics and the linked macromolecular fluctuations described in detail by Debrunner and Frauenfelder in Chapter 25. Tom Pederson's investigations in low temperature biochemistry took him to the Physics department laboratories where he was instrumental in bringing analytical and organic chemical understanding to the investigations which were rapidly getting deeper and deeper into protein chemistry. Tom proved to be yet another example of the ease with which the interactions of Gunny, Frauenfelder, and Debrunner allowed branching and development of young scientists' careers. Tom, who had completed a degree in classical biochemistry with little exposure to the hardware of the physicist, developed and constructed a flash photolysis optical bench consisting of light source, collection and focusing optics, monochromators, photomultiplier tubes, high-voltage power supplies, trigger transformers, spark gaps, and the extensive shielding needed to keep the megawatt electrical pulses from destroying the data collection electronics. The development of a wet biochemist to a man comfortable with soldering iron and integrated circuits is an accomplishment of an open and rather unique collaborative environment.

The rapid reaction techniques initiated by Tom led to the precise measurement of putidaredoxin–P450 electron transfer rates and the resultant equilibrium constants for the redox transfer process. This latter parameter, though measured by a dear friend, was accomplished using an entirely different approach from the potentiometric titrations I had made. I was ecstatic, therefore, when the measurements confirmed the redox potential of substrate-free cytochrome P450 as -300 mV (Sligar and Gunsalus, 1976b; Sligar, 1976), the 0.5 μM disassociation constant for the putidaredoxin–P450 complex (Sligar et al., 1974a), and the net shift in the redox potential of putidaredoxin on binding to cytochrome P450 (Sligar and Gunsalus, 1976a). Tom's elegant measurement of electron transfer rates (Pederson et al., 1976), though never published in complete fashion, finished the kinetic and equilibrium documentation of the ferric–ferrous reduction of the P450 heme by putidaredoxin.

With the first electron transfer process under our belt, we initiated the study of the proton coupling to this reaction process, a task which was completed during my first year at Yale (Sligar and Gunsalus, 1979). Tom began work on the second electron transfer process. Beginning with the oxygenated intermediate (Fig. 1), the addition of a second electron results in the rapid appearance of oxidized cytochrome and hydroxylated substrate. Using flash photolysis, this second electron transfer process documented the *simultaneous* loss of reduced putidaredoxin signal and the concomitant appearance of the ferric cytochrome P450 absorbance. Thus it appeared from this investigation that the actual transfer of the electron from reduced putidaredoxin into cytochrome P450 is rate limiting in the chemical steps involved in oxygen–oxygen bond scission and substrate oxygenation. These facts were extremely important to me at the time, as I was beginning to think about the chemical means by which this alkane hydroxylation occurred, and in particular was looking for a common mechanism between the NADH and dioxygen and peroxide-dependent reactivities. The acylation of heme-bound dioxygen, found from our recent studies (Sligar et al., 1980), could indeed be this linking process, although it must be remembered that no real unique mechanism may be operating in all P450-catalyzed oxygenation events (Estabrook et al., 1980; Heimbrook and Sligar, 1981).

The search for spectral intermediates in the peroxide-dependent reactivities of cytochrome P450 began in cryobiochemical experiments in a low temperature nitrogen cooler built into an old Cary 14 spectrophotometer. Simultaneously, Tom Pederson began to look into the stopped flow at the reaction of m-chloroperbenzoic acid and ferric P450, which resulted in one of the first demonstrations of a spectrally distinct intermediate in this process (Peterson et al., 1976). The use of low temperature techniques had brought Tom and me in close contact with the "Paris group" of Pierre Douzou, Pascale Debey, Reinhardt Lang, and their colleagues. Tom had advanced the use of low temperature, mixed solvent systems by development of the ternary solvents (Bon Hoa and Douzou, 1973), and the general interactions with our French colleagues have been extremely beneficial over the years.

The completion of the electron transfer work and the beginning of a chemical understanding of the mixed-function oxidation process brought us to the summer of 1976 when Tom Pederson and I traveled with Gunny to Germany to attend the Third International Symposium of Microsomes and Drug Oxidations held in Berlin, followed by the IUB Congress in Hamburg. Again the *Gunny Third Rule of Science* applied. There must be two separate talks: I spoke in Berlin on the peracid and peroxide reactivities of cytochrome $P450_{cam}$ and the general reaction of nucleophiles with oxygenated heme (Sligar *et al.*, 1976b) and in Hamburg on the spin state interconversion processes of ferric P450 and the regulation of redox flow through the thermodynamic linkage of spin and substrate equilibria (Sligar and Gunsalus, 1976b; Sligar, 1976). Tom presented a poster on the dynamics of electron transfer in Berlin (Pederson *et al.*, 1976) and on the ligand-binding reactions in Hamburg. Following these two meetings we traveled for a few weeks in southern Europe, finally meeting for a week in Montpelier where we visited Douzou, Debey, and their colleagues. The sunshine of southern France prohibited any intensive scientific investigations, though we learned extensively of the latest techniques in low temperature chromatography and potential measurements. From Nice, I left the group and again went to Greece with Gunny for a refresher course in Molecular Biology at the summer school.

Returning from the summer meetings of 1976 brought a new outlook. This had completed my first year as a postdoctoral with Gunny and new frontiers lay ahead. This transition period saw Tom Pederson leave for the research department at General Motors, Bill Toscano depart for a postdoctoral in Washington, and a general flux as the natural turnover of a scientific laboratory ensued. From these pages it should be clear that I was not eager to leave the excellent research environment created by Gunny, Peter Debrunner, and Hans Frauenfelder, and yet the opportunity of joining the Yale faculty could not be ignored. Our research here in the Molecular Biophysics and Biochemistry Department over the past 3 years has seen the rapid thrust into the precise chemical mechanisms of mixed-function oxidation. The time has certainly been ripe. Through the interactions with Joe Fruton, linked in heritage and philosophy to Gunny through an uncompromising thirst for hard science; my excellent and hardworking students, Dave Heimbrook, Mike Gelb, Marc Besman, Andy Keller, and Peter Gould; and our pharmacologist friends and colleagues, John Schenkman, Dominick Cinti, Gordon Gibson, and Ingela Jansson, we have extended the thermodynamics of fundamental P450 interactions (Sligar *et al.*, 1979; Cinti *et al.*, 1979; Backes *et al.*, 1980; Gibson *et al.*, 1980) and pushed the chemical definition of P450 catalysis (Sligar *et al.*, 1980, 1981; Heimbrook and Sligar, 1981; Gould *et al.*, 1981). We are now organic chemists. The flashing lights, electronic components, computers, and epr machines have, to some extent, been replaced by rotary evaporators, distillation columns, and gc/ms and ir spectrophotometry. The lab even smells now. Though in some ways it has been a long 9 years since joining the biochemical community, another change looms ahead in 1 year. The Fourth Gunny Rule of Science is explicit: *Always change your scientific direction and project every 10 years.* Is it too optimistic to say that by 1983 P450 cytochromes will have yielded their most important secrets? Already now the new vistas in mammalian physiology, ion transport processes in epithelia, antitumor medicinal chemistry, and new oxygenase mechanisms are apparent and being exploited in our research efforts. I look forward to sharing the excitement of the next scientific decade with Gunny, the scientist and friend.

REFERENCES

Backes, W., Sligar, S., and Schenkman, J. (1980). *Biochem. Biophys. Res. Commun.* **97,** 860.
Bon Hoa, G., and Douzou, P. (1973). *J. Biol. Chem.* **248,** 4649–4654.
Cinti, D., Sligar, S., Gibson, G., and Schenkman, J. (1979). *Biochemistry* **18,** 36.
Estabrook, R., Capdevila, J., Renneberg, R., and Prough, R. (1980). *In* "Genetic and Environmental Factors in Experimental and Human Cancer" (H. Gelboin *et al.*, eds.), pp. 45–58. Japan Soc. Press, Tokyo.
Gelb, M., Hambrook, D., Malkonen, P., and Sligar, S. (1982). *Biochemistry* (in press).
Gibson, G., Sligar, S., Cinti, D., and Schenkman, J. (1980). *J. Biol. Chem.* **255,** 1867.
Gould, P., Gelb, M., and Sligar, S. (1981). *J. Biol. Chem.* **256,** 6686–6691.
Hamilton, G. (1974). *In* "Molecular Mechanisms of Oxygen Activation" (O. Hayaishi, ed.), pp. 405–448. Academic Press, New York.
Hedegaard, J., and Gunsalus, I. C. (1965). *J. Biol. Chem.* **240,** 4038.
Heimbrook, D., and Sligar, S. G. (1981). *Biochem. Biophys. Res. Commun.* (in press).
Hennes, J., Briggs, M., Sligar, S., and Fruton, J. (1980). *Proc. Natl. Acad. Sci. U.S.A.* **77,** 940.
Lipscomb, J., Sligar, S., Namtvedt, M., and Gunsalus, I. C. (1976). *J. Biol. Chem.* **251,** 1116.
Pederson, T., Austin, R., and Gunsalus, I. C. (1976). *In* "Microsomes and Drug Oxidations" (V. Ullrich, ed.), pp. 275–283. Plenum, New York.
Sligar, S. (1975). Ph.D. Thesis, Univ. of Illinois, Urbana.
Sligar, S. (1976). *Biochemistry* **15,** 5399.
Sligar, S., and Gunsalus, I. C. (1976a). *Proc. Natl. Acad. Sci. U.S.A.* **73,** 1078.
Sligar, S., and Gunsalus, I. C. (1976b). *Proc. Int. Congr. Biochem. 10th, 1976,* p. 349.
Sligar, S., and Gunsalus, I. C. (1979). *Biochemistry* **18,** 2290.
Sligar, S., Debrunner, P., Lipscomb, J., and Gunsalus, I. C. (1973a). "Chemical Modification of Putidaredoxin: The Role of the Carboxy Terminus in Camphor Hydroxylation by P450," p. 61. Int. Union Biochem., Stockholm.
Sligar, S., Debrunner, P., Lipscomb, J., and Gunsalus, I. C. (1973b). *Proc. Int. Congr. Biochem., 9th, 1973,* p. 390.
Sligar, S., Debrunner, P., Lipscomb, J., Namtvedt, M., and Gunsalus, I. C. (1974a). *Proc. Natl. Acad. Sci. U.S.A.* **71,** 3906.
Sligar, S., Lipscomb, J., Debrunner, P., and Gunsalus, I. C. (1974b). *Biochem. Biophys. Res. Commun.* **61,** 290.

Sligar, S., Shastry, B., and Gunsalus, I. C. (1976a). *In* "Microsomes and Drug Oxidations" (V. Ullrich, ed.), pp. 202–209. Plenum, New York.

Sligar, S., Namtvedt, M., Ellis, R., and Gunsalus, I. C. (1976b). *Hoppe-Seyler's Z. Physiol. Chem.* **357,** 1056.

Sligar, S., Cinti, D., Gibson, G., and Schenkman, J. (1979). *Biochem. Biophys. Res. Commun.* **90,** 925.

Sligar, S., Kennedy, K., and Pearson, D. (1980). *Proc. Natl. Acad. Sci. U.S.A.* **77,** 1240.

Wagner, G., and Gunsalus, I. C. (1978). *In* "Methods in Enzymology" (S. Fleischer and L. Packer, eds.), Vol. 52, p. 166. Academic Press, New York.

Yasunobu, K., Hanin, M., Tonalla, M., and Gunsalus, I. C. (1980). *In* "Microsomes, Drug Oxidations, and Chemical Carcinogenesis" (M. J. Coon *et al.,* eds.), p. 85. Academic Press, New York.

21

Purification
and Characterization
of Adrenal
P450 Cytochromes

Masayuki Katagiri
and
Katsuko Suhara

I. INTRODUCTION

The first demonstration of the P450 nature of the substrate-binding and oxygen-activating component of a soluble monooxygenase system in *Pseudomonas putida* (Katagiri *et al.*, 1968), the camphor 5-exohydroxylase (Hedegaard and Gunsalus, 1965), conflicted with the then-accepted concept that both the unique spectral properties of P450 cytochromes and their functions in monooxygenase systems reflect their unusual state of existence in the membrane structure (Omura and Sato, 1964; Cooper *et al.*, 1965). Such an idea further suggested to us the possibility that the membrane-bound P450 occurring in organelles might be purified without losing its basic physicochemical properties and enzymatic functions. However, earlier attempts to separate cytochrome P450 from the membrane uniformly failed leading to the extensive formation of altered forms of the P450, "P420," possessing no monooxygenase activity. For this reason and because of many additional advantages of its use, this bacterial P450, termed $P450_{cam}$, has received considerable attention from numerous investigators. Indeed, after subsequent success in further purifying and characterizing $P450_{cam}$ (Yu *et al.*, 1974), there has been a rapid increase in the number of reports on the separation and purification of different multiple forms of P450

EXPERIENCES IN BIOCHEMICAL PERCEPTION
Copyright © 1982 by Academic Press, Inc.
All rights of reproduction in any form reserved.
ISBN 0-12-528420-9

associated not only with liver microsomes (Imai and Sato, 1974; Haugen *et al.,* 1975; Welton *et al.,* 1975; Thomas *et al.,* 1976) but also with microsomes of other organs (Serabjit-Singh *et al.,* 1979). Evidence provided by these studies contradicts the temporarily accepted hypothesis that a common cytochrome P450 in the same organelles catalyzes various monooxygenase reactions of most substrates (Orrenius and Ernster, 1974).

In adrenal cortex mitochondria, presence of the two P450-mediated monooxygenase reactions, the cholesterol desmolase reaction splitting the cholesterol side chain between C-20 and C-22, and the corticoid 11β-hydroxylase reaction, has long been recognized. By this time, additional catalytic components with NADPH-linked electron transfer functions, adrenal ferredoxin (adrenodoxin) and NADPH:adrenal ferredoxin oxidoreductase (adrenodoxin reductase), had been purified and characterized (Kimura and Suzuki, 1967; Omura *et al.,* 1966). Subsequently, Young *et al.* (1970) and independently Jefcoate *et al.* (1970) achieved the first partial separation of the two adrenal P450 activities by ammonium sulfate fractionation. Shikita and Hall (1973) further purified the P450 with cholesterol desmolase function to near homogeneity, although the preparation possessed some 11β-hydroxylase activity. At that time, it could not be determined whether the 11β-hydroxylase activity represented an inherent activity of the cholesterol desmolase P450. Although much has been learned at this stage about the role of cytochrome P450 in the hydroxylation of steroids, knowledge of highly purified preparations has been awaited to complete our understanding concerning the nature of the P450-mediated reactions.

We have succeeded in separating and purifying these P450 cytochromes to apparently homogeneous states in amounts sufficient for studying molecular properties of P450 (Takemori *et al.,* 1975a,b). These preparations, termed $P450_{scc}$ and $P450_{11\beta}$, each independently exhibit specific monooxygenase functions, one catalyzing cholesterol desmolase reaction and the other 11β-hydroxylation of steroid (detailed in Section V), respectively. Both function in the presence of the same reconstituted adrenal electron transfer system composed of NADPH, adrenodoxin reductase, adrenodoxin, and O_2.

The two cytochromes appeared to be the only major P450 enzymes which corresponded to 5–6% of the total mitochondrial proteins. Direct measurement of adrenal mitochondria for absolute amounts of $P450_{scc}$ and $P450_{11\beta}$ indicated that the bovine mitochondria contained the two P450 enzymes in a ratio of approximately 5:2, comprising all of the CO reactive mitochondrial P450 (Katagiri and Suhara, 1980).

The purpose of this chapter is to summarize our purification and characterization of the two distinct adrenal P450 cytochromes, in the hope of contributing to the general understanding of the molecular properties of P450 cytochromes, as well as forming the basis for further studies on the mechanism of the steroid hormone biosynthesis.

II. PURIFICATION OF THE TWO P450 PROTEINS

The purification procedure described here is part of our program of successive solubilization and purification of all of the protein participants in the steroid oxygenase enzyme system from mitochondrial preparations of bovine adrenal cortices (Katagiri et al., 1978). Approximately 60 mg of crystalline adrenodoxin (Suhara et al., 1972a) and 10 mg of purified adrenodoxin reductase (Suhara et al., 1972b) can be obtained from the extracts of 1 kg of the cortices. The residual mitochondrial pellet is then solubilized for P450 proteins with cholate in a buffer supplemented with deoxycorticosterone, on which the stability of $P450_{11\beta}$ is highly dependent. The cholate-solubilized supernatant is fractionated with ammonium sulfate and the fractions 0–32% saturation and 32–45% saturation are further purified for $P450_{scc}$ and $P450_{11\beta}$, respectively. A typical protocol for the purification of the two cytochromes is summarized in Table I.

All buffers used throughout the purification of $P450_{11\beta}$ are supplemented with 100 μM EDTA, 100 μM dithiothreitol, and 10 μM deoxycorticosterone. After the $P450_{11\beta}$-rich ammonium sulfate fraction (0–32% saturation) is briefly treated with alumina Cγ, the supernatant fraction is dialyzed against a cholate-free buffer. The importance of this dialysis step is that most of the $P450_{11\beta}$ protein

TABLE I

Summary of Purification Procedure

Step	$P450_{scc}$ (nmol)	$P450_{11\beta}$ (nmol)
Crude extract	1280	660
$P450_{11\beta}$		
Ammonium sulfate precipitate (0–32% saturation)	160	250
Aniline-Sepharose	0	99
$P450_{scc}$		
Ammonium sulfate precipitate (32–45% saturation)	920	100
Aniline-Sepharose I	590	32
Aniline-Sepharose II	250	0

precipitates during the dialysis, while the contaminated $P450_{scc}$ remains soluble. The precipitated $P450_{11\beta}$ can be resolubilized with similar buffer supplemented with 200 mM KCl and 0.7% cholate. The extract is applied to an aniline-substituted Sepharose 4B column, referred to as "aniline-Sepharose" (Katagiri et al., 1978), with the same cholate–KCl buffer and then eluted with similar buffer supplied with 500 mM KCl, 0.5% cholate, and 0.5% Tween 20. Although there are several methods of affinity chromatography available, including those on commercial preparations of octyl- and phenyl-Sepharose, aniline-Sepharose was found to yield better results in the separation of coexisting $P450_{scc}$ from the $P450_{11\beta}$ preparation. After the active fractions eluted from the aniline-Sepharose column are combined and concentrated on an Amicon Centriflo CF25 Membrane Cone, the buffer is replaced through a Sephadex G-25 column with a similar buffer supplemented with 0.3% cholate and 0.3% Tween 20.

The $P450_{scc}$-rich ammonium sulfate fraction (32–45% saturation) is, after dialysis, also subjected to aniline-Sepharose chromatography. The active fractions are combined and further chromatographed on a second aniline-Sepharose column. The eluted $P450_{scc}$ fractions are combined and concentrated on an Amicon Centriflo CF25. The concentrated $P450_{scc}$ solution is then dialyzed against the desired buffer.

The procedures described above yielded the two preparations with nanomoles of P450 heme to milligram protein ratios of 11 and 12, for $P450_{scc}$ and $P450_{11\beta}$, respectively. Either preparation was obtained in the substrate-complexed form showing a high-spin type (H-type*) absorption spectrum in its ferric state, having the Soret peak at 393 nm. Both preparations retained full activity for many months when stored at −80°C, and activity was unaffected by freezing and thawing.

The separation and purification of adrenal P450 cytochromes with the use of aniline-Sepharose chromatography, first described by Hashimoto et al. (1971) and Katagiri and Takemori (1973), established the principle that a hydrophobic chromatography could be used in efficiently separating multiple forms of P450 cytochromes. A few conflicting reports have appeared. Wang and Kimura (1976) noted some difficulty in using our method for chromatographic separation of adrenal P450. Although they examined several affinity columns under various experimental conditions, they did not consider the critical fact that the presence of 50 mM or higher concentrations of phosphate buffer is essential when

---

*Reference is made to absolute spectra of ferric cytochrome P450 indicating either an H-type or an L-type spectrum. The former refers to a high-spin type of absorption spectrum of P450 showing typical maxima at 393 nm and 645 nm, and a shoulder around 540 nm, frequently seen on binding substrate. The latter is a typical low-spin type of cytochrome P450 showing maxima at 418, 537, and 570 nm. In either form of the preparation, the cytochrome P450 must have potential activities both in inducing typical CO spectrum of P450 upon binding CO in its ferrous state, and in catalyzing a specific monooxygenase reaction.

the P450 preparation is applied to the column. In contrast to this report, the other report from the same laboratory described the use of an aniline-Sepharose as an important step for their purification of $P450_{scc}$ (Kido and Kimura, 1979). Watanuki et al. (1977) also reported difficulty in eluting $P450_{11\beta}$ from an aniline-Sepharose column.

There have now been increasing numbers of reports employing use of hydrophobic affinity columns for efficient and reproducible separation of multiple forms of P450 both in mitochondria (Ingelman-Sundberg et al., 1978; Lambeth et al., 1980) and in microsomes (Imai and Sato, 1974; Kominami et al., 1980).

III. CATALYTIC ACTIVITY OF ADRENAL P450

We measured the $P450_{11\beta}$-mediated hydroxylase activities according to the method of Mitani et al. (1975), except that [^{3}H]deoxycorticosterone was used as substrate (Sato et al., 1978). This assay easily quantitates the $P450_{11\beta}$-mediated hydroxylase activities by measuring the rate of formation of the radioactive products, corticosterone and 18-hydroxydeoxycorticosterone, in the presence of an adrenodoxin-dependent electron-donating system from NADPH. The low estimates of the activities reported so far can be accounted for by low $P450_{11\beta}$ contents of the sample, rather than by inadequacy of the assays, since the activity was measured under proper conditions (see Section IV).

In the case of $P450_{scc}$, however, additional comment must be made on the cause of low specific activities reported, since the rate of the $P450_{scc}$-mediated cholesterol desmolase reaction was found to be highly dependent on how the substrate cholesterol had been dispersed in the assay medium. In our newly developed assay, the substrate was prepared by treating [^{3}H]cholesterol at 70°C for 5 minutes in a Tween 20-containing buffer (Katagiri et al., 1978). The assay measured conversion of the cholesterol to pregnenolone at 37°C in a reconstituted electron-donating system from NADPH via adrenodoxin reductase, adrenodoxin, and $P450_{scc}$, to cholesterol and O_2. Among various surfactants tested, such as Emulgen 210, Emulgen 913, Triton X-100, and other Tween series detergents, Tween 20 was most effective (Fig. 1).

The reconstituted desmolase system showed optimal activity in 0.3% Tween 20 and at phosphate buffer concentration of 30 mM at pH 7.4 (Takikawa et al., 1978). The purified $P450_{scc}$ had a turnover number of 16 mol/minute/mol of P450 heme under these assay conditions. This value was nearly an order of magnitude greater than that which we measured in the absence of the detergent. The turnover number of 16 is equivalent to 48 monooxygenase cycles/minute/ P450 heme, since six electrons from NADPH are required for the conversion of one molecule of cholesterol to one molecule of pregnenolone. Very recently, Lambeth et al. (1980) reported similar activity for their $P450_{scc}$ preparations

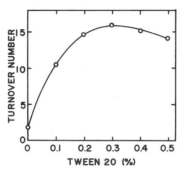

Fig. 1. Effect of Tween 20 on cholesterol desmolase activity mediated by $P450_{scc}$ at 37°. The procedures were as in the standard assay using 30 mM potassium phosphate buffer, pH 7.2.

using cholesterol embedded in liposome vesicles as a substrate. Thus far, other assays developed to date for $P450_{scc}$, including ones employing Tween 80 to disperse cholesterol (Doering, 1969; Hochberg *et al.*, 1974), have frequently underestimated the activities giving turnover numbers of 2 mol/minute/mol of P450 heme, or less.

Although definite conclusions may not be drawn at the present time as to the theoretical basis of the effect of Tween 20, the fact that the presence of a nonionic detergent markedly affected the catalytic activity of a cytochrome P450 isolated from the membrane structure is of great interest. Tween 20 is also effective in activating the rate of reduction of $P450_{scc}$ by hydrosulfite even in the absence of added cholesterol (Takikawa *et al.*, 1978). These observations along with the protective effects of Tween 20 on the thermal stability of $P450_{scc}$ may reflect the conformational and thus the functional changes of the protein in the presence of this detergent. Therefore, it seems likely that the Tween micelle mimics the membrane structure affecting the organization of cholesterol and cytochrome P450, so that the potential activity of the system is manifested.

IV. MOLECULAR PROPERTIES OF THE TWO CYTOCHROME P450 PROTEINS

Polyacrylamide gel electrophoresis of the purified $P450_{scc}$ and $P450_{11\beta}$ in sodium dodecyl sulfate revealed single protein bands. By comparing the mobilities on the gel with marker proteins, apparent molecular weights of 51,000 and 46,000 were estimated for $P450_{scc}$ and $P450_{11\beta}$, respectively.

Rabbit antibodies prepared against the two P450 proteins interacted with respective, but not alternative, cytochrome P450, whether it was in the crude mitochondrial preparation or in the purified form. Neither antibody immuno-precipitated with $P450_{cam}$. The observed patterns of immunoprecipitin and inhibition of catalytic activity of adrenal P450 cytochromes indicated that the two cytochromes are immunochemically different from each other (Suhara *et al.*, 1978). Additional experiments on the amino acid composition of the two proteins (Katagiri *et al.*, 1976) indicated that a significant difference existed between the two P450 proteins. A difference index of about 10 was calculated according to the method of Metzger *et al.* (1968).

To ascertain whether any significant differences occurred in the chemical compositions of P450 proteins, we analyzed the preparations for phospholipids, sugars, and metals. The results indicated that both preparations contained a maximum of 5 mol phospholipids per mole of P450 heme, although the values were not always constant, the results varying from preparation to preparation in a range between 0.7 and 5 mol/mol of P450 heme (Katagiri and Suhara, 1980). These values, however, indicate that both proteins are essentially phospholipid-depleted compared to the equivalent mitochondrial value of approximately 500 mol/mol of P450 heme. Each preparation contained about 3 mol of neutral sugar and 2 mol of amino sugar per mole, but no detectable amounts of sialic acids. Assays for non-heme iron and copper were performed with negative results.

More recently, Watanuki *et al.* (1977) described a procedure for the preparation of a cytochrome P450 from bovine adrenocortical mitochondria which catalyzed 11β- and 18-hydroxylation of steroids. Their purified preparation gave a single band on sodium dodecyl sulfate–polyacrylamide gel electrophoresis, but, unlike our preparation, exhibited a stable Soret peak around 420 nm. According to our study (Takemori *et al.*, 1975b), the substrate-depleted $P450_{11\beta}$, which is the only known active species of ferric $P450_{11\beta}$ that exhibits the Soret peak at around 420 nm, is an extremely unstable enzyme rapidly losing its hydroxylase function with a half-time of approximately 100 minutes at 0°C under the best conditions tested. In addition, their preparation had a turnover number of 0.6 in deoxycorticosterone 11β-hydroxylation, which can be compared with a turnover number of 110 that we reported for $P450_{11\beta}$. The puzzling results may be readily explained if their preparation had been degraded extensively during the course of the purification process. Similar low values in turnover numbers of $P450_{11\beta}$ have been reported ranging from 5 to 19 mol/minute/mol of P450 (Schleyer *et al.*, 1972; Mitani *et al.*, 1975; Ingelman-Sundberg *et al.*, 1978).

In addition to the above problems in estimating $P450_{11\beta}$, most assays reported so far for $P450_{scc}$ undervalued the cholesterol desmolase activity (see Section III). This obviously leads to erroneous conclusions as to the nature of "$P450_{11\beta}$." It should be pointed out that, in a $P450_{11\beta}$ preparation, any contaminating $P450_{scc}$, the presence of which may have frequently been ignored based on improper assays, is a typical P450 in terms of the physicochemical properties on one site and has no 11β-hydroxylase activity at all on the other, which could mask the actual properties of the preparation.

V. COMPARISON OF SUBSTRATE SPECIFICITY AND SPECTRAL PROPERTIES

The purified preparation of P450$_{scc}$ has been shown to interact solely with the side chain of cholesterol. No other classes of steroids, such as various C$_{21}$- and C$_{19}$-steroids could serve as substrates able to be hydroxylated by purified P450$_{scc}$ under similar assay conditions.

P450$_{11\beta}$ is an efficient enzyme with high turnover numbers catalyzing hydroxylation of various steroids such as deoxycorticosterone, deoxycortisol, 4-androstene-3,17-dione, testosterone, and progesterone. Cortisol, corticosterone, 18-hydroxycorticosterone, 11β-hydroxy-4-androstene-3,17-dione, and 11β-hydroxytestosterone were also hydroxylated but at much slower rates.

A number of steroids have been known to induce an H-type absorption spectrum of adrenal P450. In their earlier work with crude adrenal preparations, Mitani and Horie (1969) extensively analyzed the spectral interactions of the cytochrome with various steroids. To examine further this type of interaction with individual P450 cytochrome, we prepared the substrate-free preparations of P450 by incubating the purified P450 and NADPH in the presence of catalytic amounts of adrenodoxin and its reductase. After the reaction was completed as indicated by the complete shift of the Soret peak from 393 nm to 418 nm, i.e., the conversion of the H-type form to the L-type form, the reaction mixture was applied to a Sephadex G-25 column. The combined P450 fractions were shown to be free of cholesterol, cholate, and pregnenolone (P450$_{scc}$), and deoxycorticosterone (P450$_{11\beta}$), respectively. When the substrate-free P450$_{scc}$ was tested for a number of steroids, only cholesterol caused a shift of the spectrum to an H-type form. In contrast to P450$_{scc}$, the substrate-free P450$_{11\beta}$ interacted with any one of the steroids that were the substrates of the P450$_{11\beta}$-mediated hydroxylase reactions to induce H-type spectra. Since the magnitude of such spectral changes were dependent on the concentration of the substrate, one can calculate the affinity of the steroid to P450$_{11\beta}$ from the titration curve. The results indicated that a positive correlation can be drawn between the calculated affinity constant for the substrate and the ability of substrate to undergo hydroxylase reactions. In contrast, the nonsubstrates for P450$_{11\beta}$, such as cholesterol, pregnenolone, aldosterone, estrogens, and D-camphor, were all without significant effect in inducing H-type absorption spectrum of ferric P450$_{11\beta}$. In this respect, P450$_{11\beta}$ appears to be active toward the general structure of 3-keto-Δ^4-steroids, on which the presence of additional hydroxyl groups at the positions 17, 21, and either 11β or 18 may not be critical. The group at the 17-position on the C_{19}-steroid may be either a keto or hydroxyl group (Katagiri and Suhara, 1980).

Having established the substrate specificity of $P450_{11\beta}$, it was of interest to study the position specificity of the $P450_{11\beta}$-mediated hydroxylase reactions. Deoxycorticosterone has been known to be hydroxylated at both the 11β- and 18-positions by intact mitochondria of adrenal cortex, as well as by crude adrenal P450 preparations (Björkhem and Karlmer, 1977). Various lines of evidence from several experimental approaches show that the same species of $P450_{11\beta}$ is involved in both 11β-methylene and 18-methyl hydroxylations of deoxycorticosterone, the C_{21}-steroid(Katagiri et al., 1976; Sato et al., 1978). In the case where the substrate is 4-androsterne-3,17-dione, the C_{19}-steroid, the sites able to be hydroxylated appeared to be its 11β- and 19-positions. Although the mechanism and physiological roles of the $P450_{11\beta}$-mediated dual hydroxylations are not known at present, these results might provide evidence in support of the hypothesis of Rapp and Dahl (1976) that a single cytochrome P450 could bind a steroid in two, somewhat loose, stereospecific ways and that binding one way results in 11β-hydroxylation and binding the other way, 18- or 19-hydroxylation. This explanation may further be rationalized by the fact that the interatomic distances between the 11β- and 18-(19-) positions are very close on the steroid structure.

VI. ADRENAL STEROID HYDROXYLASES AS SECOND MODEL P450 SYSTEMS

This chapter has illustrated some of the properties of P450 cytochromes in the adrenal cortex mitochondria. According to a recent report by Kominami et al. (1980), a microsomal cytochrome P450, termed $P450_{C21}$, which is specific in hydroxylating a steroid at the 21-position, has also been solubilized and extensively purified from bovine adrenal cortex. Thus, the combination of all three P450 cytochromes from the same bovine adrenal cortex catalyzing a series of monooxygenase reactions in the steroid hormone metabolism, may provide the following advantages in a comparative sense.

1. All of the P450 proteins are available in purified forms in sufficient amounts.

2. Each of the P450 cytochromes in this class is known to be unique in both substrate and position specificities, representing the two types of monooxygenase mechanisms, the C–C lyase and the hydroxylase. The latter reaction may further be subdivided to methyl and methylene hydroxylations.

3. These P450 systems include both mitochondrial and microsomal types of

P450, representing the two typical examples of the mechanism of the P450-mediated electron transfer systems.

4. In the mitochondria, a common electron-donating chain consisting of adrenodoxin reductase and adrenodoxin are shared by the two distinct P450 systems (Masters *et al.*, 1973).

Therefore, the study of these characteristics of each of the multiple forms of P450 cytochromes in the adrenal may form a basis of knowledge in steroid hormone metabolism, on one hand, and may contribute to general working model systems for various classes of P450 cytochromes, on the other, offering great promise for future lines of research in these fields.

ACKNOWLEDGMENTS

We are indebted to many colleagues who have contributed to various aspects of this work. This work was supported in part by grants from the Ministry of Education, Science, and Culture, Japan, and from the Yamada Science Foundation.

REFERENCES

Björkhem, I., and Karlmer, K.-E. (1977). 18-Hydroxylation of deoxycorticosterone by reconstituted systems from rat and bovine adrenals. *Eur. J. Biochem.* **51**, 145-154.

Cooper, D. Y., Levin, S., Narashimulu, S., Rosenthal, O., and Estabrook, R. W. (1965). Photochemical action spectrum of the terminal oxidase of mixed function oxidase systems. *Science* **147**, 400-402.

Doering, C. H. (1969). A microassay for the enzymatic cleavage of the cholesterol side chain. *In* "Methods in Enzymology" (R. B. Clayton, ed.), Vol. 15, pp. 591-596. Academic Press, New York.

Hashimoto, S., Suhara, K., Takemori, S., and Katagiri, M. (1971). Steroid hydroxylase systems in bovine adrenal cortex. Purification of cytochomre P-450. *Seikagaku* **43**, 535.

Haugen, D. A., Van der Hoeven, T. A., and Coon, M. J. (1975). Purified liver microsomal cytochrome P-450. Separation and characterization of multiple forms. *J. Biol. Chem.* **250**, 3567-3570.

Hedegaard, J., and Gunsalus, I. C. (1965). Mixed function oxidation. IV. An induced methylene hydroxylase in camphor oxidation. *J. Biol. Chem.* **240**, 4083-4043.

Hochberg, R. B., Van der Hoeven, T. A., Welch, M., and Lieberman, S. (1974). A simple and precise assay of the enzymatic conversion of cholesterol into pregnenolone. *Biochemistry* **13**, 603-609.

Imai, Y., and Sato, R. (1974). A gel-electrophoretically homogeneous preparation of cytochrome P-450 from liver microcomes of phenobarbital pretreated rabbits. *Biochem. Biophys. Res. Commun.* **60**, 8-14.

Ingelman-Sundberg, M., Montelius, J., Rydström, J., and Gustafsson, J.-Å. (1978). The active form of cytochrome P-450$_{11\beta}$ from adrenal cortex. *J. Biol. Chem.* **253**, 5042-5047.

Jefcoate, C. R., Hume, R., and Boyd, G. S. (1970). Separation of two forms of cytochrome P-450 from adrenal cortex mitochondria. *FEBS Lett.* **9**, 41-44.

Katagiri, M., and Suhara, K. (1980). Comparison of the two adrenal cortex mitochondrial cytochrome P-450 (P-450$_{scc}$ and P-450$_{11\beta}$). *In* "Biochemistry, Biophysics, and Regulation of Cytochrome P-450" (J.-Å. Gustafsson, ed.), pp. 97-100. Elsevier/North-Holland Biomedical Press, Amsterdam.

Katagiri, M., and Takemori, S. (1973). Hydroxylase components of adrenal mitochondria. *Abstr. Book, Int. Congr. Biochem., 9th, 1973*, p. 327.

Katagiri, M., Ganguli, B. N., and Gunsalus, I. C. (1968). A soluble cytochrome P-450 functional in methylene hydroxylation. *J. Biol. Chem.* **243**, 3543-3546.

Katagiri, M., Takemori, S., Itagaki, E., Suhara, K., Gomi, T., and Sato, H. (1976). Characterization of purified cytochrome P-450$_{scc}$ and P-450$_{11\beta}$ from bovine adrenocortical mitochondria. *In* "Iron and Copper Proteins" (K. T. Yasunobu, H. F. Mower, and O. Hayaishi, eds.), pp. 281-289. Plenum, New York.

Katagiri, M., Takemori, S., Itagaki, E., and Suhara, K. (1978). Purification of adrenal cytochrome P-450. *In* "Methods in Enzymology" (S. Fleischer and L. Packer, eds.), Vol. 52, pp. 124-132. Academic Press, New York.

Kido, T., and Kimura, T. (1979). The formation of binary and ternary complexes of cytochrome P-450$_{scc}$ with adrenodoxin and adrenodoxin reductase · adrenodoxin complex. *J. Biol. Chem.* **254**, 11806-11815.

Kimura, T., and Suzuki, K. (1967). Components of the electron transport system in adrenal steroid hydroxylase. Isolation and properties on non-heme iron protein (adrenodoxin). *J. Biol. Chem.* **242**, 485-491.

Kominami, S., Ochi, H., Kibayashi, Y., and Takemori, S. (1980). Studies on the steroid hydroxylation system in adrenal cortex microsomes. *J. Biol. Chem.* **255**, 3386-3394.

Lambeth, J. D., Seybert, D. W., and Kamin, H. (1980). Phospholipid vesicle-reconstituted cytochrome P-450$_{scc}$. *J. Biol. Chem.* **255**, 138-143.

Masters, B. S. S., Taylor, W. E., and Isaacson, E. L. (1973). Studies on the function of adrenodoxin and TPNH-cytochrome *c* reductase in the mitochondria and microsomes of adrenal cortex, utilizing immunochemical techniques. *Ann. N.Y. Acad. Sci.* **212**, 76-93.

Metzger, H., Shaprio, M. B., Mosimann, J. E., and Vinton, J. E. (1968). Assessment of compositional relatedness between proteins. *Nature (London)* **219**, 1166-1168.

Mitani, F., and Horie, S. (1969). Studies on P-450. On the substrate-induced spectral change of P-450 solubilized from bovine adrenocortical mitochondria. *J. Biochem. (Tokyo)* **65**, 269-280.

Mitani, F., Ichiyama, A., Masuda, A., and Ogata, I. (1975). Enzymic studies on adrenocortical deoxycorticosterone 11β-hydroxylase system. *J. Biol. Chem.* **250**, 8010-8015.

Omura, T., and Sato, R. (1964). The carbon monooxide-binding pigment of liver microsomes. I. Evidence for its hemoprotein nature. *J. Biol. Chem.* **239**, 2370-2378.

Omura, T., Sanders, E., Estabrook, R. W., Cooper, D. Y., and Rosenthal, O. (1966). Isolation from adrenal cortex of a nonheme iron protein and a flavoprotein functional as a reduced triphosphopyridine nucleotide-cytochrome P-450 reductase. *Arch. Biochem. Biophys.* **117**, 660-673.

Orrenius, S., and Ernster, L. (1974). Microsomal cytochrome P-450-linked monooxygenase systems in mammalian tissues. *In* "Molecular Mechanisms of Oxygen Activation" (O. Hayaishi, ed.), pp. 215-244. Academic Press, New York.

Rapp, J. R., and Dahl, L. K. (1976). Mutant forms of cytochrome P-450 controlling both 18- and 11β-steroid hydroxylation in the rat. *Biochemistry* **15**, 1235-1242.

Sato, H., Ashida, N., Suhara, K., Itagaki, E., Takemori, S., and Katagiri, M. (1978). Properties of an adrenal cytochrome P-450 (P-450$_{11\beta}$) for the hydroxylations of corticosteroids. *Arch. Biochem. Biophys.* **190**, 307-314.

Schleyer, H., Cooper, D. Y., and Rosenthal, O. (1972). Preparation of the heme protein P-450 from the adrenal cortex and some of its properties. *J. Biol. Chem.* **247**, 6103-6110.

Serabjit-Singh, C. J., Wolf, C. R., and Philpot, R. M. (1979). The rabbit pulmonary monooxygenase system. Immunochemical and biochemical characterization of enzyme components. *J. Biol. Chem.* **254**, 9901–9907.

Shikita, M., and Hall, P. F. (1973). Cytochrome P-450 from bovine adrenocortical mitochondria: An enzyme for the side chain cleavage of cholesterol. *J. Biol. Chem.* **248**, 5598–5604.

Suhara, K., Takemori, S., and Katagiri, M. (1972a). Improved purification of bovine adrenal iron–sulfur protein. *Biochim. Biophys. Acta* **263**, 272–278.

Suhara, K., Ikeda, Y., Takemori, S., and Katagiri, M. (1972b). The purification and properties of NADPH-adrenodoxin reductase from bovine adrenocortical mitochondria. *FEBS Lett.* **28**, 45–47.

Suhara, K., Gomi, T., Sato, H., Itagaki, E., Takemori, S., and Katagiri, M. (1978). Purification and immunochemical characterization of the two adrenal cortex mitochondrial cytochrome P-450-proteins. *Arch. Biochem. Biophys.* **190**, 290–299.

Takemori, S., Suhara, K., Hashimoto, S., Hashimoto, M., Sato, H., Gomi, T., and Katagiri, M. (1975a). Purification of cytochrome P-450 from bovine adrenocortical mitochondria by an "aniline-Sepharose" and the properties. *Biochem. Biophys. Res. Commun.* **63**, 588–593.

Takemori, S., Sato, H., Gomi, T., Suhara, K., and Katagiri, M. (1975b). Purification and properties of cytochrome P-450$_{11\beta}$ from adrenocortical mitochondria. *Biochem. Biophys. Res. Commun.* **67**, 1151–1157.

Takikawa, O., Gomi, T., Suhara, K., Itagaki, E., Takemori, S., and Katagiri, M. (1978). Properties of an adrenal cytochrome P-450 (P-450$_{scc}$) for the side chain cleavage of cholesterol. *Arch. Biochem. Biophys.* **190**, 300–306.

Thomas, P. E., Lu, A. Y. H., Ryan, D., West, S. B., Kawalek, J., and Levin, W. (1976). Multiple forms of rat liver cytochrome P-450. *J. Biol. Chem.* **251**, 1385–1391.

Wang, H.-P., and Kimura, T. (1976). Purification and characterization of adrenal cortex mitochondrial cytochrome P-450 specific for cholesterol side chain cleavage activity. *J. Biol. Chem.* **25**, 6068–6074.

Watanuki, M., Tilley, B. E., and Hall, P. F. (1977). Purification and properties of cytochrome P-450 (11β- and 18-hydroxylase) from bovine adrenocortical mitochondria. *Biochim. Biophys. Acta* **484**, 236–247.

Welton, A. F., O'Neal, F. O., Chaney, L. C., and Aust, S. D. (1975). Multiplicity of cytochrome P-450 hemoproteins in rat liver microsomes. *J. Biol. Chem.* **250**, 5631–5639.

Young, D. G., Holroyd, J. D., and Hall, P. F. (1970). Enzymatic and spectral properties of solubilized cytochrome P-450 from bovine adrenocortical mitochondria. *Biochem. Biophys. Res. Commun.* **38**, 184–190.

Yu, C.-A., Gunsalus, I. C., Katagiri, M., Suhara, K., and Takemori, S. (1974). Cytochrome P-450$_{cam}$. 1. Crystallization and properties. *J. Biol. Chem.* **249**, 94–101.

22

Application of Affinity and Photoaffinity Probes to Cytochromes P450$_{cam}$ and P450$_{11\beta}$: New Insights into the Mode of Substrate Binding and Orientation

Karl M. Dus,
John A. Bumpus,
and
Ralph I. Murray

I. INTRODUCTION

It is a great pleasure and an honor to contribute to this volume dedicated to Irwin C. Gunsalus at the advent of his seventieth birthday. Since much of the work to be reported in the following pages emanated from research initiated jointly by him and one of us (K.M.D.) several years ago, we are particularly grateful that he has now also, albeit indirectly, provided the proper occasion for us to summarize, update, and project into the near future. It is a wonderful opportunity to pause and reflect at this festive moment and to share our reflections, thoughts, and anticipations with him, his other students, and his collaborators. This is a joyous occasion to look back at the numerous outstanding

EXPERIENCES IN BIOCHEMICAL PERCEPTION
Copyright © 1982 by Academic Press, Inc.
All rights of reproduction in any form reserved.
ISBN 0-12-528420-9

achievements during a very distinguished scientific career that is still very much in progress today through his continued bold advances into new frontier areas. The enormous impact of Gunny's intellect and profound insight into the intricate processes of living organisms, and his powerful yet warm personality will continue to be a guiding light for future generations of biochemists.

It certainly was a memorable experience for one of us (K.M.D.) to have the privilege to work with Gunny for several years, exchanging ideas and sharing in the excitement of scientific conjecture and discovery. And it was during this time that the seeds for our current work were planted. During the last few years we have pondered the question of how the structurally diversified, yet generally very hybrophobic substrates are bound to P450 heme proteins to permit hydroxylation or other, related catalytic reactions, to occur at a specific carbon atom. As in past investigations of the structural characteristics of their heme-binding domain (Swanson and Dus, 1979) and the immunochemical properties of P450 heme proteins (Dus et $al.$, 1980), the highly soluble and crystalline $P450_{cam}$ of the bacterial camphor hydroxylase has offered itself as the natural model to search out a unifying concept for P450 heme proteins. It is good to remember that exploring molecular detail of one member of a set of related proteins may be informative about all members of the set. That is, the detailed structure and mechanism of one member provides a model for understanding the structure, mechanism, and specificity of other members of the same set. We will apply this simplifying concept to P450 heme proteins and compare the $P450_{11\beta}$ of the bovine adrenocortical mitochondrial 11β-hydroxylase of deoxycorticosterone to $P450_{cam}$ and see to what extent our model of the substrate-binding site is applicable.

II. THE SUBSTRATE-BINDING SITE OF CYTOCHROME $P450_{cam}$

A. Rationale

Cytochrome $P450_{cam}$ is the substrate-binding component of the camphor methylene hydroxylase of $Pseudomonas$ $putida$, converting $(+)-$camphor to 5-exo-hydroxycamphor. The crucial role of cysteines in heme ligation and substrate binding of $P450_{cam}$ has long been recognized (Dus, 1976). Titrations with mercurials such as PCMB* have shown the presence of 6–7 Cys/2 in this protein,

*Key to abbreviations used: PCMB, p-chloromercuribenzoate; NEM, N-ethylmaleimide; NES-, N-ethylsuccinimido-; IBA, isobornyl bromoacetate; API, 1-(4-azidophenyl)imidazole; BPI, 1-(4-bromoacetamidophenyl)imidazole; IAC, isobornyl acetate; CMC, S-carboxymethyl-cysteine; PIA, 1-(4-acetamidophenyl)imidazole; DBA, deoxycorticosterone bromoacetate.

and all of them were accounted for as free sulfhydryl groups. Alkylation studies with NEM have allowed partial characterization of these cysteines (Lipscomb *et al.*, 1978). Under mild conditions four sulfhydryls were converted to NES-cysteine, while vigorous treatment produced six NES-cysteine residues. Kinetic studies under the mild alkylating conditions showed the presence of three distinct reactivities. A single residue reacted very rapidly and has been correlated with a surface-exposed cysteine capable of generating a still functional P450$_{cam}$ dimer. Two further equivalents titrated with an intermediate reactivity. Alkylation of these resulted in loss of the substrate-induced Soret transition from 417 nm to 390 nm and a concomitant change in E_0' shift necessary for transfer of the first electron from putidaredoxin to P450$_{cam}$ during the oxygenation cycle. The fourth cysteine titrated at a relatively slow rate. The rate of alkylation of the intermediate and slow-reacting sulfhydryls was reduced by an order of magnitude when substrate was present, suggesting the close proximity of these groups to the substrate-binding site. Dus (1976) proposed that a cysteine sulfhydryl plays a role in the binding and orientation of camphor in the active site of P450$_{cam}$. Murray and Dus (1980) suggested that this interaction might lead to the formation of a thiohemiketal bond (**I**), resulting from addition of the sulfhydryl to the camphor carbonyl group. Such a bond would require the carbonyl and sulfhydryl groups to be in close proximity and proper alignment. Since this implied that a suitable alkylating derivative of camphor could serve as a specific covalent affinity label for the substrate-binding cysteine, we selected isobornyl bromoacetate (**II**) for our initial studies. In an ancillary study we exploited isobornylmercaptan for similar purposes (Murray and Dus, 1980).

I   **II**

N-Phenylimidazole, on the other hand, is a general inhibitor of P450 heme proteins. Previous work in our laboratory has shown 1-(4-azidophenyl)imidazole (**III**) to be an excellent photoaffinity label for the active site of P450$_{cam}$ (Swanson and Dus, 1979). However, as photolysis of API produces a reactive nitrene targeted to hydrophobic side chains, we have now prepared 1-(4-bromoacetamidophenyl)imidazole (**IV**), an alkylating analog, to allow comparison of the nucleophilic environment at the substrate- and inhibitor-binding sites.

III   IV

B. Application of Substrate-Derived Labels

Due to the rapid, irreversible reaction of IBA, equilibrium could not be established to allow determination of the dissociation constant (K_D) for the $P450_{cam}$–IBA complex. Table I shows instead the K_D for the binding of the close analog, isobornyl acetate (IAC), as determined by Lineweaver–Burk analysis of the titration difference spectrum. The favorable K_D seen there supported the expectation that the label would be highly specific for the substrate-binding site.

Binding of IBA to $P450_{cam}$ in 1:1 stoichiometry resulted in an immediate type I spectral shift of strong intensity (Fig. 1). From this rapid spectral response we concluded that the label was bound in the correct orientation, analogous to the substrate, camphor. Immediately after the addition of the reagent, an aliquot of the reaction mixture was dried and hydrolyzed. Amino acid analysis revealed that 0.57 nmol of CMC were present per nmole hydrolyzed protein. This is in keeping with the expectation that acid hydrolysis will cleave the ester bond of the S-alkylcysteine to yield CMC and isoborneol. Amino Acid analysis of an aliquot taken after 24 hours alkylation showed 0.74 nmol of CMC per nmole of protein. It should be noted, however, that during this additional incubation period the

TABLE I
$P450_{cam}$ Ligands

Ligand	Structure	Spectral type	K_D (μM)
Camphor		I	2
Isobornyl acetate (IAC)		I	5
Acetamidophenyl imidazole (PIA)		II	42
Azidophenyl imidazole (API)		II	1

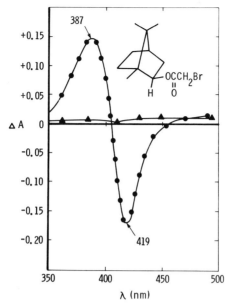

Fig. 1. Difference spectrum of P450$_{cam}$-IBA complex versus P450$_{cam}$. Substrate free P450$_{cam}$ (10 μM), in 50 mM K-PO$_4$, pH 7.5, was incubated with IBA (1:1) added as a 95% EtOH solution. Incubation was in the dark, at 25°C, for 24 hours. ●, Zero time spectrum; ▲, 24-hour spectrum.

Soret maximum of P450$_{cam}$ had shifted back to 417 nm. Thus, the P450$_{cam}$-(IBA)$_1$ complex was spectrally indistinguishable from substrate-free P450$_{cam}$. Subsequent addition of excess camphor regenerated the type I spectrum characteristic of P450$_{cam}$.

It should be remembered that after alkylation with NEM to the level of the NES$_4$-P450$_{cam}$, the protein derivative had also lost the substrate-induced spectral characteristics, but did not have the ability to respond to addition of excess camphor. Clearly, NEM labeling is a function of sulfhydryl reactivity while labeling with IBA is affinity directed and limited to the substrate-binding site. This was further emphasized by studies with higher ratios of label to protein which resulted in increased CMC values upon acid hydrolysis, approaching 3 nmol per nmole of protein at 10:1. No more than 3 CMC were found with reagent to protein ratios as high as 100:1, a level at which NEM produced the NES$_6$-P450$_{cam}$ derivative. The rapid spectral and chemical response at low label to protein ratios underscores the role of binding affinity in promoting the alkylation reaction with IBA. Preincubation of P450$_{cam}$ with camphor dramatically reduced the rate of labeling with IBA.

C. Application of Inhibitor-Derived Labels

As with IBA, the rapid reaction of BPI with P450$_{cam}$ required that the corresponding acetate be used for approximation of K_D values (Table I). Addition of BPI to substrate-free P450$_{cam}$ in 1:1 stoichiometry produced a weak type II spectrum (Fig. 2). In contrast to IBA, however, the spectrum with BPI continued to develop with time until it reached a maximal amplitude. Amino acid analysis of an aliquot taken after 24 hours of alkylation with BPI showed 0.95 nmol of CMC per nmole of protein. Treatment with a reagent to protein ratio of 10:1 for 24 hours also resulted in the time-dependent development of a type II spectrum, but in this case the initial response was much more rapid. The final response was virtually identical to that seen with a 1:1 BPI to protein ratio. From the amino acid analysis of a hydrolyzed aliquot of the alkylation mixture having a 10:1 BPI to protein ratio, a value of 2.3 nmol of CMC per nmol of protein was obtained. This finding suggests that the limiting value for cysteines alkylated by this reagent would also be 3 CMC, as was found with IBA. In view of the pronounced spectral transitions induced by both affinity reagents, and the high specificity of active site directed affinity labels, it is reasonable to assume that both probes label the same three cysteines. Thus the substrate- and inhibitor-binding sites must be largely coincident.

The first affinity label used in this laboratory for P450$_{cam}$ was the photoaffinity probe API (Swanson and Dus, 1979). In this case a ninefold molar excess of reagent produced monolabeled P450$_{cam}$ when applied to a 40-μM solution of the protein. In addition, it was determined that the label was localized entirely in the

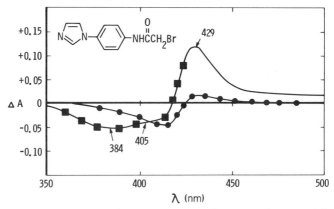

Fig. 2. Difference spectrum of P450$_{cam}$–BPI complex versus P450$_{cam}$ Substrate free P450$_{cam}$ (10 μM), in 50 mM K–PO$_4$, pH 7.5, was incubated with BPI (1 : 1) added as a 95% EtOH solution. Incubation was in the dark, at 25°C, for 24 hours. ●, Zero time spectrum; ■, 24-hour spectrum.

smallest BrCN derived heme peptide. When the experiment was repeated with 100 μM P450$_{cam}$ it produced a dilabeled P450$_{cam}$ derivative, with both labels appearing quantitatively in the heme peptide. Based on these photoaffinity-labeling experiments, together with the results outlined above with the nucleophilic alkylating agents, we have developed a model for P450$_{cam}$ with two discrete binding sites, one for substrate and one for product.

D. The Two-Site Hypothesis

The K_D of the P450$_{cam}$-substrate complex, as deduced from binding studies, is about 1–2 μM. Using radiolabeled (^{14}C or ^{3}H) camphor it has been shown that a single equivalent of substrate binds at substrate concentrations not greatly exceeding this value. At much higher concentrations, however, a second equivalent of camphor can be accommodated (Gunsalus *et al.*, 1974). This was the first indication of the existence of two binding sites on P450$_{cam}$. The subsequent findings of Swanson and Dus with the photoaffinity probe API, again suggested the presence of a second binding site, when high protein and label concentrations favored the dilabeled P450$_{cam}$-API complex. Since then, no further discussion of this problem has occurred.

The unexpected spectral response we observed with IBA may be closely related to the presence of two binding sites, or more specifically, to the presence of a substrate- and a product-binding site. A stoichiometric reagent to protein ratio generated an initial rapid spectral shift equivalent to about 45% of the spectral amplitude produced by a saturating amount of camphor (about 200:1, substrate to enzyme ratio). After acid hydrolysis we found a value of 0.57 CMC indicative of the extent of cysteine alkylation by IBA. From this finding we may conclude that the covalent label is initially lodged in the substrate-binding site with a position and orientation nearly identical to that of camphor. Yet within minutes one can observe a spectral decay that after 24 hours leads to an apparently substrate-free spectrum. Concurrent amino acid analyses, however, confirm unequivocally that covalent attachment of label to protein has occurred, as ascertained by increasing amounts of CMC.

Since the substrate-induced spectral shift is reversed with time, a question about the location of the covalently bound label is raised, especially as the P450$_{cam}$-(IBA)$_1$ complex shows a normal response to further additions of camphor, restoring the type I spectral transition. In search for the position of the label a binding titration difference spectrum for camphor was recorded using the IBA complex (0.77 CMC). As seen in Fig. 3, this spectrum is nearly identical in form to that seen with camphor applied to native P450$_{cam}$, but the amplitude is only 70–80% that obtained with native enzyme. The K_D (about 5 μM) is, however, within the limits of error, equivalent to that observed with the P450$_{cam}$-camphor complex. Thus we conclude that for all practical purposes the substrate-binding site has been vacated by IBA and is now again free and intact for a second occupancy.

The schematic drawing in Fig. 4 presents a simple model for the envisioned transfer of covalently bound IBA from the substrate to the product-binding site. This concept of translocation is suggested to apply equally to the hydroxylation of camphor by native $P450_{cam}$. The motivating force behind a rapid transfer of camphor to a site of lower affinity may be derived from the change in binding characteristics after hydroxylation has occurred; the substrate-binding site will no longer provide a perfect fit for the hydroxy compound and the binding affinity will have been lowered commensurately with the increase in hydrophilicity. We suggest that this change, in turn, permits the translocation by a simple rotation around the C–C bond mediated by the transient covalent link to the adjacent cysteine. For IBA the net effect of this transfer is that the substrate-binding site of $P450_{cam}$-$(IBA)_1$ is very rapidly vacated due to an irreversible covalent bond. The site is now ready for occupancy by a second molecule of label or substrate. The strength of our model lies in the ease with which this mechanism of translocation to the product site could be carried out by a transient thiohemiketal bond of camphor to a nearby cysteine, thus providing a convenient and reversible shuttle service. In the case of binding with IBA, however, the guiding cysteine is obviously lost in the transfer irreversibly. Since binding with large excess of

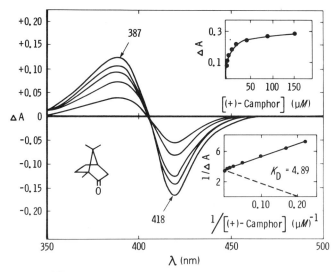

Fig. 3. Titration difference spectrum of $P450_{cam}$-$(IBA)_1$ complex with (+)-camphor. Substrate free $P450_{cam}$ (10 μM), in 50 mM K-PO_4, pH 7.5, was incubated with IBA (1 : 1) added as a 95% EtOH solution. Incubation was in the dark, at 25°C, for 24 hours. Aliquots were then taken as reference and sample, and camphor was added as a 95% EtOH solution.

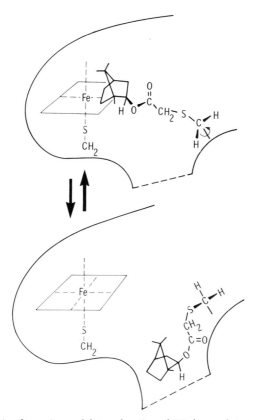

Fig. 4. Schematic of two-site model: translocation of IBA from substrate to product site.

label caused alkylation of up to three cysteines, but never in excess of three, we have to postulate that the active site of P450$_{cam}$ contains two additional sulfhydryl groups so placed as to provide close to native binding interactions for camphor as well as IBA and BPI.

III. THE SUBSTRATE-BINDING SITE OF CYTOCHROME P450$_{11\beta}$

A. General Information

P450$_{11\beta}$ of the steroid 11β-hydroxylase of adrenocortical mitochondria has been selected here for an initial comparison of its substrate-binding characteristics to those of the bacterial P450$_{cam}$ because of obvious similarities. Both heme proteins function as part of a similar enzyme system, and act on structurally similar terpenoid substrates. Moreover, all three enzyme constituents of these hydroxylases—P450, redoxin, and reductase—closely parallel each other in structure, function, and immunochemical behavior, although none of these protein constituents can effectively substitute for one another in mixed reconstitution assays. Adrenodoxin and putidaredoxin show extensive sequence homology (Tanaka *et al.*, 1974). Based on our immunochemical data (Dus *et al.*, (1980), and based on the ability of P450$_{11\beta}$ to generate a BrCN-derived small hemepeptide which closely resembles that of P450$_{cam}$ (Bumpus *et al.*, 1980), it may be expected that comparable sequence homology also extends to P450$_{11\beta}$ and P450$_{cam}$, especially since their amino acid compositions and sizes are strikingly similar. No comparative sequence data are, however, as yet available. But it is important for our comparison here that the number of available cysteines in P450$_{11\beta}$ (Bumpus *et al.*, 1980) is comparable to that found in P450$_{cam}$ because our two-site model of substrate-binding requires the participation of several sulfhydryl groups. Since P450$_{11\beta}$ is an intrinsic component of the adrenocortical mitochondrial membrane, its solubility, even in high detergent concentrations, is limited and the protein denatures much more readily in aqueous buffers than does P450$_{cam}$. While these limitations made a complete comparison between these two proteins impossible at this time, we have been able to secure enough detailed information to prove that pronounced similarity exists in the principal mode of binding of substrate and inhibitor derivatives to P450$_{cam}$ and P450$_{11\beta}$.

B. Affinity and Photoaffinity Experiments

As with P450$_{cam}$, we synthesized and applied both an inhibitor-derived and a substrate-derived affinity label of the bromoacetyl type to probe the possible involvement in the mechanism of substrate binding and processing by P450$_{11\beta}$ of nucleophilic amino acid side chains, particularly of sulfhydryl groups located at the active site. In this case the substrate derivative was deoxycorticosterone bromoacetate (**V** = DBA) which is readily synthesized from deoxycorticosterone while the inhibitor derivative was again BPI (**IV**) to permit a direct comparison to the results obtained with P450$_{cam}$.

V

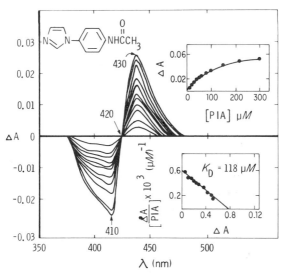

Fig. 5. Difference spectrum of 1-(4-acetamidophenyl)imidazole binding to cytochrome P450$_{11\beta}$ After recording a baseline of equal light absorbance with 1 ml of a 1.4-μM cytochrome P450$_{11\beta}$ solution in each cuvette, aliquots of an ethanolic solution of PIA and an equal volume of ethanol were added to the sample and reference cuvette, respectively. A plot of the peak to trough change in optical density (ΔA) versus PIA yields a hyperbolic curve (upper inset). Eadie–Hofstee analysis gives a straight line and the K_D is determined by calculating the reciprocal of the slope. The buffer was 50 mM potassium phosphate, pH 7.4, containing 100 μM EDTA, 100 μM dithiothreitol, 0.3% sodium cholate, and 0.3% Tween 20.

The corresponding acetates were used to determine the approximate K_D values from spectral titrations based on the respective type I and type II shifts of the Soret band of P450$_{11\beta}$: $K_D = 94 \ \mu M$ for deoxycorticosterone acetate and $K_D = 120 \ \mu M$ for PIA (Fig. 5). It should be noted that the responses of P450$_{11\beta}$ to these reagents were slower than those of P450$_{cam}$ with IBA and BPI due both to less favorable K_D values and lower temperature. Most of the reactions with P450$_{11\beta}$ had to be performed at 4°C instead of room temperature to protect this labile hemeprotein.

Specifically, addition of BPI to P450$_{11\beta}$ in ratios 1:1 and 10:1 instantly resulted in type II transitions. The amplitude of the difference spectra, however, did not at first exceed 40% of the maximal value seen with PIA, and gradually increased with time to a final amplitude after 24 hours of 50% of the maximal value. After addition of BPI in a ratio of 50:1, the initial amplitude was 90% and approached 100% of the maximal value after 24 hours at 4°C. P450$_{11\beta}$ is isolated as the substrate complex in the presence of excess deoxycorticosterone, which statilizes this labile heme protein. Therefore the whole reconstituted steroid 11β-hydroxylase system, including NADPH, was included in both the sample and reference cells to metabolize deoxycorticosterone. Addition of DBA in a ratio of 10:1 was made to the sample cuvette. This resulted in oxidation of NADPH, monitored at 340 nm, and a concomitant type I spectral transition which reached its maximal amplitude within 25 minutes. Addition of excess DBA after NADPH oxidation had been completed did not elicit any further change. After a 24-hour incubation at 4°C the spectral amplitude in the difference spectrum had declined to 88% of the maximal value, somewhat reminiscent of the complete disappearance of the type I spectral transition observed with IBA and $P450_{cam}$. Aliquots of the covalent $P450_{11\beta}$-substrate or inhibitor complexes, resulting from interactions at 1:1 to 10:1 ratios, were hydrolyzed after 24 hours incubation and submitted to amino acid analysis. About 0.5–0.6 residues of CMC were found with one equivalent while values of 0.9–1.0 residues of CMC were recovered at a ratio of 10:1. Higher reagent to protein ratios yielded a maximum of 2–3 nmol of CMC per nmol P450.

Although these results require further study we conclude at this point that the covalent interactions of our affinity reagents with $P450_{11\beta}$ reflect the same pattern of sulfhydryl labeling and attendant spectral shifts observed with $P450_{cam}$, but occur at a much slower pace due to lower temperature and lower affinities of the reagents employed. This conclusion is reemphasized by results we obtained with our generally applicable photoaffinity probe, API, which preferentially lables hydrophobic amino acid side chains. When applied tp $P450_{11\beta}$ it caused significant covalent label incorporation, specifically in the heme environment. Again, due to lower affinity of the reagent for $P450_{11\beta}$, the quantitative recoveries were lower but the qualitative picture of the interaction was essentially the same.

IV. APPLICABILITY OF THE TWO-SITE HYPOTHESIS TO P450 HEME PROTEINS

The limited comparison, presented in the preceding pages, of two prominent P450 heme proteins, the bacterial $P450_{cam}$ and the mitochondrial $P450_{11\beta}$, leads us to several important conclusions. The mode of binding of the substrate, its orientation relative to the oxygen-activating heme iron, and its subsequent conversion to product with attendant transfer from the substrate-binding to the product-binding site from which release is favored, can be conveniently rationalized by the proposed two-site hypothesis. This hypothesis apparently applies quite well to both P450 heme proteins investigated here, and probably to many others as well. One attractive feature of this concept is its reliance on cysteine sulfhydryl groups adjacent to the substrate-binding site which can form thiohemiketal bonds with suitably oriented carbonyl groups of the properly bound substrate. This provides a simple means for reinforcing the correct alignment of the substrate as well as for its rapid and fail-safe, unidirectional transfer from one site to the other with regeneration of the active site for the next cycle. It also makes the hypothesis readily accessible to experimental testing by affinity reagents, both of the bromoacetyl and the sulfhydryl types. Suitable derivatives of substrates and inhibitors are readily accessible by simple synthetic procedures. Considering the common occurrence of strategically placed carbonyl groups on a large group of steroids which are known or potential substrates for P450 heme proteins, this aspect carries considerable appeal. For the liver microsomal P450's and their poorly defined substrate specificities, however, the applicability of the sulfhydryl-mediated two-site concept is not yet apparent.

REFERENCES

Bumpus, J. A., Murray, R. I., and Dus, K. M. (1981). Covalent modifications of P450$_{scc}$ and P450$_{11\beta}$ of bovine adrenocortical (BAC) mitochondria by substrate and inhibitor derived affinity reagents. American Society for Biological Chemists, 72nd Annual Mtg., June 1981, St. Louis, Abstract No. 13.

Dus, K. (1976). On the structure and function of cytochromes P450. *Enzymes Biol. Membr.* **4,** 199–238.

Dus, K. M., Litchfield, W. J., Hippenmeyer, P. J., Bumpus, J. A., Obidoa, O., Spitsberg, V., and Jefcoate, C. R. (1980). Comparative immunochemical studies of cytochrome P450$_{cam}$ of *Pseudomonas putida* and of cytochrome P450$_{scc}$ of bovine adrenocortical mitochondria. *Eur. J. Biochem.* **111,** 307–314.

Gunsalus, I. C., Meeks, J. R., Lipscomb, J. D., Debrunner, P., and Münck, E. (1974). Bacterial monooxygenases—The P-450 cytochrome system. *In* "Molecular Mechanisms of Oxygen Activation" (O. Hayaishi, ed.), pp. 559–613. Academic Press, New York.

Lipscomb, J. D., Harrison, J. E., Dus, K. M., and Gunsalus, I. C. (1978). Cytochrome P450$_{cam}$: SS-dimer and -SH derivative reactivities. *Biochem. Biophys. Res. Commun.* **83,** 771–778.

Murray, R. I., and Dus, K. M. (1980). Camphor-derived affinity reagents for specific labeling of cytochrome P450$_{cam}$: Synthesis and application of isobornyl mercaptan. *In* "Microsomes, Drug Oxidations and Chemical Carcinogenesis" (M. J. Coon *et al.*, eds.), Vol. 1, pp. 367–370. Academic Press, New York.

Swanson, R. A., and Dus, K. M. (1979). Specific covalent labeling of cytochrome P-450$_{cam}$ with 1-(4-azidophenyl)imidazole, an inhibitor-derived photoaffinity probe for P-450 heme proteins. *J. Biol. Chem.* **254,** 7238–7246.

Tanaka, M., Haniu, M., Yasunobu, K. T., Dus, K., and Gunsalus, I. C. (1974). The amino acid sequence of putidaredoxin, an iron–sulfur protein from *Pseudomonoas putida*. *J. Biol. Chem.* **249,** 3689–3701.

23

NADH Peroxidase of
Streptococcus faecalis

M. I. Dolin

I. OXYGEN AS ELECTRON ACCEPTOR FOR *Streptococcus faecalis*

As a beginning graduate student in the laboratory of Dr. Gunsalus, I was given the opportunity to investigate the pyruvate oxidase system of *Streptococcus faecalis*. O'Kane and Gunsalus (1948) had recently found that cells of *S. faecalis*, grown in a semisynthetic medium, would oxidize pyruvate only in the presence of a new cofactor, now known as lipoic acid (Gunsalus, 1953, 1954). An obvious next step was to isolate the enzyme responsible for pyruvate oxidation and to show, if possible, that the activity of the enzyme depended on the presence of the new cofactor. It was assumed that the pyruvate oxidase of *S. faecalis*, like that of another cytochrome-free lactic acid microorganism, *Lactobacillus delbrueckii* (Lipmann, 1939), would be a relatively simple flavoprotein that reacted directly with oxygen. No special difficulties were anticipated in the isolation of the streptococcal enzyme.

Streptococcus faecalis had some surprises in store, however. First, whereas intact cells of *S. faecalis* formed only small amounts of acetoin from pyruvate, cell-free extracts contained a potent acetoin-forming system that competed strongly with the pyruvate oxidase reaction (Dolin and Gunsalus, 1951). Second,

EXPERIENCES IN BIOCHEMICAL PERCEPTION
Copyright © 1982 by Academic Press, Inc.
All rights of reproduction in any form reserved.
ISBN 0-12-528420-9

as it eventually turned out, pyruvate oxidation by *S. faecalis* is catalyzed by a multienzyme system (Dolin and Gunsalus, 1952). With NAD as the electron acceptor for pyruvate oxidation, the components of the system and the mechanism of dehydrogenation were quite analogous to those that had been demonstrated for the pyruvate dehydrogenase system of *Escherichia coli* (Korkes *et al.,* 1951; Gunsalus, 1953, 1954; Hager, 1953). In this sequence of reactions, lipoic dehydrogenase catalyzes the reduction of NAD to NADH, with reduced lipoic acid as the hydrogen donor. The question then became, how does *S. faecalis* handle the reoxidation of NADH when O_2 is the ultimate hydrogen acceptor for pyruvate oxidation?

Under anaerobic conditions, pyruvate can serve as electron acceptor for both *E. coli* and *S. faecalis,* the reaction then being the dismutation of two molecules of pyruvate to lactate, acetyl phosphate, and CO_2 (Korkes *et al.,* 1951; Dolin and Gunsalus, 1952). Under aerobic conditions, *E. coli* can reoxidize NADH through its cytochrome-containing electron transport chain, but *S. faecalis* contains no heme enzymes when grown in conventional media (Dolin, 1961).

Earlier work by Gunsalus and some of his colleagues had already established that *S. faecalis,* and certain other lactic acid streptococci, are more aerobic than would be expected for homofermentative lactic acid bacteria. It was shown that cell suspensions of *S. faecalis* catalyzed rapid O_2 uptake with glycerol (Gunsalus and Umbreit, 1945), pyruvate (O'Kane and Gunsalus, 1948), or glucose (O'Kane, 1950) as substrates. Resting cell suspensions of *S. agalactiae* (formerly *mastitidis*) oxidized alcohol rapidly with oxygen as hydrogen acceptor (Greisen and Gunsalus, 1944). Where tested, these reactions were not inhibited by cyanide and were assumed to be catalyzed by flavoproteins. By analogy to the properties of "old yellow enzyme," H_2O_2 was expected to be the product of O_2 reduction (Dolin, 1961). It was found, however, that some of the oxidase reactions listed above (alcohol, glucose, pyruvate as substrates) took place without H_2O_2 accumulation. Of particular interest were the findings that cell suspensions of *S. agalactiae* (Greisen and Gunsalus, 1943) and *S. faecalis,* B 33a (Seeley and VanDemark, 1951), could oxidize alcohol or glucose, respectively, with H_2O_2 as oxidant, and that the reactions were resistant to cyanide.

As of 1951, it was known that cell suspensions of certain lactic acid streptococci could use O_2 as an efficient oxidant for various substrates; lack of H_2O_2 formation in some of these presumed flavoprotein oxidase reactions could be accounted for by the ability of the cells to use H_2O_2 as an electron acceptor.

After leaving the laboratory of Dr. Gunsalus to take a position at the Biology Division of the Oak Ridge National Laboratory, I did some further work on the ketoacid oxidase system of *S. faecalis* (Dolin, 1955a), and then decided to investigate the fate of the NADH generated by the dehydrogenase portion of the system.

It was soon found that extracts prepared from cells of *S. faecalis,* 10C1 grown fermentatively on glucose, contained a series of flavoprotein enzymes concerned with NADH oxidation (Dolin, 1953, 1955b). Among these enzymes was a cyanide-resistant NADH oxidase system that catalyzed rapid four electron reduction of O_2 to H_2O.

$$NADH + H^+ + \quad O_2 \rightarrow NAD^+ + H_2O_2 \tag{1}$$

$$NADH + H^+ + H_2O_2 \rightarrow NAD^+ + 2H_2O \tag{2}$$

$$2\ NADH + 2H^+ + O_2 \rightarrow 2\ NAD^+ + 2\ H_2O \tag{3}$$

Reactions (1) and (2) are catalyzed by separate flavoproteins, NADH oxidase and NADH peroxidase, respectively. This sequence allows O_2 to function as a hydrogen acceptor without the accumulation of peroxide, a compound that is toxic for catalase-free lactic acid bacteria. With crude extracts, and under conditions in which the peroxidase reaction is limiting, the oxidase, in the presence of manganous ions, yields H_2O_2 stoichiometrically (Dolin, 1953). Recent work (Britton *et al.*, 1978) with a different strain of *S. faecalis* has shown that a portion of the H_2O_2 formed when NADH is oxidized by O_2 in the presence of crude extracts of *S. faecalis*, is generated via the dismutation between two superoxide radicals. It is not known which of the NADH oxidizing enzymes of *S. faecalis* is responsible for the one electron reduction of O_2 to O_2^-, but it is clear that NADH peroxidase is able to deal efficiently with the H_2O_2 that is formed when two O_2^- radicals are converted to $H_2O_2 + O_2$ by streptococcal superoxide dismutase.

Although NADH oxidation by the cytoplasmic enzymes that catalyze reactions (1) and (2) is not coupled to oxidative phosphorylation, the NADH oxidase system is physiologically useful. For instance, since pyruvate can be oxidized to acetyl phosphate, the oxidation of glucose can yield $4\sim P$ per hexose (two from fermentation of glucose to pyruvate, and two from oxidation of two molecules of pyruvate to two molecules of acetyl phosphate). Under fermentative conditions, only $2\sim P$ per hexose are obtained, since pyruvate must be used as the electron acceptor for the NADH generated by the oxidation of triose phosphate. Direct growth experiments have demonstrated the energetic advantage conferred by the NADH oxidase system of *S. faecalis*, 10C1 (Dolin, 1955b; Smalley *et al.*, 1968). The pyruvate dehydrogenase and NADH oxidase system can obviously compete very well with lactic dehydrogenase, since *S. faecalis*, 10C1, growing aerobically with glucose as energy source, is reported to convert 85% of the hexose to acetate $+ CO_2$ (Smalley *et al.*, 1968).

The oxidase catalyzing reaction (1) has not been studied further. Because of the novelty of finding a non-heme peroxidase, most of my work with the NADH oxidizing enzymes of *S. faecalis* has focused on the peroxidase. This enzyme probably accounts for the cyanide-resistant peroxidase reactions catalyzed by intact cells of streptococci and lactobacilli with substrates whose oxidation is

NAD-linked. NADH peroxidase has been isolated from *S. faecalis,* strains 10C1 and B 33a, and also from *S. agalactiae* (Dolin, 1961), the organism in which Greisen and Gunsalus (1943) demonstrated that peroxide serves as acceptor for alcohol oxidation. Flavoprotein NADH peroxidases have also been found in extracts of *L. casei* (Walker and Kilgour, 1965) and *Bacillus subtilis* (Lightbown and Kogut, 1959).

During a search for flavoprotein peroxidases in organisms lacking heme enzymes, the surprising finding was made that the anaerobe, *Clostridium perfringens,* contains a very active flavoprotein NADH oxidase that catalyzes a cyanide-resistant, four electron reduction of O_2 to H_2O (reaction 3) (Dolin, 1959a,b). Only a single enzyme is involved and free peroxide is not an intermediate. In crude extracts, the specific activity for NADH oxidation is as great as found for *Azotobacter agile.* It is possible that the clostridial oxidase functions as a scavenger of oxygen, a reaction that would help to explain the finding that *C. perfringens* will grow at oxygen tensions that inhibit the growth of stricter anaerobes (Gordon *et al.,* 1953). This hypothesis is consistent with the observation that the clostridial oxidase has a high affinity for O_2. Subsequently, a flavoprotein NADH oxidase, catalyzing the reduction of O_2 to H_2O, was also isolated from aerobically grown *S. faecalis,* 10C1 (Hoskins *et al.,* 1962). This enzyme had no peroxidase activity. Aerobically grown cells still contain NADH peroxidase. In fact, with efficient aeration the yield of peroxidase can increase ~15-fold (M. I. Dolin, unpublished data).

In part because one of the NADH-oxidizing enzymes of *S. faecalis* is a diaphorase for which quinones are the best oxidants (Dolin and Wood, 1960), a search was made for a naturally occurring quinone in *S. faecalis,* 10C1. This resulted in the isolation of 2-solanesyl-1,4-naphthoquinone, the first example of a biologically occurring demethylmenaquinone (Baum and Dolin, 1963, 1965).* All of the naphthoquinone, along with 30% of the total cellular flavin, were located in membranes prepared from osmotically lysed protoplasts (Dolin and Baum, 1965). Analysis of the supernatant and membrane fractions of the lysate showed that the supernatant contained all the lactic dehydrogenase and NADH peroxidase, and 80% of the NADH oxidase activity. The membranes contained all the NADH-cytochrome *c* reductase and 50% of the NADH-menadione reductase. Earlier work (Dolin, 1955b) had shown that after sonic oscillation of cell suspensions, a considerable portion of the cytochrome *c* reductase is solubilized. Cytochrome *c* may be a nonspecific oxidant for some flavoproteins, but in view of later findings, the occurrence of NADH-cytochrome *c* reductase in the membranes may be significant.

---

*Dr. Robert Baum, who worked on the naphthoquinone problem as a postdoctoral fellow, received his Ph.D. degree from the University of Illinois, where his research mentor was Dr. I. C. Gunsalus.

The levels of demethylmenaquinone, flavin, and non-heme iron in the membranes are, respectively, 3.5. 1.77, and 21.6 nmol/mg membrane protein (Dolin and Baum, 1965), a composition that suggests the presence of a respiratory chain lacking cytochromes. This idea is not as far-fetched as it seems. In a development that was rather startling to investigators familiar with the characteristics of lactic acid bacteria, it was found that some of these microorganisms, when grown in the presence of hematin, synthesize catalase, and a few strains synthesize cytochromes (Whittenbury, 1964). With two strains of *S. faecalis*, the cytochromes were shown to be functional, since membrane preparations containing the bound cytochrome carry out oxidative phosphorylation with a P/O ratio of ~0.3, when NADH is the electron donor (Bryan-Jones and Whittenbury, 1969; Ritchey and Seeley, 1974). A P/O ratio of ~0.7 has been estimated from oxygen-induced proton pulses measured in hematin-grown cells of *S. faecalis* var. *zymogenes* (Pritchard and Wimpenny, 1978).

There are reports, however, that *S. faecalis*, 10C1, grown in the absence of hematin, is still able to catalyze oxidative phosphorylation. Molar growth yields, with glucose as substrate, suggest the occurrence of oxidative phosphorylation coupled to electron transport with a P/O ratio of ~0.6 (Smalley *et al.*, 1968). It is also reported that membrane preparations from *S. faecalis*, 10C1 (grown in the absence of hematin) couple electron transport between NADH and fumarate to ATP formation, with a P/O ratio of ~0.2 (Faust and VanDemark, 1970). These results suggest that membranes of *S. faecalis*, 10C1, with the composition of naphthoquinone, flavin, and non-heme iron noted above, may carry out "site 1" oxidative phosphorylation. With other strains of *S. faecalis*, oxidative phosphorylation has not been detected in cells lacking cytochrome (Bryan-Jones and Whittenbury, 1969; Ritchey and Seeley, 1974); however, it has not been reported whether the membranes of these cytochrome-free bacteria contain any electron transport coenzymes.

As emphasized previously, flavoprotein respiration by lactic acid bacteria can be physiologically useful even when the electron transport per se is not linked to ATP formation. In general, a pathway to oxygen makes it possible for an organism to use substrates that cannot be metabolized under anaerobic conditions, because the hydrogen acceptors necessary for a balanced fermentation may not be available. A portion of the energy in such oxidations is conserved through substrate-linked phosphorylation. Glycerol oxidation by *S. faecalis* (strain 24), one of the strains of *S. faecalis* that grows on glycerol only under aerobic conditions, furnishes an example of such a physiologically useful oxidation (Gunsalus and Sherman, 1943; Gunsalus and Umbreit, 1945). The oxidation of glycerol to triose phosphate permits the subsequent energy-linked fermentation of the triose phosphate to lactate.

As mentioned above, the presence of an NADH oxidase system in *S. faecalis*, 10C1, allows a potential doubling of the energy yield during aerobic growth on glucose, even in the absence of oxidative phosphorylation coupled to electron transport. A more detailed treatment of flavoprotein respiration and its physiological significance has been given elsewhere (Dolin, 1961).

II. NADH PEROXIDASE FROM FERMENTATIVELY GROWN
S. faecalis, 10C1; DEMONSTRATION OF AN
ENZYME–SUBSTRATE COMPLEX

NADH peroxidase, isolated from cells grown fermentatively on glucose, was identified as a flavoprotein containing FAD as prosthetic group (Dolin, 1955, 1957). Zone electrophoresis of the purified enzyme showed that enzyme activity, FAD and protein, migrated as a single peak (Dolin, 1957). No heme components were present and only traces of Fe or Mn were detected in the purified enzyme.

A totally unexpected result of this early work was the finding that NADH does not cause a net reduction of enzyme-bound flavin. Instead, a complex is formed between NADH and enzyme; complex formation is accompanied by partial bleaching of the 450-nm band of the flavin and by formation of a new long wavelength absorption band extending from ~520 nm to beyond 620 nm (λ_{max} at ~540 nm) (Dolin, 1956, 1957). Addition of H_2O_2 to the complex causes the regeneration of oxidized enzyme. The complex, however, is not dissociated by the chemical reducing agent, dithionite, although in the absence of NADH, dithionite bleaches (reduces) the bound FAD without causing formation of a long wavelength band. Further work showed that the complex may be a kinetically significant species, since it forms only in the presence of NADH or analogs of NADH that are substrates for the peroxidase activity of the enzyme (Dolin, 1960a).

Substrate-induced spectral changes very similar to those obtained with NADH peroxidase were also reported for another flavoprotein, one of the acyl-CoA dehydrogenases (Beinert and Crane, 1956); within the next few years, several other flavoproteins were shown to form long wavelength bands in the presence of substrate (see Beinert and Sands, 1961; Massey et al., 1961). Most of these absorption bands were assigned to substrate-stabilized flavin radicals. This seemed plausible at the time, since Beinert (1956) had shown that reoxidation of reduced FMN in air gave rise to a transient long wavelength absorption band (λ_{max} ~565 nm) that was attributed to the semiquinone of FMN. However, a simple semiquinone hypothesis could not explain the characteristics of the NADH peroxidase complex, in part because the absorbance changes at 450 and 540 nm could be obtained independently, by choosing the appropriate NADH analog (Dolin, 1960a).

It was soon recognized that not all substrate-induced long wavelength absorption bands of flavoprotein could be attributed to flavin semiquinones (Beinert, 1961; Massey *et al.*, 1961, 1966), and it is now known, from work on model systems (Blankenhorn, 1975) and a variety of flavoproteins (Massey and Ghisla, 1974), that charge-transfer complexes between reduced substrate (including reduced pyridine nucleotide) and oxidized flavoprotein, or between reduced flavoprotein and oxidized substrate, can account for the long wavelength bands formed by many flavoproteins. Some of these complexes have been shown to be obligatory intermediates in flavoprotein catalysis.

Although flavin radicals seemed to be ruled out as the explanation for the spectral properties of the NADH peroxidase complex, the reduction state of the complex was ambiguous because of the unusual finding that the complex would form on addition of either oxidized or reduced pyridine nucleotide to enzyme that had been reduced by high concentrations of dithionite. These results suggested that the complex was formed between reduced NAD and reduced enzyme. Such a formulation did not seem realistic and an alternative explanation was proposed, (Dolin, 1966) but the problem was not solved until large amounts of enzyme became available and it was possible to carry out stoichiometric titration of oxidized enzyme with dithionite or NADH under strict anaerobic conditions (see Section III).

III. NADH PEROXIDASE FROM AEROBICALLY GROWN
S. faecalis

A. Purification and Properties of the Enzyme*

1. Crystallization

Early work (Dolin, 1955b) had shown that aeration of growth medium through a sparger caused a twofold increase in the NADH peroxidase content of *S. faecalis*. It was found later that the more efficient aeration possible in a fermentor (4.5 ft^3/min of air) led to a doubling of the growth yield, compared to fermentative conditions, and to an approximate tenfold increase in the level (per cell) of NADH peroxidase. It then became possible to answer some of the questions raised by the earlier work.

Enzyme was purified essentially as before, to the stage of the calcium phosphate gel eluate (Dolin, 1955b). Then, in brief, the eluate was concentrated by ammonium sulfate precipitation, dissolved in 0.02 M potassium phosphate buffer, pH 7.0, and dialyzed overnight against 0.04 M sodium acetate buffer, pH 5.0, at 4°C. After removal of the precipitated protein by centrifugation, the super-

*M. I. Dolin, unpublished data.

natant was dialyzed overnight against 0.04 *M* sodium acetate buffer, pH 4.5. The precipitate was collected by centrifugation, dissolved in 0.05 *M* potassium phosphate buffer, pH 7.0, and crystallized from 0.51 saturated ammonium sulfate at 4°C. The crystals are shown in Fig. 1.

2. Minimum and Subunit Molecular Weight

The subunit molecular weight of crystalline enzyme, determined by electrophoresis on sodium dodecyl sulfate–polyacrylamide gel (Weber and Osborn, 1969) is 63,000; the minimum molecular weight, per molecule of bound FAD, is 61,000–67,000. A tentative molecular weight of 134,000 was obtained by thin layer chromatography of enzyme on Sephadex G-200.

On electrophoresis of crystalline enzyme on 7.5% polyacrylamide gel at either pH 6.5 or 8.4, two bands are detected at each pH, with relative mobilities (compared to bromphenol blue) of 0.46 and 0.62. The ratio of protein in the faster moving band to protein in the slower moving band is 0.14 at pH 6.5 and 0.55 at pH 8.4. If the enzyme in the major band is eluted, from gels run at either pH 6.5 or 8.4, and again subjected to electrophoresis at the original pH, two bands appear once more on each gel, at the same positions as before. It appears, therefore, that the enzyme can dissociate and that this tendency is much more pronounced at alkaline pH.

There is a difference in the minimum molecular weight (per flavin) determined

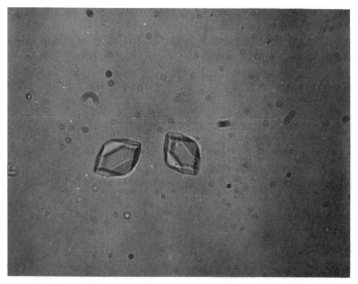

Fig. 1. Crystals of NADH peroxidase in 0.05 *M* potassium phosphate buffer, pH 7.0, containing 2 *M* ammonium sulfate.

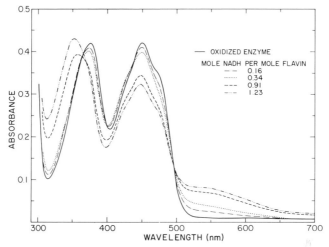

Fig. 2. Spectrophotometric titration of NADH peroxidase with NADH; formation of the first and second intermediates. A 2-ml volume of enzyme (0.04 mM as bound flavin) was titrated anaerobically with a solution containing 4.2 mM NADH in 0.02 M Tris base. (From Dolin, 1975. Published with permission of *J. Biol. Chem.*)

for enzyme isolated from fermentatively and aerobically grown cells. Although enzyme from fermentatively grown cells has the same specific activity under standard assay conditions as enzyme from aerobically grown cells, the minimum molecular weight for the former was given as 120,000 (Dolin, 1957). There may, therefore, be a real difference in the flavin content of the two kinds of enzyme, but this possibility has not been further investigated.

3. Assays for Bound Prosthetic Groups

It was verified, with enzyme from aerobically grown cells, that FAD is the sole flavin present. Neutron activation analysis of two samples of enzyme, containing 0.014 and 0.021 mmol of bound FAD, showed that the selenium content of the enzyme was <0.002 gm atom of Se per mole FAD. It was important to rule out the presence of Se because the non-heme (and non-flavin) enzyme, glutathione peroxidase, contains one atom of Se per subunit (Flohe *et al.*, 1973).

B. Enzyme Species Detected During Anaerobic Titration of NADH Peroxidase

Anaerobic titration of the flavoprotein with dithionite revealed that the active site contains three electron acceptors—the two bound FAD groups and in addition a non-flavin acceptor tentatively identified as a disulfide group (Dolin, 1975). NADH reacts with only two of these acceptors (the non-flavin group and

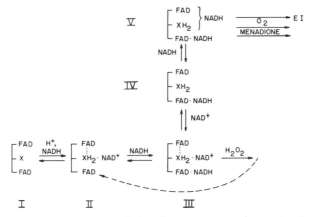

Fig. 3. A mechanism consistent with the effector properties of NAD. Species I is oxidized enzyme; II and III are the intermediates detected during anaerobic titration of the enzyme with NADH. Enzyme species involved in the oxidation of III to II are not shown. X, the non-flavin acceptor; EI, inactive enzyme. (From Dolin, 1977. Published with permission of Academic Press.)

one of the bound flavins); thus, when oxidized enzyme is titrated with NADH, two sequential and spectrally distinct intermediates are formed. Figure 2 shows two stages in the development of each of these intermediates; proposed structures are shown in Fig. 3 (species II and III).

The first molecule of NADH reacts with oxidized enzyme (species I) and reduces the non-flavin acceptor, X. The reduced acceptor (XH_2) then forms a complex with one of the bound FAD groups, to give species II. The spectrum of II is shown in Fig. 2, at 0.16 and 0.34 mol NADH per mole flavin. A second molecule of NADH then complexes with the second molecule of bound FAD, to produce species III; the spectrum of III is shown in Fig. 2, after addition of 0.91 and 1.23 mol NADH per mole flavin. The NADH titration curves (not shown) can be fitted with dissociation constants of 1×10^{-7} M for the equilibrium between I and II, and 3×10^{-6} M for the equilibrium between II and III. Species III, in the presence of O_2, is slowly oxidized to II. Species II is air-stable, but is stoichiometrically oxidized by H_2O_2 to species I. Treatments that cause the enzyme to lose its peroxidase activity cause an equivalent loss in ability of the enzyme to form species II. It is believed, therefore, that the $XH_2 \cdot NAD^+ \cdots FAD$ complex is the site at which peroxide is reduced.

Since both the subunit molecular weight and the minimum molecular weight per flavin are ~60,000, whereas titration data indicate that there are two flavins per active site, the presence of only one X group per flavin seems anomalous. If two identical monomers combine to form active enzyme and each monomer contains an X group, either (1) one of the X groups is shielded in the dimer, or (2) the enzyme may show half-site reactivity (Levitzki *et al.*, 1971), so that after the first molecule of NADH reacts with enzyme to form species II, the second X group cannot be reduced.

In earlier studies (Dolin, 1960a) there was not enough enzyme available for anaerobic titration experiments. It was possible, however, to titrate small amounts of enzyme (0.1 ml volumes) with NAD or NADH in the presence of ~0.06 M dithionite. Under these conditions, the air-stable intermediate (species II) was not detected. The titration results suggested that reduced flavoprotein forms a complex with reduced NAD. Such a structure for the complex is obviously in disagreement with the stoichiometry observed when the enzyme from aerobically grown cells is titrated with NADH under anaerobic conditions, in the absence of dithionite (Fig. 3). The discrepancy can be resolved if it is assumed that under the conditions of the earlier experiments—that is, in the presence of bisulfite and H_2O_2, generated by the continued reaction of dithionite with dissolved O_2—NADH can compete successfully with dithionite for oxidized enzyme. This mechanism seems likely for the following reasons: (1) Mayhew (1978) has clearly shown that the dithionite/bisulfite couple is a reversible redox system. (2) The dissociation constant for the complex between NADH and enzyme, in the presence of dithionite, is much higher (1.6 $\times$ 10^{-5} M) than the dissociation constants for the first and second steps detected during anaerobic titration of the enzyme in the absence of dithionite. (3) Complexes formed between oxidized enzyme and weakly bound NADH analogs, such as the reduced forms of 3-pyridine aldehyde–adenine dinucleotide and 3-pyridine aldehyde–hypoxanthine dinucleotide, can be partially or almost completely dissociated, respectively, in the presence of dithionite (Dolin, 1960a).

C. Effector Activities of NAD

NAD is an activator of NADH peroxidase and, at the same time, an inhibitor of several reactions of the enzyme that compete with peroxidase activity (Dolin, 1977). Figure 3, a postulated mechanism for peroxidase activity under steady state conditions, offers an explanation for the effector activities of NAD. Oxidized enzyme (I) is reduced to the air-stable intermediate (II) in a pre-steady state step. Species II is converted to III with a second molecule of NADH. Peroxide then oxidizes the upper locus of species III, after which the air-stable intermediate (II) is regenerated at the expense of enzyme-bound NADH.

In order to account for the effector role of NAD, it is assumed that at low concentrations of enzyme, NAD can dissociate from species III; this step allows the formation of IV and V. Species V is considered to be the intermediate that is responsible for the weak oxidase activity of the enzyme and for the menadione reductase reaction. It is also regarded as the intermediate that decays slowly to inactive enzyme in the presence of NADH, at suboptimal concentrations of H_2O_2 (Dolin, 1960b). NAD forces the equilibrium between species III, IV, and V toward III, the enzyme intermediate that is oxidized by H_2O_2. This mechanism accounts for the ability of NAD to activate the peroxidase reaction and to cause a large decrease in the Michaelis constant for peroxide. The activation is accompanied by strong inhibition of the rate of enzyme decay and of the rate at which NADH is oxidized by nonspecific acceptors such as O_2 and menadione, because, in terms of the mechanism, the concentrations of species IV and V become very small in the presence of optimal concentrations of NAD.

After the effector role of NAD was recognized, steady-state studies of peroxidase activity were carried out over a wide range of NADH, NAD, and H_2O_2 concentrations. Some of the kinetic parameters determined in these experiments have been reported (Dolin, 1977). The turnover of the enzyme and the Michaelis constant for H_2O_2 are different from those reported previously (Dolin, 1957) because the earlier experiments were done in the absence of added NAD.

IV. CONCLUSIONS

In his early work on the oxidative metabolism of lactic acid streptococci, Gunsalus pointed out that the characteristics of the reactions he studied contradicted the prevalent assumption that non-heme (presumably flavoprotein) respiration is unphysiological. These studies showed that O_2 uptake by streptococci could be rapid, did not require high O_2 concentrations (Gunsalus and Umbreit, 1945), and that peroxide need not be the final produce of oxygen reduction (Greisen and Gunsalus, 1943, 1944). The years since then have seen the identification of the enzymes that make possible functional, cyanide-resistant flavoprotein respiration (Section I).

When electron transport to oxygen is catalyzed by flavoproteins, H_2O_2 may arise either by two-electron reduction of O_2 to H_2O_2 (Dolin, 1961) or by one-electron reduction of O_2 to O_2^-, followed by dismutation (in the presence of superoxide dismutase) between two O_2^- radicals, to yield H_2O_2 and O_2 (Britton *et al.*, 1978). The lactic acid bacteria, as a group, have several methods of coping with H_2O_2: (1) H_2O_2 can be reduced to water by NADH in the presence of NADH peroxidase, a reaction that can be part of a physiologically useful oxidase system (Section I). (2) Some strains of *S. faecalis* (but not strain 10C1) and various other lactic acid bacteria contain an azide-resistant, presumably non-heme enzyme with catalase activity (Johnston and Delwiche, 1965). (3) Finally, certain lactic acid bacteria, when grown in the presence of hematin, synthesize the classical hemoprotein catalase (Whittenbury, 1964).

Of course, peroxide accumulation could also be prevented during flavoprotein respiration if organisms used only flavoproteins of the type that catalyze four-electron reduction of O_2 to water (Section I). Even under such (theoretical) conditions, there might still be a need for enzymes that decompose H_2O_2, since it is known from work with one strain of *S. faecalis,* that relatively high concentrations of superoxide anion (equivalent to ~17% of the O_2 used) can be formed when oxygen is reduced by NADH, in a reaction catalyzed by an as yet unidentified enzyme (Britton *et al.,* 1978).

Some 20 years ago, it was suggested that the flavoprotein respiratory system of *S. faecalis* represented a transitional stage in aerobic development (Dolin, 1961). At that time, it was not known that *S. faecalis,* 10C1, contained membrane-bound flavins, demethylmenaquinone, and non-heme iron (Baum and Dolin, 1965; Dolin and Baum, 1965), nor was it known that functional membrane-bound cytochromes could be synthesized by various strains of *S. faecalis* and some other lactic acid bacteria, if they were grown in media containing hematin (Bryan-Jones and Whittenbury, 1969; Ritchey and Seeley, 1974). These later findings reinforce the view that certain of the lactic acid bacteria have a good deal to teach us about the steps that lead from flavoprotein respiration to the synthesis of more advanced aerobic respiratory systems.

REFERENCES

Baum, R. H., and Dolin, M. I. (1963). Isolation of a new naphthoquinone from *Streptococcus faecalis,* 10C1. *J. Biol. Chem.* **238,** PC4109–PC4111.

Baum, R. H., and Dolin, M. I. (1965). Isolation of 2-solanesyl-1,4-naphthoquinone from *Streptococcus faecalis,* 10C1. *J. Biol. Chem.* **240,** 3425–3433.

Beinert, H. (1956). Spectral characteristics of flavins at the semiquinoid oxidation level. *J. Am. Chem. Soc.* **78,** 5323–5328.

Beinert, H., and Crane, F. L. (1956). The function of the electron-transferring flavoprotein in the first oxidative step of the fatty acid cycle. *In* "Inorganic Nitrogen Metabolism" (W. D. McElroy and B. Glass, eds.), pp. 601–627. Johns Hopkins Press, Baltimore, Maryland.

Beinert, H., and Sands, R. H. (1961). Semiquinone formation of flavins and flavoproteins. *In* "Free Radicals in Biological Systems" (M. S. Blois, H. W. Brown, R. M. Lemmon, R. O. Lindblom, and M. Weissbluth, eds.), pp. 17–52. Academic Press, New York.

Blankenhorn, G. (1975). Flavin–nicotinamide biscoenzymes: Models for the interaction between NADH (NADPH) and flavin in flavoenzymes. *Eur. J. Biochem.* **50,** 351–356.

Britton, L., Malinowski, D. P., and Fridovich. I. (1978). Superoxide dismutase and oxygen metabolism in *Streptococcus faecalis* and comparisons with other organisms. *J. Bacteriol.* **134,** 229–236.

Bryan-Jones, D. G., and Whittenbury, R. (1969). Haematin-dependent oxidative phosphorylation in *Streptoccus faecalis. J. Gen. Microbiol.* **58,** 247–260.

Dolin, M. I. (1953). The oxidation and peroxidation of DPNH$_2$ in extracts of *Streptococcus faecalis,* 10C1. *Arch. Biochem. Biophys.* **46,** 483–485.

Dolin, M. I. (1955a). Diacetyl oxidation by *Streptococcus faecalis,* a lipoic acid dependent reaction. *J. Bacteriol.* **69,** 51–58.

Dolin, M. I. (1955b). The DPNH-oxidizing enzymes of *Streptococcus faecalis.* II. The enzymes utilizing oxygen, cytochrome c, peroxide and 2,6-dichlorophenolindophenol or ferricyanide as oxidants. *Arch. Biochem. Biophys.* **55,** 415–435.

Dolin, M. I. (1956). Evidence for an enzyme–substrate complex between pyridine nucleotides and DPNH peroxidase flavoprotein. *Arch. Biochem. Biophys.* **60**, 499-501.

Dolin, M. I. (1957). The *Streptococcus faecalis* oxidases for reduced diphosphopyridine nucleotide. III. Isolation of a flavin peroxidase for reduced diphosphopyridine nucleotide. *J. Biol. Chem.* **225**, 557-573.

Dolin, M. I. (1959a). Oxidation of reduced diphosphopyridine nucleotide by *Clostridium perfringens*. I. Relation of peroxide to the over-all reaction. *J. Bacteriol.* **77**, 383-392.

Dolin, M. I. (1959b). Oxidation of reduced diphosphopyridine nucleotide by *Clostridium perfringens*. II. Purification of the oxidase; relation to cytochrome c reductase. *J. Bacteriol.* **77**, 393-402.

Dolin, M. I. (1960a). The *Streptococcus faecalis* oxidases for reduced diphosphopyridine nucleotide. IV. Properties of the enzyme–substrate complex formed between reduced diphosphopyridine nucleotide peroxidase and pyridine nucleotides. *J. Biol. Chem.* **235**, 544-550.

Dolin, M. I. (1960b). The *Streptococcus faecalis* oxidases for reduced diphosphopyridine nucleotide. VI. Inhibition of the flavin peroxidase by its electron donor. *Biochim. Biophys. Acta* **42**, 61-69.

Dolin, M. I. (1961). Cytochrome-independent electron transport enzymes of bacteria. *In* ''The Bacteria'' (I. C. Gunsalus and R. Y. Stanier, eds.), Vol. 2, pp. 425-460. Academic Press, New York.

Dolin, M. I. (1966). NADH Peroxidase. *In* ''Flavins and Flavoproteins'' (E. C. Slater, ed.), pp. 171-182. Elsevier, Amsterdam.

Dolin, M. I. (1975). Reduced diphosphopyridine nucleotide peroxidase. Intermediates formed on reduction of the enzyme with dithionite or reduced diphosphopyridine nucleotide. *J. Biol. Chem.* **250**, 310-317.

Dolin, M. I. (1977). DPNH peroxidase: Effector activities of DPN$^+$. *Biochem. Biophys. Res. Commun.* **78**, 393-400.

Dolin, M. I., and Baum, R. H. (1965). Localization of electron transport components in *Streptococcus faecalis*, 10C1. *Bacteriol. Proc.* pp. 96-97.

Dolin, M. I., and Gunsalus, I. C. (1951). Pyruvic acid metabolism. II. The acetoin-forming enzyme system in *Streptococcus faecalis*. *J. Bacteriol.* **62**, 199-214.

Dolin, M. I., and Gunsalus, I. C. (1952). A soluble pyruvate-αketobutyrate dehydrogenase system from *Streptococcus faecalis*. *Fed. Proc., Fed. Am. Soc. Exp. Biol.* **11**, 203.

Dolin, M. I., and Wood, N. P. (1960). The *Streptococcus faecalis* oxidases for reduced diphosphopyridine nucleotide. V. A flavin mononucleotide-containing diaphorase. *J. Biol. Chem.* **235**, 1809-1814.

Faust, P. J., and VanDemark, P. J. (1970). Phosphorylation coupled to NADH oxidation with fumarate in *Streptococcus faecalis*, 10C1. *Arch. Biochem. Biophys.* **137**, 392-398.

Flohe, L., Günzler, W. A., and Shock, H. H. (1973). Glutathione peroxidase: A selenoenzyme. *FEBS Lett.* **32**, 132-134.

Gordon, J., Holman, R. A., and McLeod, J. W. (1953). Further observations on the production of hydrogen peroxide by anaerobic bacteria. *J. Pathol. Bacteriol.* **66**, 527-537.

Greisen, E. C., and Gunsalus, I. C. (1943). Hydrogen peroxide destruction by streptococci. *J. Bacteriol.* **45**, 16-17.

Greisen, E. C., and Gunsalus, I. C. (1944). An alcohol oxidation system in streptococci which functions without peroxide accumulation. *J. Bacteriol.* **48**, 515-525.

Gunsalus, I. C. (1953). The chemistry and function of the pyruvate oxidation factor (lipoic acid). *J. Cell. Comp. Physiol.* **41**, Suppl. 1, 113-136.

Gunsalus, I. C. (1954). Group transfer and acyl-generating functions of lipoic acid derivatives. *In* ''The Mechanism of Enzyme Action'' (W. D. McElroy and B. Glass, eds.), pp. 545-580. Johns Hopkins Press, Baltimore, Maryland.

Gunsalus, I. C., and Sherman, J. M. (1943). The fermentation of glycerol by streptococci. *J. Bacteriol.* **45**, 155-162.

Gunsalus, I. C., and Umbreit, W. W. (1945). The oxidation of glycerol by *Streptococcus faecalis*. *J. Bacteriol*. **49**, 347–357.

Hager, L. P. (1953). Enzymatic steps in alpha-keto acid oxidation. Thesis, Univ. of Illinois, Urbana.

Hoskins, D. D., Whitely, H. R., and Mackler, B. (1962). The reduced diphosphopyridine nucleotide oxidase of *Streptococcus faecalis:* Purification and properties. *J. Biol. Chem*. **237**, 2647–2651.

Johnston, M. A., and Delwiche, E. A. (1965). Distribution and characteristics of the catalases of Lactobacillaceae. *J. Bacteriol*. **90**, 347–351.

Korkes, S., Del Campillo, A., Gunsalus, I. C., and Ochoa, S. (1951). Enzymatic synthesis of citric acid. IV. Pyruvate as acetyl donor. *J. Biol. Chem*. **193**, 721–735.

Levitzki, A., Stallcup, W. B., and Koshland, D. E. (1971). Half-of-the-sites reactivity and the conformational states of cytidine triphosphate synthetase. *Biochemistry* **10**, 3371–3378.

Lightbown, J. W., and Kogut, M. (1959). Soluble enzymes catalyzing the oxidation of reduced diphosphopyridine nucleotide by molecular oxygen and hydrogen peroxide, isolated from *Bacillus subtilis*. *Biochem. J*. **73**, 14P–15P.

Lipmann, F. (1939). An analysis of the pyruvate oxidation system. *Cold Spring Harbor Symp. Quant. Biol*. **7**, 248–259.

Massey, V., and Ghisla, S. (1974). Role of charge-transfer interactions in flavoprotein catalysis. *Ann. N.Y. Acad. Sci*. **227**, 446–465.

Massey, V., Gibson, Q. H., and Veeger, C. (1961). Intermediates in the catalytic action of lipoyl dehydrogenase (diaphorase). *In* "Free Radicals in Biological Systems" (M. S. Blois, H. W. Brown, R. M. Lemmon, R. O. Lindblom, and M. Weissbluth, eds.), pp. 75–90. Academic Press, New York.

Massey, V., Palmer, G., Williams, C. H., Swoboda, B. E. P., and Sands, R. H. (1966). Flavin semiquinones and flavoprotein catalysis. *In* "Flavins and Flavoproteins" (E. C. Slater, ed.), pp. 133–152. Elsevier, Amsterdam.

Mayhew, S. G. (1978). The redox potential of dithionite and SO_2^- from equilibrium reactions with flavodoxins, methyl viologen and hydrogen plus hydrogenase. *Eur. J. Biochem*. **85**, 535–547.

O'Kane, D. J. (1950). Influence of the pyruvate oxidation factor on the oxidative metabolism of glucose by *Streptococcus faecalis*. *J. Bacteriol*. **60**, 449–458.

O'Kane, D. J., and Gunsalus, I. C. (1948). Pyruvic acid metabolism. A factor required for oxidation by *Streptococcus faecalis*. *J. Bacteriol*. **56**, 499–506.

Pritchard, G. G., and Wimpenny, J. W. T. (1978). Cytochrome formation, oxygen-induced proton extrusion and respiratory activity in *Streptococcus faecalis* var. *zymogenes* grown in the presence of haematin. *J. Gen. Microbiol*. **104**, 15–22.

Ritchey, T. W., and Seeley, H. W. (1974). Cytochromes in *Streptococcus faecalis* var. *zymogenes* grown in a haematin-containing medium. *J. Gen. Microbiol*. **85**, 220–228.

Seeley, H. W., and VanDemark, P. J. (1951). An adaptive peroxidation by *Streptococcus faecalis*. *J. Bacteriol*. **61**, 27–35.

Smalley, A. J., Jahrling, P., and VanDemark, P. J. (1968). Molar growth yields as evidence for oxidative phosphorylation in *Streptococcus faecalis*, 10C1. *J. Bacteriol*. **96**, 1595–1600.

Walker, G. A., and Kilgour, G. L. (1965). Pyridine nucleotide oxidizing enzymes of *Lactobacillus casei*. II. Oxidase and peroxidase. *Arch. Biochem. Biophys*. **111**, 534–539.

Weber, K., and Osborn, M. (1969). The reliability of molecular weight determinations by dodecyl sulfate-polyacrylamide gel electrophoresis. *J. Biol. Chem*. **244**, 4406–4412.

Whittenbury, R. (1964). Hydrogen peroxide formation and catalase activity in the lactic acid bacteria. *J. Gen. Microbiol*. **35**, 13–26.

24

Biochemical
Investigations
at Subzero Temperatures

Pierre Douzou

Although not cited frequently in the following chapter, Gunny is certainly intimately associated with the development of all facets of cryobiochemistry.

The preliminary experiments using fluid hydroorganic solvents and subzero temperature to slow down biochemical reactions seemed of great potential interest for the study of complex multienzyme systems, where the whole activity depends on a delicately adjusted sequence of events, including chemical and structural transformations as well as protein–protein interactions, all worthy of a subzero temperature approach. We chose the monooxygenases of the cytochrome P450 type for their general importance as oxygen-activating enzymes and their occurrence in almost all mammalian tissues and many microorganisms.

With his extreme sense of generosity and his enthusiasm for any new approach, Gunny provided us with a few milliliters of the precious "$P450_{cam}$," which represented a dream of purity and simplicity, and the best model for all cytochrome P450-type monooxygenases.

Starting with the stabilization and purification of the ternary oxy compound, the studies were rapidly extended to other reaction steps, and this fascinating enzyme was used as a tool to solve problems raised by the use of mixed solvents and to gain some insight in the conformational expressions of the structural flexibility of proteins.

309

EXPERIENCES IN BIOCHEMICAL PERCEPTION
Copyright © 1982 by Academic Press, Inc.
All rights of reproduction in any form reserved.
ISBN 0-12-528420-9

His wide and sensible perception of the molecular mechanisms of enzyme action, his acute critical sense combined with a constant enthusiasm and an overwhelming curiosity, placed him as one of the most active supporters of the development of cryobiochemistry.

It was during Gunny's sabbatical year in Paris that we polished many of the studies presented in this chapter as a tribute to one of our best friends.

I. INTRODUCTION

Kinetic studies of fast biochemical reactions have rapidly developed as improvements in time resolution have evolved. It is now unthinkable to study a biochemical process without reporting the direct observation of the intermediates involved. It becomes increasingly possible to carry out measurements in the shorter time periods of nanoseconds and picoseconds, and to record characteristic relaxation times and, therefore, reaction intermediates. However, many of the fast kinetic techniques provide no structural information about the systems as a function of time and then no direct observation of the rate of biochemical processes at the molecular level.

Visible and ultraviolet spectroscopy is used far more than all other spectrometric techniques and merely gives optical kinetic traces just indicative of the existence of transient intermediates on reaction pathways. Improvements in sensitivity of the measurements permit new useful recordings in shorter intervals of time, using spectroscopic techniques yielding much more detailed information about the pathways. However, it is still difficult to combine the highly sophisticated techniques for the study of molecular structure (circular dichroism, electron microscopy, X-ray diffraction, electron and nuclear magnetic resonance measurements) with dynamic techniques. The aim of low temperature biochemistry is to reach experimental conditions allowing such combination, by dramatically slowing down the reactions and even by obtaining a suitable step-by-step "quenching" of processes with a subsequent structure analysis of the intermediates. Such structure determinations might permit a direct observation of the rate of many biochemical processes at the molecular level.

Cryobiochemistry, involving enzymology and analytical investigations at subzero temperatures, is mainly concerned with the use of fluid mixed solvents of low freezing points. Such mixed solvents, which are, in general, binary mixtures of water and miscible polar solvents in high concentration (then used as antifreeze), have been intensively studied and used. Their physicochemical properties as a function of temperature have been analyzed and a wealth of data allowing to recreate suitable conditions of pH, ionic strength, etc., are now available (Douzou, 1977b).

For most biochemical systems investigated to date, it has been possible to find media in which activity is retained at subzero temperatures. We found that unavoidable reversible effects on such activity are linked to the presence of high concentration in cosolvent. All the results clearly indicate that cosolvents lead only to a change, but not a loss of, catalytic capacity. Such change occurs over a broad range of cosolvent concentration and appears to be reversible, gradual, and, in most cases, moderate. More recently, it has been shown unambiguously that the abnormal conditions of medium are not fundamentally different from conditions obtainable in pure water by changes in the "physiological" parameters involved in enzyme-specific activity (Douzou, 1979).

This chapter briefly summarizes the main results obtained on a number of enzyme systems investigated in fluid mixed solvents at subzero temperatures, and, in particular, the stabilization and isolation of ground-state enzyme–substrate complexes and related studies. It will be shown that the absorption and fluorescence spectra of these complexes are just indicative of the existence of these transient species, that their structures are still disputed, and that those of other complexes are even more speculative in the absence of data about detailed structural features. Such features have been and are now intensively studied.

Recent results obtained in crystals as well as in solution will be described. They clearly indicate the trends of present and forthcoming structural investigations of a number of transient intermediates in biochemical systems and processes, and more precisely at the level of resting as well as of working proteins.

No further attempt will be made to give a detailed theoretical and experimental background of the low temperatures procedure. We will show rather the type of insight brought to biochemical problems illustrated by a few examples, as well as the present limitations of the procedure. We will, in fact, focus our attention on reactions which may be sufficiently decreased in rate to affect the different steps of their pathway and then to permit reaction intermediates to be stabilized, accumulated, isolated, and next analyzed by all available spectroscopic techniques.

II. TEMPORAL RESOLUTION OF ENZYME-CATALYZED REACTIONS

Many enzyme-catalyzed reactions occurring in seconds or minutes can be sufficiently reduced in rate at subzero temperatures to obtain their "temporal" resolution step by step and permit enzyme–substrate intermediates to be accumulated in the test tube and then spectroscopically characterized. Since the magnitudes of the activation energies differ from one intermediate step to another, resolution among them becomes possible at low temperatures according to the Arrhenius relationship, and a number of overall reactions can be resolved into intermediate stages. Suitable cooling $\rightleftharpoons$ warming "cycles" then permit obtaining the resolution of such reactions. The first reaction to be "resolved" by thermal control has been the peroxidatic reaction involving horseradish peroxidase (HRP), catalyzing the oxidation of hydrogen donors (AH, AH_2) by hydrogen peroxide (H_2O_2). Consecutive intermediates (compounds I and II) have been sequentially stabilized and studied by all available spectroscopic techniques (Douzou *et al.*, 1970; Leterrier and Douzou, 1970) and later used as "pure" starting reagents to study side reactions (Douzou, 1971).

Such results were in the nature of confirmation of what was already known about these reactions, while further attempts on other enzyme systems brought new contributions to our knowledge of the reactions and opened the way to much more precise studies of the intimate mechanisms of enzymes. There have been investigations of serine proteases (Fink, 1973b, 1976), luciferase (Hastings *et al.*, 1975; Hastings and Balny, 1975), cytochrome oxidase (Chance *et al.*, 1975a,b), and bacterial and microsomal cytochrome P450 (Debey *et al.*, 1973, 1976, 1979). These and several other results have been reviewed elsewhere (Douzou, 1977a; Cox, 1978).

A. Enzyme-Catalyzed Hydroxylation of Camphor

The potential as well as the limitations of the temporal resolution of enzyme-catalyzed reactions can be illustrated by the work carried out in this laboratory on the reaction cycle of bacterial cytochrome P450 (extracted from *Pseudomonas putida*), an enzyme catalyzing camphor hydroxylation and termed $P450_{cam}$. This enzyme is a hemoprotein acting as a monooxygenase according to the overall reaction:

$$RH \text{ (camphor)} + O_2 + 2\ e^- + 2H^+ \xrightarrow{P450} R-OH + H_2O$$

The mechanism of hydroxylation has been resolved to show four main steps (Fig. 1). These steps are

1. Binding of the substrate camphor (RH) by the free ferric cytochrome (Fe^{3+})

$$Fe^{3+} + RH \leftrightarrow Fe^{3+} \cdot RH$$

2. Reduction of this E–S complex by an iron–sulfur protein putidaredoxin (Pd)

$$Fe^{3+} \cdot RH + e^- \rightarrow Fe^{2+} \cdot RH$$

3. Binding of molecular oxygen to give a ternary oxy–ferrous compound

$$Fe^{2+} \cdot RH + O_2 \leftrightarrow Fe^{2+} \cdot RH \diagdown O_2$$

4. Uptake of a second electron initiating the reactions leading to the hydroxylated substrate (ROH) with restoration of the free enzyme (Fe^{3+})

$$Fe^{2+} \cdot RH \diagdown O_2 + e^- \rightarrow Fe^{3+} + ROH + H_2O$$

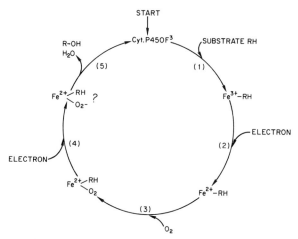

Fig. 1. Reaction cycle of bacterial cytochrome P450.

Cytochrome P450 has been characterized in four stable states (Fe^{3+}, $Fe^{3+} \cdot RH$, $Fe^{2+} \cdot RH$, $Fe^{2+} \cdot RH$ metastable) of an oxygenase reaction cycle.
$$\overset{}{\underset{O_2}{\diagdown}}$$

In the complete native system a flavoprotein and a redoxin (putidaredoxin) act as electron donors but also as effectors that complement the cytochrome.

Electron transfer reactions, especially step (4), are too fast and the intermediates are too fleeting to be properly characterized and discriminated; they are moreover "contaminated" by recycling of the free ferric cytochrome (Fe^{3+}) and by spontaneous nonhydroxylating decay of the oxy–ferrous compound. Consistent knowledge is lacking of the nature and reactivity of unstable intermediates occurring beyond the metastable oxy-ferrous compound $Fe^{2+} \cdot RH$ in the reaction cycle.

Single steps (1), (2), (3), and (4) of the reaction cycle are quite temperature-sensitive. Work at subzero temperatures permits their "temporal" resolution; cytochrome P450 is not denatured in polyol–water mixtures. The mixture generally used is ethylene glycol and buffered water (1:1 v/v), which freezes at about −50°C. Cytochrome P450 is stable at −30°C in this mixture, which remains fluid and thus may be maintained in its native form without repetitive freezing-thawing. This is even more important for the iron–sulfur protein, putidaredoxin, which is very sensitive to thawing and moreover decays quite rapidly when stored in fluid solution at 4°C.

The various redox states of cytochrome P450 (Fe^{3+}, $Fe^{3+} \cdot RH$, $Fe^{2+} \cdot RH$), as well as the metastable oxy–ferrous compound ($Fe^{2+} \cdot RH$), are obtained in the ethylene glycol–water mixture; their absorption spectra and formation rates are similar to those recorded in pure aqueous media.

These identical spectra demonstrate that the intermediates obtained in the mixed solvent at normal and subzero temperatures are similar to those found in the productive enzyme pathway under normal conditions. This is an essential observation since the low temperature procedure permits one to stabilize and accumulate intermediates and offers the opportunity of obtaining structural information about such intermediates—a result unattainable by the "classical" fast kinetic techniques. So far observations in these conditions fit well with results obtained in normal conditions of medium and temperature.

Binding of the carbon [reaction (1)] and oxygen [reaction (3)] substrates are by far the most rapid reactions of the cycle. Formation of the stable camphor–ferric cytochrome ($Fe^{3+} \cdot RH$) accompanied by a major change of the spin equilibrium could be directly studied for the first time at temperatures lower than 0°C, revealing a strong pa_H dependence of the ON and OFF rates and thermodynamic parameters. Proton (and cation) concentration proved later to be an essential parameter in the modulation of iron spin state and other functional properties of the starting enzyme–substrate complex $Fe^{3+} \cdot RH$.

The mixed solvent induces only discrete and reversible perturbations of conformational equilibria (seen through high-spin $\rightleftharpoons$ low-spin balance) of $Fe^{3+} \cdot RH$. These changes do not differ from reversible alterations induced by physiological parameters and can be corrected by changes in the last ones, or used as tools to study structural aspects of the heme pocket.

In suitable buffered polyol–water mixtures each step of the pathway is unaltered. Intrinsic temperature effect on single steps is then obtained by cooling–heating cycles.

The most interesting effects of cooling are

1. The stabilization and isolation of the metastable oxy–ferrous compound ($Fe^{2+} \cdot RH$) which can then be used as pure reactant.
$$\quad\diagdown \atop O_2$$

2. The possibility of starting reactions from the preformed dienzyme complex $Pd^- - Fe^{2+} \cdot RH$ to obtain the complex

$$Pd^- - Fe^{2+} {\diagup O_2 \atop \diagdown RH}$$

and to "uncouple" its decomposition from subsequent recycling

$$Fe^{3+},\ Fe^{3+} \cdot RH,\ Fe^{2+} \cdot RH,\ Fe^{2+} \cdot RH \atop \diagdown O_2$$

and from spontaneous nonhydroxylating decay leading to $Fe^{3+} \cdot RH + O_2 + e^-$.

Thus, the reaction cycle can be viewed through only one turnover, which is not possible in usual conditions of temperature, and insight gained into the dynamics of cytochrome P450–putidaredoxin interaction (formation and dissociation accompanying electron transfer). In addition, investigation in ethylene glycol (or glycerol)-water mixtures at subzero temperatures does not alter the reaction pathway of the hydroxylating multienzyme systems under consideration. Cosolvent effects on protein-protein interactions, equilibria, and rate constants are fully reversible and sometimes helpful to strengthen the temperature effects and allow the resolution of elementary steps with accumulation of given intermediates. Changes in the balance of the multistep reactions, when suitably controlled and recorded, give an opportunity to select and analyze normally fleeting intermediates as pure "signals" devoid of the "noise" usually represented by several consecutive steps and intermediates appearing simultaneously in the time scale of recording.

The most valuable results are probably temperature-controlled "uncoupling" of reactions, the conditions for single turnover, and the isolation of concentrated solutions of a pure intermediate, normally unstable and present as only 60% under steady state conditions.

However, some intermediates are too short-lived and therefore fleeting to be detected optically at subzero temperatures. This is obviously the case of intermediates involved during the evolution of the oxy-ferro compound. More refined spectroscopic techniques used over a broader range of low temperatures might permit the "trapping" of such intermediates and further study of the study of reaction pathways.

Cosolvents effects as well as subzero temperatures sometimes offer another alternative to the detection of normally fleeting intermediates and their accumulation. Changes in the balance of multistep reactions then give an opportunity to observe still hypothetical intermediates.

The different steps of a reaction pathway may be affected to different extents at low temperature in the presence of a cosolvent and might permit observation of enzyme-substrate intermediates that do not occur in measurable concentrations in usual conditions of medium temperature. Such observation was obtained recently (Yagi et al., 1980) in this laboratory on the reaction between D-amino acid oxidase and its substrate, D-alanine.

B. D-Amino Acid Oxidase Intermediates

An intermediate of the reaction between D-amino acid oxidase [D-amino acid : O_2 oxidoreductase (deaminating), EC 1.4.3.3] and its substrate, D-alanine, has been isolated by crystallization (Yagi and Ozawa, 1964). This purple-colored crystal is an equimolar complex of the enzyme and the substrate, and involves a strong charge-transfer interaction between them (Yagi et al., 1968). Accordingly, the occurrence of an enzyme-substrate adduct prior to the electron transfer is suspected as shown in the following scheme of the reaction in anaerobic conditions:

$$E_{ox} + S \xrightarrow{K_1} E_{ox} \cdot S \xrightarrow{K_2} E' \cdot S' \xrightarrow{K_3} E_{red} \cdot P$$

where $E_{ox} \cdot S$ is an oxidized enzyme–substrate adduct, $E' \cdot S'$, the purple complex, and $E_{red} \cdot P$, the fully reduced enzyme–product complex. The occurrence of $E_{ox} \cdot S$ was, at least partly, verified by the spectroscopic study of the reaction of this enzyme with a substrate analog, D-lactate. However, the demonstration of $E_{ox} \cdot S$ with ordinary substrates, D-amino acids, has never been successful.

To observe $E_{ox} \cdot S$ easily, the rate constant, k_2, must be smaller than k_1. For this purpose, a slow reaction method (Yagi, 1965) seemed to be useful. Since it is known that k_3 is very small in the reaction of this enzyme with D-α-aminobutyric acid (Yagi and Ohishi, 1978), we used this substrate for the observation of the preceding event. To achieve a small rate constant, k_2, the pH and temperature of the reaction were decreased from their maxima.

After a systematic investigation using the enzyme purified from pig kidney, we found that $E_{ox} \cdot S$ can be observed by an ordinary spectrophotometer on lowering both pH and temperature of the reaction medium under anaerobic conditions.

Figure 2 shows a typical result. Curve I represents the absorption spectrum of the oxidized enzyme in 100 mM phosphate buffer (pH 6.5) containing 35% glycerol measured at $-10°C$ (pa_H at $-10°C$: 7). This spectrum is not significantly different from the spectrum of an aqueous solution on the enzyme at $+20°C$. After anaerobiosis was attained by argon gas flushing, D-α-aminobutyric acid was anaerobically added to its final concentration of 10 mM and mixed rapidly. By self-recording spectrophotometry, curve I was found to change to curve II and then to curve III. It is noted that the fine structure existing in the second absorption band of the oxidized form disappeared and a new fine structure appeared in the first absorption band. This change in the absorption spectrum is in principle similar to that observed in the formation of an adduct between this enzyme and D-lactate or benzoate (Yagi and Ozawa, 1962). This indicates the change in the environment surrounding the flavin chromophore of the enzyme, and consequently the occurrence of an interaction between the enzyme and the substrate. In curves I, II, and III, an isosbestic point appeared at 469 nm, which indicates the occurrence of a stoichiometric equilibrium between the oxidized enzyme and a newly appearing adduct. The spectrum then changed to curve IV and gradually approached the typical spectrum of the purple complex, $E' \cdot S'$. During this period, an isosbestic point again appeared at 516 nm. This indicates a stoichiometric equilibrium between the adduct represented by curve III and the purple complex. All these results indicate that the entity of curve III is $E_{ox} \cdot S$.

Although the same spectral change was observed upon changing the phosphate buffer to cacodylate buffer (100 mM), the elevation of pa_H up to 8.0 failed to demonstrate the whole typical spectrum of $E_{ox} \cdot S$. This was also the case for the

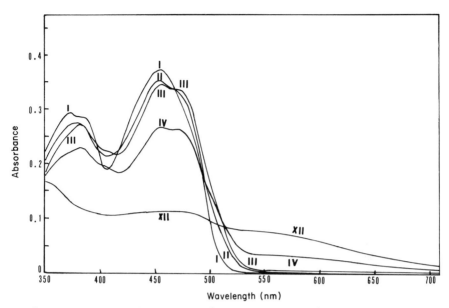

Fig. 2. Spectroscopic demonstration of a primary enzyme–substrate complex. D-Amino acid oxidase (31 μM) and D-α-aminobutyric acid (10 mM) were mixed anaerobically in 100 mM sodium phosphate buffer (pH 6.5) containing 35% glycerol at −10°C (pa_H at − 10°C: 7). Curve I, the enzyme; curve II, immediately after the addition of the substrate. Scanning speed of curves II and III is 20 nm/sec; that of curves IV–XII is 5 nm/sec (Yagi et al., 1980).

elevation of the temperature up to +1°C. Therefore, it was clear that the decrease in both pH and temperature resulted in the marked decrease in k_2. When the concentration of the cosolvent was increased up to 50%, the typical spectrum of $E_{ox} \cdot S$ could not be observed. Even in this case, the isosbestic point at 516 nm appeared clearly. These results indicate that k_1 was smaller than k_2 in the presence of 50% of cosolvent (glycerol).

The elucidation of the mechanism of the decrease in k_2 on the decrease in pH and temperature has been made by further investigation: the shift of the monomer–dimer equilibrium of this enzyme was considered to be involved, since it had been found previously that the rate of formation of the purple intermediate is larger in the dimer than in the monomer (Yagi et al., 1972).

Electrophoretic and ultracentrifugal studies have shown that the binding of a substrate substitute shifts the monomer–dimer equilibrium of the enzyme (Yagi and Ohishi, 1972), which exhibits, in fact, a multiple-state equilibrium between dimer and monomer, apo- and holoenzyme forms (Tanaka and Yagi, 1979). Applying electrophoresis at subzero temperatures (R. Lange and Y. Yagi, personal communication), it has been possible to resolve the substrate-free enzyme into four components which can be ascribed to the above forms. The monomer-dimer equilibrium was shifted toward the monomer form by lowering the temperature from $+20$ to $-10°C$, in addition to the effects of salt concentration and of glycerol as antifreeze. In fact, the cosolvent effect appears to be more important than the temperature effect on the displacement of the dimer $\rightarrow$ monomer equilibrium and might explain the observed decrease in the rate constant k_2.

III. PURIFICATION OF REACTION INTERMEDIATES AND STRUCTURAL STUDIES

A. Purification

In favorable conditions, stabilized intermediates represent 80–99% of the initial enzyme concentration and their spectroscopic detection is possible but sometimes made difficult by the fact that a major fraction of the substrates, often nonenzymically transformed, remains in the mixture as a background absorption or fluorescence. On the other hand, it would be advantageous to separate intermediates from the initial enzyme and excess substrate to find direct evidence of their participation in given steps, by using them as pure starting reagents. Low temperature chromatography procedures have been used successfully to isolate and purify a number of stabilized intermediates. The first attempts were made almost simultaneously by Fink (1973a,b) and Hastings *et al.* (1975) in this laboratory using gel filtration on Sephadex LH-20 to purify the acyl enzyme of chymotryspin and the oxygen adduct intermediate of the bacterial luciferase, respectively. Later, the oxy–ferrous intermediates of bacterial cytochrome P450 were purified using the same procedure (Debey *et al.*, 1976). These successful operations prompted us to adapt several other protein fractionation techniques to subzero temperatures in an attempt to increase their potential (Douzou and Balny, 1978).

As an example of the purification of reaction intermediates to initiate additional structural and functional studies, the results obtained with the oxygenated compound of cytochrome P450$_{cam}$ will be presented.

The enzyme–substrate complex $Fe^{2+} \cdot RH$ binds O_2 rapidly to form the ternary complex $Fe^{2+} \cdot RH$, which is the real starting species leading to hydroxylation. At 25°C a spontaneous decomposition occurs without product formation via the side reaction

$$Fe^{2+} \cdot RH \xrightarrow{K_a} Fe^{3+} \cdot RH + O_2 + e^-$$

The kinetics are first order with a half time of ca. 18 minutes at 4°C in 50 mM phosphate buffer, pH 7.4. In the ethylene glycol–phosphate buffer (1 : 1) mixture

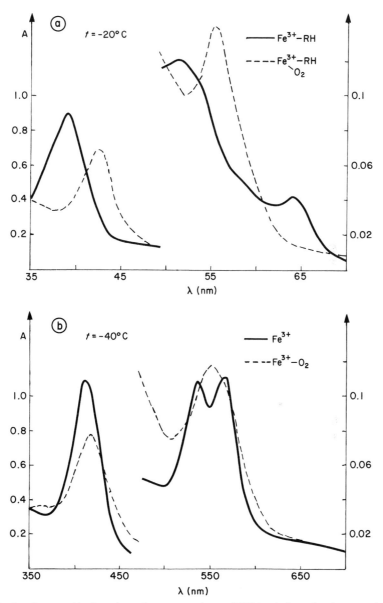

Fig. 3. Spectra of ferric and oxy‑ferrous cytochrome P450 in ethylene glycol‑water mixture (50 : 50 v/v) at subzero temperatures: (a) camphor-bound; (b) camphor-free (from Debey *et al.*, 1979, with permission of Dr. W. Junk bv Publishers, The Hague, The Netherlands).

at $-30°C$, half time is 48 hours. Thus, the stabilized ternary oxy compound can be used as a pure reagent. The optical spectra of the oxygenated intermediate can be recorded and ϵ values can be measured with high precision (Fig. 3).

Arrhenius plots of the decomposition reaction are linear in both the aqueous phosphate and cosolvent system. The activation energy is unaffected by the cosolvent, E in kcal/mol = 18 ± 0.5 in aqueous phosphate and 19 ± 0.5 in 1:1 ethylene glycol–phosphate buffer (Fig. 4).

As shown in Fig. 3, an oxy–ferro compound can also be formed from the substrate-free protein, which exhibits similar spectral characteristics at subzero temperatures. Sephadex gel shows an abnormal affinity toward the reducing agent (proflavine) which is thus retained on the column.

Chromatography was performed with a column 2.5 × 10 cm. During elution, the temperature was maintained at $-20° ± 0.5°C$ at the flow rate 0.4 ml/min, regulated with both a peristaltic pump and a nitrogen pressure (0.2 bar); the penetration speed of the compounds was identical to the elution speed; 1.3-ml fractions were collected at $-20°C$. The time required to elute the pure complex was 30 minutes, with a maximum concentration of 10 μm in 1.3 ml (best tube), only three times less than the starting solution. The overall recovery of the chromatography was nearly 100%. These values were highly reproducible.

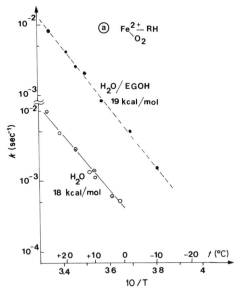

Fig. 4. Arrhenius plots of the camphor-bound oxy–ferrous compound autoxidation rate constants obtained in fluid mixed solvent (ethylene glycol–water, 50:50 v/v) (from Debey et al., 1979, with permission of Dr. W. Junk bv Publishers, The Hague, The Netherlands).

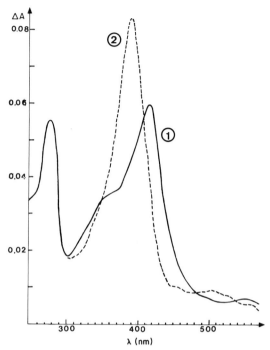

Fig. 5. uv Visible spectra of the chromatographed oxy-ferro compound before (1) and after (2) autoxidation. Of the elution peak tube, 0.1 ml was rapidly diluted at 2°C in 0.9 ml of 50 mM phosphate buffer containing 0.1 M KCl and 3 mM camphor. The decomposition was then performed by heating and the spectrum of the product again taken at 2°C (spectrum 2) (from Debey et al., 1979, with permission of Dr. W. Junk bv Publishers, The Hague, The Netherlands).

Figure 5 shows the uv visible absorption spectrum of the elution peak tube after tenfold dilution in pure aqueous buffer (so that the proportion of ethylene glycol falls down to 5%), recorded at 2°C immediately after chromatography and corrected for camphor absorption. The spectrum demonstrates the absence of contaminating proflavine. Furthermore, the 280-mm absorption does not change on decomposition of the complex into $Fe^{3+} \cdot RH$ (spectrum 2, Fig. 5); the ratio of the absorbancies at 392 nm and 280 nm, $A_{392}/A_{280} = 1.48$, is in good agreement with the previously obtained value of 1.47. The solution of pure compound may be stored frozen at 77°K, without appreciable reoxidation.

A similar fractionation at −35°C with camphor-free mixed solvent as eluant allows purification of the substrate-free oxy–ferro cytochrome while both camphor and proflavine are retained on the LH 20 column. The highly concentrated compound is then stored frozen at 77°K for further use as a reactant. The transfer of an electron from putidaredoxin to this compound triggers a reaction sequence leading to the production of ROH, with regeneration of the free enzyme. The purified oxy-ferro cytochrome complex is presently under intense investigation using a number of spectroscopic techniques to obtain information about its detailed structure.

B. Structural Studies

1. Solution

In spite of the fact that a number of intermediates can be stabilized, purified, and solubilized again in mixed solvents at subzero temperatures, the use of the sophisticated spectrometric techniques for the analysis of molecular structure is still rather limited.

However, interesting nmr studies (Ghisla *et al.*, 1978) are being carried out on the oxygen adduct intermediate of a bacterial luciferase reaction, the absorption spectrum of which cannot be considered to be demonstrative of the flavin C-4 peroxide structure postulated for such types of adduct (Kemal and Bruice, 1976; Favaudon, 1977). The intermediate formed upon addition of molecular oxygen to the reduced flavin mononucleotide/enzyme complex

$$\text{E-FMNH}_2 + \text{O}_2 \rightarrow \text{E} \overset{\text{FMNH}_2}{\underset{\text{O}_2}{\diagdown}}$$

can be almost indefinitely stabilized at low temperature ($-20°$ to $-30°C$), isolated by chromatography, and spectrally characterized (Hastings *et al.*, 1975; Becvar *et al.*, 1978). The flavin C-4 carbon is generally considered as the best candidate for the electrophilic addition of molecular oxygen; other positions (including C-6, C-8, C-9, and C-10) were considered until direct evidence showed that they had no role in the addition. The direct evidence was obtained using ^{13}C nmr under conditions where the oxygen adduct is stabilized.

These successful experiments offer the opportunity to investigate the conditions of application of ^{13}C nmr for the structural analysis of enzyme intermediates stabilized at subzero temperatures. Other "stop-action" structural studies using other available spectroscopic techniques are now in progress, in solution as well as in single crystals, and should provide missing information about reaction mechanisms at the molecular level.

2. Crystals

The contribution of X-ray diffraction to the determination of three-dimensional structure of "productive" enzyme-substrate intermediates at room temperature is very limited because of the dramatic inequality between the rapidity of the enzyme reaction and the length of time required to complete an X-ray experiment.

The only productive intermediates that can possibly be examined in normal conditions are the Michaelis complexes of certain enzymes whose reactions and equilibrium constants are favorable.

In spite of the inability to observe true enzyme–substrate intermediates, X-ray diffraction produced some important results on the activity of certain enzymes, e.g., lysozyme, the serine proteinases, and carboxypeptidase. With these enzymes, results from the study of the interactions of inhibitors could be extended by structural and chemical considerations to produce plausible models of the productive complexes from which generally accepted hypotheses of their hydrolytic activity have been deduced.

Fink and Ahmed (1976) have investigated the behavior of chymotrypsin, trypsin, and elastase toward specific ester substrates at temperatures between $-20°$ and $-70°C$ in aqueous–organic solvents to test the feasibility of obtaining stable crystalline intermediates of these enzymes suitable for X-ray studies. They showed that under these conditions the rate of acylation is several orders of magnitude faster than the rate of deacylation, and that for each enzyme, conditions can be achieved in which the rate of deacylation becomes so low that acyl-enzyme intermediates accumulate in high concentrations. At temperatures of $-50°$ to $-70°C$ in aqueous dimethyl sulfoxide or methanol at pH values of maximum activity, they have prepared well-defined acyl-enzyme intermediates in almost stoichiometric quantities for all three enzymes, both in the dissolved and crystalline states. These intermediates are stable for days at low temperatures, but when warmed to $0°C$, are turned over at the expected rate.

A preliminary X-ray analysis of one of the stable acyl-elastase intermediates characterized by Fink and Ahmed was reported by Alber *et al.* (1976). Elastase was chosen because its active site is accessible and it exhibits low solubility and high stability in aqueous methanol, which is necessary for the X-ray studies because its low viscosity allows the substrate to diffuse easily into the crystal. Using a flow cell they were able to change the mother liquor from 0.01 M sodium acetate to aqueous methanol in a series of stages of increasing concentration and lower temperature until 70% methanol was attained at $-55°C$. Under these conditions, the substrate, *N*-carbobenzoxyalanyl *p*-nitrophenol ester, could be added to the cell and its binding followed by crystallography. After equilibrium was attained, three-dimensional X-ray data were collected to 3.5 Å resolution. These authors determined the structure of the native enzyme at room temperature, and also collected native data at $-55°C$. This enabled them to ascertain that the enzyme structure was essentially undisturbed by the transfer from an ionic liquid at room temperature to an organic liquid at low temperature. The difference map calculated from the data sets collected at $-55°C$ was consistent with the expected productive acyl-enzyme intermediate in the catalytic process as predicted by Fink and Ahmed. The control experiment of raising the temperature of the crystal to $-10°C$ caused the binding curve to reverse, and the corresponding difference map showed no density remaining in the active site.

It seems certain that this technique should be used to produce detailed structural information on the acyl-enzyme intermediate and possibly other intermediates of the reaction. This would permit X-ray diffraction studies to be able to give "stop action" pictures of enzymes at work at subzero temperatures. This, along with further studies of stabilized enzyme–substrate intermediates in cooled fluid solution, would indeed make a major contribution to the understanding of enzyme mechanism and, therefore, open new perspectives in biochemical perception in such unusual, but useful, but new conditions of medium and temperature.

ACKNOWLEDGMENTS

This work was supported by the Institut National de la Santé et de la Recherche Médicale (INSERM). We thank our colleagues, C. Balny, P. Debey, G. Hui Bon Hoa, R. Lange, and K. Yagi who collaborated in the investigations reported in this work.

REFERENCES

Alber, T., Petsko, G. A., and Tsernoglou, D. (1976). Crystal structure of elastase–substrate complex at −55°C. *Nature (London)* **263,** 297–300.

Becvar, J. E., Tu, S. C., and Hastings, J. W. (1978). Activity and stability of the luciferase–flavin intermediate. *Biochemistry* **17,** 1807–1812.

Chance, B., Saronio, C., and Leigh, J. S. (1975a). Functional intermediates in the reaction of membrane-bound cytochrome oxidase with oxygen. *J. Biol. Chem.* **250,** 9226–9237.

Chance, B., Saronio, C., and Leigh, J. S. (1975b). Functional intermediates in reaction of cytochrome oxidase with oxygen. *Proc. Natl. Acad. Sci. U.S.A.* **72,** 1635–1640.

Cox, R. P. (1978). Cryoenzymology: The use of fluid solvent mixtures at subzero temperatures for the study of biochemical reactions. *Biochem. Soc. Trans.* **6,** 689–697.

Debey, P., Balny, C., and Douzou, P. (1973). Enzyme assay in microsomes below zero degree. *Proc. Natl. Acad. Sci. U.S.A.* **70,** 2633–2636.

Debey, P., Balny, C., and Douzou, P. (1976). The sub-zero temperature chromatographic isolation of transient intermediates of a multi-step cycle: Purification of the substrate-bound oxy–ferrous cytochrome P450. *FEBS Lett.* **69,** 231–235.

Debey, P., Gunsalus, I. C., and Douzou, P. (1979). Testing cosolvent cryoenzymology on multienzyme systems. *Mol. Cell. Biochem.* **26,** 33–45.

Douzou, P. (1971). Le contrôle thermique de réactions enzymatiques. *Biochimie* **53,** 17–23.

Douzou, P. 1977a). Enzymology at subzero temperatures. *Adv. Enzymol.* **45,** 154–272.

Douzou, P. (1977b). "Cryobiochemistry: An Introduction." Academic Press, New York.

Douzou, P. (1979). The study of enzyme mechanisms by a combination of cosolvent, low-temperature and high-pressure techniques. *Q. Rev. Biophys.* **12,** 521–571.

Douzou, P., and Balny, C. (1978). Protein fractionation at subzero temperatures. *Adv. Protein Chem.* **32,** 77–189.

Douzou, P., Sireix, R., and Travers, F. (1970). Temporal resolution of individual steps in an enzymic reaction at low temperature. *Proc. Natl. Acad. Sci. U.S.A.* **66,** 787–790.

Favaudon, V. (1977). Oxidation kinetics of 1,5-dihydroflavin by oxygen in non-aqueous solvent. *Eur. J. Biochem.* **78,** 293–307.

Fink, A. L. (1973a). The isolation of N-acetyl-L-tryptophanyl-α-chymotrypsin. *Arch. Biochem. Biophys.* **155**, 473–474.

Fink, A. L. (1973b). The α-chymotrypsin-catalysed hydrolysis of N-acetyl-L-tryptophan p-nitrophenil ester in dimethyl sulfoxide at subzero temperatures. *Biochemistry* **12**, 1736–1742.

Fink, A. L. (1976). Cryoenzymology of chymotrypsin: The detection of intermediates in the catalysis of a specific anilide substrate. *Biochemistry* **15**, 1580–1586.

Fink, A. L., and Ahmed, A. I. (1976). Formation of stable crystalline enzyme–substrate intermediates at sub-zero temperatures. *Nature (London)* **263**, 294–297.

Ghisla, S., Hastings, J. W., Favaudon, V., and Lhoste, J. M. (1978). Structure of the oxygen adduct intermediate in the bacterial luciferase reaction: ^{13}C nuclear magnetic resonance determination. *Proc. Natl. Acad. Sci. U.S.A.* **75**, 5860–5863.

Hastings, J. W., and Balny, C. (1975). The oxygenated bacterial luciferase–flavin intermediate: Reaction products via the light and dark pathways. *J. Biol. Chem.* **250**, 7288–7293.

Hastings, J. W., Balny, C., Le Peuch, C., and Douzou, P. (1975). Spectral properties of an oxygenated luciferase–flavin intermediate isolated by low temperature chromatography. *Proc. Natl. Acad. Sci. U.S.A.* **70**, 3468–3472.

Kemal, C., and Bruice, T. C. (1976). Simple synthesis of a 4a-hydroperoxy adduct of a 1,5-dihydroflavine: Preliminary studies of a model for bacterial luciferase. *Proc. Natl. Acad. Sci. U.S.A.* **73**, 995–999.

Leterrier, F., and Douzou, P. (1970). Electron spin resonance of intermediates in the catalytic reaction of peroxidase at low temperature. *Biochim. Biophys. Acta* **220**, 338–340.

Tanaka, F., and Yagi, K. (1979). Cooperative binding of coenzyme in D-amino-acid oxidase. *Biochemistry* **18**, 1531–1536.

Yagi, K. (1965). Mechanism of enzyme action. An approach through the study of slow reactions. *Adv. Enzymol.* **27**, 1–36.

Yagi, K., and Ohishi, N. (1972). Structure and function of D-amino acid oxidase. IV. Electrophoretic and ultracentrifugal approach to the monomer-dimer equilibrium. *J. Biol. Chem.* **250**, 993–998.

Yagi, K., and Ohishi, N. (1978). Lifetime of the purple intermediate of D-amino acid oxidase under anaerobic conditions. *J. Biochem. (Tokyo)* **84**, 1653–1655.

Yagi, K., and Ozawa, T. (1962). Complex formation of apo-enzyme, coenzyme and substrate of D-amino acid oxidase. II. Spectrophotometric analysis using a substrate-substitute. *Biochim. Biophys. Acta* **56**, 413–419.

Yagi, K., and Ozawa, T. (1964). Mechanism of enzyme action. I. Crystallization of Michaelis complex of D-amino acid oxidase. *Biochim. Biophys. Acta* **81**, 29–38.

Yagi, K., Sugiura, N., Okamura, K., and Kotaki, A. (1968). Mechanism of enzyme action. III. Crystallization of the semiquinoid form of D-amino acid oxidase. *Biochim. Biophys. Acta* **151**, 343–352.

Yagi, L., Nishikimi, M., and Ohishi, N. (1972). Identity of the rapidly appearing purple intermediate of D-amino acid oxidase. *J. Biochem. (Tokyo)* **72**, 1369–1377.

Yagi, K., Lange, R., and Douzou, P. (1980). *Biochem. Biophys. Res. Commun.* **97**, 370–374.

25

Dynamic Proteins

Peter G. Debrunner
and
Hans Frauenfelder

How does it happen that nuclear physicists turn their attention to the study of proteins? In our case the conversion, as frequently happens in academic research, can be traced back to the stimulating influence of a student. About 15 years ago, we were deeply involved in studying various phenomena with the Mössbauer effect. One day Roger Cooke, then a graduate student in physics, came by to ask if he could investigate the Mössbauer spectra of iron proteins as a thesis project. Knowing little about proteins, we agreed. This work resulted in two publications (Cooke *et al.*, 1968; Cooke and Debrunner, 1968) and, what was much more important to us, brought us in close contact with Professor I. C. Gunsalus. Over the years this contact became ever stronger; it taught us a great deal of biochemistry, shaped our thinking, and strongly influenced our approach to biomolecular problems. We also learned to appreciate the remarkable perfection to which many biological systems have evolved. The collaboration with Gunny resulted in a number of papers on the active centers in heme and iron–sulfur proteins, most importantly those on the various reaction intermediates in the cytochrome $P450_{cam}$ system (Frauenfelder *et al.*, 1972; Gunsalus *et al.*, 1972; Münck *et al.*, 1972; Sharrock *et al.*, 1973, 1976; Champion *et al.*, 1975a). The work also led to the organization in 1969 of a small meeting on "Mössbauer Spectroscopy in Biological Systems" held at the Allerton House (Debrunner *et*

EXPERIENCES IN BIOCHEMICAL PERCEPTION
Copyright © 1982 by Academic Press, Inc.
All rights of reproduction in any form reserved.
ISBN 0-12-528420-9

al., 1969). During extended discussions at Allerton House, it became clear to us that static studies alone would only tell part of the story. We consequently began to consider kinetic approaches as well. Two of our students opted to work on the new and exciting cytochrome P450, studying substrate interactions by equilibrium and kinetic methods (Sligar *et al.*, 1974; Gunsalus *et al.*, 1975; Sligar, 1975) and using nmr to observe proton and substrate exchange (Philson *et al.*, 1979). At the same time we began, in a rather inexperienced way, to look at processes that can be initiated by radiolysis (Chan *et al.*, 1975) and by photons (Greenbaum *et al.*, 1972). (Incidentally, as physicists, we were not aware of the beautiful work that had already been done in flash photolysis and, as a result, reinvented many of the standard techniques.) We had all along been interested in extending our studies to low temperatures, when a chance observation by Vince Marshall provided the impetus to explore this regime more systematically. Vince looked at the low temperature optical absorption of carbon monoxy cytochrome P450 and, in checking the helium level in his glass dewar with a flashlight, noticed that the sample changed color. He had photodissociated the complex, and at 4.2 K the CO would not rebind! We extended our flash photolysis experiment on P450 to the temperature range of liquid helium and found a remarkable richness of phenomena, similar to the earlier observations of Chance and collaborators (Chance *et al.*, 1965). It soon became clear that the rate at which we physicists used the precious enzyme was frightening the biochemists, and we asked Gunny for a more easily obtainable test protein. He suggested myoglobin, a rather simple and boring protein as far as biochemists are concerned. To us, it proved to be a nearly ideal model system—easy to obtain, nearly indestructible even in the hands of physicists, well studied, and with apparently simple function. Myoglobin shows unexpectedly rich phenomena and we are still studying it! In the following pages we will describe the concepts that evolved, to a considerable extent, out of this early work with myoglobin (Austin *et al.*, 1973).

CONFORMATIONAL SUBSTATES—CONCEPTS AND EXISTENCE

Myoglobin (Mb) and other heme proteins show a remarkable feature at temperatures below about 200 K: rebinding of small ligands such as CO or O_2 after photodissociation still occurs, but the kinetics approximately follows a power law in time rather than an exponential (Austin *et al.*, 1974). This observation is made in the following experiment: Mb with bound ligand L (MbL) is placed in a cryostat and photolyzed by a light flash. The subsequent rebinding, Mb + L → MbL, is followed optically. The rate of change in the absorbance yields the fraction $N(t)$ of Mb molecules that have not rebound a ligand (CO) at the time t after the flash. In Fig. 1, log $N(t)$ is plotted versus log t, and the curves demonstrate that $N(t)$ cannot be described by a single exponential: $N(t) \neq \exp(-kt)$. A

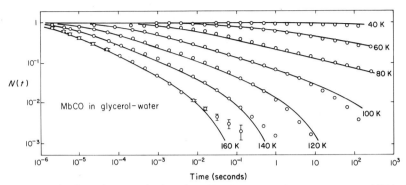

Fig. 1. Rebinding of CO to Mb after photodissociation at various temperatures. $N(t)$ is the fraction of molecules that have not bound CO at a time t after the flash.

power law, $N(t) = (1 + t/t_0)^{-n}$, where t_0 and n are temperature-dependent parameters, fits the data well. At low temperatures the photodissociated ligand remains trapped within the protein, and in order to interpret the kinetics of Fig. 1, one has to consider the immediate surrounding of the heme group. In Fig. 2 we sketch the crystallographer's current view of the heme pocket. In state A, Fig. 2a, the ligand is bound to the heme iron, the heme group is planar, and the iron lies in the heme plane and has spin $S = 0$. After photodissociation, state B in Fig. 2b, the ligand is in the heme pocket, the heme group is domed, and the iron has moved out of the heme plane, thereby changing its spin to $S = 2$. Rebinding at low

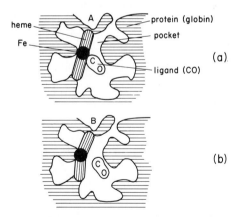

Fig. 2. The states involved in the binding of CO within Mb. Binding occurs from the "free" state B to the bound state A. (a), In state A, the CO is bound to the heme iron, the heme group is planar, and the iron lies in the heme plane. (b), After photodissociation, the Fe–CO bond is broken, the CO molecule has moved away from the iron into the pocket, the iron has moved out of the heme plane, and the heme is domed.

temperatures corresponds to the transition B → A. In moving from B to A, the system must overcome a barrier. The details are complicated because many factors contribute to the barrier: the ligand will experience a repulsion from the four pyrrole nitrogens as it approaches the binding site, and the iron has to change spin state as it moves back into the heme plane. If we represent the entire process by a potential barrier of height H, then the rate coefficient for the transition B → A can be written as

$$k = C \exp(-H/RT) \tag{1}$$

and the return rate is a simple exponential,

$$N(t) = \exp(-kt)$$

The observed power-law dependence of $N(t)$ can be understood if we assume that the barrier between B and A differs somewhat from molecule to molecule. We denote with $g(H)dH$ the probability for finding a barrier with height between H and $H + dH$. The function $N(t)$ then becomes

$$N(t) = \int dH\ g(H)\ \exp[-k(H)/RT] \tag{2}$$

With considerable effort and sophisticated computer analysis, Eq. (2) can be inverted: From the measured rebinding rate $N(t)$, we can determine the probability density $g(H)$. Figure 3 gives one example, $g(H)$ for the binding of CO to Mb.

What then, causes this distribution of barrier heights, and why is it not observed in ordinary room temperature kinetics? A likely explanation is based on the structure of proteins. Proteins are linear chains of 100 or more amino acids folded into a specific three-dimensional structure. This native form is stabilized by numerous relatively weak interactions in dynamic equilibrium, and at any given instant the protein will be found in one of a very large number of *conformational substates*. These substates have the same overall structure and biological function, but their reaction rates will differ. We obtain a crude esti-

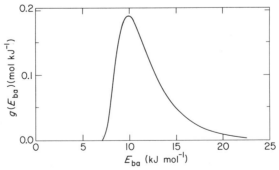

Fig. 3. Activation enthalpy spectrum of the innermost barrier in the binding of CO to Mb.

mate for the number of possible substates by noting that, on the average, each residue has about two states of equal energy. The total number of possible substates hence exceeds $2^{100} \sim 10^{30}$. Obviously, many of these states are very close in structure and function, and we mention the number mainly to stress that it is large, and that we can treat the resulting distributions as continuous. At low temperatures, e.g., below 200 K, each protein molecule will be frozen into a particular substate, characterized in the special case of ligand binding to Mb by the corresponding activation enthalpy H. The nonexponential rebinding in Fig. 1 and the activation enthalpy spectrum in Fig. 3 thus find a natural explanation.

Nonexponential binding and activation enthalpy spectra are not limited to Mb (Austin, et al., 1975), but have been found equally well in all other ligand-heme protein combinations studied (Gunsalus et al., 1977; Alberding et al., 1978). Evidence for freezing in conformational substates also comes from many other low temperature experiments. In paramagnetic resonance, for instance, the experimental line shape can be accounted for by a distribution of crystal-field parameters both in single crystals and in frozen solution (Devaney, 1980). The same distribution, referred to as "g-strain," is responsible for line broadening observed in Mössbauer spectra (Dwivedi et al., 1979). Similar examples are found in other spectral regimes (e.g., Champion and Sievers, 1980; Andrew et al., 1980). The fact that a given protein assumes a large number of functionally and structurally closely related substates in a given conformation can be assumed to be established.

CONFORMATIONAL TRANSITIONS

If we postulate the freezing-in of conformational substates in order to explain the nonexponential low temperature kinetics, we also have to demonstrate the compatibility of this postulate with the "normal," exponential kinetics observed at physiological temperatures. Because of the enormous number of substates, conformational motion will involve a continuum of transition rates. Nevertheless, we simplify the discussion to the extreme by assuming only two substates, 1 and 2, separated by a barrier of fixed height as shown in Fig. 4. At a given temperature T, transitions between the two substates are characterized by the rate coefficients

$$k_{12} = A_{12} \exp[-(Q + E)/RT]$$

$$k_{21} = A_{21} \exp[-E/RT]$$

(3)

At sufficiently low temperatures, k_{12} and k_{21} will be so small that any given molecule remains locked in its substate over the time span of an experiment. The rebinding discussed in the previous section will therefore be nonexponential in

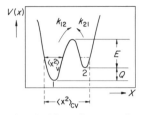

Fig. 4. Schematic diagram of a double-well potential representing two conformational substates of a molecule. The vibrational mean square displacement in well (1) is indicated by $\langle x^2 \rangle_v$; $\langle x^2 \rangle_{cv}$ is the sum of the vibrational and conformational mean square displacements.

time. At higher temperatures, however, k_{12} and k_{21} will become large compared to the rebinding rates, hence the latter should become exponential (Austin *et al.*, 1975). Indeed, experiments that observe the rebinding B $\rightarrow$ A (Figs. 1 and 2) near 300 K see a fast exponential (Alpert *et al.*, 1979; Morris *et al.*, 1982). An exponential fast component has also been found in the binding of O_2 to hemerythrin (Alberding *et al.*, 1981); the corresponding curve is shown in Fig. 5.

Studies of the transition from nonexponential to exponential time dependence promise to provide information about conformational motion at the active center. Another approach is based on the Mössbauer effect and uses ^{57}Fe in the heme active center as a probe (Parak *et al.*, 1981; Keller and Debrunner, 1980). The recoil-less fraction, f, of a Mössbauer transition is related to the mean square displacement, $\langle x^2 \rangle$, of the iron nucleus by the expression

$$f = \exp\{-4\pi^2 <x^2>/\lambda^2\} \tag{4}$$

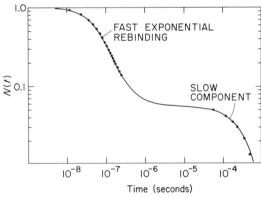

Fig. 5. Recombination of O_2 with deoxy hemerythrin in glycerol–water at 5°C after flash photolysis. $N(t)$ is the fraction of molecules that have not rebound at a time t after the flash. The solid line is the sum of two exponentials fit to the data points (Alberding *et al.*, 1981).

where λ is the wavelength of the gamma rays. Ordinarily $\langle x^2 \rangle$ is given by the vibrational amplitude of the (harmonically) bound nucleus, indicated schematically as $\langle x^2 \rangle_v$ in Fig. 4. If substates exist, we can model them by the double potential well for the bound iron sketched in Fig. 4. At low temperatures the iron stays in well (1) or (2) for a time that exceeds the lifetime τ_M of the nuclear excited state, and $\langle x^2 \rangle$ equals $\langle x^2 \rangle_v$. At high temperatures, however, the iron moves many times from well (1) to (2) and back within the time τ_M, and $\langle x^2 \rangle >$ $\langle x^2 \rangle_v$ then depends on the distance between the wells and on the rate coefficients k_{12} and k_{21}. Analysis of the experimental data in Fig. 6 yields $Q \sim 6$ kJ/mol, $E \sim$ 27 kJ/mol, and $A_{21} \sim 10^{13}$ sec^{-1} for the parameters in Eq. (3). At 300 K, the conformational transition rate is about 2×10^8 sec^{-1}. Of course, this treatment is still very crude, and the numbers apply only to one particular process within the protein. Nevertheless, the basic concepts are probably valid, and corresponding phenomena can be expected to appear in many proteins and nucleic acids.

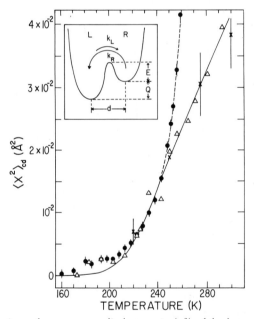

Fig. 6. Comparison of mean square displacements $\langle x^2 \rangle$ of the heme iron deduced from Mössbauer ($\bullet$, $\triangle$) and X-ray data ($\times$,$\times$). Only the difference between the total $\langle x^2 \rangle$ and the vibrational contribution $\langle x^2 \rangle_v$ is shown, where $\langle x^2 \rangle_v$ is proportional to temperature. For crystalline metMb($\triangle$,$\times$), the difference is interpreted as conformational mean square displacement, $\langle x^2 \rangle - \langle x^2 \rangle_v = \langle x^2 \rangle_c$, and the solid line is a fit to the data based on the model sketched in the inset. In frozen solution of MbO$_2$, ($\bullet$), an additional, diffusional contribution $\langle x^2 \rangle_d$ to the mean square displacement is seen for $T > 240$ K; $\langle x^2 \rangle_d$ is proportional to the excess line broadening observed at these temperatures (Keller and Debrunner, 1980).

Here we have restricted the discussion to the experimental evidence for conformational substates. Impressive support for the concept of substates comes from computer calculations of molecular dynamics. Karplus and collaborators, in particular, have studied the motion of some proteins and have found that molecular dynamics provides a way to understand the properties of conformational substates in considerable detail (McCammon and Karplus, 1980).

THE SPATIAL STRUCTURE OF CONFORMATIONAL SUBSTATES

At first sight, the existence of protein single crystals and the beautiful three-dimensional models produced by the X-ray crystallographers would appear to leave no room for conformational substates in protein crystals. A closer look, however, shows that X-ray diffraction provides further support for the concept of substates and even allows study of their spatial properties.

In a hypothetical ideal crystal, each atom can be considered fixed at its proper lattice position, and each diffraction spot exhibits maximum intensity. In a real crystal each atom vibrates, and the diffraction peaks are correspondingly less intense. In a protein crystal, a further decrease in intensity is caused by the large displacements of many atoms from their mean position. The contribution of a particular atom to the scattered intensity at the scattering angle 2θ is given by the Debye–Waller factor (temperature or displacement factor)

$$T = \exp(-8\pi^2 \langle x^2 \rangle \sin^2\theta/\lambda^2) \tag{5}$$

Here $\langle x^2 \rangle$ is the mean square displacement of the atom from its average position in the direction of the momentum transfer. Often the mean square displacement is assumed to be isotropic, $\langle x^2 \rangle = \langle y^2 \rangle = \langle z^2 \rangle$, and $\langle u^2 \rangle = \langle x^2 \rangle + \langle y^2 \rangle + \langle z^2 \rangle = 3\langle x^2 \rangle$ is quoted. From the observed X-ray intensities it is possible to not only determine the mean positions of the non-hydrogen atoms, but also their mean square displacements. The connection with conformational substates can now be discussed easily: if no conformational substates existed, the mean square displacement of each atom (after correction for lattice disorder) would arise from lattice vibrations only, i.e., it would be small, typically less than 0.05 Å², and proportional to T. The existence of substates, however, leads to much larger values of $\langle x^2 \rangle$ with temperature dependences that deviate markedly from linearity. Since the substates are an inherent property of proteins, no improvement in crystal-growing techniques will eliminate the large $\langle x^2 \rangle$ values.

Low-intensity diffraction spots have always plagued protein crystallographers; in an extreme case a whole segment of polypeptide chain could not be located in the electron density map because of excessive motion (Huber et al., 1976). The concept of substates implies that not only some special parts of the protein can perform large motion, but that nearly every atom will occupy multiple sites.

X-rays consequently should provide information about the substates of essentially every non-hydrogen atom. These predictions have been verified (Frauenfelder *et al.*, 1979; Artymiuk *et al.*, 1979; Frauenfelder and Petsko, 1980), and we present here some examples to demonstrate that X-ray diffraction can provide

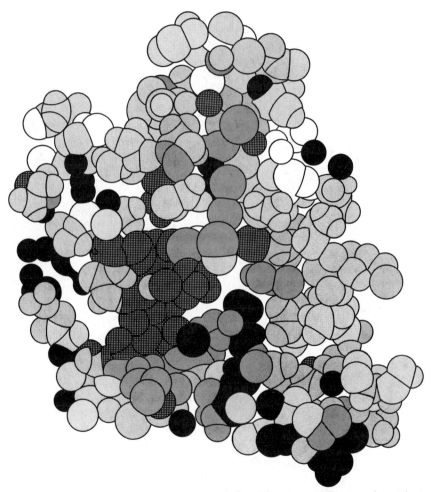

Fig. 7. Atomic mean square displacements deduced from X-ray diffraction of metMb. A 5-Å slice perpendicular to the heme plane is shown, and $\langle x^2 \rangle$-values are indicated by shading, darker shades corresponding to smaller $\langle x^2 \rangle$. The heme plane is seen in cross section as a dark horizontal row of atoms in the middle left. Below the heme the bound water is visible as a light crescent in the tighly packed ligand pocket. The cavity of the proximal histidine, seen above the heme, is less tightly packed. The highly mobile atoms near the C-terminus are in the upper right (unshaded) (after computer graphics by R. J. Feldmann).

specific and unique information concerning protein dynamics. Figure 7 represents a 5-Å slice of myoglobin taken perpendicular to the heme plane. Values of $\langle x^2 \rangle$ are indicated by shading—the darkest shading corresponds to the smallest $\langle x^2 \rangle$. The figure shows that different regions of the protein have very different properties. The parts around the oxygen-binding site are rigid and look like a protective case; the proximal side is much more flexible and atoms may move rather freely in this "semi-liquid" region. Figure 8 shows the atomic mean square displacements of one particular residue, Lys-147. Lys-147 is charged, and the side chain presumably extends into the solvent. As Fig. 8 shows, the residue is very flexible.

More information comes from the temperature dependence of $\langle x^2 \rangle$ (Frauenfelder *et al.*, 1979; Gavish, 1981). For a harmonic potential, $\langle x^2 \rangle$ is proportional to T for temperatures above $\theta/2$, where $\theta = h\nu/k$ is a characteristic temperature. Measurements at 220, 250, 275, and 300 K reveal that few atoms satisfy this classical law. The empirically observed relation between the magnitude and the temperature dependence of $\langle x^2 \rangle$ is at first surprising: small $\langle x^2 \rangle$ values depend strongly on T, large ones are often temperature independent! This unexpected relation can, however, be easily understood. In the rigid part of the protein, atoms occupy a unique position in their ground state, and considerable energy may be required to reach other substates. Such a situation leads to an exponential dependence of $\langle x^2 \rangle$ on $1/T$ and rigid parts consequently have $\langle x^2 \rangle$ that depend strongly on T. In the more flexible regions, where $\langle x^2 \rangle$ is large, many substates with essentially equal energies may exist; the potential can be approximated by a square well, and $\langle x^2 \rangle$ is nearly temperature independent.

A comparison between liganded and unliganded forms of Mb is given in Fig. 9 (Frauenfelder and Petsko, 1980). For clarity only a small fraction of the data is

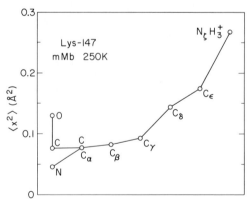

Fig. 8. Mean square displacements $\langle x^2 \rangle$ of the carbon and nitrogen atoms of Lys-147 in metMb single crystals at 250 K.

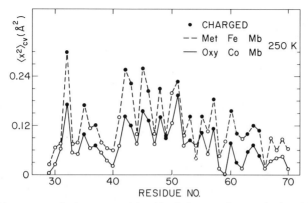

Fig. 9. Mean square displacements of the side chain atoms in crystals of metMb and cobalt MbO$_2$ at 250 K plotted against residue number. Only the atom with the largest displacement is plotted for each residue.

shown. Figure 9 demonstrates two points: (1) the dependence of $\langle x^2 \rangle$ on residue number for the two different forms is remarkably similar, and (2) the liganded form nearly always has smaller $\langle x^2 \rangle$ values than the unliganded form.

The examples of protein dynamics presented here relate to our own work, but other powerful techniques are available to study different aspects of the same phenomena. We only mention that molecular dynamics calculations, particularly those by Karplus and his collaborators, yield more detailed evidence of the internal motions in a protein (McCammon and Karplus, 1980).

STRUCTURE AND FUNCTION

One goal of dynamic studies is an understanding of the relation between structure and function, and of the role played by conformational fluctuations. In most cases we are far from achieving this goal, but in simple systems some of the crucial aspects are emerging. Here we treat the binding of O$_2$ and CO to myoglobin—a reaction that is not very complicated but can serve as a model for more complex processes. Perutz and Matthews (1966) have pointed out that the static X-ray structure does not allow O$_2$ to enter or leave Mb because it does not show a channel or opening large enough for a diatomic molecule. The binding and release consequently must involve conformational motion.

We have studied the binding of CO and O$_2$ to Mb and to the separated Hb chains over a wide temperature and time range (Austin *et al.*, 1975; Alberding *et al.*, 1978). Initially we described the binding processes as being governed by a series of static potential barriers and evaluated the barrier parameters (activation

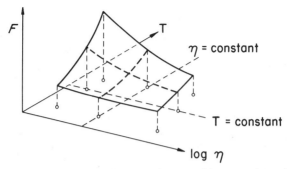

Fig. 10. Idealized plot of an observable F as a function of the two independent variables T and $\log \eta$, where T is temperature and η the viscosity. Isothermal (T = constant) and isoviscosity (η = constant) sections are indicated.

enthalpy and entropy) by using standard transition state theory. This approach leads to a satisfactory description of all observations in a given solvent, but is internally inconsistent with the notion of a dynamic protein: if proteins are indeed flexible, their motion and hence their activity will be influenced by the solvent. Specifically, the transition rates between conformational substates depend on the solvent viscosity. Indeed, such an influence has been discussed by a number of authors (Damjanovich and Somogyi, 1973; Gavish and Werber, 1979). In order to follow this idea, we note that the solvent viscosity is a function of temperature. As the temperature is changed, the protein feels a different damping; the barrier parameters determined by standard methods characterize the protein–solvent system and not the protein alone. We have therefore used a novel approach to obtain the relevant observables for the protein alone. The approach should be applicable not only for ligand binding to heme proteins, but more generally to any observable F, be it sound velocity or reaction rate. The observable F is measured in a

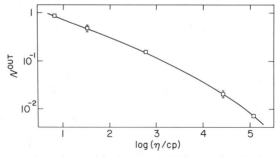

Fig. 11. Viscosity dependence of the fraction N^{out} of CO molecules that reach the solvent after photodissociation of MbCO at 240 K (Beece *et al.*, 1980).

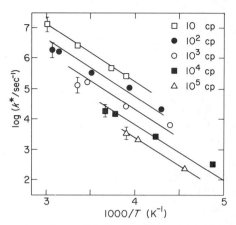

Fig. 12. Temperature dependence of the rate coefficient k^* for the escape of O_2 from the outermost potential well in Mb to the solvent measured at the viscosities 10^5cp($\triangle$), 10^4cp($\blacksquare$), 10^3cp($\bigcirc$), 10^2cp($\bullet$), and 10 cp($\square$) (Beece et al., 1980).

wide variety of solvents as a function of T, keeping parameters other than the viscosity constant (Douzou, 1977). Thus F is found as function of the two variables T and η, $F(T, \eta)$, and it represents a surface in the T-log η plane as shown in Fig. 10. If the surface is smooth, it can be assumed that the various solvents do not change the protein in an unacceptable manner. *Isothermal* cuts through the surface show how the viscosity affects a particular observable; one example is given in Fig. 11. *Isoviscosity* cuts provide the temperature dependence of $F(T, \eta)$ at given fixed viscosity; an example is shown in Fig. 12. Experiments on ligand binding to Mb (Beece *et al.*, 1980) and on the photoinduced reaction cycle in bacteriorhodopsin (Beece *et al.*, 1981) prove that most biomolecular processes indeed depend strongly on viscosity. The approach described here is therefore not a luxury, but a necessity.

REACTION THEORY

The data in Fig. 12 present a new problem: what equation should be used to evaluate the temperature dependence of biomolecular rate coefficients? Perusal of the literature of the past 40 years reveals a striking dichotomy: experimental chemists and biochemists almost exclusively use standard transition state theory to deduce activation enthalpies and entropies from experimental data. On the other hand, starting with the seminal work of Kramers (1940), theoretical chemists and physicists have been demonstrating with increasing sophistication and rigor that transition state theory in its conventional form is not adequate. In the following we will give the transition state equation, contrast it with the Kramers approach, and discuss how a generalized Kramers equation can be applied to biomolecular reactions.

In transition state theory (Glasstone *et al.*, 1941), the rate coefficient is written as

$$k^{TST} = \nu \, \tau \, \exp(-G^{\ddagger}/RT) \qquad (6)$$

Here $\nu = k_B T/h$ is the attempt factor, τ a transmission coefficient, R the gas constant, and $G^{\ddagger} = H^{\ddagger} - TS^{\ddagger}$ the activation Gibbs energy; $H^{\ddagger}$ and $S^{\ddagger}$ are activation enthalpy and entropy. The derivation of Eq. (6) assumes that the system undergoing the transition is in thermal equilibrium with the surrounding heat bath; the coefficient τ is not explicitly given. In the approach pioneered by Kramers, equilibrium is not assumed, and an explicit expression for the transmission coefficient is obtained. The original paper by Kramers is difficult to read, and no easily accessible account is known to us. Kramers' result has been generalized and verified; we quote here only some of the most recent papers with extensive lists of earlier references (Skinner and Wolynes, 1978; Larson and Kostin, 1978; Ishioka, 1980; Coffey, 1980). Rather than describe Kramers' approach we indicate how Eq. (6) is modified. Consider a particle in a potential well, for instance well (2) in Fig. 4, which is coupled to the surrounding heat bath with a strength characterized by the viscosity η. The problem is to find the rate coefficient k for escape from well (2) over the barrier as a function of η. In transition state theory, k is independent of viscosity as indicated in Fig. 13. Approach to equilibrium and transmission over the barrier both depend on viscosity, however, and k^{TST} thus will give, at best, a correct description over a narrow range of viscosities. At low viscosities, particles with energies below the barrier height will acquire energy through interaction with the heat bath; the time required for

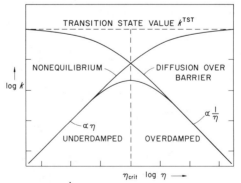

Fig. 13. Schematic diagram of the viscosity dependence of a reaction rate k according to Kramers' model.

this "diffusion in energy space" will be larger than the average transition time $1/k$ over the barrier and thus the rate coefficient will be reduced below the transition state value. Since the energy gain is proportional to the viscosity ($dE/dt \propto \eta$), k will also be proportional to η at low viscosities, as shown in Fig. 13. At higher viscosities, the time required to reach equilibrium is shorter than $1/k$ and the equilibrium assumption is justified. However, the transmission coefficient now reduces k. At low viscosities, any particle with sufficient energy moves over the barrier on the first attempt. At higher viscosities, however, the particle "diffuses" over the barrier. Even if sufficient energy is available, the particle may cross and recross the barrier many times before escaping completely. Ordinary diffusion is proportional to $1/\eta$ and it is therefore not surprising that Kramers' theory gives $k \propto 1/\eta$ at high viscosities. The dependence of k on η is shown as a solid line in Fig. 13 for both the underdamped and overdamped regime. It is clear from Fig. 13 that standard transition state theory is valid in a narrow region at best, and consequently should not be used for biomolecular processes.

The next question to be answered concerns the value of η_{crit}, the dividing line between the underdamped and the overdamped region. A simple model suggests that even reactions in water are overdamped; the rate equation to be used for biomolecular reactions therefore is

$$k(T, \eta) = [A/\eta + A^\circ] \, exp(-H^*/RT) \tag{7}$$

Here we have added the viscosity-independent term A° because some reactions take place even in the limit of extremely high viscosities. The asterisk on H denotes that the data are evaluated along isoviscosity lines, as sketched in Fig. 10.

The final question concerns the value of η to be used in Eq. (7). The viscosity describes the coupling between the system undergoing the transition and the surrounding heat bath. If a process takes place deep inside a protein, the pertinent coupling coefficient may be very different from the external solvent viscosity. Experimental data suggest that the internal viscosity is related to the solvent viscosity η by (Beece et al., 1980)

$$\eta_{\text{int}} \propto \eta^\kappa \tag{8}$$

The power κ indicates the degree to which the external solvent affects a particular protein process; $\kappa = 1$ means complete coupling and $\kappa = 0$ implies complete shielding.

The suggested evaluation of protein reactions can be summarized as follows: the rate is studied over a wide range of temperature and solvents and determined as a function of the two independent variables T and η: $k(T, \eta)$. Arrhenius plots, $\log k$ versus $1/T$, are then fit with Eqs. (7) and (8), and the parameters H^*, A, κ, and A° are determined.

A DYNAMIC MODEL FOR LIGAND BINDING

As one example of a dynamic structure–function relation, we select the binding of dioxygen to myoglobin (Beece *et al.*, 1980). The migration of O_2 from the solvent to the heme iron is controlled by three barriers which, in the simplest model, are assumed to be in sequence. Initially, we assumed these barriers to be static and determined activation enthalpies and entropies by using standard transition state theory (Austin *et al.*, 1975). The concept of a dynamic protein permits a simpler and more satisfactory description. Assume, as shown in Fig. 14, that O_2 moves between the states C and B, where B is the pocket already drawn in Fig. 2, and C is a semiliquid region. In the "old" model, the barrier between B and C would be static. In the new approach we assume that the protein has two substates, "open" and "closed." In the open state, O_2 can move without hindrance between B and C; in the closed it cannot. The transition between the open and the closed substates is described by the Kramers equation, [Eq. (7)], together with the relation [Eq. (8)]. In this model, the transitions B $\rightarrow$ C and C $\rightarrow$ B are characterized by the same activation enthalpy H^* and the same parameter κ: $H^*_{BC} = H^*_{CB}$ and $\kappa_{BC} = \kappa_{CB}$. Consequently the ratio of rate coefficients is given by the entropy factors or, in the simplest interpretation, by the volumes of the states B and C: $k_{BC}/k_{CB} = V_C/V_B$. The effect of the solvent on the ligand migration is easy to understand: opening and closing of the gate between B and C can be damped by the solvent. Similarly, inhibitor molecules may immobilize part of a protein and thus prevent easy opening of gates. This dynamic approach and the simple model introduced in Fig. 14 give a satisfactory prediction of the binding of small ligands to myoglobin.

A successful model often raises more questions than it answers. Can the residues representing the gate be unambiguously identified, the entropy factors related objectively to volumes? Does the Kramers equation adequately describe substrate binding to enzymes, which may involve large conformational motion? We do not know the answers to these questions yet, and much work remains to be done. Looking back we note that our views of biomolecules have changed

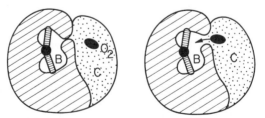

Fig. 14. Gate model for ligand binding to Mb. As explained in the text, the ligand O_2 can enter or leave the heme pocket B whenever the "gate" is open.

considerably. What we originally modeled as an isolated system has turned into a dynamically interacting one. As we probe deeper, the questions keep changing, but the fascination with biomolecular systems remains the same as when Gunny first introduced them to us.

REFERENCES

Alberding, N., Chan, S. S., Eisenstein, L., Frauenfelder, H., Good, D., Gunsalus, I. C., Nordlund, T. M., Perutz, M. F., Reynolds, A. H., and Sorensen, L. (1978). Binding of carbon monoxide to isolated hemoglobin chains. *Biochemistry* **17,** 43–51.

Alberding, N., Lavalette, D., and Austin, R. H. (1981). Hemerythrin's oxygen binding reaction studied by laser photolysis. *Proc. Natl. Acad. Sci. U.S.A.* **78,** 2307–2309.

Alpert, B., El Moshni, S., Lindquist, L., and Tfibel, F. (1979). Transient effects in the nanosecond laser photolysis of carboxyhemoglobin: "Cage" recombination and spectral evolution of the protein. *Chem. Phys. Lett.* **64,** 11–16.

Andrew, E. R., Bryant, D. J., and Cashell, E. M. (1980). Proton magnetic relaxation of proteins in the solid state: Molecular dynamics of ribonuclease. *Chem. Phys. Lett.* **69,** 551–554.

Artymiuk, P. J., Blake, C. C. F., Grace, D. E. P., Oatley, S. J., Phillips, D. C., and Sternberg, M. J. E. (1979). Crystallographic studies of the dynamic properties of lysozyme. *Nature (London)* **280,** 563–568.

Austin, R. H., Beeson, K., Eisenstein, L., Frauenfelder, H., Gunsalus, I. C., and Marshall, V. P. (1973). Dynamics of carbon monoxide binding by heme proteins. *Science* **181,** 541–543.

Austin, R. H., Beeson, K., Eisenstein, L., Frauenfelder, H., Gunsalus, I. C., and Marshall, V. P. (1974). Activation energy spectrum of a biomolecule: Photodissociation of carbonmonoxy myoglobin at low temperatures. *Phys. Rev. Lett.* **32,** 403–405.

Austin, R. H., Beeson. K. W., Eisenstein, L., Frauenfelder, H., and Gunsalus, I. C. (1975). Dynamics of ligand binding to myoglobin. *Biochemistry* **14,** 5355–5373.

Beece, D., Bowne, S. F., Czégé, J., Eisenstein, L., Frauenfelder, H., Good, D., Marden, M. C., Marque, J., Ormos, P., Reinisch, L., and Yue, K. T. (1981). The effect of viscosity on the photocycle of bacteriorhodopsin. *Photochem. Photobiol.* **33,** 517–522.

Beece, D., Eisenstein, L., Frauenfelder, H., Good, D., Marden, M. C., Reinisch, L., Reynolds, A. H., Sorensen, L. B., and Yue, K. T. (1980). Solvent viscosity and protein dynamics. *Biochemistry* **19,** 5147–5157.

Champion, P. M., and Sievers; A. J. (1980). Far infrared magnetic resonance of deoxyhemoglobin and deoxymyoglobin. *J. Chem. Phys.* **72,** 1569–1582.

Champion, P. M., Lipscomb, J. D., Münck, E., Debrunner, P., and Gunsalus, I. C. (1975a). Mössbauer investigations of high-spin ferrous heme proteins I. Cytochrome P450. *Biochemistry* **14,** 4151–4158.

Champion, P. M., Münck, E., Debrunner, P. G., Moss, T. H., Lipscomb, J. D., and Gunsalus, I. C. (1975b). The magnetic susceptibility of reduced cytochrome $P450_{cam}$. *Biochim. Biophys. Acta* **376,** 579–582.

Chan, S. S., Nordlund, T. M., Frauenfelder, H., Harrison, J. E., and Gunsalus, I. C. (1975). Enzymatic reduction of $NADP^+$ induced by radiolysis. *J. Biol. Chem.* **250,** 716–719.

Chance, B., Schoener, B., and Yonetani, T. (1965). The low-temperature photodissociation of cytochrome $a_3^{2+} \cdot CO$. *In* "Oxidases and Related Redox Systems" (T. E. King, H. S. Mason, and M. Morrison, eds.), pp. 609–621. Wiley, New York.

Coffey, W. T. (1980). Rotational and translational Brownian motion. *Adv. Mol. Relaxation Interact. Processes* **17,** 169–337.

Cooke, R., and Debrunner, P. (1968). Mössbauer studies of the iron atom in cytochrome c. *J. Chem. Phys.* **48**, 4532–4537.

Cooke, R., Tsibris, J. C. M., Debrunner, P. G., Tsai, R., Gunsalus, I. C., and Frauenfelder, H. (1968). Mössbauer studies on putidaredoxin. *Proc. Natl. Acad. Sci. U.S.A.* **59**, 1045–1052.

Damjanovich, S., and Somogyi, B. (1973). A molecular enzyme model based on oriented energy transfer. *J. Theor. Biol.* **41**, 567–569.

Debrunner, P. G., Tsibris, J. C. M., and Münck, E., eds. (1969). "Mössbauer Spectroscopy in Biological Systems." Proceedings of a meeting held at Allerton House, Monticello, Illinois, March 17 and 18, 1969. Engineering Publications Office, Univ. of Illinois at Urbana.

Devaney, P. (1979). Electron spin resonance study of single crystals of cytochrome P450 from *Pseudomonas putida*. Ph.D. Thesis, Univ. of Illinois at Urbana (unpublished).

Douzou, P. (1977). "Cryobiochemistry." Academic Press, New York.

Dwivedi, A., Toscano, W. A., Jr., and Debrunner, P. G. (1979). Mössbauer studies of cytochrome c_{551}: Intrinsic heterogeneity related to g-strain. *Biochim. Biophys. Acta* **576**, 502–508.

Frauenfelder, H., and Petsko, G. A. (1980). Structural dynamics of liganded myoglobin. *Biophys. J.* **32**, 465–478.

Frauenfelder, H., Gunsalus, I. C., and Münck, E. (1972). Iron–sulfur proteins and Mössbauer spectroscopy. *In* "Mössbauer Spectroscopy and Its Applications," pp. 231–255. IAEA, Vienna.

Frauenfelder, H., Petsko, G. A., and Tsernoglou, D. (1979). Temperature-dependent X-ray diffraction as a probe of protein structural dynamics. *Nature (London)* **280**, 558–563.

Gavish, B. (1981). Modeling the unusual temperature dependence of atomic displacements in proteins by local nonharmonic potentials. *Proc. Natl. Acad. Sci. U.S.A.* **78**, 6868–6872.

Gavish, B., and Werber, M. M. (1979). Viscosity dependent structural fluctuations in enzyme catalysis. *Biochemistry* **18**, 1269–1275.

Glasstone, S., Laidler, K. J., and Eyring, H. (1941). "The Theory of Rate Processes." McGraw-Hill, New York.

Greenbaum, E., Austin, R. H., Frauenfelder, H., and Gunsalus, I. C. (1972). Photoreduction of $NADP^+$ sensitized by synthetic pigment systems. *Proc. Natl. Acad. Sci. U.S.A.* **69**, 1273–1276.

Gunsalus, I. C., Lipscomb, J. D., Marshall, V., Frauenfelder, H., Greenbaum, E., and Münck, E. (1972). Structure and reactions of oxygenase active centers: Cytochrome P450 and iron–sulfur proteins. *In* "Biological Hydroxylation Mechanisms" (G. S. Boyd and R. M. S. Smellie, eds.), pp. 135–157. Academic Press, New York.

Gunsalus, I. C., Sligar, S. G., and Debrunner, P. G. (1975). Product formation from ferrous oxy-cytochrome P450. *Biochem. Soc. Trans.* **3**, 821–825.

Gunsalus, I. C., Sligar, S. G., Nordlund, T., and Frauenfelder, H. (1977). Oxygen sensing heme proteins: Monooxygenases, myoglobin and hemoglobin. *In* "Tissues Hypoxia and Ischemia" (M. Reivich, R. Coburn, S. Lahiri, and B. Chance, eds.), pp. 37–50. Plenum, New York.

Huber, R., Deisenhofer, J., Colman, P. M., Matsushima, M., and Palm, W. (1976). Crystallographic structure studies of an IgG molecule and an Fc fragment. *Nature (London)* **264**, 415–420.

Ishioka, S. (1980). Quantization of Kramers' rate theory. *J. Phys. Soc. Jpn.* **48**, 367–376.

Keller, H., and Debrunner, P. G. (1980). Evidence for conformational and diffusional mean square displacements in frozen aqueous solutions of oxymyoglobin. *Phys. Rev. Lett.* **45**, 68–71.

Kramers, H. A. (1940). Brownian motion in a field of force and the diffusion model of chemical reactions. *Physica (Amsterdam)* **7**, 284–304.

Larson, R. S., and Kostin, M. D. (1978). Kramers' theory of chemical kinetics: Eigenvalue and eigenfunction analysis. *J. Chem. Phys.* **69**, 4821–4829.

McCammon, J. A., and Karplus, M. (1980). Simulation of protein dynamics. *Annu. Rev. Phys. Chem.* **31**, 29–45.

Morris, R. J., Duddell, D. A., and Richards, J. T. (1982). Ultrafast CO rebinding following nanosecond laser photolysis of human HbCO in viscous solvents at low temperature. *In* "Hemoglobin and Oxygen Binding" (C. Ho, ed.), pp. 339–343. Elsevier, New York.

Münck, E., Debrunner, P. G., Tsibris, J. C. M., and Gunsalus, I. C. (1972). Mössbauer parameters of putidaredoxin and its selenium analog. *Biochemistry* **11**, 855–863.

Parak, F., Frolov, E. N., Mössbauer, R. L., and Goldanskii, V. I. (1981). Dynamics of metmyoglobin crystals investigated by nuclear gamma resonance absorption. *J. Mol. Biol.* **145**, 825–833.

Perutz, M. F., and Matthews, F. S. (1966). An X-ray study of azide methemoglobin. *J. Mol. Biol.* **21**, 199–202.

Philson, S. B., Debrunner, P. G., Schmidt, P. G., and Gunsalus, I. C. (1979). The effect of cytochrome P450$_{cam}$ on the nmr relaxation rate of water protons. *J. Biol. Chem.* **254**, 10173–10179.

Sharrock, M., Münck, E., Debrunner, P. G., Marshall, V., Lipscomb, J. D., and Gunsalus, I. C. (1973). Mössbauer studies of cytochrome P450$_{cam}$. *Biochemistry* **12**, 258–265.

Sharrock, M., Debrunner, P. G., Schulz, C., Lipscomb, J. D., Marshall, V., and Gunsalus, I. C. (1976). Cytochrome P450$_{cam}$ and its complexes. Mössbauer parameters of the heme iron. *Biochim. Biophys. Acta* **420**, 8–26.

Skinner, J. L., and Wolynes, P. G. (1978). Relaxation processes and chemical kinetics. *J. Chem. Phys.* **69**. 2143–2150.

Sligar, S. G. (1975). Coupling of spin, substrate and redox equilibria in cytochrome P450. *Biochemistry* **15**, 5399–5406.

Sligar, S. G., Debrunner, P. G. Lipscomb, J. D., Namtvedt, M. J., and Gunsalus, I. C. (1974). A role of the putidaredoxin COOH-terminus in P450$_{cam}$ (cytochrome m) hydroxylation. *Proc. Natl. Acad. Sci. U.S.A.* **71**, 3906–3910.

V
Microbiology

26

The Microbes'
Contribution
to Nutritional Science

Herman C. Lichstein

INTRODUCTION

My first meeting with Professor I. C. Gunsalus was during the summer of 1945 when I was offered the privilege of working with him as a junior colleague. That brief period, only 6 weeks, initiated a change in my perspective to microbiological research and shaped the future course of my professional career.

Coming from a parochial background as a predoctoral student the excitement and brilliance of the Gunsalus–Umbreit laboratory at Cornell was unbelievable. The techniques learned, although "crude" by today's standards, provided the basis for my work and that of others for some period of time. Techniques for harvesting large batches of bacterial cells, methods for the preparation of dried and often stable microbial cells, followed by disruption of such cells to provide cell-free enzyme systems without permeability barriers were a source of wonder to me and enabled us in but a few weeks to work out the kinetics of the glutamic–oxaloacetate transaminase system in *Streptococcus faecalis* and to identify pyridoxal phosphate as the coenzyme (Lichstein *et al.*, 1945).

Emphasis was placed repeatedly on the fact that we were or were training to be microbial physiologists. While utilizing biochemical methods we were hopefully asking questions and accumulating data that would help to explain a specific

349

EXPERIENCES IN BIOCHEMICAL PERCEPTION
Copyright © 1982 by Academic Press, Inc.
All rights of reproduction in any form reserved.
ISBN 0-12-528420-9

physiological or metabolic system. In time perhaps the information might be used to understand better the intact proliferating microbial cell. Perhaps my early contacts with Gunny explain in part the position expressed in the preface to a laboratory manual on experimental microbial physiology published many years later (Lichstein and Oginsky, 1965):

> The tremendous growth of the field of microbial physiology in the past several years has been accompanied by surprisingly little development of techniques that are specific for, and peculiar to, the field itself. Many of the procedures used by physiologists are classical microbiological techniques; many others are borrowed, with only little modification, from mammalian biochemistry. The design of an experiment in microbial physiology thus becomes dependent for its usefulness and originality on the recognition of the intrinsic qualities of the fabric—that is, the microorganism studied—and on the manner in which the stock pieces of the pattern are put together. It is on these two selective processes that the laboratory science of microbial physiology is primarily based.

Like Marjory Stephenson, Gunny taught the several levels of microbiological investigation from growing cultures, both pure and mixed grown in complex or chemically defined media, to viable cell suspensions and finally nonviable cell preparations (vacuum dried, acetone dried, disrupted cells with enzyme systems at various levels of purification). These concepts as expressed by Stephenson may be found in the Inaugural Marjory Stephenson Memorial Lecture given by Woods (1953) and in the Harvey Lecture presented by Gunsalus (1952).

The atmosphere at the Cornell laboratories was both relaxed and vibrant. A number of intriguing problems were under investigation and the exchange of ideas was both easy and productive. Teaching was informal and took place during the planning of an experimental protocol, discussion of the results, and finally a decision regarding the next step. The ever present pad and pencil was used freely and at the conclusion one had a reasonably decipherable copy of the ideas that Gunny had scribbled on paper. Technical mistakes were treated with the chiding remark—''what can you expect from a medical bacteriologist''—but errors in judgment and failure to make appropriate correlations were considered serious and not treated lightly at all. One learned very quickly to be well prepared for a research discussion with Gunny.

Toward the conclusion of my summer visit Gunsalus and his colleague Wayne Umbreit suggested that I seriously consider a career change from medical bacteriology to microbial physiology. They felt that an extended period of time in their laboratories should provide sufficient experience for me to "go it alone." I was most fortunate in receiving a National Research Council Fellowship for the year 1946–1947 and traveled back to Cornell with great enthusiasm and great expectations.

My work that year led via a series of unexpected events to a partial elucidation of a function for biotin in the oxaloacetate decarboxylase system (Lichstein and

Umbreit, 1947). It is with this vitamin that I have spent a large share of my research career.

STUDIES ON BIOTIN

So much of my research has been influenced by my tenure at Cornell that it would be at best arbitrary to cite specific papers directly traceable to that period. Suffice it to say that it was not merely experimental design that influenced me but a philosophy to the approach of microbial physiology and especially microbial nutrition. My most successful ventures with biotin did originate from earlier discussions at Cornell and in later years at meetings in various parts of the country.

Most important was my developing concern that progress from my own laboratory on the elucidation of the coenzyme form of biotin was slow and that basically I was uncomfortable with the biochemical aspects of the vitamin. I was reminded that Gunny often said that one does best what one can do and what one feels comfortable with. With time I began to consider the more physiological aspects of the microbial cells requirement and utilization of biotin. This was stimulated further by the remarkable progress being made during the latter part of the 1950's on physiological control mechanisms studied largely with microbial systems.

Almost by serendipity we obtained preliminary results which were best explained by the fact that biotin itself influences its permeation into cells auxotrophic for the vitamin and that it controls its own biosynthesis in microbial cells having the biosynthetic pathway. The elucidation of these mechanisms in our laboratory as well as others proved most exciting especially at a time when the direction of most workers in the field of control mechanisms involved amino acids. I shall record here only the general aspects of our work. Details are manifestly recorded in the literature and an excellent review of much of the work has been provided by Eisenberg (1973).

As a consequence of the results of numerous investigations, conclusive evidence was available that the biosynthesis of amino acids, purines, and pyrimidines in microorganisms is under strict physiological control via feedback and/or repression mechanisms. In contrast to such compounds, which are subsequently incorporated into macromolecules of the cell, vitamins, which are required only in catalytic amounts, had been reported to be overproduced suggesting a lack or inefficiency of biosynthetic control. The earliest detailed inspection of vitamin B synthesis was reported by Thompson in 1942 shortly after the introduction of the microbiological assay method. He surveyed five microorganisms and eight of the B vitamins. While the amount of a particular vitamin retained within the bacterial cell was relatively constant among the different species, the amount found in the medium varied widely. Thus the overproduction of the B vitamins was reflected by their accumulation in the growth medium.

Our initial experiments involved a study of the time course of biotin synthesis by growing cells of *Escherichia coli* (Crookes) (Pai and Lichstein, 1965a). Microbiological assays for biotin were performed with *Saccharomyces cerevisiae* (Fleischmann strain 139) and *Lactobacillus plantarum* (17-5). Later studies utilized ^{14}C-labeled biotin. Biotin synthesis occurred immediately upon the introduction of the cells into the growth medium with the rate of synthesis reaching a maximum just prior to the initiation of the exponential phase of growth. The vitamin was produced by the cells until cessation of growth, with the bulk of the biotin accumulated in the medium at the end of the exponential phase. The influence of exogenous biotin was studied by the addition of graded amounts to the basal medium at zero time. It was ascertained quite promptly that the total amount of biotin synthesized by *E. coli* varied inversely with the concentration of biotin present in the culture medium prior to the inoculation of bacteria. Essentially complete inhibition of biotin synthesis was seen in the presence of 5 ng of biotin per ml of medium.

Since a number of synthetic and naturally occurring biotin vitamers can replace the biotin requirement for growth of some microorganisms, their effect on the biosynthesis of biotin was investigated with the finding that only d-biotin was inhibitory. Thus, a high degree of specificity for d-biotin in the control of biotin synthesis is suggested. This specificity is in contrast to the situation with analogs of some amino acids which have been shown to mimic the action of the amino acid by causing repression or feedback inhibition of their biosynthetic pathway (Pai and Lichstein, 1965b).

Attention was directed next to the mechanism of regulation of biotin synthesis. Cells grown in the absence of exogenous biotin synthesized a significant amount of the vitamin under conditions where new protein synthesis was inhibited by either ultraviolet irradiation or chloramphenicol. The cells grown in the presence of exogenous biotin, however, could not synthesize biotin under the same conditions. The results suggest that exogenous biotin controls its own synthesis in *E. coli* by repression of one or more enzymes involved in the biosynthetic pathway. No evidence for feedback control has been obtained. Since biotin is required only in catalytic amounts, repression alone might be adequate from the point of view of cell economy.

Subsequent growth studies from our laboratory and others (Eisenberg, 1973) revealed that the addition of biotin to culture media prevents the accumulation of several intermediates in the pathway to biotin but to different degrees. The lack of feedback inhibition and the presence of multiple sties of different sensitivities to repression by biotin may explain the accumulation of some intermediates of the biotin pathway, which appears to be a unique phenomenon in metabolic control. The pathway to biotin synthesis has been elucidated principally by the work of Pai and of Eisenberg (1973). In those studies the specific activities of four enzymes in the biosynthetic pathway were assayed. When cells were grown in as little as 1 ng of biotin per ml of medium the specific activities of the enzymes were almost nil, although 5 ng of biotin per ml were required in order to inhibit completely the *de novo* synthesis of total biotin vitamers. The results also suggested that the biotin pathway is coordinately repressed by biotin.

Finally, the effect of avidin on biotin repression was examined in our laboratory (Pai and Lichstein, 1966). Avidin is a glycoprotein which binds extracellular biotin thus making the vitamin unavailable to the cells. It was found, as already stated, that the specific activity of the biotin synthesizing system in cells harvested from the basal medium lacking biotin increased rapidly thereafter. In the biotin-supplemented medium, no enzyme activity was found until after the addition of avidin. Derepression by avidin was found to follow the pattern characteristic of other repressible biosynthetic enzymes.

Turning now to another aspect of control mechanisms related to biotin, we found quite unexpectedly during studies on biotin uptake by *S. cerevisiae* that the transport system for biotin was controlled by the level of biotin in the growth medium. When the concentration of biotin exceeded that needed for maximum growth (0.25 ng/ml), the ability of cells to take up biotin decreased as the concentration of the vitamin in the medium increased; at a level of 9 ng/ml, transport was inhibited maximally (Rogers and Lichstein, 1969b).

The parameters of biotin permeation were identified using nonproliferating cells of the yeast harvested from media containing optimal levels of the vitamin. Biotin transport exhibited temperature and pH optima of 30°C and pH 4.0, respectively. Glucose markedly stimulated biotin uptake and this effect was overcome by iodoacetate. Inhibition of biotin uptake by homobiotin demonstrated the stereospecificity of the system. Biotin transport displayed saturation kinetics with an apparent K_m of 4.34×10^{-7} M. Such data suggested that biotin transport in *S. cerevisiae* is mediated by a finite carrier system having characteristics associated with active transport (Rogers and Lichstein, 1969a).

In support of the growth data, studies with resting cells revealed that while biotin-sufficient cells took up large amounts of the vitamin, cells grown in excess biotin took up little or none (Rogers and Lichstein, 1969b). In an attempt to understand this control system we addressed ourselves next to the effect of avidin on the transport system of cells grown in media containing excess biotin. Measurements were made both of residual biotin in the medium and free biotin uptake by the cells. Prior to the addition of avidin the level of medium biotin was high and the cells took up little or none of the vitamin. At the mid-logarithmic phase of growth, avidin was added to the medium. The concentration of biotin in the medium decreased rapidly to zero and the cells gained the ability to take up large quantities of biotin. Of interest was the fact that after maximum biotin was accumulated, the vitamin appeared to flow out of the cells. This "overshoot" phenomenon was investigated with the finding that the greater the amount of biotin offered the cells initially, the greater was the rate of biotin uptake, the higher was the level of biotin reached intracellularly, and the faster was the rate of biotin efflux (Becker and Lichstein, 1972).

It is pertinent that avidin was not able to release repression of excess biotin grown cells when such cells were suspended in a menstruum which did not support growth. This observation suggested an examination of the effect of avidin on cells pretreated with cycloheximide, an inhibitor of protein synthesis in yeast. Cycloheximide was added to the culture after removal of the 12-hour sample (mid-logarithmic phase) followed by the addition of avidin 20 minutes later. Although the concentration of biotin in the medium dropped to zero after the addition of avidin, the cells did not regain their ability to take up biotin. Thus, repression release did not occur under conditions which inhibited protein synthesis. It is pertinent that cycloheximide had little or no effect on biotin transport in optimally grown cells suggesting that once the transport system is formed protein synthesis is not required for biotin uptake (Rogers and Lichstein, 1969b).

The results outlined here indicate that biotin permeation in *S. cerevisiae* is under physiological control by a mechanism having the characteristics of repression. Biotin itself is the repressor since clearly the level of this vitamin in the growth medium controls the uptake of biotin by the cells.

It is manifest from our results with *E. coli* and *S. cerevisiae* that both organisms control the intracellular level of biotin quite rigidly. In the yeast, which requires an exogenous source of biotin for growth, this level appears to be restricted by controlling the synthesis of a component(s) of the transport system. In the case of *E. coli* which synthesizes biotin, overproduction is controlled by repression of one or more of the enzymes in the biosynthetic pathway. In agreement with the results of numerous investigations with a variety of metabolites, the physiological significance of the observations with biotin may be that such controls conserve both energy and building blocks thus providing for cellular economy. We are, however, also compelled to question whether high intracellular concentrations of biotin may exert a deleterious effect on the metabolism of some cells. The literature does reveal examples of microorganisms whose growth is inhibited by concentrations of biotin considered optimal for the growth of other organisms. Clark and Mitchell (1944) reported marked inhibition of the growth of *Clostridium thermosaccharolyticum* by the presence of 0.01 μg of biotin per ml of medium. More recently, Murphy and Elkan (1963) demonstrated complete growth inhibition of *Rhizobium japonicum* by levels of medium biotin from 0.001 to 0.1 μg/ml. A later report (Elkan, 1965) demonstrated that avidin prevented the inhibition. The nature or site of such a toxic effect remains unresolved. Perhaps the "overshoot" phenomenon may be a mechanism which enables the cell to release excess biotin. Possibly *C. thermosaccharolyticum* and *R.*

japonicum lack such a system which appears to operate by feedback inhibition of the biotin transport system by large intracellular biotin concentrations.

THE MICROBES' CONTRIBUTION TO NUTRITIONAL SCIENCE

Microbiologists are perhaps the oldest experimental nutritionists. Since the very foundation of microbiology rests on the ability to grow microorganisms in pure culture, it has been a daily practical problem for them. It was recognized quite early that the incorporation into artificial media of certain natural materials such as blood, milk, extracts of beef and yeast, and numerous other substances provided good growth of many microorganisms. These earlier complex and empirically designed media have to a large measure been replaced by chemically defined media containing precisely known ingredients. In addition to the goals set by earlier investigators in microbial nutrition, the "spin-offs" were indeed remarkable. These included support for the concept of the unity of biochemistry, much of our knowledge of biosynthetic pathways, and the discovery of previously unknown metabolites.

Sufficient credit has not, I believe, been given to the elegant work of J. Howard Mueller and the purposes enunciated so well in his first paper (1922a). In that year he initiated a program designed to define the growth requirements of bacteria in precise chemical terms. In the introduction of the paper he stated:

> Perhaps the most important results to which success in such a piece of work might lead, are the applications of the findings to problems of more general biological importance, particularly to those of animal metabolism. For, whatever may prove to be the nature of these substances which cause growth of bacteria, they are largely or entirely components of animal tissue, and it is probable that they are either needed also by the animal body and supplied by plant or other sources, or else are synthesized by the animal itself to fill some metabolic requirement. When it is possible to catalogue the substances required by pathogenic bacteria for growth, it will probably be found that most of them are either required by, or important in, animal metabolism, and while many of them will surely be compounds at present familiar to the physiological chemist, it is equally probable that some will be new, or at least of hitherto unrecognized importance. This point is sufficiently clear in the light of many recent publications in connection with the relation of vitamines to the growth of bacteria and of yeast.

As a result of the fractionation of hydrolytic products of casein which are required for the growth of streptococci he isolated and identified the amino acid, methionine (Mueller, 1922a,b,c, 1923). This was the first positive identification of a new compound of general biological importance through the study of bacterial nutrition.

One of the major discoveries in microbial nutrition was reported in 1901 by Wildiers. He noted that *S. cerevisiae* failed to grow appreciably in a minimal medium when small inocula were used, but did grow well when extracts of yeast or certain other natural materials were added. He called the factor "bios." Since yeast ash was inactive it was clear that an organic compound(s) was involved. Considerable study by a number of laboratories was required before the resolution of the "bios" problem. A major consequence of such studies was the independent publications in 1919 of Williams and of Bachmann calling attention to the similarity in properties of the yeast growth factor(s) and the vitamin B complex. During the exciting decades of the 1930's, 1940's, and 1950's, a number of B vitamins was discovered first as a growth factor for one or more microorganisms before its requirement in animal nutrition was described. These include folic acid, para-aminobenzoic acid, biotin, nicotinic acid, pantothenic acid, lipoic acid, and vitamin B_{12}—an impressive contribution of the microbe to the nutrition of man.

One of the most interesting later studies on the nutritional requirements of bacteria was the demonstration by Herbst and Snell (1949) of the effect of putrescine on the growth of *Hemophilus parainfluenzae*. Within a few years a number of polyamines were demonstrated to stimulate markedly the growth of *Neisseria perflava, Pasteurella tularensis,* and *Lactobacillus casei.* These first indications for a biological role for the polyamines have been followed by numerous studies in both prokaryotic and eukaryotic cells. They have been implicated in the stabilization of membranes and ribosomes and to play a role in maintaining the tertiary structure of macromolecules such as deoxyribonucleic and ribonucleic acids. A provocative article on the organization of tRNA structure and activity by spermine has appeared recently (Cohen, 1978). Thus, the relatively simple techniques involved in the study of microbial nutrition led to the demonstration of a physiological role for a class of compounds which had been until that time not appreciated. This was then followed by highly sophisticated biochemical and biophysical studies that continue to shed light on these highly important polyamines. The discovery that α-difluoromethylornithine causes a specific and irreversible inhibition of ornithine decarboxylase, the rate-controlling step for the formation of polyamines in mammals, has been employed effectively in the treatment of experimental trypanosome infections in mice. The possibility for its use in the treatment of human trypanosome disease is truly exciting (Bacchi *et al.,* 1980). These compounds have come a long distance in biology and medicine from their incorrect implication in "ptomaine or food poisoning" by Italian toxicologists in the late nineteenth century.

An important practical application of the absolute requirement by microorganisms of a specific B vitamin was the development of rapid, inexpensive, accurate, and highly sensitive microbiological methods for the assay of vitamins and later amino acids. The first such method was reported for riboflavin using *L. casei* (Snell and Strong, 1939). This was followed quickly by the description of assay methods specific for all the known B vitamins and amino acids employing microorganisms of exacting nutritional requirements, especially various lactobacilli and yeasts and later a variety of auxotrophic mutants. While such methods were at one time very widely employed, microbiological assay has been replaced in many instances by more sophisticated technology. However, in the medical sciences microbiological assay is still employed especially for folic acid, biotin, and vitamin B_{12}. Matthews and Linnell (1979) state, "... we should say that cases of serious discrepancies between the results of microbiological and radioisotopic assays for total cobalmins are now giving rise to controversy and concern. We think that every laboratory should specify on its reports the assay method used to obtain its values for total cobalmins, and that the term 'vitamin B_{12}' should be abandoned and replaced by 'the cobalmins.'" It should be emphasized that microbiological assay is the only practical method available whenever estimation of biological activity is required.

The role of the intestinal microflora in both health and disease is of considerable importance and continues to be studied, although the methodology is indeed formidable and has been the primary factor contributing to a lack of decisive data. It is known that the intestinal tract of man and other animals have a flora abundant in microorganisms capable of synthesizing vitamins of the B complex as well as vitamin K. The amount synthesized and subsequently available to the host must certainly vary considerably but indirect evidence suggests that in some instances it may be sufficient to satisfy the minimal daily requirements of the host. This is most clearly seen with biotin deficiency or egg white injury. Studies with experimental animals including human volunteers have demonstrated that avidin must be incorporated in the diet in order to precipitate frank biotin deficiency. It appears a reasonable deduction, therefore, that it is necessary to bind the biotin synthesized by the intestinal microflora. The occurrence of vitamin B deficiencies in humans on a prolonged regimen of wide-spectrum antibiotics taken by mouth is recognized by clinicians and such patients are usually given vitamin B supplementation during such therapy. These deficiencies are presumed to be caused by the documented alteration of the normal intestinal microflora by the antibiotics.

More recent has been the recognition that bacterial overgrowth consequent to intestinal stasis contributes to vitamin B_{12} maladsorption in such patients. Several mechanisms may be operative in this situation but perhaps most likely is the competitive uptake by bacteria of bound B_{12}, thus preventing adsorption of the vitamin by the intestinal mucosa (Tabaqchali et al., 1974).

Another facet is the recognition that many microorganisms have the ability to degrade a number of vitamins. In vitro studies have been carried out especially with thiaminase, pantothenate hydrolyase, and the degradation of nicotinic acid via oxidation. The possible importance of these observations to human nutrition is not at all clear. A recent letter in Science by Rogers (1979) is provocative in this regard. Commenting on the possibility that the sudden infant death (SID) syndrome is caused by botulism he suggests a different role for Clostridium *botulinum*. Because of previously noted similarities between certain symptoms of thiamin deficiency and that of SID, and the marginal level of thiamin in cow's milk or breast milk, he wonders whether thiaminase-I produced by *C. botulinum* could contribute to a vitamin deficiency by decomposition in the gut of the low concentration of thiamin ingested.

I am compelled to mention another provocative study on the possible etiology of SID, because it involves biotin. Johnson *et al.* (1980) reported that young chickens exposed to mild stress died suddenly. When the birds' diet was supplemented with biotin the disorder was eliminated. They noted, further, that livers of such chickens had a very low level of biotin. Work with infants who had died of SID revealed a statistically lower level of biotin than livers from normal infants. They suggest that infants may require an exogenous source of biotin until their intestinal microflora develops a mixed population. Finally, they point out that SID occurs more commonly in bottle-fed than in breast-fed infants and that considerable biotin is lost during the processing of some infant formulations.

The exhaustive studies of the biochemical functions of B vitamins, much of them done with microorganisms, led clearly to the recognition that these vitamins are converted by cells to a more complex form and function as coenzymes of a variety of important enzyme reactions. The availability of the biochemical machinery required to synthesize the active or coenzyme form from the free vitamin is widespread in the biological world. However, there are a number of reports on the requirement by some microorganisms of one or more coenzymes. Such requirements reflect not only a deficiency in the biosynthetic system but remarkable permeation mechanisms for such large molecules. The earliest and best documented example is the requirement by *Hemophilus influenzae* for nicotinamide adenine dinucleotide. Neither niacin or niacinamide will support the growth of the organism. In 1952, this author made the following statement. "By analogy, it is at least provocative to suggest that metabolic dysfunctions may exist in man wherein an individual may be unable to convert effectively a vitamin present in his diet to the coenzyme form required for its proper biochemical performance." It is noteworthy that such biochemical deficiencies do exist in man and have been demonstrated with pyridoxine, thiamin, and vitamin B_{12} (Matthews and Linnell, 1979).

Finally, one of the more interesting and perhaps clinically useful aspects of nutrition is the concept of "nutritional immunity" (Kochan, 1977; Weinberg, 1975). The dynamic interaction between animals including man and pathogenic microbes involves well-defined humoral and cellular factors of the host as well as many factors characteristic of the invading microorganism. Relatively recently has there been the enunciation of the obvious fact that an organism invading a host must find a suitable nutritional environment which would permit its growth and multiplication. From this has come the concept, now based on experimental evidence, that the host–parasite relationship involves among other factors a competition for essential nutrilites, especially minerals such as iron. The competition for iron appears to occur in the fluids and tissues of the host and involves biological iron carriers of both the host and the microorganism. The organic iron transport compounds of microorganisms are called siderophores. Evidence is becoming increasingly available demonstrating that when the host is invaded by pathogenic microorganisms the level of host iron is often quite promptly reduced, thus hindering microbial growth. However, if the pathogen can mobilize sufficient quantities of siderophores it may be capable of obtaining sufficient growth-essential iron from host cells or fluids.

A recent reference to this interesting example of "immunity" relates both fever and iron concentration (Kluger and Rothenburg, 1979). Working with rabbits and *Pasteurella multocida* data were obtained that support the possibility that one of the beneficial effects of fever is the reduced ability of pathogenic bacteria to grow well at elevated temperatures in an iron-poor medium. The authors conclude that if their data can be extrapolated to organisms pathogenic to man, then we should reevaluate the advisability of using drugs to reduce moderate fever, that the fortification of our diets with iron is questionable, and that iron chelators such as deferoxamine mesylate may have therapeutic value in certain bacterial infections.

Finally, Crosa (1980) presented compelling evidence that the virulence plasmid of *Vibrio anguillarum* (a marine fish pathogen) specifies a very efficient iron-sequestering system enabling bacteria to survive in conditions of limited iron availability. On losing the plasmid the organism loses its virulence and also its ability to grow under conditions of iron restriction.

REFERENCES

Bacchi, C. J., Nathan, H. C., Hunter, S. H., McCann, P. P., and Sjoerdsma, A. (1980). Polyamine metabolism: A potential therapeutic target in trypanosomes. *Science* **210**, 332–334.

Bachmann, F. M. (1919). Vitamine requirements of certain yeasts. *J. Biol. Chem.* **39**, 235–257.

Becker, J. M., and Lichstein, H. C. (1972). Transport overshoot during biotin uptake by *Saccharomyces cerevisiae*. *Biochim. Biophys. Acta* **282**, 409–420.

Clark, F. M., and Mitchell, W. R. (1944). Studies on the nutritional requirements of *Clostridium thermosaccharolyticum*. *Arch. Biochem.* **3**, 459–466.

Cohen, S. S. (1978). What do polyamines do. *Nature (London)* **274**, 209–210.

Crosa, J. H. (1980). A plasmid associated with virulence in the marine fish pathogen *Vibrio anguillarum* specifies an iron-sequestering system. *Nature (London)* **284**, 566–568.

Eisenberg, M. A. (1973). Biotin: Biogenesis, transport, and their regulation. *Adv. Enzymol.* **38**, 317–372.

Elkan, G. H. (1965). Factors affecting biotin inhibition of growth of a *Rhizobium japonicum* strain. *Bacteriol. Proc.* p. 75.

Gunsalus, I. C. (1952). Comparative metabolism: Bacterial nutrition and metabolic function. *Harvey Lect.* **45**, 40–63.

Herbst, E. J., and Snell, E. E. (1949). Putrescine and related compounds as growth factors for *Hemophilus parainfluenzae*. *J. Biol. Chem.* **181**, 47–54.

Johnson, A. R., Hood, R. L., and Emery, J. L. (1980). Biotin and the sudden infant death syndrome. *Nature (London)* **285,** 159–160.

Kluger, M. J., and Rothenburg, B. A. (1979). Fever and reduced iron: Their interaction as a host defense response to bacterial infection. *Science* **203,** 374–376.

Kochan, I. (1977). Role of siderophores in nutritional immunity and bacterial parasitism. *In* "Microorganisms and Minerals" (E. D. Weinberg, ed.), pp. 251–288. Dekker, New York.

Lichstein, H. C. (1952). Metabolic functions of the vitamin B complex. *Bull. Univ. Minn. Hosp. Minn. Med. Found.* **23,** 221–235.

Lichstein, H. C., and Oginsky, E. L. (1965). "Experimental Microbial Physiology." Freeman, San Francisco, California.

Lichstein, H. C., and Umbreit, W. W. (1947). A function for biotin. *J. Biol. Chem.* **170,** 329–336.

Lichstein, H. C., Gunsalus, I. C., and Umbreit, W. W. (1945). Function of the vitamin B_6 group: Pyridoxal phosphate (codecarboxylase) in transamination. *J. Biol. Chem.* **161,** 311–320.

Matthews, D. M., and Linnell. J. C. (1979). Vitamin B_{12}: An area of darkness. *Br. Med. J.* **2,** 533–535.

Mueller, J. H. (1922a). Studies on cultural requirements of bacteria. I. *J. Bacteriol.* **7,** 309–324.

Mueller, J. H. (1922b). Studies on cultural requirements of bacteria. II. *J. Bacteriol.* **7,** 325–338.

Mueller, J. H. (1922c). A new sulphur-containing amino acid isolated from casein. *Proc. Soc. Exp. Biol. Med.* **19,** 161–163.

Mueller, J. H. (1923). A new sulfur-containing amino acid isolated from the hydrolytic products of protein. *J. Biol. Chem.* **56,** 157–169.

Murphy, S. G., and Elkan, G. H. (1963). Growth inhibition by biotin in a strain of *Rhizobium japonicum*. *J. Bacteriol.* **86,** 884–885.

Pai, C. H., and Lichstein, H. C. (1965a). The biosynthesis of biotin in microorganisms. I. The physiology of biotin synthesis in *Escherichia coli. Biochim. Biophys. Acta* **100,** 28–35.

Pai, C. H., and Lichstein, H. C. (1965b). The biosynthesis of biotin in microorganisms. II. Mechanism of the regulation of biotin synthesis in *Escherichia coli. Biochim. Biophys. Acta* **100,** 36–42.

Pai, C. H., and Lichstein, H. C. (1966). Biosynthesis of biotin in microorganisms. IV. Repression and derepression of (+)−biotin synthesis from (+)−desthiobiotin. *Arch. Biochem. Biophys.* **114,** 138–144.

Rogers, E. F. (1979). Sudden infant death. *Science* **203.**

Rogers, T. O., and Lichstein, H. C. (1969a). Characterization of the biotin transport system in *Saccharomyces cerevisiae. J. Bacteriol.* **100,** 557–564.

Rogers, T. O., and Lichstein, H. C. (1969b). Regulation of biotin transport in *Saccharomyces cerevisiae. J. Bacteriol.* **100,** 565–572.

Snell, E. E., and Strong, F. M. (1939). The microbiological assay for riboflavin. *Ind. Eng. Chem., Anal. Ed.* **11,** 346–350.

Tabaqchali, S., Schjönsby, H., and Gompertz, D. (1974). Role of microbial alterations in the pathogenesis of intestinal disorders. *In* "Anaerobic Bacteria" (A. Balows, ed.), pp. 106–110. Thomas, Springfield, Illinois.

Thompson, R. C. (1942). Synthesis of B vitamins by bacteria in pure culture. *Univ. Tex. Publ.* **4237,** 87–96.

Weinberg, E. D. (1975). Metal starvation of pathogens by hosts. *BioScience* **25,** 314–318.

Wildiers, E. (1901). Une nouvelle substance indispensible au développement de la levure. *Cellule* **18,** 313–331.

Williams, R. J. (1919). The vitamine requirement of yeast, a simple biological test for vitamine. *J. Biol. Chem.* **38,** 465–486.

Woods, D. D. (1953). The integration of research on the nutrition and metabolism of microorganisms. *J. Gen. Microbiol.* **9,** 151–173.

27

Pseudomonas
aeruginosa —
A Highly Evolved Aerobe

Jack J. R. Campbell

I am not sure that Gunny would want it to be widely known but his early training and research interests involved those rather pallid bacteria, the streptococci. However, his interests evolved to the finer things and he moved on to the study of the biochemistry of the pseudomonads. As evidenced by the topics dealt with in this volume, his scientific friends seemed to have been cloned for their interest in the pseudomonads.

In common with other inquisitive young microbiologists, Gunny was intrigued by bacteria that had unusual colonies, formed startling pigments, or had pronounced extracellular activity; thus as graduate students we helped to build up his collection of interesting-looking bacteria. When grown on appropriate media, *Pseudomonas aeruginosa* meets Gunny's criteria as an interesting-looking bacterium. In appropriate media it will convert 10% of the carbon compounds to pyocyanine and the medium will be as blue as dark blue ink, whereas under other nutritional conditions, no pyocyanine is formed but the concentration of pyoverdine (bacterial fluorescein) is so great that it appears to crystallize from the medium. Gunny's interest in colorful bacteria was passed on to his students.

Anyone who has worked with natural populations of bacteria has encountered fluorescent pseudomonads in a great variety of situations. These organisms comprise about 7% of the normal flora of soil, account for almost 100% of the

EXPERIENCES IN BIOCHEMICAL PERCEPTION
Copyright © 1982 by Academic Press, Inc.
All rights of reproduction in any form reserved.
ISBN 0-12-528420-9

psychrotroph population of dairy products, are the principal spoilage organisms of fish, meat, and eggs, and are present in freshwater lakes and in the oceans. The fact that they are part of the normal flora of soil, oceans, lakes, and rivers means that they are in a position to gain entry to almost any environment on our planet. Because of their superior ability to survive and grow in adverse environments, they become even more prominent when selective pressures are imposed on a mixed flora. As Gunny's graduate student, I became involved in a variety of ad hoc microbiological problems. In one such instance, Gunny decided to help members of the Animal Husbandry Department at Cornell explain the poor fertility rates of certain bulls at the Central New York State artificial insemination center. We found that *P. aeruginosa* had invaded the bulls' reproductive tract and had established a venereal disease (Gunsalus *et al.*, 1944). The observation permitted us to predict the effectiveness of the various bulls without waiting for conception data. On another occasion when I spent a summer at Urbana, Gunny was directing the bacteriological aspects of the Ph.D. thesis of a graduate student in the field of nutrition. The student was trying to sterilize the gut of rats by feeding a combination of antibiotics in order to determine whether or not, in the absence of intestinal flora, rats could utilize urea as a sole source of nitrogen. The preliminary results were encouraging—the bacterial count went almost to zero. However, soon a few green colonies began to appear on the plates and within days the bacterial numbers in the feces, as determined by the aerobic plate count, were back to normal and the population consisted entirely of *P. aeruginosa*. So even in Gunny's lab, where the thrust was at the molecular level, it was difficult not to work on pseudomonads. Tarr *et al.* (1950) introduced the practice of incorporating a broad-spectrum antibiotic such as aureomycin into ice for the purpose of preserving fish and other perishable foods. It worked well on an experimental basis and when first practiced on an industrial scale doubled the time that fishing vessels could stay at sea and still bring in a salable product. However, after a few trips the process lost its advantage because aureomycin-resistant strains of fluorescent pseudomonads had become the dominant population in the fish holds. The same results were experienced in poultry-eviscerating plants across the United States.

A rather specialized habitat for the pseudomonads was discovered by Ophel (1960) in Canada and Fowler *et al.* (1960) in the United States when they observed massive bacterial growth in nuclear reactors with levels of radiation 1000-fold greater than could be withstood by *Escherichia coli*. In each case the radiation-resistant organisms were found to be pseudomonads.

A possible role for pseudomonads as agents in petroleum exploration may have been found by Campbell (1939) when, in experiments designed to determine the organism responsible for a severe odor problem in Canadian butter, he found that the causative organism was *P. aeruginosa* and that its source was water from the wells of the town of Leduc, Alberta. Leduc later became famous as a center of the oil industry and oil wells were drilled within the city limits. The bacterium isolated could utilize paraffins and presumably this was its carbon source in the well water.

One definition of the world's best bacteriologist is the one who knows the most about the greatest variety of bacteria. This could be paraphrased to "the world's smartest bacterium is the one which thrives under the greatest variety of environmental situations." I am not prepared to commit myself to answering the first statement but on the basis of the above criterion, my nomination for the smartest bacteria would be the fluorescent pseudomonads and, in particular, *P. aeruginosa*.

An explanation for the range of environments that *P. aeruginosa* successfully invades is that, by virtue of its array of extracellular products, it modifies its immediate surroundings to create a more compatible environment for itself, often at the expense of a host.

Pyocyanine, which is the characteristic blue pigment of *P. aeruginosa,* has a variety of interesting properties, some of which may have been more important to the organism at an earlier stage in its evolution. For instance, it is an electron transport agent and this does not appear to be an advantage to the organism as we currently know it. Some of its properties are undoubtedly important contributing factors to the organism's ability to establish itself in a variety of environmental niches.

Pyocyanine was shown by Judah and Williams-Ashman in 1951 to be an uncoupler of oxidative phosphorylation and it has the possibility of inhibiting energy generation in tissue. It was one of the earliest antibiotics to be used but proved to be too toxic. However, this toxicity may be of value in destroying host cells, thus permitting the organism to colonize animal tissue. It may also be helpful in a habitat such as soil by inhibiting the growth of competing organisms. Pyocyanine is a strong chelating agent and this property could be important to *P. aeruginosa* in natural situations where the level of cations is marginal. It is a sufficiently strong chelating agent to cause metabolic reactions to stop at enzymatic steps which require a cation such as Mg^{2+} as a cofactor. A common reaction which requires Mg^{2+} is the oxidation of α-keto acids. Campbell *et al.* in 1957 found that, in the presence of pyocyanine, susceptible bacteria such as *Pseudomonas fluorescens* and *Proteus vulgaris* oxidized substrates only to the keto acid level. *Pseudomonas aeruginosa* was not affected by high concentrations of pyocyanine and so it could scavenge these acids.

The production of pyoverdin, which is the fluorescent pigment produced by *P. aeruginosa,* is derepressed under conditions of iron limitation. The pigment is an extremely strong chelator of ferric iron and Meyer and Abdallah (1978) concluded that it acts as a siderophore. Other pigments are produced by strains of *P.*

aeruginosa but have not been identified with any specific functions (Leisinger and Margraff, 1979). Liu and Shokrani (1978) have termed other sideophores which are capable of competing with tissue for limiting iron *pyochelins*.

Although in general the antibiotics produced by *P. aeruginosa* have proved to be too toxic for therapeutic use, nonetheless they may be significant in fostering the growth of *P. aeruginosa* in a mixed population. Leisinger and Margraff (1979) have stated that pseudomonads represent the major group of nondifferentiating microorganisms producing antibiotics.

Pseudomonas aeruginosa is one of the most successful opportunistic pathogens and differs from other gram-negative bacteria in that its pathogenic activity is due to its range of extracellular products and not to its endotoxin. Its proteases and elastase cause necrotic lesions and destroy permeability defenses. These enzymes would appear to play a role in the pathology of such diverse diseases as pneumonia, dermatitis, and keratoconjunctivitis (Jensen *et al.*, 1980). The organism may also have the advantage of phospholipase which will hydrolyze erthrocytes and other cells and thus participate in the formation of local lesions (Stinson and Hayden, 1979). In addition, a hemolysin, which is a glycolipid, may be available to lyse erthrocytes, thus damaging the host and providing nutrients for invading bacteria (Liu, 1957).

The most harmful product produced by this bacterium is its lethal toxin, exotoxin A. The toxin is very similar in action to diphtheria toxin in its mechanism (Iglewski and Kabat, 1975). In addition to producing these proteins, pigments, and chelating agents, *P. aeruginosa* secretes a slime that protects it against phagocytosis. So the total picture is that *P. aeruginosa* possesses an unusually wide array of extracellular compounds that contribute to its success as an opportunistic pathogen.

The ability of bacteria to destroy or inactivate antibiotics is a widely held property. By chemical modification we can create antibiotics that resist this type of bacterial action. If this were its only basis of antibiotic resistance, *P. aeruginosa* would be no smarter than other bacteria or man. However, by a mechanism that is not yet fully understood *P. aeruginosa* can acquire resistance to a variety of antibiotics and this resistance is not due to modification or destruction of antibiotics. A good model of this property was revealed by the work of Kay and Gronlund (1969) who were endeavoring to isolate mutants of *P. aeruginosa* which had lost the ability to transport particular amino acids. They found that when *P. aeruginosa* was grown in the presence of sublethal concentrations of amino acid analogs it became impermeable to the analogs and to related amino acids but not to unrelated amino acids. Thus the organism was able to selectively change its permeability in response to an inducer and prevent the entry of the toxic compound and its analogs. Kay and Gronlund did not determine whether the phenomenon was associated with the outer membrane or with the transport enzyme in the cytoplasmic membrane. However, Hamilton (1970) has shown that this type of resistance is not present in spheroplasts and so the resistance is associated with the cell wall. The outer membrane of gram-negative bacteria acts as a sieve by virtue of pores formed by aggregations of protein molecules. The pores in the outer membrane of *P. aeruginosa* are similar to those in the outer membrane of mitochondria, being five to six times larger than those in *E. coli* (Hancock and Nikaido, 1978). However, whereas the pores in mitochondria are considered to be "leaky," those in *P. aeruginosa* are very impermeable to certain molecules. R. E. W. Hancock (personal communication, 1980) has suggested that the diameter of the orifice of the pores in *P. aeruginosa* is controlled by "gates" and that these "gates" can be induced to close, rendering the organism resistant.

In common with other fluorescent pseudomonads, *P. aeruginosa* has a tremendous range of enzymes that permit it to degarde at least 100 different organic compounds. In that the degradation of many of these compounds involves a series of enzymes, the total enzyme complement of the organisms available for the degradation of its nutrients is vast. In order to accommodate this great catabolic potential the organism resorts to several shortcuts. First, it regularly uses convergent pathways for the degradation of substrates so that for many substrates only the first few enzymatic steps are unique. Also, almost all strains of *P. aeruginosa* are lysogenic and genetic information can be transferred from one strain to another by transduction or conjugation. Moreover, the genetic information for an entire metabolic pathway may be closely linked and so a large amount of catabolic activity may be transferred on a relatively small fragment of DNA.

The pathways of carbohydrate degradation available to *P. aeruginosa* are quite usual for an obligate aerobe. However, there are several unexplained observations which suggest that we do not know everything about the operation of the various pathways of carbohydrate metabolism. Gunny's philosophy was that "if an organism carries out a reaction, there is probably a very good reason for it." The statement will not always be true but it is a good working principle. The dominant pathway of glucose oxidation by *P. aeruginosa* is via 2-ketogluconic acid, yet there appears to be little purpose to this route. The reactions leading to 2-ketogluconate occur in the periplasm (Roberts *et al..* 1973). It is difficult to visualize what advantages accrue to the organism by being bathed in gluconate and 2-ketogluconate; until we know otherwise we should assume there is a useful purpose to this. *Pseudomonas aeruginosa* excretes α-ketoglutarate under conditions of nitrogen starvation and the cell is impermeable to the reentry of α-ketoglutarate, so the carbon source is essentially stored until ammonium ions become available and then the α-ketoglutarate reenters the cell. Extracts of these cells contained the apoenzyme for the oxidation of α-ketoglutarate, yet the compound was secreted. In some way the level of α-ketoglutarate controls its own secretion from the cell (von Tigerstrom and Campbell, 1966). Thus, even when the organism does not possess a unique metabolic pathway, it still manages to incorporate a novel twist that works to its advantage.

Many bacteria display remarkable properties but the factor that sets *Pseudomonas aeruginosa* apart is its high level of sophistication in every facet of its activities.

REFERENCES

Campbell, J. J. R. (1939). Surface taint in butter. Undergraduate Thesis, Univ. of British Columbia.

Campbell, J. J. R., McQuillan, A. M., Eagles, B. A., and Smith, R. A. (1957). The inhibition of keto acid oxidation by pyocyanine. *Can. J. Microbiol.* **3,** 313–318.

Fowler, E. B., Christerson, C. W., Jurney, E. T., and Schafer, W. D. (1960). Bacterial "infection" of the Omega west reactor. *Nucleonics* **18,** 108.

Gunsalus, I. C., Campbell, J. J. R., Beck, G. H., and Salisbury, G. W. (1944). The bacteriology of bull semen. II. The effect of bacteria upon rapid tests for semen quality. *J. Dairy Sci.* **27,** 357–364.

Hamilton, W. C. (1970). The mode of action of membrane active antibacterials *FEBS-Symp.* **20,** 71–79.

Hancock, R. E. W., and Nikaido, H. (1978). Outer membranes of gram-negative bacteria. XIX. Isolation from *Pseudomonas aeruginosa* PA01 and use in reconstitution and definition of the permeability barrier. *J. Bacteriol.* **136,** 381–390.

Iglewski, B. H., and Kabat, D. (1975). NAD-dependent inhibition of protein synthesis by *Pseudomonas aeruginosa* toxin. *Proc. Natl. Acad. Sci. U.S.A.* **72,** 2284–2293.

Jensen, S. E., Phillippe, L., Tseng, T., Stembe, G. W., and Campbell, J. N. (1980). Purification and characterization of exocellular proteases produced by a clinical isolate and a laboratory strain of *Pseudomonas aeruginosa. Can. J. Microbiol.* **26,** 77–86.

Judah, J. D., and Williams-Ashman, H. G. (1951). The inhibition of oxidative phosphorylation. *Biochem. J.* **48,** 33–42.

Kay, W. W., and Gronlund, A. F. (1969). Isolation of amino acid transport-negative mutants of *Pseudmonas aeruginosa* and cells with repressed transport activity. *J. Bacteriol.* **98,** 116–123.

Leissinger, T., and Margraff, R. (1979). Secondary metabolites of the fluorescent pseudomonads. *Microbiol. Rev.* **43,** 422–442.

Liu, P. V. (1957). Survey of hemolysin production among species of Pseudomonads. *J. Bacteriol.* **74,** 718–727.

Liu, P. V., and Shokrani, F. (1978). Biological activities of pyochelins: Iron-chelating agents of *Pseudomonas aeruginosa. Infect. Immun.* **22,** 878–890.

Meyer, J. M., and Abdallah, M. A. (1978). The fluorescent pigment of *Pseudmonas fluorescens:* Biosynthesis, purification and physicochemical properties. *J. Gen. Microbiol.* **107,** 319–328.

Ophel, I. L. (1960). Reactor antibiotics. *Nucleonics* **18,** 7.

Roberts, B. K., Midgley, M., and Dawes, E. A. (1973). The metabolism of 2-oxogluconate by *Pseudmonas aeruginosa. J. Gen. Microbiol.* **78,** 319–329.

Stinson, M., and Hayden, C. (1979). Secretion of phospholipase C by *Pseudmonas aeruginosa. Infect. Immun.* **25,** 558–564.

Tarr, H. L. A., Southcott, B. A., and Bissett, H. M. (1950). Effect of several antibiotics and food preservatives in retarding bacterial spoilage of fish. *Fish. Res. Board Can., Prog. Rep. Pac. Coast Stn.* **83,** 35–38.

von Tigerstrom, M., and Campbell, J. J. R. (1966). The tricarboxylic acid cycle, the glyoxylate cycle and the enzymes of glucose oxidation in *Pseudomonas aeruginosa. Can. J. Microbiol.* **12,** 1015–1022.

Index

A

Acetate, stimulation, lactic acid bacteria, 47
Acetolactate isomeroreductase, induction, 133
Acetone preparation, bacteria, 16
Acetyl-CoA
  citrate synthesis 4
  pyruvate oxidation, 6
Acetyl-CoA dehydrogenase
  amino acid metabolism, 24, 25
  spectral analysis, 298
Acetyl phosphate, pyruvate oxidation, 4–7
Acid-hydrolyzed casein, bacterial media, 10
Acid-hydrolyzed gelatin, bacterial media, 10
Acinetobacter calcoaceticus, β-ketoadipate
  pathway, 122–124
Acinetobacter NCIB 9871, cyclohexanol degra-
  dation, 64–66
Actinoplanes utahensis, steffimycin metabolism,
  81
Aclacinomycin A, cleavage, reductive
  glycosidic, 79
Activation energy, enzyme–substrate inter-
  mediate, 311
Acylation, vectorial mechanism, 88, 89
Acyl-CoA:octanoate-CoA transferase, 90
Acyl-CoA synthetase, fatty acid transport, 88–90
Acyl thiokinase, *see* Acyl-CoA synthetase
Adenosine monophosphate, L-threonine dehy-
  drase, 149–160
Adenosine triphosphate, protein degradation,
  234, 236, 237, 241–248
Adenosine triphosphate/adenosine diphosphate
  ratio, 18

Adenylation, glutamine synthetase inactivation,
  241–243
Adrenal ferredoxin, characterization, 268, *see
  also* Adrenodoxin
Adrenodoxin
  purification, 269
  sequence homology, putidaredoxin, 288
Adrenodoxin reductase, purification, 269
Adriamycin
  cleavage, reductive glycosidic, 78
  metabolism, 75, 76, 78
  structure, 77
Aeromonas hydrophila, anthracycline
  metabolism, 78, 79
Agrobacterium tumefaciens, plasmid, chromo-
  some transfer, 105
Alcaligenes, cyclohexane carboxylic acid
  metabolism, 66, 67
Alcohol dehydrogenase, genetics, 113, 114
Alicyclic biodegradation, 60–72
Alkane hydroxylase, genetics, 113, 114
Alkane hydroxylation, cytochrome P450, 262
Alkane oxidation, gene regulation, 113
Amino acid catabolism, *Pseudomonas,* 24, 25
Amino acid, microbiological assay, 356
D-Amino acid oxidase
  absorption spectrum, 316, 317
  D-amino acid metabolism, 24, 25
  intermediate, 315–318
  isosbestic point, 316, 317
  kinetic mechanism, low temperature, 317,
    318
  pH effect, absorption spectrum, 316, 317

D-Amino acid oxidase (*continued*)
  reaction, 316
  temperature effect, absorption spectrum, 316, 317
D-Amino acid:oxygen oxidoreductase, *see* D-Amino acid oxidase
α-Aminoadipate, catabolism, bacteria, 87
Aminoacylation, TRNA, 175
p-Aminobenzoic acid, microbial growth factor, 356
AMP, *see* Adenosine monophosphate
Anthracycline antibiotic
  metabolism, 75–82
  structure, 77
Anthracycline, carbonyl reduction, 80, 81
Anthranilate, tryptophan synthase induction, 131, 132
Antibiotic resistance, *Pseudomonas,* plasmid, 107
Antiobiotic therapy, vitamin B deficiency, 357
Antitumor agent, biomodification, 76–82
Apotyrosine decarboxylase, bacterial media, 10
L-Arabinose, metabolite, bacteria, 46
Aromatization, cyclohexane carboxylic acid, 68
Arterial occlusion, cyclic nucleotide role, 215
Arteriovenous anastomosis, cyclic nucleotide role, 215
Arthrobacter CA1, cyclohexylacetic acid, 67–69
Aspartokinase III, nitrogen starvation, 234
Atomic mean square displacement
  metmyoglobin, 335–337
  protein, 334, 337
  temperature dependence, 336
Autogenous regulation hypothesis, 135, 138
Avidin, biotin derepression, 353, 354
1-(4-Azidophenyl)imidazole, cytochrome P450$_{cam}$, active site label, 281, 282
Azospirillum brasiliensis, plasmid, chromosome transfer, 105
Azurin, 91–95
  chemical properties, 94
  purification, 93

B

B1 fragment, *Escherichia coli,* 178–182, 186
Bacillus subtilis
  NADH peroxidase, 296
  tryptophan auxotroph, 131

Bacteria
  purple, non-sulfur, 49, 50
  purple, sulfur, cytochrome, 50
Bacteriophage *pf*16, *Pseudomonas putida,* 104
Bacteriophage *pfdm, Pseudomonas putida,* 104
Bacteriorhodopsin, photoinduced reaction cycle, 339
Benzaldehyde–benzoic system, 39
Benzaldehyde oxidation, 39
Benzenoid compound, degradation, 49, 51
Betacocci, fermentation, 41
Biomolecular reaction, rate equation, 341
Biotin
  biosynthetic control, 351
  biosynthetic pathway, 352, 353
  deficiency, turkey, 48
  microbial growth factor, 356
  microbiological assay, 357
  sudden infant death, 358
  transport system, *Saccharomyces cerevisiae,* 353, 354
Bornan-2α-ol-6-one dehydrogenase, 206, 207
6-Bornanone, *see* Camphor
Branched-chain ketoacid dehydrogenase
  Hill coefficient, 31
  induction, 32
  kinetics, 31–34
  Michaelis constant, 31
  purification, 26–29
  regulatory subunit, 32
  substrate, maximum velocity, 31
1-(4-Bromoacetamidophenyl)imidazole, cyto-chrome P450$_{cam}$, 281, 284, 288, 289

C

Calmodulin, protein kinase activation, 208–214
Camphor
  catabolic enzyme induction, 87
  degradation, bacteria, 60–63, 69–72
  degradation, plasmid control, 114, 115
  microbial catabolism, 46, 49
Camphor 5-*exo*hydroxylase, 60, 267
Camphor hydroxylase, induction, 114, 115
Camphor 1,2-monooxygenase complex, 62, 63
Carbohydrate metabolism, *Pseudomonas aeruginosa,* 365
Carbon cycle, 48, 49
Carbon monoxycytochrome P450, optical absorption, low temperature, 328

Carbonyl reduction, ketonic, anthracycline, 76

β-Carboxymuconate lactonizing enzyme, 123

γ-Carboxymuconolactone decarboxylase, 123, 124

Carboxypeptidase, X-ray diffraction, 323

Carrier transport system, octanoate, 90

Catabolism
eukaryote versatility, 54, 55
evolution, 49

Catachol, degradation, 51-53

Catalase, glutamine synthetase inactivation, 235-244, 247, 248

Catechol 1,2 oxygenase, 123

Cell-free preparation, bacteria, 36

Chaetomium UC4634, steffimycin metabolism, 81

Chlorinated aromatic compound, degradation, 117, 118

3-Chlorobenzoate, oxidation, 117, 118

Chlorophyll, photosynthetic bacteria, 50

Cholesterol, cytochrome P450$_{scc}$ substrate, 274

Cholesterol desmolase, activity assay, 271-273

Chromatophore, electron energy transfer, 256

Chromosome, complementation mapping, 106, 107

Chromosome map, camphor degradative genes, 111

Chymotrypsin
acyl-enzyme intermediate, 323
acyl-enzyme isolation, 318

Cinerubin A, cleavage, reductive glycosidic, 78

Cinerubin, structure, 77

Citrate, enzymatic synthesis, 4

Citrate lyase, bacteria, 45

Citric acid cycle, *see also* Krebs cycle
pyruvate oxidation, 4

Citrobacter freundii, anthracycline metabolism, 78

Cloning, *Pseudomonas aeruginosa trp* gene in *Escherichia coli*, 135-139

Clostridium, pyruvate oxidation, 13

Clostridium botulinum, sudden infant death, 358

Clostridium perfringens, NADH peroxidase, 296

Clostridium thermosaccharolyticum, growth inhibition, biotin, 354

Coenzyme A
requirement, of branched-chain ketoacid dehydrogenase, 28

Coenzyme I, *see* Nicotinamide adenine dinucleotide

Coenzyme II, *see* Nicotinamide adenine dinucleotide phosphate

Complementation mutant
pheS, λ p2 bacteriophage, 175
pheT, λ p2 bacteriophage, 175
thrS, λ p2 bacteriophage, 175

Corynebacterium, camphor oxidation, 206, 207

Cosolvent, *see* Fluid mixed solvent

Cryobiochemistry, 309-324

Crystalline condensing enzyme, 4, 5

Cycloalkyl alkane, degradation, 67

Cyclohexane carboxylic acid, metabolism, 66-68

Cyclohexanol, degradation, 63-66, 68

Cyclohexanone monooxygenase, characteristics, 65, 66

Cyclohexylacetic acid, metabolism, 67-69

Cyclopentanol, degradation, 63-66

Cysteine, cytochrome P450$_{cam}$ substrate binding, 280, 281

Cysteine-S-phosphate, 221

Cytochrome b_5, 258

Cytochrome c, evolution, 49, 50

Cytochrome c_{551}, 91-95
chemical properties, 94
purification, 93
anthracycline metabolism, 79
glutamine synthetase inactivation, 237-239

Cytochrome oxidase system, *Pseudomonas aeruginosa*, 91, 93-95
chemical properties, 94
purification, 93

Cytochrome P420, 267

Cytochrome P450
active site, sulfhydryl role, 259
amino acid composition, 273
camphor degradation, 61, 62
catalysis, 264
characterization, 47
chemical composition, 273
m-chloroperbenzoic acid reaction, 262
cholesterol desmolase, 268
corticoid 11β-hydroxylase, 268
dioxygen, heme-bound acylation, 262
effector, 313
heme iron, 254
heme protein, immunochemical property, 280
heme reduction, 262

Cytochrome P450 (*continued*)
  hemoprotein, fluorescence properties, 259
  hydroxylation, 261
  immunoprecipitation, 273
  iron spin state, 314
  liver microsome, purification, 268
  metastable oxy–ferrous compound, 314
  monooxygenase reaction, 268
  nonionic detergent, effect on catalytic activity, 272
  oxy–ferrous intermediate
    isolation, 318
    spectra, 319
  reaction cycle, 260
  redox potential, 262
  redox state, 313, 314
  sequence, 260
  spin state interconversion, 263
  stable states, 313
  thermodynamic, 263
Cytochrome P450–putidaredoxin, interaction, 314, 315
Cytochrome P450 monoxygenase, fluorescence, 255, 256
Cytochrome P450 reductase, anthracycline metabolism, 79
Cytochrome P450$_{cam}$
  alkylation, 283
  characterization, 267
  cytochrome P450$_{11\beta}$ similarity, 287–288
  decomposition reaction, ternary oxy intermediate, 320, 321
  dissociation constant, isobornyl acetate, 282
  dissociation constant, substrate, 285
  glutamine synthetase inactivation, 237–244
  hydroxylation mechanism, 312
  inhibitor binding site, 284
  isobornyl acetate translocation, 286, 287
  low temperature chromatography, 320, 321
  peracid reactivity, 263
  peroxide reactivity, 263
  product binding site, 285–287, 290
  purification, 91, 267
  reaction cycle, 312, 313
  spectral analysis, substrate binding site, 282, 283
  substrate binding site, 280–287, 290
  ternary oxy intermediate, 320–322
  two-site model, 287

Cytochrome P450$_{C21}$
  purification, 275
  specificity, 275
Cytochrome P450$_{scc}$
  catalytic activity, 271–273
  cholesterol desmolase reaction, 268
  molecular weight, 272
  purification, 269–271
  Soret peak, 270
  substrate specificity, 274
  thermal stability, Tween 20, 272
  turnover number, 271, 272
Cytochrome P450$_{11\beta}$
  catalytic activity, 271
  cytochrome P450$_{cam}$ similarity, 287–288
  dissociation constant, 289
  11 β-hydroxylation, 268
  molecular weight, 272
  position specificity, 275
  purification, 269–271
  Soret peak, 270, 273
  spectral analysis, binding site, 289, 290
  substrate binding site, 287–291
  substrate specificity, 274
  sulfhydryl labeling, 289, 290
  turnover number, 273

D

Daunomycin
  cleavage, reductive glycosidic, 78
  metabolism, 75, 76, 78, 80
  structure, 77
Debye–Waller factor, 334
Decarboxylase–dehydrogenase
  subunit, of branched-chain ketoacid dehydrogenase, 32
Demethylmenaquinone, *Streptococcus faecalis*, 297, 298
Dewey problem-solving system, 12
Deletion analysis, p*trpAB* plasmid, 137, 138
Difference spectrum
  cytochrome P450$_{11\beta}$–
    1-(4-acetamidophenyl)imidazole complex, 289
  cytochrome P450$_{cam}$–
    1(4-bromoacetamidophenyl)imidazole complex, 284

cytochrome P450$_{cam}$–isobornyl acetate complex, 285–286
cytochrome P450$_{cam}$–isobornyl bromoacetate complex, 283, 285, 286
α-Difluoromethylornithine, ornithine decarboxylase inhibition, 356
13-Dihydrodaunomycin, cleavage, reductive glycosidic, 78
10-Dihydrosteffimycinone, cleavage, reductive glycosidic, 78
Dioxygen, activation, 48, 49
Displacement factor, *see* Debey–Waller factor
Dithioctanoic acid, *see* Lipoic acid
Dithionite, NADH peroxidase, 303
Double-well potential, 332, 333

E

Elastase
    acyl-enzyme intermediate, 323
    Pseudomonas aeruginosa pathogenicity, 364
    substrate binding, 323
Electrochemical membrane potential, membrane transport, 89
Electron transfer
    dynamics, 263
    putidaredoxin–cytochrome P450, 262
Embden–Meyerhoff pathway, 17
Enoyl-CoA hydratase, amino acid metabolism, 24, 25
Entropy factor, myoglobin ligand binding, 342
Enzyme regulation, plasmid code, 112–115
Enzyme–substrate intermediate
    structural analysis, 322, 323
    temporal resolution, 311, 312
    X-ray diffraction study, 322, 324
Enzyme transition rate coefficient, 331
Erwinia chrysantheni, plasmid, chromosome transfer, 105
Escherichia coli
    anthracycline metabolism, 78
    biotin biosynthesis, 352, 354
    butyrate transport, 88
    catalase level, glutamine synthetase inactivation, 247
    energy source shift-down, 192–202
    enzyme induction, 133
    fatty acid transport, 88
    glutamine synthetase inactivation, 236

glutamine synthetase proteolysis, 242–245
growth curve, 193
lactate dehydrogenase, 5
messenger ribonucleic acid, functional half-life, 193, 198
plasmid, chromosome transfer, 105
protein degradation, 234–244, 247
translational initiation control mutant, 199–202
tryptophan biosynthesis, 106
tryptophan synthesis, regulation, 135
Escherichia coli K12
    chromosome map, 102
    conjugation, 103
Euglena, cytochrome c_{558}, 49
Evolution, eukaryotic, 49–51
Exotoxin A, *pseudomonas aeruginosa,* 364

F

F dehydrogenase, induction, 114
FAD, *see* Flavin adenine dinucleotide
Feedback inhibition, amino acid synthesis, 352
Ferriprotoporphyrin IX, cytochrome P450, 47
Fever, bacterial growth, 359
Fick's first law of diffusion, 159
meta-Fission pathway, benzenoid catabolism, 51–53
ortho-Fission pathway, benzenoid catabolism, 52, 53
Flavin adenine dinucleotide, camphor, 1,2-monooxygenase, 62
Flavin mononucleotide, camphor, 1,2-monooxygenase, 62
Flavin semiquinone, 298, 299
Flavoprotein
    catalysis, 298, 299
    glycerol oxidation, 16
Flow dialysis, vesicle transport measurement, 88, 89
Fluid mixed solvent, low temperature enzyme study, 310–324
Fluorescein, bacterial, *see* Pyoverdine
FMN, *see* Flavin mononucleotide
Folic acid
    microbial growth factor, 356
    microbiological assay, 357
Formylmethionyl-tRNA[fmet] binding, thermolability, 173

G

Galactaric acid, degradation, bacteria, 60
β-Galactosidase synthesis, *Escherichia coli,*
  197, 198
Gate model, myoglobin ligand binding, 342
Gene
  arrangement, *Pseudomonas,* 106
  duplication, 125, 126
  expression, *trp* gene, 135, 136, 138, 139
  homologous divergence, 125
  linkage, 102
  order determination, 101
  regulation, positive control, 113
  regulation, *Pseudomonas,* 106
  structural rearrangements, 124, 125
Gene cluster regulation, *trpEGDC,* 139
Gene *infC*
  cotranscription, 181–186
  gene dosage effect, 186
  location, 178–181
Gene map
  trpAB region, *Pseudomonas putida,* 134
  trp gene, *Pseudomonas putida,* 132, 133
Gene order, λ p2 bacteriophage, 175–178
Gene *pheS*
  complementation mutant, 178
  cotranscription, 181–186
  gene dosage effect, 186
  location, 180, 181
  map position, λ p2 bacteriophage, 177–181
Gene *pheT*
  complementation mutant, 178
  cotranscription, 181–186
  gene dosage effect, 186
  location, 180, 181
  map position, λ p2 bacteriophage, 177–181
Gene P12, map position, 177–179
Gene *thrS*
  complementation mutant, 178
  cotranscription, 181
  location, 178–181
Gene transcription, λ+ heavy strand promoter,
  181–186
Gene *trpDC,* derepression, *Pseudomonas,* 139
Gene *trpEG,* derepression, *Pseudomonas,* 139
Gene *trpF, Pseudomonas,* 140
Gene *trpI,* regulatory, *Pseudomonas,* 139–141
Genetic cluster, 112

Gentisate, catabolism, 51, 54
Glucaric acid, degradation, bacteria, 60
Glucose, biotin uptake, 353
Glucose 6-phosphate, mammalian tissue, 223
Glucose-6-phosphate phosphatase, mammalian
  tissue, 223
Glutamate, glutamine synthetase degradation,
  246–248
Glutamate dehydrogenase, nitrogen starvation,
  234
Glutamic–aspartic transaminase, pyridoxal 5'-
  phosphate requirement, 148
Glutamine metabolism, glutamine synthetase
  degradation, 246, 247
Glutamine synthetase
  degradation, regulation, 246–248
  inactivation, 235–244, 247, 248
  inactivation system, properties, 239–241
  nitrogen starvation, 234
  proteolytic degradation, 242–244
3-Glyceraldehyde phosphate, oxidation, 13
Glycosidic cleavage, reductive, anthracycline,
  76, 78, 79
Glyoxylate metabolism, 46
Growth condition, bacteria, metabolically active, 10

H

Heart, catacholamine sensitivity, cyclic nu-
  cleotide role, 215
Hemerythrin, oxygen binding, 332
Hemolysin, *Pseudomonas aeruginosa*
  pathogenicity, 364
Hemophilus influenzae, NAD requirement, 358
Hemophilus parainfluenzae, nutrition, 356
Hemoprotein
  catalase, 304
  low temperature ligand binding, 261
Heptadecylcyclohexane, degradation, 67
Heteroduplex analysis, plasmid R68.45, 105
Hexaric acid metabolism, 46
Hill coefficient, l-threonine dehydrase, 150
Histone H1, lysine phosphorylation, 229
Histone H4
  kinase, 224
  phosphate, half-life, 224
  phosphorylated, conformation, 224, 226–228
  phosphorylation, 224, 225

Homogentisate, catabolism, 51, 54
Homoprotocatechuate, catabolism, 51, 54
Horseradish peroxidase, enzyme–substrate intermediate, 312
Hutner mineral salt, 93
Hybridization, λ p2 bacteriophage deoxyribonucleic acid, 182
Hydrogen peroxide, streptococcal oxidation, 294
Hydrogen sulfide, reducing power, 50
Hydrophobic chromatography, cytochrome P450 separation, 270, 271
p-Hydroxybenzoate hydroxylase, 66
Hydroxydicarboxylic acid, degradation, bacteria, 60
Hydroxylase activity, putidaredoxin, 261
Hydroxyproline, metabolite, bacteria, 46
4-Hydroxy-2-ketovaleric acid, 46
Hypertension, cyclic nucleotide role, 215
Hysteretic activation, L-threonine dehydrase, 154, 155

I

IF, see Initiation factor
Indole, Pseudomonas putida growth, 131
Indoleglycerol phosphate, tryptophan synthase regulation, 132–134, 136
Inhibitor molecule, mechanism, myoglobin, 342
Initiation complex, protein synthesis, 170
Initiation factor, thermal inactivation, 172
Initiation factor 1
  map position, 187
  protein synthesis, 169, 170
Initiation factor 2
  map position, 187
  protein synthesis, 169, 170
  protein synthesis, control, 199
Initiation factor 3
  Escherichia coli gene cluster, 168–169
  infC gene, 173
  protein synthesis, 169–171
  thermosensitive mutant, 171, 172
  translational control, 169
Initiation monosome, 199
Initiation sequence, ribosome, protein synthesis, 170
Initiation triplet, selection specificity, 170, 171
Initiator tRNA, 169, 170

Internal viscosity, protein, 341
Iron
  glutamine synthetase inactivation, 239–241
  pathogenic bacterial requirement, 359
Isobornyl bromoacetate, cytochrome $P450_{cam}$, substrate binding, 281–287
Isobutyrate, induction, 115, 116
Isopropylmalate dehydrogenase, induction, 133
Isopropylmalate isomerase, induction, 133

K

α-Keto acid, terminal oxidation, 36
β-Ketoadipate pathway, 122–126
  evolution, 124–126
β-Ketoadipate enol–lactone hydrolase I, 123, 125, 126
β-Ketoadipate enol–lactone hydrolase II, 123, 125, 126
β-Ketoadipate succinyl-CoA transferase I, 123
β-Ketoadipate succinyl-CoA transferase II, 123
β-Ketoadipyl-CoA thiolase, 123
α-Ketoglutarate
  Pseudomonas aeruginosa, 365
  semialdehyde, 45, 46
2-Ketoglutarate dehydrogenase, 28, 29
2-Ketoisocaproate, 24, 25
2-Ketoisovalerate, 24, 25
2-Ketoisovalerate oxidation, Pseudomonas putida, 33
Ketolactonase, induction, 114
Klebsiella aerogenes, protein degradation, 234–244
Klebsiella pneumoniae, polychlorinated biphenyl degradation, 117
Kramer theory, protein dynamics, 339–341
Krebs cycle, see also Citric acid cycle
  function, evolution, 50

L

Lactate dehydrogenase, 5
Lactobacillus casei
  growth factor, 47
  NADH peroxidase, 296
  nutrition, 356
Lactobacillus plantarum, biotin biosynthesis, 352
Lactone hydrolase, induction, 70
Lag phase, bacterial culture, 18

Leuconostoc
  fermentation, 41
  sucrose phosphorylase, 9
Ligand migration, myoglobin ligand binding, 342
Lignin, fermentation, 49
Limonene, degradation, 70
Lipoamide dehydrogenase
  branched-chain ketoacid dehydrogenase, 26–29
  culture effect, *Pseudomonas putida,* 30–34
  mutant, *Escherichia coli,* 29
  mutant, *Pseudomonas putida,* 29–31
  requirement, *Pseudomonas putida,* 30, 31
  subunit, of branched-chain ketoacid dehydrogenase, 32
Lipoic acid
  characterization, 47
  microbial growth factor, 356
  pyruvate oxidation, bacteria, 6, 11
Lipoic dehydrogenase, *Stretococcus faecalis,* 294
Liver regeneration, cyclic nucleotide role, 215
Luciferase, bacterial.
  enzyme intermediate isolation, 318
  oxygen adduct intermediate, 322
Lysosyme, X-ray diffraction, 323

M

Magnesium, requirement, of branched-chain ketoacid dehydrogenase, 28, 29
Mandelate oxidative pathway, 37
Maple syrup urine disease, 26
2-keto-3-Methylvalerate, 24, 25
Membrane transport, bacteria, 87–90
Messenger ribonucleic acid, inactivation, 195, 202
Metabolic reaction, bacteria as model, 10
Methionine, identification, 355
Methylene carbon
  oxygenation, cytochrome P450, 260
  conversion to secondary alcohol, 259
Microbial nutrition, 355–359
Microflora, intestinal, 357
Mixed-function oxidation, glutamine synthetase inactivation, 237–239
Modulator
  inhibitory, cyclic adenosine monophosphate-dependent protein kinase, 207, 209

  inhibitory, effects, 208
  stimulatory, cyclic guanosine monophosphate-dependent protein kinase, 207, 209
  stimulatory, effects, 208
Monocylic terpenes, degradation, 70
Monooxygenase, ring oxygen insertion, 70
Mössbauer probe, cytochrome oxidase system, 95
Mössbauer spectra, g-strain, 331
Mössbauer transition, heme protein, 332, 333
Muconate lactonizing enzyme, 123
Muconolactone isomerase, 123, 125
Mucor spinosus, daunomycin metabolism, 80
Multienzyme complex
  branched-chain ketoacid dehydrogenase, 32
Mycobacterium rhodochrous T1, camphor degradation, 60, 61
Myelin basic protein, phosphorus–nitrogen bond, 229, 230
Myoglobin
  activation enthalpy, 330, 331
  conformational substate, 328–331
  dioxygen binding, 342
  heme pocket, 329
  kinetic study, binding, 329–331
  kinetics, nonexponential low temperature, 330, 331
  ligand binding, 339

N

NAD
  coenzyme research, 19, 20
  effector, NADH peroxidase, 303, 304
  pyruvate oxidation, 6
  requirement, of branched-chain ketoacid dehydrogenase, 28
NADH oxidase, *Streptococcus faecalis,* 295
NADH peroxidase
  activator, 303
  active site, 301–303
  characterization, *Streptococcus faecalis,* 298–304
  crystallization, 299, 300
  mechanism, 301–303
  menadione reductase reaction, 303
  molecular weight, 300–302
  prosthetic group, 301
  spectral analysis, 298, 299

Streptococcus faecalis, 295, 298–305
titration, 302, 303
NADP, coenzyme research, 19
NADPH:adrenal ferredoxin oxidoreductase, *see also* Adrenodoxin reductase, characterization, 268
NADPH-linked electron transfer, 268
Naphthoquinone, *Streptococcus faecalis,* 297, 298
Neisseria perflava, nutrition, 356
Neoplasia, cyclic nucleotide role, 215
Neuberg concept, 16
Neurobiochemistry, membrane transport, 87
Neurospora, enzyme induction, 133
Nicotinamide adenine dinucleotide, *see* NAD
Nicotinamide adenine dinucleotide phosphate, *see* NADP
Nicotinamide adenine dinucleotide phosphate, reduced, *see* NADPH
Nicotinamide adenine dinucleotide, reduced, *see* NADH
Nicotinic acid, microbial growth factor, 356
Nigericin, octanoate uptake, spheroplast, 89
Nocardia globerula CL1, cyclohexanone monooxygenase, 65, 66
Nogalamycin
cleavage, reductive glycosidic, 78
metabolism, 75, 78
structure, 77
Nuclear magnetic resonance spectra, phosphorylated histone H4, 226–228
Nutritional immunity, 358, 359
Nutritional versatility, soil microorganisms, 116–119

O

Octane hydroxylase, OCT plasmid, 112
Octanoate transport, *Pseudomonas oleovorans,* 88–90
Octanol dehydrogenase, induction, 112
Ontogeny, cyclic nucleotide role, 215
Organic acid metabolism, bacteria, 10
Organic phosphate ester analysis, 17
Ornithine decarboxylase, inhibition, 356
Osmotic fragility, *Pseudomonas aeruginosa,* 93
Oxaloacetate, citrate precursor, 4
β-Oxidation
Arthrobacter CA1, 69
cyclohexane carboxylic acid, 68
Rhodopseudomonas palustris, 68
Oxidative phosphorylation, pyocyanine uncoupling, 363
Oxygen
glutamine synthetase inactivation, 239
fixation, carbon cycle, 49

P

P site, protein synthesis, 169
Pantothenic acid, microbial growth factor, 356
Paracoccus denitrificans, cytochrome c_{550}, 49, 50
Pasteurella multocida
fever effect, iron requirement, 359
Pasteurella tularensis, nutrition, 356
PCB, *see* Polychlorinated biphenyl
Pentose, metabolism, 46
Phenylacetic oxidation, 40
Phenylalanyl-tRNA synthetase
overproduction, 186
pheS gene, 173
pheT gene, 173
N-Phenylimidazole, cytochrome P450, inhibition, 281
Phosphate bond energy, 16
Phosphatidylserine, protein kinase, 210
Phosphohistidine
formation, 223–229
myelin basic protein, 229
π Phosphohistidine, rat liver, 228
τ Phosphohistidine, Walker-256 carcinosarcoma, 228
Phospholipase, *Pseudomonas aeruginosa* pathogenicity, 364
Phospholipid, protein kinase activation, 208
Phospholysine, myelin basic protein, 229
Phosphoramidase, *Escherichia coli,* 222, 223
Phosphoramidate, dephosphorylation, 221–227
Phosphoramidate hexose transferase, mammalian tissue, 223
Photosynthesis, carbon cycle, 49
Plasmid
camphor metabolism, 91
2,4-D degradation, 116
degradative types, 118
enhanced chromosome mobilization, 105
enzyme inheritance, 52, 53
genetic influence, 102

Plasmid (*continued*)
  hybrid generation, 105
  incompatibility group P1, 104, 105
  substrate utilization, *Pseudomonas*, 107
Plasmid CAM, 112–115
  size, 114
Plasmid NAH, 112–114
Plasmid OCT, 113–115
Plasmid pAC2I, polychlorinated biphenyl degradation, 117
Plasmid pAC25, 3-chlorobenzoic acid degradation, 117, 118
Plasmid pGA39, structure, 183, 185
Plasmid pGA46, structure, 183
Plasmid pGA87
  structure, 183
  tetracycline resistance, 185
Plasmid pMG2, incP2 antibiotic resistance, 115
Plasmid p*trpAB*-1, tryptophan synthase, 136
Plasmid p*trpAB*-2, tryptophan synthase, 136
Plasmid pZAZ167, restriction site map, 137
Plasmid R68.45, 105
Plasmid R'EC1, 105
Plasmid R'PA1, 105
Plasmid TOL, 112–114
Plasmid XYL, 113
Pneumococcus, transformation, 102
Polyamine, bacterial growth promotion, 356
Polychlorinated biphenyl, biodegradation, 117
Polypeptide chain propagation, *Escherichia coli*, 197, 199
Polyribosome, loss, *Escherichia coli*, 193
Power law, enzyme kinetics, 329, 330
Preinitiation complex, protein synthesis, 170, 171
Probability density, myoglobin binding, carbon monoxide, 330
Protease, *Pseudomonas aeruginosa* pathogenicity, 364
Protein
  conformational motion, 336–339
  conformational transition, 331–334
  ligand binding, 342
  X-ray crystallography, conformational substate, 334–337
Protein degradation, 234–244
  nutritional factors, 235
Protein kinase
  activation, 208–214
calcium-dependent, 208–216
calcium-dependent, calmodulin-sensitive, 208, 209
calcium-dependent, phospholipid-sensitive, 208, 210
cyclic adenosine monophosphate-dependent, 207, 208, 215, 216
cyclic guanosine monophosphate-dependent, 207, 208, 215, 216
regulation, 207–216
Protein phosphorylation
  basic amino acids, 223–225
  biologic regulation, 214, 215
  calcium, 208–221
  calcium-dependent, bioregulation, 215
  camphor metabolism, 209–217
Protein synthesis
  adenosine triphosphate, intracellular pool, 200, 201
  guanosine triphosphate, intracellular pool, 200, 201
  initiation, 169, 170
  initiation complex, 194, 199
  polypeptide chain initiation, 194, 199
  posttranscriptional control, 192–203
  relative translational yield, 195, 198, 199
  rifampicin effect, 196
  transcriptional control, 202
  translational control, *Escherichia coli*, 199–202
Protein transition
  temperature dependence, 337–339
  solvent viscosity dependence, 338–340
Proteus, pyruvate oxidation, 13
Protocatechuate, catabolism, 51, 54
Protocatechuate 3,4 oxygenase, 123, 126
Pseudomonas
  carbon sources, 24, 365
  enzyme induction, 122
  glycine carbon source, 45
  nutritional classification, 122
  radiation resistance, 362
Pseudomonas aeruginosa
  antibiotic production, 364
  antibiotic resistance, 364, 365
  catabolic potential, 365
  chromosome map, 106
  chromosome mobilization, 103
  growth curve, 92, 93

lysogeny, 103, 365
paraffin utilization, 362, 363
pathogenicity, 364
plasmid, FP, 107
selective pressure, 362
transduction, 103
tryptophan auxotroph, 105
veneral disease, 362
Pseudomonas B3, 118
Pseudomonas cytochrome oxidase, *see* Cytochrome oxidase system
Pseudomonas glycinea, plasmid, chromosome transfer, 105
Pseudomonas oleovorans, fatty acid transport, 88–90
Pseudomonas putida
  amino acid auxotroph, 129
  camphor methylene hydroxylase, 280
  chromosome map, 106
  gene regulation, tryptophan, 132, 135
  glutamine synthetase inactivation, 236–239
  2-ketoglutarate dehydrogenase deficiency, 29–31
  mandelate adaption, 37
  methylene hydroylase system, 47
  mutant, *lpd* locus, 34
  plasmid, chromosome transfer, 105
  protein degradation, 235–244
  pyruvate dehydrogenase deficiency, 30
  toluic acid degradation, 53
  transduction, 103, 104
  tryptophan biosynthesis, 106
  tryptophan mutants, 131–134
  tryptophan synthase regulation, 133–135, 138
Pseudomonas putida C1B, camphor degradation, 60–63
Pseudomonas putida PpG2
  ketoacid dehydrogenase, branched-chain, 24–34
Pseudomonas Pxy, 113
Pseudomonas U, 46
Pseudopyridoxine, *see* Pyridoxal
Purine, bacterial media, 11
Putidaredoxin
  chemical modification, 259
  des-Trp compound, 261
  glutamine synthetase inactivation, 241
  identification, 254
  tryptophan content, 260, 261

tryptophan fluorescence, 258
sequence homology, adrenodoxin, 288
Putidaredoxin–cytochrome P450 complex
  binding reaction, 258, 259
  dissociation constant, 262
  electron transfer rate, 262
Putrescine, growth stimulation, 356
Pyochelin, *see* Siderophore
Pyocyanine, *Pseudomonas aeruginosa,* 361, 363
Pyoverdine, *Pseudomonas aeruginosa,* 361, 363
Pyridoxal, 18
Pyridoxal phosphate
  vitamin B_6 coenzyme, 19, 20
  coenzyme, tyrosine decarboxylase, 47
Pyridoxine
  animal deficiency, 20
  coenzyme deficiency disease, 358
  synthesis, bacteria, 18, 19
Pyrimidine, bacterial media, 11
Pyrophosphate phosphotransferase, mammalian tissue, 223
Pyrophosphate-resistant bacteriophage λp2
  characterization, 175, 176
  coding context, 176
Pyruvate, oxidative decarboxylation, 36
Pyruvate dehydrogenase, 5
Pyruvate dehydrogenase regulation, 26
Pyruvate desmutation, 5
Pyruvate oxidation
  animal tissue, 3, 4, 6
  bacteria, 3–6, 10
Pyruvate oxidation factor, *see* Lipoic acid

R

Rate equation
  first-order, integrated, 156
  second-order, integrated, 156
Red-edge effect, 256
Redoxin, glutamine synthetase inactivation, 238–244
Redoxin reductase, glutamine synthetase inactivation, 238, 244
Regulator gene *xylR,* 113
Regulator gene *xylS,* 113
Repression, biosynthesis, biotin, 352

Repressor gene, *trpR, Pseudomonas,* 139
Restriction endonuclease analysis, plasmid
　　R68.45, 105
Restriction map
　　λp2 bacteriophage, 176, 177
　　pB1 plasmid, 179
　　λ512 bacteriophage, 176
Rhizobium japonicum, growth inhibition, biotin,
　　354
Rhizobium leguminosarum, plasmid, chromo-
　　some transfer, 105
Rhizobium meliloti, plasmid, chromosome trans-
　　fer, 105
Rhodopseudomonas sphaeroides
　　plasmid, chromosome transfer, 105
　　photosynthesis, 50
Riboflavin, microbiological assay, 356
Ring-fission dioxygenases, stringency, 51
mRNA, *see* Messenger ribonucleic acid

S

Saccharomyces cerevisiae, biotin biosynthesis,
　　352–355
Salicylate hydroxylase, 66
Salmonella typhimarium, genetic study, 103
SDS-gel electrophoresis, branched-chain
　　ketoacid dehydrogenase, 27
Sequential induction, *see* Simultaneous adapta-
　　tion
Serine deaminase, *see* L-Threonine dehydrase
Serine proteinase, X-ray diffraction, 323
Shine and Dalgarno sequence, 170, 171
Shizuta–Hayaishi model, L-threonine catalysis,
　　154, 160
Siderophore, 359, 363
Simultaneous adaptation
　　aromatic catabolism, 53–55
　　concept, 35, 36
Southern hybridization, plasmid R68.45, 105
Spermine, bacterial growth promotion, 356
Spheroplast, octanoate uptake, 89
Steffimycin
　　cleavage, reductive glycosidic, 78
　　metabolism, 75
　　structure, 77
Steffimycin B
　　cleavage, reductive glycosidic, 78
　　structure, 77

Steffimycinone
　　cleavage, reductive glycosidic, 78
　　structure, 77
3-keto-Δ^4-Steroid, cytochrome P450$_{11\beta}$ sub-
　　strate, 274
Streptococcus allantoicus, 46
Streptococcus, glycerol oxidation, 16
Streptococcus agalactiae
　　NADH peroxidase, 296
　　oxidase reaction, 294
Streptococcus faecalis
　　acetoin, 293
　　catalase synthesis, 297
　　cytochrome synthesis, 297
　　formate production, 13
　　gluconate fermentation, 23
　　glycerol oxidation, 297
　　growth requirements, 47
　　lactate dehydrogenase, 5
　　NADH, reoxidation, 294
　　oxidase-catalyzing reaction, 295, 296
　　oxidative phosphorylation, 297
　　pyruvate oxidation, 10–13, 294
Streptomyces nogalates
　　anthracycline metabolism, 78, 79
　　steffimycinone metabolism, 80, 81
Streptomyces peucetius, steffimycinone
　　metabolism, 80, 81
Streptomyces steffiburgensis, anthracycline
　　metabolism, 78
Substrate adaptation, *Escherichia coli,* 192–203
Succinyl-CoA synthetase
　　phosphorylation, lypoate succinylation, 221
　　phosphorylation, basic protein, 229, 230
Succinyl lipoate, synthesis, 221
Sucrose phosphorylase, 9
Sudden infant death syndrome, 357, 358
Sulfhydryl group, cytochrome P450$_{cam}$, 281
Superoxide anion, carbon cycle, 48
Superoxide dismutase
　　glutamine synthetase inactivation, 241
　　hydrogen peroxide production, 304
　　reaction, 48, 49
　　streptococcal, 295
Superoxide ion, cytochrome P450, 260

T

Tartronate, semialdehyde, 45, 46
Temperature factor, *see* Debye–Waller factor

Tetracycline resistance gene, 183–185
Thermosensitive mutant selection, suicide
    method, 171
Thiamin
    coenzyme deficiency disease, 358
    deficiency, sudden infant death, 358
Thiamin pyrophosphate
    branched-chain ketoacid dehydrogenase, 26,
      28, 29
    pyruvate oxidation, 5
Thiobacillus thiooxidans sulfuric acid produc-
    tion, 16, 17
Thiohemiketal bond, cytochrome $P450_{cam}$, 281,
    286, 290
Thiophosphoramidate, basic amino acid, 229
Thioredoxin system, bacteria, 221
L-Threonine dehydrase, 148–163
    activation, 151, 154–157, 162, 163
    boundary sedimentation velocity, 162
    characterization, 150
    concentration effect, 154–157
    dimerization, 158–163
    ligand-induced association, 150–154
    oligomer formation, 149–152
    rate constant, catalytic, 160
    rate constant, second-order, 157–159
    sedimentation velocity, 152–154
    velocity at maximum activation, determina-
      tion, 156, 157
    viscosity effect, 160–161
Threonyl-tRNA synthetase
    posttranscriptional control, 186
    thrS gene, 173
Toluene degradation, gene regulation, 113
Transacetylase, 4
Transaminase, 20
Transcyclase, subunit, of branched-chain
    ketoacid dehydrogenase, 32
Transition state theory, protein dynamics, 339–
    342
Translational initiation frequency, *Escherichia*
    coli, 198, 199, 202
Transposon, alkane oxidation, 114
Trifluoperazine, protein kinase, 210
Trichosporon cutaneum, enzyme induction, 54,
    55
3,4,4-Trimethyl-5- carboxymethyl-Δ^2-
    cyclopentenone, metabolic cleavage, 71

Trypanosome disease, treatment, 356
Trypsin, acyl-enzyme intermediate, 323
Trypsin-hydrolyzed casein, bacterial media, 11
Tryptone-yeast extract, bacterial media, 10
Tryptophan
    biosynthetic pathway, 130
    gene order, 137, 138
Tryptophan synthase
    positive regulation, 138, 139
    pyridoxal 5'-phosphate requirement, 148
    repression, 130
Tryptophanase, pyridoxal 5'-phosphate re-
    quirement, 148
Tween 20, cytochrome $P450_{scc}$ reduction, 272
Tyramine, 18
Tyrosine decarboxylase
    coenzyme requirement, 47
    pyridoxal 5'-phosphate requirement, 148
    tyramine formation, 18, 19
Tyrosine oxidation, 40

U

Ubiquitin, protein degradation, 234
Uncoupling, enzyme reaction, 315
Urea, synthesis, 48

V

L-Valine, branched-chain ketoacid dehy-
    drogenase, 26–29, 31–34
Valinomycin, octanoate uptake, spheroplast, 89
Vibrational mean square displacement, 332, 333
Vibrio anguillarum, virulence plasmid, 359
Vitamin B synthesis, microbial control, *see also*
    specific B vitamins, 351, 352, 357
Vitamin B_6, *see* Pyridoxine
Vitamin B_{12}
    coenzyme deficiency disease, 358
    malabsorption, 357
    microbiological assay, 357
    microbial growth factor, 356
Vitamin K, microbial synthesis, 357

X

Xylene degradation, *Pseudomonas*, 113